1541
User's
Guide

Kennedy

1985

1541 User's Guide

by
Gerald Neufeld, Ph.D.
Brandon University

Technical Illustrations by
Diane M. Corralejo

DATAMOST INC ®

19821 Nordhoff Street, Northridge, CA 91324
(818) 709-1202

Acknowledgements

I would like to acknowledge the patience and forbearance of my family and friends. Without their support, producing this manual would have been considerably more difficult.

I would like to extend special thanks to Dr. Richard Immers for getting me started on writing this book and to Dr. Tom MacNeill and my wife, Nancy, for their diligent work in proofreading the manuscript. Special thanks also go to Jim Butterfield and Mike Todd for reading the manuscript and suggesting worthwhile improvements.

This manual was written on a Commodore computer system using the WordPro 4 Plus™ word processing system available from Professional Software Inc. This excellent word processor made the project much easier.

TABLE OF CONTENTS

Application Programs:

Program Name	Purpose	Page
MAIL PGM	A self-modifying mail list	142
MAIL SEQ	A mail list using SEQ files	167
MAIL REL	A mail list using REL files	194
MAIL INX	An advanced mail list using indexed relative files	214
FAST COPY	A fast, machine language file copier program	237

Disk Utility Programs:

Program Name	Purpose	Page
HOUSE HELP	Makes diskette housekeeping easy	79
RECOVER UNCLOSED	Recover data from unclosed file	257
ALLOCATE	Allocate blocks in unclosed file	258
FIND ERRORS	Scan track 18 for errors	261
REDO 18/0	Recover from errors on 18/0	262
TRACE CHAIN	Display chain given T&S pointer	268
RECOVER FILE	For files not in directory	270
ALIGN 1541	Check alignment or realign	282
MOD ENTRY	Modify name, type, or length	309
TRACE FILE	Display chain given file name	317
FULL DIRECTORY	Expanded directory listing	361
CONFIRM ALL FILE	Check that all files are OK	364
BACKUP	Make a backup of a diskette	369
MAKE FAST COPY	Create a fast file copy program	374
EDIT T&S	Edit any byte on a diskette	376
MOD DISK NAME	Modify a diskette's name	386
FIX DIRECTORY	Repair a damaged directory	387
UNSCRATCHER	Unscratch any disk file	400
PRG HEX DUMP	Hex display of BASIC program	403
PRG ANALYZER	Byte by byte look at a program	406

How to Use This Book

This book is intended to help you make more effective use of your Commodore disk drive. Although the examples and program listings are designed for use on a Commodore 64 or VIC-20 with a 1541 disk drive, many will work without modification on other Commodore computers and disk drives.

This book expands and clarifies the documentation provided by Commodore Business Machines, Inc. Some of the information covered in the *1541 User's Manual* is also presented here. However, the majority of information presented in this book is original and is the result of intensive research and testing by the author.

Beginners

If you have just purchased a 1541 disk drive, you should read the first two chapters carefully. The first chapter explains how to set up and operate your disk drive. The second chapter explains how to make use of the DOS 5.1 program included on the 1541TEST/DEMO diskette that came with your disk drive. These two chapters should get you started. If you have trouble understanding computer jargon, just check the glossary in Appendix A.

As your collection of diskettes grows you will reach the point where you will need to learn how to get rid of unwanted programs, erase and reuse an old diskette, etc. These tasks are often called diskette housekeeping. Chapter 4 tells you how to do these housekeeping tasks and explains what happens to your diskette as these tasks are performed. This chapter concludes with a listing of a menu-driven BASIC program that makes housekeeping easier. If you make a mistake, check Chapter 11 to see if you can rectify the situation.

If you are the type of person who likes to know how things work, you will want to read Chapter 13 carefully. It will help to take some of the mystery out of the inner workings of your disk drive.

Intermediate Programmers

If you already know how to operate your disk drive and know how to write simple BASIC programs, you may want to skim through Chapters 1 and 2 quickly. Once you understand how to use the command channel to read the disk drive status and do diskette housekeeping, you are ready for file handling. Make certain that you understand the fundamentals of file handling (Chapter 5) and how to use the various file types (Chapters 6 to 8) before you tackle the chapters on indexed relative files or machine language file handling.

Experienced Programmers

As an experienced programmer, you probably have some specific application in mind. Use the Table of Contents and the Index to locate the information or techniques you need. However, don't ignore the more introductory sections. They contain a great deal of information that has never been published before. For example, did you know that: DOS 5.1 has a save command, DOS 5.1 commands can be used within a program, sequential files can be saved and loaded, or that there is a Modify (M) mode that allows you to read an unclosed file?

Note that the chapter on file handling from machine language uses only the standard Commodore 64 Kernal jump table. If you use other ROM entry points, your program may not work on some future versions of the Commodore 64 because there is no guarantee that Commodore will retain the same entry points.

About the Programs

This book contains many listings of ready to use programs written in BASIC. There are three main types of programs: instructional, application and utility.

Instructional Programs

Many chapters contain one or more programs that are designed to help you learn more about how your computer or disk drive works. Some of these programs will not have much lasting value. Others, such as the one to merge programs or those to analyze a program, will probably find a place in your tool kit.

Application Programs

Each of the main chapters on file handling from BASIC concludes with a mailing list program. Chapter 10 on machine language file handling concludes with a fast file copy program. These programs are designed to illustrate a practical application of the file handling techniques discussed in that chapter. Even if you do not bother to type in these programs, you should study them to be certain that you understand the techniques used. Although the programs work quite well as is, you may want to modify them by adding color or sound. Some possible modifications and improvements are suggested at the end of the program listings.

Utility Programs

This book also contains several disk utility programs. Some of these are scattered throughout the text. Several more are given in Appendix E. These are powerful tools. Remember, any tool can be dangerous. Be sure you read and understand the operating procedures before you use one of these programs. It is always a good idea to practice using a disk utility program with a test diskette before you use it with one that contains valuable programs or data.

Typing the Programs

Program listings in books and magazines often suffer from two problems: typographical errors that occur when the program is retyped into a word processor, and the readability of the Commodore's control characters (e.g., the reverse-field heart that means clear the screen). To overcome these problems, the program listings for this book were created using a special lister program. The lister program takes a working program and converts it into a WordPro file. At the same time, the control characters are converted into English language code words surrounded by curly brackets. For example, the reverse-field heart which is used to clear the screen is converted to {CLR}. The table below lists the code words, their meaning, and the proper key or keys to press on your Commodore 64 or VIC-20.

Code	Meaning	Press these Keys
{CLR}	Clear the screen	Hold SHIFT and press CLR/HOME
{HOME}	Home the cursor	Press CLR/HOME
{DOWN}	Cursor down	Press CRSR (up/down)
{UP}	Cursor up	Hold SHIFT and press CRSR (up/down)
{RIGHT}	Cursor right	Press CRSR (right/left)
{LEFT}	Cursor left	Hold SHIFT and press CRSR (right/left)
{RVS}	Reverse field ON	Hold CTRL and press 9
{ROFF}	Reverse field OFF	Hold CTRL and press 0

Notes:

1. When a number appears inside the curly brackets, it means you repeat the operation immediately to the left of the number, that many times. For example, {DOWN 5} means to press CRSR (up/down) five (5) times.

2. All programs have been listed in a column 40 characters wide. Except where special characters have been spelled out between curly brackets, the lines are listed exactly as they appear on a Commodore 64 display. Spaces must be typed in as listed. Where necessary, count the character columns to determine the appropriate number of spaces.

Using the Programs

This book contains listings of over fifty programs written in BASIC. These programs are copyrighted. They may not be used commercially nor may they be sold. Since many of the programs are long, typing them all in would be a time consuming, tedious process. Feel free to share your typing efforts with your friends who have also purchased a copy of this book. However, please do not share these programs with those who do not own a copy of the book.

If you do not have the time to type in the programs, you may purchase a diskette containing all the programs from DATAMOST.

CHAPTER 1

GETTING STARTED

This chapter is designed for the new 1541 owner. It covers such topics as setting up your system, operating procedures, running a program and saving a program. Experienced 1541 users may want to skim through this chapter quickly.

1.1 Setting Up Your System

Before you unpack your new drive you should decide where you are going to put it. It should be on a sturdy, level surface near your computer. If your computer is on a desk or table, you can set the drive beside the computer or on a shelf above or below the desk or table top. Try to keep it at least six inches away from your monitor or TV set (stray magnetic fields can cause problems). Avoid locations where you will be tempted to set a cup of coffee or ashtray on it.

Remember that you will need a place to store your diskettes. They should go on a shelf or in a drawer. You do not want to leave them lying around loose. Be sure you have lots of space, diskette collections tend to grow rapidly!

When you unpack your 1541 you should find the following items in the packing case:

1. The 1541 disk drive.
2. A grey three-prong power cord.
3. A black serial bus cable with a DIN connector on each end.
4. A copy of the *1541 User's Manual.*
5. A copy of the 1541TEST/DEMO diskette.

If one or more pieces are missing, contact the store where you bought it. It is a good idea to keep the box and protective packaging in case you move or have to take your drive in for service.

You may see a cardboard tab sticking out of your 1541. Pull on it gently and remove the floppy diskette-sized piece of cardboard. Keep it. You should slip it into your drive whenever you will be transporting your 1541. The cardboard helps protect the read/write head.

Follow these steps to set up your disk drive:

Step 1: Take the female end of the grey power cable and plug it into the back of the disk drive. Plug the other end into any grounded, three-prong electrical outlet.

If the drive makes any sounds when you plug it in, turn OFF the disk drive before you go any further. The power switch is at the back of the drive. Be sure *both* your *computer* and *disk drive* are OFF before you connect any other cables.

Step 2: Plug the black serial bus cable into either of the serial bus sockets on the back of your disk drive. It doesn't matter which end of the cable you use, they're identical.

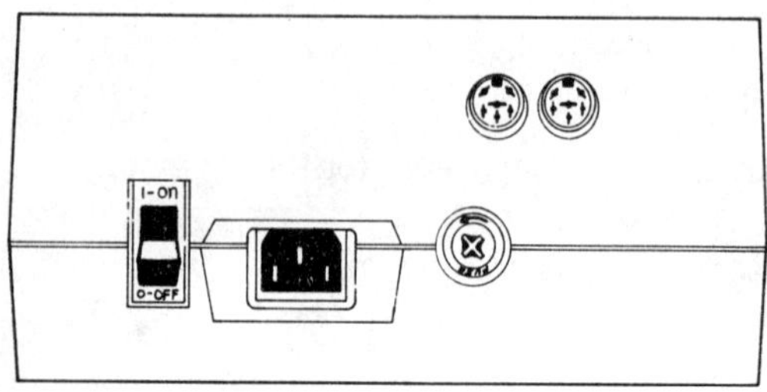

Left: Rear view of 1541 disk drive. *Below:* Rear view of the Commodore 64 computer.

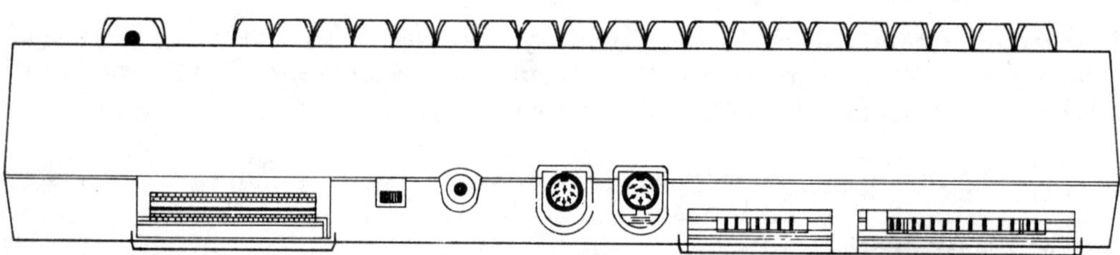

Step 3: Make sure your computer is switched OFF. Now, plug the other end of the black serial bus cable into the back of the computer. If you do not have a printer or other peripherals to attach, the hookup is now complete.

Step 4: If you have a printer or a second disk drive, plug its serial bus cable into the second serial port on the back of the 1541.

1.2 Powering ON Your System

Once you have connected all the parts of your computer system, it is time to start switching it ON. Your *1541 User's Manual* suggests that your computer should be the last thing you switch on. However, many people who had several peripherals attached to the serial bus encountered difficulties. As a result, Commodore released a technical bulletin suggesting the following power ON sequence.

Computer → disk drive
Computer → disk drive → printer
Computer → disk drive → disk drive
Computer → disk drive → disk drive → printer

Note that the computer is always switched on first and the printer, if any, is switched on last. The use of a power bar to switch everything ON at once is not recommended; particularly if you have several peripherals hooked up to the serial bus. The system may lock up.

WARNING:

Always remove all diskettes from a disk drive before you turn it OFF or ON. If a diskette is left in the drive, you may create a magnetic spike on it that may make important data or programs unreadable.

When you switch the disk drive ON, the motor will start, the green power-on LED will come on, and the red drive-active LED will light up. After a few seconds, the motor will stop and the red drive-active LED will go out. It is now safe to insert a diskette and begin working.

1.3 Inserting a Diskette

To open the door of your 1541 drive, simply press the door catch lightly inwards. The catch will move upward and the door will pop open. Any diskette in the drive will be ejected automatically when the door is opened. To insert a diskette, slide it into the drive with the label side up. The edge nearest the large opening goes in first. The write protect notch should be on the left like this:

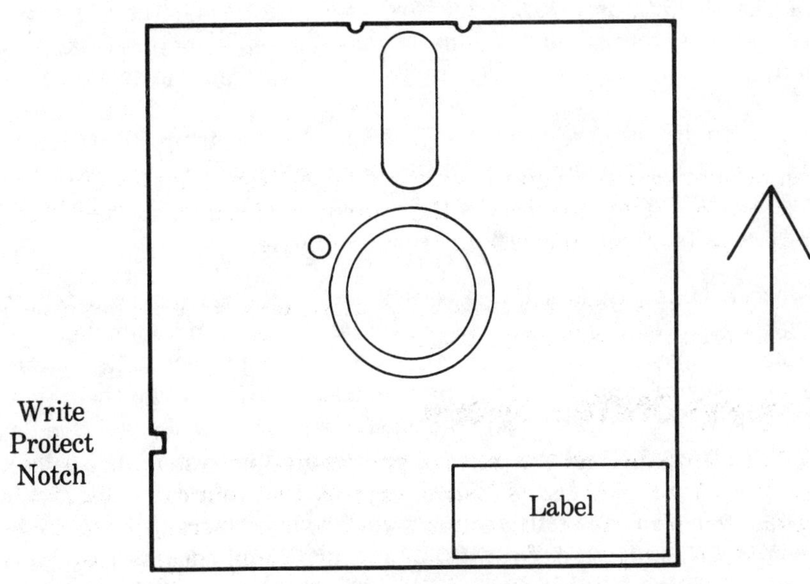

The diskette should slide in easily. If it sticks or binds, slowly pull it out and try again. When the diskette is almost completely into the drive, you will feel a slight spring resistance. This is normal. You will know that you have inserted the diskette completely when you hear a click and the spring resistance stops. Close the disk drive door by pushing downward on the catch. When the catch has moved downward about half an inch it will spring outward. The door is now closed and the diskette is firmly locked into place. You may now begin working with the diskette.

WARNINGS:

1. *Always* remove the diskette before you switch your disk drive OFF or ON.

2. Never open the drive door while the red drive-active LED is glowing steadily and the motor is running. If you do this while the drive is writing, part of your program or data may be lost. For the one time when you should ignore this rule, see Section 11.6.

1.4 Using a 1541 with a VIC-20

The *1541 User's Manual* suggests that, if you are using a 1541 with a VIC-20, you should send a "UI-" command to the 1541 to switch it to VIC-20 data transmission speed. Current 1541 drives do not require this speed adjustment. As a result, this section of the *1541 User's Manual* may be ignored.

1.5 Rules for Using Floppy Diskettes

Floppy diskettes are quite reliable but they must be handled with care. Follow these rules to ensure long and satisfactory service from your diskettes:

1. Keep things clean. Dust and grit will cause rapid wear of your diskettes and the 1541's record/play head. Don't set up your system in a dusty environment. It is a good idea not to smoke while using your system.

2. Do not turn the disk drive ON or OFF while a diskette is in the disk drive. If you do, the surge of current may produce a magnetic spike on the diskette surface. Depending on where this spike occurs, you may lose valuable data or programs.

3. Never touch a diskette's recording surface; handle it by its protective jacket. If you touch the recording surface, the oil from your fingers will contaminate the surface and make the diskette unusable. Be particularly careful about the back side of the diskette because the data is stored on that side.

4. Keep your diskettes cool and dry. Diskettes work best at normal room temperature. Too high a temperature can cause the disk jacket to warp and make the diskette unusable. Too cold a temperature can cause moisture problems. If you must transport your diskettes and disk drive in very cold weather, wrap them in a plastic bag and allow them to warm up in the plastic bag for at least an hour before using them. This prevents moisture from condensing on them.

5. Keep your diskettes away from magnetic fields. Electric motors, TV sets and other electrical appliances produce magnetic fields that can destroy the programs and data recorded on your diskettes. This means you should never put your diskettes on top of your monitor!

6. Put your floppy diskettes back into their paper storage envelopes when you are not
   using them. This helps to protect them from dust.

7. Make backup copies of important programs and data files. You never know when
   disaster may strike!

1.6 Viewing a Diskette's Directory

One floppy diskette can store many different programs. In order to make use of a
program stored on a floppy diskette you need to know its name. The names of all the
programs and data files stored on a diskette are kept in the diskette's directory. To
view a diskette's directory on the Commodore 64 or VIC-20 you must LOAD it into
memory and then LIST it.

Let's practice this using the 1541TEST/DEMO diskette that comes with your 1541.
Here is what to do:

Step 1: Insert the 1541TEST/DEMO diskette into your disk drive.

Step 2: Load the directory by typing the following command and pressing the
RETURN key.

```
LOAD "$",8    or    LOAD "$0",8
```

When you enter this command the red drive-active LED will light up and the motor
will run. After a few seconds the drive-active LED and motor should turn OFF. If the
drive-active LED keeps flashing after the motor turns off, a disk error has occurred.
Turn your computer OFF and ON and try again. If you cannot load the directory of
the 1541TEST/DEMO diskette, take your drive back to where you bought it.

HINT:

Instead of turning your Commodore 64 OFF and ON to reset things, you can hold
down the RUN/STOP key and press the RESTORE key. The screen should clear and
the READY prompt and the cursor should appear. Now type in SYS 64738 and press
the RETURN key. Presto!

Step 3: List the directory by typing LIST and pressing the RETURN key. You
should see the following display on your video screen.

```
0  "1541TEST/DEMO     "  ZX  2A
13    "HOW TO USE"          PRG
5     "HOW PART TWO"        PRG
4     "VIC-20 WEDGE"        PRG
1     "C-64 WEDGE"          PRG
4     "DOS 5.1"             PRG
11    "COPY/ALL"            PRG
9     "PRINTER TEST"        PRG
4     "DISK ADDR CHANGE"    PRG
4     "DIR"                 PRG
6     "VIEW BAM"            PRG
```

```
 4      "CHECK DISK"        PRG
 14     "DISPLAY T&S"       PRG
 9      "PERFORMANCE TEST"  PRG
 5      "SEQUENTIAL FILE"   PRG
 13     "RANDOM FILE"       PRG
558 BLOCKS FREE.
```

Let's look at this directory listing piece by piece.

```
0  "1541TEST/DEMO    "  ZX  2A          Drive number
```

The first line begins with the drive number zero. This is a carry over from the Commodore dual drives. It will always be zero on your 1541.

```
0  "1541TEST/DEMO    "  ZX  2A          Diskette name
```

The drive number is followed by the diskette name. This is the name specified when the diskette was prepared for use (see Section 1.11 on formatting a diskette). The name is padded with blank spaces to make it exactly 16 characters long.

```
0  "1541TEST/DEMO    "  ZX  2A          Diskette formatting ID
```

The next two characters are the diskette identification (ID) characters. They were also specified when the diskette was prepared for use. In this case the diskette ID is ZX.

```
0  "1541TEST/DEMO    "  ZX  2A          Diskette DOS type
```

The last two characters on the first line identify the diskette format. These will be 2A on any diskette formatted for use on a 1541 drive.

```
558 BLOCKS FREE.                        Storage space remaining
```

The last line of the directory listing indicates how much space is still available on the diskette for storing new programs or data. In this case there are 558 blocks of storage space left. Each block can hold 256 characters (bytes) of information. On a newly formatted diskette there are 664 blocks available for your use (free). This means that you can store a total of 664 x 256 = 169,984 characters (bytes) of information.

The lines between the first and last lines are the directory entries for the various programs and data files stored on the diskette.

```
 13     "HOW TO USE"        PRG
 5      "HOW PART TWO"      PRG
 4      "VIC-20 WEDGE"      PRG
 1      "C-64 WEDGE"        PRG
 4      "DOS 5.1"           PRG
```

```
11      "COPY/ALL"          PRG
9       "PRINTER TEST"      PRG
4       "DISK ADDR CHANGE"  PRG
4       "DIR"               PRG
6       "VIEW BAM"          PRG
4       "CHECK DISK"        PRG
14      "DISPLAY T&S"       PRG
9       "PERFORMANCE TEST"  PRG
5       "SEQUENTIAL FILE"   PRG
13      "RANDOM FILE"       PRG
```

This diskette contains a total of 15 directory entries. There is one entry for each file of information stored on the diskette. The listing gives the size, name and type of each of these files. Let's examine the first entry in detail.

```
13      "HOW TO USE"        PRG        Length of file
```

The number on the left indicates the size (length) of the file in blocks. The file corresponding to this entry is 13 blocks long.

```
13      "HOW TO USE"        PRG        File name
```

The directory entry also gives the name of the file. This file is named HOW TO USE. You must know a file's name in order to make use of the file. A file name may be up to 16 characters in length. Almost any combination of letters, numbers or graphics symbols may be used for a file name.

```
13      "HOW TO USE"        PRG        File type
```

The last part of the directory entry is the file type. All the files on the 1541TEST/DEMO diskette are program (PRG) files. The other common file types are:

File type	Entry
Sequential file	SEQ
Relative file	REL
User file	USR

Now that you know how to load and list a diskette's directory to find out what files are stored on the diskette, let's see how wild cards can make your life a bit easier.

1.7 Wild Cards and Pattern Matching

In order to make use of a program or data file stored on a diskette you must give its name. On a Commodore disk drive you do not have to give a file's complete name when you want to access it. You can use wild card characters that will match one or more characters in the name. There are two wild card characters: the question mark (?), and the asterisk (*). The question mark (?) will match any single character in a name. The asterisk (*) will match any number of characters at the end of a file name.

When using wild cards you type some combination of ordinary characters (A, B, C,...) and wild card characters (? and *). This creates a pattern. When you send the pattern to the drive, it will compare the names of the programs and data files in the directory with the pattern and see which ones match. This is called pattern matching.

Let's take a look at a few examples of patterns to see how this works. We'll begin with the question mark (?). Since the ? matches any single character in a file name, the pattern ?EST will match the names BEST, TEST and REST. However, since it matches one and only one character, it will not match BLEST, GUEST or TEST1. The ?EST pattern specifies a four character name with any first character followed by the letters EST.

The * will match any number and combination of characters at the end of a name. This makes it more powerful. For example, the pattern CHE* will match any name starting with the three letters CHE such as CHECK DISK, CHECKERS or CHESTNUT. If you use the * in a pattern, there is no point in putting any characters following the *, such as TE*ER, because any ending will match.

You may use both wild cards in a pattern. For example, the pattern ?ON* will match any name having ON as the second and third characters in the name (e.g., BONZO, CONSUMER GRIPES and CONTEST).

You can use wild cards whenever you have to type the name of a program or data file stored on a diskette. You will find them handy for loading programs, doing disk housekeeping, and accessing files. They are especially handy for creating selective directory listings.

1.8 Creating Selective Directory Listings

Occasionally you will run across a diskette with many, many files stored on it (the directory can hold up to 144 entries). In this case you may want to look at only some of the entries. All you have to do is include a file name pattern in your LOAD command like this:

```
SYNTAX:
  LOAD "$:xxxx",8

ALTERNATE:
  LOAD "$0:xxxx",8

EXAMPLES:
  LOAD "$:DIR",8
  LOAD "$:?IR",8
  LOAD "$:DI*",8
  LOAD "$0:?I*",8
```

WHERE:

xxxx   = a file name pattern which may contain one or more wild card
              characters.

If the load command contains a complete file name with no wild card characters, the directory listing will contain the diskette name line, the one entry whose name you specified, and the blocks free line like this:

```
Command:            LOAD "$:DIR",8

Resulting           O "1541TEST/DEMO    " ZX 2A
listing:            4      "DIR"              PRG
                    558 BLOCKS FREE.
```

If there is no file on the diskette with the name you specified, you will just get the first and last lines of the directory display.

To create a selective listing containing more than one entry you use the wild card characters (? and *) to create a pattern that will match more than one file name. Let's examine the ? first.

Since the ? will match any single character in a file name, the pattern ?IR will match the names VIR, DIR and SIR. However, because it matches one and only one character, it will not match WHIR, HAIR or NAIR.

```
Command:            LOAD "$:?IR",8

Resulting           O "1541TEST/DEMO    " ZX 2A
listing:            4      "DIR"              PRG
                    558 BLOCKS FREE.
```

The * matches any number and combination of letters at the end of a file name. For example, the pattern DI* will match any name starting with the two letters DI.

```
Command:            LOAD "$:DI*",8

Resulting           O "1541TEST/DEMO    " ZX 2A
listing:            4      "DISK ADDR CHANGE" PRG
                    4      "DIR"              PRG
                    14     "DISPLAY T&S"      PRG
                    558 BLOCKS FREE.
```

The two wild cards can be used together. The * is always used last because it will match any number or combination of letters from that point on. For example, the pattern ?E* will match any file with an E as the second letter in its name.

```
Command:            LOAD "$:?E*",8

Resulting           O "1541TEST/DEMO    " ZX 2A
listing:            9      "PERFORMANCE TEST" PRG
                    5      "SEQUENTIAL FILE"  PRG
                    558 BLOCKS FREE.
```

Practice using pattern matching to load selective directory listings until you get a feel for how to use the wild card characters. It will be useful later for loading programs and doing diskette housekeeping.

1.9 Loading Programs

Now that you know how to examine a diskette's directory you can start to make use of the programs stored on the diskette. In order to use a program that is stored on a diskette you must bring a copy of the program into the computer's memory. This is called loading the program. Loading a copy of a program does not destroy or affect the copy of the program stored on the diskette. To bring a copy of a program into memory use a LOAD command like this:

```
SYNTAX:
  LOAD "name",8            (Program relocated)


ALTERNATE:
  LOAD name$,8


SYNTAX:
  LOAD "name",8,1          (Program not relocated)


ALTERNATE:
  LOAD name$,8,1


EXAMPLES:
  LOAD "HOW TO USE",8
  LOAD "HOW T*",8
  LOAD "DOS 5.1",8,1
  F$ = "VIEW BAM"
  LOAD F$,8
```

WHERE:

name	= the name of the desired program. It may contain one or more wild card characters.
8	= the device number of the disk drive.
1	= the channel number (secondary address).
name$	= the name of a string variable containing the desired program name.

NOTE:

Our last example illustrates how you can store part or all of the file name in a string variable. If you are not familiar with string variables, don't worry. Just type out the file name.

If several different program names match the one specified in the load command, the first program in the directory that matches the specified name will be loaded. For example, the name DI* matches three different entries in the directory: DISK ADDR CHANGE, DIR, and DISPLAY T&S. The command LOAD "DI*",8 will load the first entry, DISK ADDR CHANGE.

As soon as you press the RETURN key, the drive motor will start and the red drive-active LED will light up. The program is being loaded. After a few seconds, or minutes if the program is a very long one, the drive motor should stop, the red drive-active LED should go out, your computer should print the word READY on the screen, and the flashing cursor should return. This indicates that the program has been loaded successfully. If the computer prints the message, ?FILE NOT FOUND ERROR, the program name you gave in the LOAD command does not match the name of any program stored on that diskette. Check the directory and try again.

If the cursor doesn't return and your computer appears to have locked up, hold down the RUN/STOP key and press the RESTORE key. This should get the cursor back. The program did not load properly. Check the directory and try again.

Once the program has been loaded into the computer's memory simply type the word RUN and press the RETURN key to begin the program. Some commercial programs have an auto-run feature. These programs will start running automatically as soon as they have been loaded into memory. An auto-run program must be loaded using the LOAD "name",8,1 form of the LOAD command. Most auto-run programs cannot be listed.

Practice loading and running a program using the program named HOW TO USE on your 1541TEST/DEMO diskette. This program gives a brief description of the various programs on the diskette. Here is what you should see on your screen as you do this:

```
LOAD"HOW TO USE",8            Remember to press RETURN.

SEARCHING FOR HOW TO USE      Computer response.
LOADING                       Computer response.
READY.                        Load completed successfully.
```

Once a program has been loaded into the computer's memory you can list the program by typing LIST and pressing the RETURN key. To slow down the listing, hold down the CTRL key. To stop the listing, press the RUN/STOP key. Most commercial programs are protected and cannot be listed. If you see something like this when you list a program, 0 SYS 2038, the program is either a machine language program or a compiled BASIC program and cannot be listed.

HINTS:

1. Instead of pressing RETURN after typing a LOAD command, try this. Type a colon (e.g., LOAD "COP*",8:) and then hold down the SHIFT key while you press the RUN/STOP key. The program will not only load, it will run automatically.

2. The 1541TEST/DEMO diskette contains a program that tests your disk drive to make sure that it is working properly. The program is called PERFORMANCE TEST. You should load and RUN this program to check out your new drive. You will need either a new, blank diskette or one that you don't mind being erased to use this program.

You may be wondering about the significance of the ",1" at the end of some of the LOAD commands. The ",1" is a signal to your computer to load the program into the same part of memory from which it was saved. This is used mainly when loading commercial programs or special machine language routines. It is not needed when loading a BASIC program. There is only one non-BASIC program on your 1541TEST/DEMO diskette, DOS 5.1. Try loading this program without the ",1" in the load command like this:

```
LOAD "DOS 5.1",8
```

When this program has finished loading, list it by typing the word LIST and pressing the RETURN key. You should see something like this:

```
52940 NEXTNEXTNEXTNEXTNEXTFORFORFORNEXTN
EXT!!!!! GGG  %//^^ >>@#Q
43690 ++++++++++++++++++++++++++++++++++++
++++++++++++++++++++++++++++++++++++++++++++
++++++++

    DOS MANAGER V5.1/071382

    BY  BOB FAIRBAIRN

(C) 1982 COMMODORE BUSINESS MACHINES

41676 EXPWAIT
?SYNTAX  ERROR
READY.

_
```

This is definitely *not* a normal BASIC program. It is a very useful machine language program that belongs in an entirely different part of memory. To load it into its proper location you would have to give the command:

```
LOAD "DOS 5.1",8,1
```

However, there is a program that does this automatically for you. It is called C-64 WEDGE. Load this program normally and list it. Here is what you should see:

```
LOAD "C-64 WEDGE",8

SEARCHING FOR C-64 WEDGE
LOADING
READY.
LIST

10 IFA=0THENA=1:LOAD"DOS 5.1",8,1
20 IFA=1THENSYS12*4096+12*256
30 NEW
READY.

_
```

The C-64 WEDGE program is what is known as a loader program. Line 10 loads the machine language program DOS 5.1 into its proper place in memory (note the ",1"). Line 20 activates the routine with a SYS command (begin running a machine language routine that starts at the location specified). Line 30 wipes out the loader program. Many commercial programs make use of loader programs to load program segments, sprites and high resolution pictures into memory. Usually the loader program also checks to make sure that you are using a legitimate copy of the program and not a bootleg copy. As a result, loaders are often designed so that their mode of operation is obscure.

You can use a directory listing to make loading a program even easier. Put your 1541TEST/DEMO diskette in your drive and follow these steps:

Step 1: Load and list the directory like this:

```
LOAD "$",8

SEARCHING FOR $
LOADING
READY.
LIST

0  "1541TEST/DEMO     " ZX 2A
13     "HOW TO USE"           PRG
5      "HOW PART TWO"         PRG
4      "VIC-20 WEDGE"         PRG
1      "C-64 WEDGE"           PRG
4      "DOS 5.1"              PRG
11     "COPY/ALL"             PRG
9      "PRINTER TEST"         PRG
4      "DISK ADDR CHANGE"     PRG
4      "DIR"                  PRG
6      "VIEW BAM"             PRG
4      "CHECK DISK"           PRG
14     "DISPLAY T&S"          PRG
9      "PERFORMANCE TEST"     PRG
5      "SEQUENTIAL FILE"      PRG
13     "RANDOM FILE"          PRG
558 BLOCKS FREE.
READY.
```

Step 2: Move the cursor up so that it is beside the name of the program that you want to load and type the word LOAD over the blocks column. Then use the cursor right key to move the cursor to the end of the name and type ",8:". For example, if you wanted to load COPY/ALL, your display would look like this:

```
0  "1541TEST/DEMO     " ZX 2A
13     "HOW TO USE"           PRG
5      "HOW PART TWO"         PRG
4      "VIC-20 WEDGE"         PRG
1      "C-64 WEDGE"           PRG
4      "DOS 5.1"              PRG
```

```
LOAD "COPY/ALL",8:_       PRG       Cursor on this line.
9       "PRINTER TEST"    PRG
4       "DISK ADDR CHANGE" PRG
4       "DIR"             PRG
6       "VIEW BAM"        PRG
4       "CHECK DISK"      PRG
14      "DISPLAY T&S"     PRG
9       "PERFORMANCE TEST" PRG
5       "SEQUENTIAL FILE" PRG
13      "RANDOM FILE"     PRG
558 BLOCKS FREE.
READY.
```

Step 3: Don't worry about the file type, PRG, behind the name. To load the program
into memory, just press the RETURN key. The messages, SEARCHING FOR,
LOADING and READY, will overwrite the listing, but this doesn't matter. If you
used the load only option, be sure to clear the screen once the load is completed.
Otherwise you may press RETURN on one of the other lines and enter junk into
your program.

```
0 "1541TEST/DEMO    " ZX 2A
13      "HOW TO USE"      PRG
5       "HOW PART TWO"    PRG
4       "VIC-20 WEDGE"    PRG
1       "C-64 WEDGE"      PRG
4       "DOS 5.1"         PRG
LOAD "COPY/ALL",8:        PRG
9       "PRINTER TEST"    PRG
SEARCHING FOR COPY ALL"   PRG
LOADINGIR"                PRG
READY.VIEW BAM"           PRG
_       "CHECK DISK"      PRG
14      "DISPLAY T&S"     PRG
9       "PERFORMANCE TEST" PRG
5       "SEQUENTIAL FILE" PRG
13      "RANDOM FILE"     PRG
558 BLOCKS FREE.
READY.
```

Now that you know how to load and run a program, let's take a look at how you can
make a permanent copy of a program or a diskette's directory.

1.10 Listing Programs and Directories on a Printer

Normally, once a copy of a program or diskette directory has been loaded into memory
you can list it. Simply type LIST and press the RETURN key. If you are not familiar
with examining program listings on your computer, here are a few pointers:

```
LIST              Lists the entire program or directory.
LIST 100-150      Lists only lines 100 to 150 inclusive.
LIST -200         Lists all lines up to line number 200.
LIST 125-         Lists line 125 and all subsequent lines.
```

Press RUN/STOP to abort the listing.
Press CTRL to slow down the listing.

If you have a Commodore compatible printer, you can make a printed copy of the
listing by entering the following commands:

```
OPEN 3,4                                Open file to printer.
CMD3                                    Direct output to printer.
LIST (or some variation)                Output begins.
```

Once the printer stops, enter the following commands:

```
PRINT# 3                                Switch output back to screen.
CLOSE3                                  Close file to printer.
```

HINTS:

1. If you are using a Commodore printer and would like your program listings
   double-spaced instead of single-spaced, simply use any number between 128 and
   255 in place of the three in the commands listed above.

2. If you forget to enter the PRINT# and CLOSE commands, the cursor on the
   screen may not behave properly. It may stay at the end of a line when you press
   the RETURN key. If this happens to you, you can force the cursor onto a new line
   by holding down the SHIFT key when you press RETURN. To get the cursor to
   respond properly again, you will either have to power down, or enter CLOSE3 and
   then repeat the OPEN, CMD, PRINT#, CLOSE sequence (you don't have to
   LIST).

1.11 Preparing a New Diskette for Use

NOTE:

Before you buy any new, blank diskettes read Section 13.2. It gives you some idea of
what to look for.

A new, blank diskette has nothing recorded on it. Before it can be used to store
programs or data files, a pattern of tracks and sectors must be recorded onto the
surface using your 1541 disk drive. This is called formatting or newing the diskette.
Note that the NEW command that we will be using for this job is a disk command. It
is *not* the same thing as the BASIC command you give to get rid of the program in
memory. To format a blank diskette follow these four steps:

Step 1: Turn ON your computer system. Remember that your Commodore 64 or
VIC-20 is switched on first (see Section 1.2).

Step 2: Insert the blank diskette into the disk drive.

Step 3: Start the formatting process by entering a NEW command into your
computer like this. Remember to press the RETURN key at the end of the line.

SYNTAX:
```
OPEN 15,8,15,"N:disk name,id"
```

EXAMPLES:
```
OPEN 15,8,15,"N:MY TEST DISKETTE,T1"
OPEN 15,8,15,"N:GREAT GAMES,G1"
OPEN 15,8,15,"N:DATA BASE #1,DB"
OPEN 15,8,15,"N:INCOME TAX,85"
```

WHERE:

disk name = the diskette name that will appear at the top of any directory listing. The name may be up to 16 characters long. You can use letters, numbers, spaces and graphics symbols. You may not use an asterisk (*), question mark (?), comma (,) or colon (:).

id = a two character diskette identification code. Use a different combination of characters for each of your diskettes.

CAUTION:

Use a different ID for each diskette you format! It is a good idea to develop a systematic numbering system for your diskettes as soon as you buy your first box of diskettes. This will save a lot of renaming, renumbering and recopying later. For example, you might number your word processing diskettes W1, W2,..., your games diskettes G1, G2,..., etc.

As soon as you press the RETURN key to enter the command, the red drive-active LED will light up and the drive motor will turn on. There will then be a clattering noise for a second or so. This is normal. After about 80 seconds the drive-active light and the drive motor should turn off. If the drive-active light continues to flash after the drive motor stops, the formatting operation was not successful. Close the file (Step 4) and try again. If the diskette will not format correctly after several tries, it is defective—get rid of it!

Step 4: Close the command channel by entering the following command into your computer. Remember to press the RETURN key at the end of the line.

SYNTAX:
```
CLOSE 15
```

EXAMPLE:
```
CLOSE 15
```

More information about the disk command NEW and the formatting process is given in Section 4.1.

1.12 Saving Programs

When you take the time to type in a program, you will probably want to record a copy of it on a diskette so you won't have to type it in again. This is called saving the program. Saving a copy of a program onto a diskette does not destroy or affect the copy of the program in the computer's memory. To save a copy of a program in memory you use a SAVE command. It is similar to a LOAD command. It looks like this:

```
SYNTAX:
  SAVE "name",8

ALTERNATE:
  SAVE name$,8

EXAMPLES:
  SAVE "HOW TO USE",8
  SAVE "HOW PART TWO",8
  F$ = "MY PROGRAM"
  SAVE F$,8
```

Remember to press the RETURN key after typing in a command.

WHERE:

name = the name that will appear in the directory.

name$ = the name of a string variable containing the program name desired.

8 = the device number of the disk drive.

Choosing a Name

You may save your program using any name you like. The disk drive does not care whether the name you select has any relationship to the nature of the program. But, to save you endless hours of frustration, choose a name you can remember. Otherwise, as your collection of diskettes grows, you will be unable to find anything.

A program name may be up to 16 characters long. It may not contain an asterisk (*), a question mark (?) or a comma (,). In addition, the name may not begin with an "at" sign (@). A name may contain one or more graphics characters, shifted spaces, reverse field characters, or null characters, CHR$(0). However, the use of these characters is discouraged. To use any special characters in a name, you will have to store the name as a string variable.

As soon as you press the RETURN key, the drive motor will start and the red drive-active LED will light up. The program is being saved. After a few seconds, or minutes if the program is a very long one, the drive motor should stop, the red drive-active LED should go out, your computer should print the word READY on the screen, and the flashing cursor should return. This indicates that the program has been saved successfully.

If the cursor doesn't return and your computer appears to have locked up, hold down the RUN/STOP key and press the RESTORE key. This should get the cursor back. The program did not save properly. However, the program is still in the computer's memory. Change diskettes and try again.

NOTES:

1. A new diskette must be formatted first. Before you can save any programs onto a new, blank diskette, it must be formatted. If you forgot to do this earlier, just follow Steps 2 to 4 in Section 1.11. You will not lose your program in memory.

2. Watch the drive's drive-active light. If the drive-active LED is flashing after the drive motor stops, the program has *not* been saved properly. Don't panic, your program is still in the computer's memory. Simply insert a different diskette and try again. The most common causes of an error are: the diskette has not been formatted, the diskette is full or the write protect notch is covered by a tab. See Sections 3.5 and 5.10 for more information about the error status messages. Sections 2.7, 3.6 and 3.7 tell you how to read these error messages. Appendix C contains a complete list of the error messages and what they mean.

3. You can only save normal programs this way. The simple SAVE command given above can only be used to save a copy of a BASIC or machine language program that resides in the part of memory normally occupied by a BASIC program (starting at 2049 on a Commodore 64, 4097 on an unexpanded VIC-20, or 4609 on a VIC-20 with an 8/16K expander). To save a different part of memory see Section 6.4.

Practice saving a program by typing in the short demo program listed below and saving it. Here is what your screen should look like as you do this:

```
NEW                                    Dumps old program.


READY.                                 Computer response.
10 REM TEST PROGRAM                    Enter test program.
20 INPUT"HI, WHAT'S YOUR NAME";N$
30 PRINT"IT WORKS, ";N$
SAVE"TESTER",8                         Save a copy on disk.


SAVING TESTER                          Computer response.
READY.                                 Computer response.
```

Once the program has been saved, you may want to VERIFY it to be sure that it has been saved correctly (see Section 1.13). Now, load a copy of the diskette's directory and list it. Your screen should look something like this:

```
LOAD"$",8                              Load the directory.


SEARCHING FOR $                        Computer response.
LOADING                                Computer response.
READY.                                 Computer response.
LIST


O "MY TEST DISKETTE" T1 2A
1     "TESTER"            PRG
663 BLOCKS FREE.
READY.
```

Finally, load the program back in again and run it. This time your screen should look like this:

```
LOAD"TESTER",8                        Load a copy from disk.

SEARCHING FOR TESTER                  Computer response.
LOADING                               Computer response.
READY.                                Computer response.
RUN                                   You type in RUN.
HI, WHAT'S YOUR NAME? GERRY           You type in your name.
IT WORKS, GERRY                       Computer response.

READY.                                Computer  response.
-
```

As a final check to make sure that you know how to save a program, load a copy of HOW TO USE from the 1541TEST/DEMO diskette into memory and save a copy onto another diskette. The command sequences for loading and saving programs may seem a bit complicated now, but, with a little practice, they will become second nature.

1.13 Verifying Programs

After you have saved or loaded a program, you may want to check that the copy of the program stored on the diskette is an exact copy of the program in memory. This is called verifying the program. Verifying a copy of a program does not destroy or affect the copy of the program in the computer's memory or the one stored on the diskette. It merely compares the two copies. To verify a copy of a program in memory use a VERIFY command like this:

```
SYNTAX:
   VERIFY "name",8                   (Relocated program)

ALTERNATE:
   VERIFY name$,8

SYNTAX:
   VERIFY "name",8,1                 (Non-relocated program)

ALTERNATE:
   VERIFY name$,8,1

EXAMPLES:
   VERIFY "HOW TO USE",8
   VERIFY "HOW PART TWO",8
   VERIFY "DOS 5.1",8,1
   F$ = "MY PROGRAM"
   VERIFY F$,8
```

WHERE:

name	= the name of the program as it appears in the listing of the diskette's directory (wild cards may be used).
8	= the device number of the disk drive.
1	= the channel number (secondary address).
name$	= the name of a string variable containing the program's name.

As soon as you press the RETURN key, the drive motor will start and the red drive-active LED will light up. The program is being verified. After a few seconds, or minutes if the program is a very long one, the drive motor will stop, the red drive-active LED should go out, and your computer will print one of two messages, OK or VERIFY ERROR, followed by the word READY and the flashing cursor. The message OK indicates that the two copies of the program match exactly. The message VERIFY ERROR indicates that the two copies do not match exactly.

NOTES:

1. The copies must match exactly. Unless the two copies match exactly, the VERIFY ERROR message will appear. Even one extra space will do it!

2. A relocated program will not verify correctly. When you load a BASIC program into your Commodore 64 or VIC-20 that was saved onto a diskette using a different type of Commodore computer (PET, VIC or Commodore 64), the program is automatically relocated in memory so that it will run properly. A program that has been relocated will not verify correctly because the line links have been altered. See Chapter 6 for more information about the line links and the relocation process.

3. You can verify machine language routines. If you use the ",1" form of the VERIFY command, you can verify a copy of any portion of the computer's memory.

Practice verifying programs by typing in this short demo program, saving it and then verifying it. Here is what your screen should look like as you type in, save and then verify a copy of the short demo program.

```
NEW                                     Dumps old program.

READY.                                  Computer response.
10 REM TEST PROGRAM                     Enter test program.
20 INPUT"HI, WHAT'S YOUR NAME";N$
30 PRINT"GOOD WORK, ";N$
SAVE"NEW TESTER",8                      Save a copy on disk.

SAVING NEW TESTER                       Computer response.
READY.                                  Computer response.
VERIFY"NEW TESTER",8                    Verify the copy on disk.

SEARCHING FOR NEW TESTER                Computer response.
VERIFYING                               Computer response.
OK                                      Copies match response.

READY.                                  Computer response.
–
```

Now add a single space to line 10 of the program so that it looks like this:

```
10 REM TEST  PROGRAM          Two spaces after TEST.
```

Now verify the program again. Your screen should look like this:

```
VERIFY"NEW TESTER",8          Verify the copy on disk.

SEARCHING FOR NEW TESTER      Computer response.
VERIFYING                     Computer response.
?VERIFY  ERROR                Copies don't match response.
READY.                        Computer  response.
```

QUESTION:

Should I always verify a program after I save it? In general, the 1541 disk drive is a pretty reliable device. Whenever information is recorded onto a diskette, the drive reads it back automatically to make sure that it has been recorded correctly. As long as you use good quality floppy diskettes, keep your drive in good working order, and use good work habits, you should never have to VERIFY a file. It will always be saved correctly. However, for your own peace of mind, it is always a good idea to verify important files and keep a backup copy in case anything happens. Appendix E contains two programs to help you. Use the BACKUP program to make a duplicate copy of an entire diskette. The FAST COPY program makes a duplicate copy of a single program or data file.

1.14 Where Next?

The information contained in this chapter should get you well started in using your 1541 disk drive. The next chapter describes how you can use the DOS 5.1 program to simplify the basic disk operations such as loading or saving programs. If you are interested in how your disk drive works, take a look at Chapter 13. As your diskette collection grows you will need to consult Chapter 4 on diskette housekeeping. If you run into trouble, check Chapter 11. Once you have mastered the basics, you will probably want to learn about file handling. For this, Chapter 5 is a good place to start.

Chapter 2

USING DOS 5.1

Your 1541TEST/DEMO diskette includes a powerful utility, DOS 5.1, that makes using your disk drive easier. DOS 5.1 is a short, machine language program that resides at the top of your computer's memory and adds several, disk related commands to BASIC. It is designed so that it does not affect the operation of normal BASIC programs. However, it may not be compatible with some commercial, machine language programs.

The best way to learn about DOS 5.1 is by trying the various commands yourself. To get the most benefit out of this chapter you should try all the exercises on your computer. So grab your 1541TEST/DEMO diskette and get your computer fired up.

2.1 Loading DOS 5.1

Now that you're all set, insert your 1541TEST/DEMO diskette into your 1541 and let's get started. The first thing to do is load DOS 5.1 and run it. Your 1541TEST/ DEMO diskette contains two versions of the DOS 5.1 program. One is for use with the Commodore 64 and the other for the VIC-20. Do not load DOS 5.1 directly. Use a loader program. Use the appropriate command to load the loader program:

Commodore 64   **VIC-20**

```
LOAD "C-64 WEDGE",8        LOAD "VIC-20 WEDGE",8
```

The loader program is called a wedge because the DOS 5.1 program is going to wedge (hook) into BASIC to add the new, disk related commands. Once the WEDGE program has loaded, RUN it. After a few seconds you should see a display something like this:

```
DOS MANAGER V5.1/071382

     BY   BOB FAIRBAIRN

(C) 1982 COMMODORE BUSINESS MACHINES

READY.
-
```

This display indicates that the DOS 5.1 program is active. Once you see the DOS 5.1 screen display, you are ready to begin.

2.2 Displaying a Directory

Let's begin our exploration of the DOS 5.1 commands by displaying a diskette's directory. With your 1541TEST/DEMO diskette in the disk drive, type in either of the following commands:

>$ or   @$

NOTES:

1. The two characters > and @ take on a special meaning when the DOS 5.1 program is active. They become command characters. Whenever your computer encounters either of these characters as part of a line you have entered, the DOS 5.1 program checks the characters to the right of the command character to see if this is a DOS 5.1 command. If it is, the command is carried out. The two command characters are interchangeable. Take your pick.

2. Although the > is now a command character, you can still use it as a normal "greater than" symbol in a BASIC program.

As soon as you press the RETURN key, the drive-active LED should turn on and the drive motor should start. In a few seconds you should see the following screen display:

```
0  "1541TEST/DEMO     "  ZX  2A
13    "HOW TO USE"          PRG
5     "HOW PART TWO"        PRG
4     "VIC-20 WEDGE"        PRG
1     "C-64 WEDGE"          PRG
4     "DOS 5.1"             PRG
11    "COPY/ALL"            PRG
9     "PRINTER TEST"        PRG
4     "DISK ADDR CHANGE"    PRG
4     "DIR"                 PRG
6     "VIEW BAM"            PRG
4     "CHECK DISK"          PRG
14    "DISPLAY T&S"         PRG
9     "PERFORMANCE TEST"    PRG
5     "SEQUENTIAL FILE"     PRG
13    "RANDOM FILE"         PRG
558 BLOCKS FREE.
```

This is the same display that you would get if you loaded the directory and listed it. However, there is one important difference. The program in memory is not erased when you display the directory using DOS 5.1. Let's type in a test program and see how this works. Here's what to type.

```
NEW


READY.
10 FOR K=1 TO 10
20 PRINT "IT WORKS!"
30 NEXT
```

Type NEW and press RETURN to erase any program in memory.
Computer response.

Now display the diskette's directory again by typing:

```
>$            or            @$
```

Once the directory has been displayed, type LIST and press the RETURN key. Your program is still there!

Have you ever listed a long directory and had the name you wanted scroll off the screen? With DOS 5.1 you can pause a directory listing by pressing the SPACE BAR. You can resume the listing by pressing the SPACE BAR again. You don't really need to use this feature with the 1541TEST/DEMO diskette because the directory is short enough to fit on the screen. However, practice using the SPACE BAR to pause or resume the listing so you feel comfortable with this feature.

With DOS 5.1 you can even use the wild cards (? and *) to display a selective directory listing. Let's try some examples to see how this works:

Command

Resulting directory listing

```
>$:DI*

                         0 "1541TEST/DEMO    " ZX 2A
                         4    "DISK ADDR CHANGE" PRG
Any name that            4    "DIR"             PRG
starts with DI          14    "DISPLAY T&S"     PRG
                       558 BLOCKS FREE.


>$:D?S*

                         0 "1541TEST/DEMO    " ZX 2A
                         4    "DOS 5.1"         PRG
Any name starting        4    "DISK ADDR CHANGE" PRG
with D and with S       14    "DISPLAY T&S"     PRG
as the third letter    558 BLOCKS FREE.


>$:??E*

                         0 "1541TEST/DEMO    " ZX 2A
                         6    "VIEW BAM"        PRG
Any name having E        4    "CHECK DISK"     PRG
as the third letter    558 BLOCKS FREE.
```

Now that you know how to display a diskette's directory using DOS 5.1, let's take a look at how to load a program.

2.3 Loading a Program

You can use two different commands, / and %, to load a program. The first, /, is used for loading BASIC programs. The second, %, is used for loading machine language routines, character sets, hi-res graphics screens, etc.

Let's try the / command first. We'll use it to load in the program called HOW TO
USE. Here's what your screen should look like:

```
/HOW TO USE                          The load command.

SEARCHING FOR HOW TO USE             Computer response.
LOADING
READY.

_
```

Note that you did not have to type quotation marks around the program's name. You
can put the name in quotes if you want to (e.g., /"HOW TO USE"), but you are not
required to have the name in quotes.

The reason that the / command is used for loading BASIC programs is that it relocates
the incoming program. This means that the incoming program will be stored in your
computer's memory in the proper location for a BASIC program. You can load any
BASIC program that was written on a Commodore computer into your computer's
memory. The program may not run properly if it uses a lot of PEEKs or POKEs, but
at least it will load properly.

Now let's try the % command. We'll use it to load the same program again. Here's
what your screen should look like:

```
%HOW TO USE                          The load command.

SEARCHING FOR HOW TO USE             Computer response.
LOADING
```

Oops, what's that garbage doing all over the screen?

If you are using a Commodore 64, your screen is now covered with junk. What
happened? The program HOW TO USE was not written on a Commodore 64, it was
written on a Commodore PET. When you used the % command to load it, the program
was not relocated. It loaded into the same part of memory that it originally occupied
in the Commodore PET. Unfortunately, this area of the Commodore 64's memory is
the screen.

Because the % command does not relocate the program, it is used mainly for loading
machine language routines, hi-res screen images, sprite images, etc.

SPECIAL NOTE:

At this point you must either turn your computer OFF and ON and reload DOS 5.1 or
enter one of the following commands:

```
POKE 2048,0                          Commodore 64
POKE 4096,0                          VIC-20 (unexpanded)
POKE 4608,0                          VIC-20 (8 or 16K expander)
none needed                          VIC-20 (3K expander)
```

If you forget to do this, you will get a ?SYNTAX ERROR whenever you attempt to run a program. The reason is that the memory location immediately below the start of BASIC must contain a zero. The zero that is normally there was changed when we loaded the program into the wrong part of memory. The POKE command restores the normal value.

Using Wild Cards in File Names with DOS 5.1

You can use the wild cards (? and *) as part of the program name in either type of load command. For example, try loading the program VIEW BAM using the command:

```
/VI*
```

If several different program names match the one specified in the load command, the first program in the directory that matches the specified name will be loaded. For example, the name DI* matches three different entries in the directory, DISK ADDR CHANGE, DIR and DISPLAY T&S. The command, /DI*, will load the first entry, DISK ADDR CHANGE.

2.4 Loading and Running a Program

The ↑ command is used to load and run a BASIC program. The program is relocated as it is loaded. There is no DOS 5.1 command to load and run a program without relocating it. Use the following command to load and run the program HOW TO USE from the 1541TEST/DEMO diskette.

```
↑ HOW TO USE
```

As with the / and % commands, you can use the wild cards (? and *) as part of the file name. The following command will load and run the program VIEW BAM:

```
↑ VIE*
```

Now that you know how to use DOS 5.1 to load, or load and run programs, let's take a look at how it makes it easier to save a program.

2.5 Saving a BASIC Program

The ← command is used to save a copy of the BASIC program currently in memory. To experiment with this command you will need to use a formatted diskette that does not have a write protect tab on it. If you are using a brand new, blank diskette, be sure to format it first (see Section 1.11). Let's begin by typing in this short test program:

```
10 FOR K=1 TO 10
20 PRINT "THIS IS A TEST"
30 NEXT
```

Now let's save the program onto diskette using this save command:

```
←TEST #1
```

As soon as you press the RETURN key, the drive-active LED should light up and the drive motor should turn on. After a few seconds, the light should go out and the motor turn off. The current disk error status (see Section 2.7) will be displayed to the right of the SAVE "filename" message. If the message is "00, OK,00,00," the program has been saved correctly. You can double check by using the >$ command to display the directory to be sure that it has been saved properly.

2.6 Sending Disk Commands

Disk commands are messages sent to the disk drive to tell the Disk Operating System (DOS) to carry out a particular operation. There are commands to prepare a diskette for use, rename a file, scratch (eliminate) a file name from the directory and so on. Since these disk commands are usually used for eliminating unwanted files or re-arranging the files in a diskette collection, they are often called housekeeping commands.

DOS 5.1 makes it very easy to send these diskette housekeeping commands to the 1541 disk drive. All you do is type either a > or @ command character followed by the disk command you want. For example, either of these commands will erase the program, TEST #1, from our diskette:

```
>S:TEST #1          or          @S:TEST #1
```

The various diskette housekeeping commands that you can use are explained in Chapter 4.

2.7 Reading the Error Status

The Disk Operating System (DOS) in the 1541 monitors all disk operations. Once the operation has been completed satisfactorily or aborted because of some error, the DOS prepares an error status report. This report consists of an error code number, an English language message, and the track and sector numbers of the sector where the error, if any, occurred. Section 5.10 provides more information about the error status messages. Appendix C contains a complete listing of the error messages and their meanings.

If you have DOS 5.1 active, it is very easy to read the disk drive's error status report. To display the report all you do is type either > or @ and press the RETURN key. Try it now. Hopefully, you should see the following display on your screen:

```
>
00 OK 00 00
```

This indicates that no errors have been encountered. Let's generate an error and try again. Remove the diskette from your drive and enter the command >I.

When the disk drive receives the I command, it will try to initialize the diskette in the drive (see Section 4.3). Since the drive is empty, this will produce a disk error. As soon as you press the RETURN key the drive-active light should come on and the drive motor will start. After a bit of whirring and clunking, the drive motor should shut off. The drive-active LED should be flashing to signal an error. Now use the > or @ to read the error status report. You should get the following message:

```
>
21 READ ERROR 18 00
```

This indicates a type 21 read error (no sync mark) occurred while trying to read track 18, sector 0. Appendix C summarizes the various error status messages and their meaning.

2.8 DOS 5.1 Commands in Programs

Although it is not widely known, it is possible to use the DOS 5.1 commands within a program. The only restriction is that any file names or disk commands must be enclosed in quotation marks. Here are a few test programs for you to try:

```
10 PRINT "{CLR}FANCY DIRECTORY DISPLAY{D
OWN}"
20 >"$"
30 PRINT "ISN'T THAT NICE"

10 PRINT "PRESS RETURN TO INITIALIZE DIS
KETTE"
20 GET A$:IF A$<>CHR$(13) GOTO 20
30 >"I"
40 PRINT "DISK HAS BEEN INITIALIZED"

10 PRINT "PRESS RETURN TO READ ERROR STA
TUS"
20 GET A$:IF A$<>CHR$(13) GOTO 20
30 PRINT "ERROR STATUS ";:>
```

The last example illustrates two important points. A DOS 5.1 command does not have to be on a separate program line nor does it have to be at the start of a program line. You can put a command anywhere in your program.

The only real limitation on your use of DOS 5.1 commands in a program is that each command must appear in the program listing exactly as you want it executed. You cannot store file names or disk commands in string variables. The example below illustrates what is permissible and what is not:

Permissible

```
50 >"N0:NEW DATA,D1"
```

Nonpermissible

```
45 C$="N0:NEW DATA,D1"
50 >C$
```

If you decide to use DOS 5.1 commands in a program, remember that you must always have DOS 5.1 active when you use the program. Otherwise, you will get a ?SYNTAX ERROR as soon as the computer gets to the first DOS 5.1 command.

2.9 Tips on Using DOS 5.1

With DOS 5.1 you can even make use of directory listings to save some typing. Put your 1541TEST/DEMO diskette in your drive and follow these steps:

Step 1: Display the directory using the >$ command like this:

```
>$
0  "1541TEST/DEMO     "  ZX  2A
13     "HOW TO USE"           PRG
5      "HOW PART TWO"         PRG
4      "VIC-20 WEDGE"         PRG
1      "C-64 WEDGE"           PRG
4      "DOS 5.1"              PRG
11     "COPY/ALL"             PRG
9      "PRINTER TEST"         PRG
4      "DISK ADDR CHANGE"     PRG
4      "DIR"                  PRG
6      "VIEW BAM"             PRG
4      "CHECK DISK"           PRG
14     "DISPLAY T&S"          PRG
9      "PERFORMANCE TEST"     PRG
5      "SEQUENTIAL FILE"      PRG
13     "RANDOM FILE"          PRG
558 BLOCKS FREE.
```

Step 2: Move the cursor up so that it is beside the name of the program that you want to load and type either the load or load-and-run command. If you wanted to load COPY/ALL, your display would look like this:

```
>$
0  "1541TEST/DEMO     "  ZX  2A
13     "HOW TO USE"           PRG
5      "HOW PART TWO"         PRG
4      "VIC-20 WEDGE"         PRG
1      "C-64 WEDGE"           PRG
4      "DOS 5.1"              PRG
/_     "COPY/ALL"             PRG        Cursor on this line.
9      "PRINTER TEST"         PRG
4      "DISK ADDR CHANGE"     PRG
4      "DIR"                  PRG
6      "VIEW BAM"             PRG
4      "CHECK DISK"           PRG
14     "DISPLAY T&S"          PRG
9      "PERFORMANCE TEST"     PRG
5      "SEQUENTIAL FILE"      PRG
13     "RANDOM FILE"          PRG
558 BLOCKS FREE.
```

Step 3: Don't worry about any extra digits in the blocks column or the file type, PRG, behind the name. Just press the RETURN key and the load (or load and run) command will be carried out. The display will be overprinted by the "SEARCHING

FOR," "LOADING," and "READY." messages but this doesn't matter. If you are using the load-only option, clear the screen to eliminate the garbage once the load is complete.

```
>$
0  "1541TEST/DEMO    "  ZX  2A
13    "HOW TO USE"        PRG
5     "HOW PART TWO"      PRG
4     "VIC-20 WEDGE"      PRG
1     "C-64 WEDGE"        PRG
4     "DOS 5.1"           PRG
/1    "COPY/ALL"          PRG
9     "PRINTER TEST"      PRG
SEARCHING FOR COPY ALL"  PRG
LOADINGIR"               PRG
READY.VIEW BAM"          PRG
_     "CHECK DISK"        PRG
14    "DISPLAY T&S"       PRG
9     "PERFORMANCE TEST"  PRG
5     "SEQUENTIAL FILE"   PRG
13    "RANDOM FILE"       PRG
558 BLOCKS FREE.
```

REMINDER:

If you use this technique to load, rather than load and run a program, be sure to clear the screen once the program has loaded. If you don't, and happen to press the RETURN key on one of the following lines of the listing, the computer will interpret this as a new BASIC line and add it to the program. Since the following line is not a valid BASIC statement, your program will abort with a ?SYNTAX ERROR:

```
14   "DISPLAY T&S"     PRG
```

You can use the directory listing to save a bit of typing when sending disk commands to scratch, copy or rename a file. However, you must delete the quotation marks around the file name and the file type (e.g., PRG) behind the name. As a result, it is hardly worth the effort.

Once you become familiar with the commands you will find DOS 5.1 an invaluable utility. Many people find it so helpful that they make a habit of storing a copy on each new diskette that they format. Many thanks, Bob Fairbairn.

Chapter 3

THE COMMAND CHANNEL

The command channel is used to send commands to the disk drive and read the disk drive's error status report. You can use DOS 5.1 to carry out these tasks from immediate mode. However, if you will be writing programs that use the disk drive, you will need to know how to use the command channel.

Even if you are a more experienced 1541 user you should skim through this chapter. There are a number of interesting tidbits, including four different ways to read the error status from immediate mode without using DOS 5.1!

3.1 The Command Channel

The command channel is a special communications channel between your computer and disk drive. It is used to:

1. Send diskette housekeeping commands to the disk drive.
2. Send direct-access commands to the disk drive.
3. Input the error status from the disk drive.

This chapter covers how to send diskette housekeeping commands and how to input the error status. The direct-access commands are not required for normal file handling. They are used primarily in specialized disk utility programs. As a result, they are not discussed in this book. However, many of the disk utility programs listed in this book make use of direct-access commands. The more advanced book, *Inside Commodore DOS*, by Richard Immers and Gerald G. Neufeld, (DATAMOST, 1984), discusses how to use these commands effectively.

3.2 Opening the Command Channel

To establish communications between your computer and the disk drive you use an OPEN statement. Since the command channel is channel number 15, the OPEN statement will look like this:

```
SYNTAX:
  OPEN file#,device#,cmd chnl#


EXAMPLES:
  OPEN 15,8,15
  OPEN 15,9,15
```

WHERE:

file#   = the logical file number (any integer 1-127). Often 15 is used
      as a file# for the command channel because it is easy to
      remember that this is the command channel. In this book
      the command channel will always be file# 15.

device# = the device number. Normally a 1541 is device number
      eight. A 1541's device# can be changed either temporarily
      or permanently (see Sections 5.7 and 12.3).

cmd chnl# = 15, the command channel number. The command channel
      is always channel# 15. Channels 0 and 1 are reserved for
      LOAD and SAVE. Channels 2-14 are for file handling.

You can issue an OPEN statement either by typing it in and pressing the RETURN
key (immediate mode) or from within a BASIC program. When you open the
command channel, nothing will appear to happen.

3.3 Sending Disk Commands

A disk command is a message to the 1541's Disk Operating System (DOS) that tells it
to do a particular task such as formatting a diskette or renaming a file. Disk commands are sent to the disk drive using a PRINT# statement. PRINT# is a BASIC
statement and is similar to the more familiar PRINT statement. It looks like this:

```
SYNTAX:
  PRINT# file#,"command"
```

```
EXAMPLES:
  PRINT# 15,"NO:TEST DISK,T3"
  PRINT#15,"IO"
  PRINT#15,"VO"
```

WHERE:

file#   = the logical file number used when you opened the command
      channel.

command = the diskette housekeeping command to be sent to the disk
      drive. The commands to use are described in detail in
      Chapter 4.

NOTES:

1. PRINT# is a single BASIC keyword. You may not put a space between PRINT
   and the # sign. Spaces following the # sign are optional.

2. Use the correct abbreviation. You may abbreviate PRINT# by typing P followed
   by a shifted R (pR in upper/lower case mode). Do not use ?# as an abbreviation.
   This appears to be correct in a program listing but causes a ?SYNTAX ERROR.

You can issue a PRINT# statement either by typing it in and pressing the RETURN key (immediate mode) or by including it in a BASIC program. When you send a command, the disk drive will interpret the command and carry it out. Most commands cause the drive-active LED to turn on and the drive motor to start. It may take several minutes for the command to be carried out. While the disk drive is carrying out the command, the computer is free. You can play a game, type in a new program or edit an existing program. However, if you try to access the disk drive, the computer will appear to hang up until the disk drive has completed the previous command. Once the command has been completed, the drive motor will stop and the drive-active LED should go out.

If the drive-active LED begins to flash ON and OFF regularly, an error has occurred. Either the command was incorrect or a disk error has occurred. Read the disk drive's error status to determine the cause of the error (see Sections 3.6 and 3.7).

3.4 Combining OPEN and PRINT# Statements

An alternate form of the OPEN command allows you to send a single disk command to the disk drive when you open the command channel. This combined form looks like this:

```
SYNTAX:
   OPEN file#, device#, cmd chnl#,"disk command"


EXAMPLES:
   OPEN 15,8,15,"N0:GOOD GAMES,G1"
   OPEN 15,8,15,"S0:TEST FILE"
   OPEN 15,8,15,"V0"
   OPEN 15,8,15,"I0"
```

WHERE:

file# = the logical file number used when you opened the command channel.

device# = the device number. Normally a 1541 is device number eight. A 1541's device# can be changed either temporarily or permanently (see Sections 5.7 and 12.3).

cmd chnl# = 15, the command channel number. The command channel is always channel# 15. Channels 0 and 1 are reserved for LOAD and SAVE. Channels 2-14 are for file handling.

command = the disk housekeeping command to be sent to the disk drive. The commands to use are described in detail in Chapter 4.

This form of the OPEN statement is handy when you have just a single disk command to send. If you get a ?FILE OPEN message when you use this form, this file# is already open. When this happens, it is usually easiest to close the file by typing CLOSE 15 and pressing the RETURN key (see Section 3.8). Now, move the cursor up to the OPEN statement, and press the RETURN key to reopen the command channel and send the command.

3.5 Reading the Command Channel

The most common reason for reading the command channel is to access the 1541's error status message. However, you can also use it to read the contents of the disk drive's RAM or ROM memory by using a direct access MEMORY-READ (M-R) command. Since this is not required for most operations, we will focus on reading the error status.

The Disk Operating System (DOS) in the 1541 monitors all disk operations and generates an error status report when the operation is completed or aborted. The report consists of four parts:

1. An error code number.
2. An English language error message.
3. The track number where the error, if any, occurred.
4. The sector number where the error, if any, occurred.

The various possible messages and their meanings are explained in detail in Appendix C.

You access the disk drive's error status report by reading the command channel. Normally an INPUT# statement is used to read the report. However, you can also use a GET# statement. Unfortunately, both INPUT# and GET# can only be used within a BASIC program. They may not be used in immediate mode. However, you can use simulated GET# and INPUT# commands to read the error status from immediate mode as indicated in Section 3.7.

In order to read the report you need to know a bit about the INPUT# and GET# statements. Only those characteristics of these statements that apply to reading the error channel are mentioned here. For more details regarding these statements, see Section 5.10. The usual format for the INPUT# statement is:

```
SYNTAX:
   INPUT# file#, var list
```

```
EXAMPLES:
   INPUT# 15,EN,EM$,ET,ES
   INPUT# 5,NAM$(K)
```

WHERE:

file#   = the file number used when you opened the command channel.

var list   = a list of one or more variable names. If more than one name appears, the names must be separated by commas.

NOTES:

1. INPUT# is a single BASIC keyword. You may not put a space between INPUT and the # sign. Spaces following the # sign are optional.

2. Use the correct abbreviation. You may abbreviate INPUT# by typing I followed by a shifted N (iN in upper/lower case mode).

3. INPUT# reads one or more complete numeric or string values at one time. Since the error status report consists of one string and three numeric values, the INPUT# statement can read and assign all these values quickly and easily. The INPUT# statement is the preferred way to read the drive's error status.

The usual format for the GET# statement is:

```
SYNTAX:
  GET# file#, var list

EXAMPLES:
  GET# 15,A$
  GET# 5,J$,K$,L$
```

WHERE:

file#   = the file number used when you opened the command
                  channel.

var list   = a list of one or more variable names. If more than one
                  name appears, the names must be separated by commas.

NOTES:

1. GET# is a single BASIC keyword. You may not put a space between GET and the # sign. Spaces following the # sign are optional.

2. There is no abbreviation for GET#.

3. GET# stores only one character at a time in the named variable(s). As a result, GET# is not normally used to read the disk drive's error status.

3.6 Reading the Error Status in a Program

It is a good idea to read the error status after every disk operation in your program to be sure that the operation was completed successfully. You may use either an INPUT# or a GET# statement to read the status. However, since you will probably want to interpret the status report to determine whether or not to abort the program, you will usually want to use the INPUT# form. The GET# form is only useful for displaying the disk status on the screen without interpreting it.

No matter which form you use, you will probably want to write the error status check as a subroutine. This allows you to check the disk status quickly and easily.

INPUT# form of reading the disk drive's error status report:

```
10 OPEN 15,8,15                        Open command channel.
:  :  :  :  :  :                        Program continues.
150 PRINT#15,"NO:TESTER,XY"            Disk operation.
160 GOSUB 500                          Check disk drive status.
:  :  :  :  :  :                        Program continues.
490 CLOSE 15                           Close command channel.
499 END
500 REM SUB TO CHECK STATUS
510 INPUT#15,EN,E$,ET,ES               Read error status.
520 IF EN<20 THEN RETURN               Everything is OK.
530 PRINT "FATAL DISK ERROR"           Trouble.
540 PRINT EN;E$;ET;ES                  Print status report.
550 CLOSE 15                           Close all disk files.
560 END                                Abort program.
```

GET# form of reading the disk drive's error status report:

```
10 OPEN 15,8,15                        Open command channel.
:  :  :  :  :  :                        Program continues.
150 PRINT#15,"NO:TESTER,XY"            Disk operation.
160 GOSUB 500                          Print disk drive status.
:  :  :  :  :  :                        Program continues.
490 CLOSE 15                           Close command channel.
499 END
500 REM SUB TO PRINT STATUS
510 GET#15,A$                          Read one character.
520 PRINT A$;                          Print one character.
530 IF A$<>CHR$(13) GOTO 510           Read till carriage return.
540 RETURN
```

3.7 Reading the Error Status in Immediate Mode

Normally, it is impossible to read the error status in immediate mode. The reason is that the INPUT# and GET# statements only work when they are included in a program. If you try to use them in immediate mode, you will get an ?ILLEGAL DIRECT ERROR. However, it is possible to simulate program mode, or use the Commodore 64's ROM routines to simulate these commands and read the error report from direct mode as indicated below.

Simulated GET# for reading the error status in immediate mode:

To read the error status while in immediate mode, type in the following commands. Remember to press RETURN after each line.

```
CLOSE15

POKE58,0:OPEN15,8,15:FORK=1TO30:GET#15,A
$:?A$;:IFST=0THENNEXT
```

or

```
CLOSE15:OPEN15,8,15

FORK=1TO30:SYS(43909)15,A$:?A$;:IFST=0TH
ENNEXT
```

In the first version, the POKE command causes the computer to think it is running a program. This allows the use of the normal GET# statement. If you are sure that file# 15 is not open, you can eliminate the initial CLOSE 15 line. However, if file# 15 is already open, you must close it (see Section 3.8) and then reopen it as part of the GET# line.

In the second version, the SYS command makes use of the Commodore 64's GET# ROM routine but enters it after the check for immediate mode. In this version you can eliminate the first line if file# 15 is already open to the command channel.

Simulated INPUT# for reading the error status in immediate mode:

An alternate way to read the error status while in immediate mode is to use a simulated INPUT#. As before you can use either of two versions. Take your pick. Remember to press RETURN.

```
CLOSE15

POKE58,0:POKE198,1:OPEN15,8,15:INPUT#15,
 E,E$,T,S:?E;E$;T;S
```

Note the space between the comma following INPUT# 15 and the E. This space *must* be there.

or

```
CLOSE15

POKE58,0:OPEN15,8,15:SYS(43941)15, E,E$,
T,S:?E;E$;T;S
```

Note the space between the comma following SYS(43941)15 and the E. This space *must* be there.

If you are sure file# 15 is *not* open, you may omit the CLOSE 15 line with either version. Since the check for program mode is deep within the INPUT# ROM routine, both versions use the POKE to simulate program mode and must include the OPEN command. Since the first version uses only standard BASIC commands, you will probably find it easier to remember.

3.8 Closing the Command Channel

Once you have finished using the command channel you should close it. You use the BASIC statement CLOSE to do this. It looks like this:

```
SYNTAX:
  CLOSE file#

EXAMPLES:
  CLOSE 15
  CLOSE15
```

WHERE:

file#   = the file number used when you opened the command
              channel.

NOTES:

1. Closing the command channel closes all files in the 1541. When you close the command channel, all disk files that are open will be closed automatically *in the disk drive.* Because of this, you should OPEN the command near the beginning of any program you write and leave it open until the end of your program. See the HINT below for a useful application of this. CAUTION: Although the files will be closed properly in the disk drive, they will still be open in the computer.

2. Loading, saving, running, or editing closes files in the computer. Whenever you LOAD, SAVE or RUN a program, all files that are open in the computer, including the command channel, will be closed. Adding to or editing a program will close all the files in the computer except the command channel. CAUTION: Although the files will be closed in the computer, they will still be open in the drive. If this happens, you may end up with one or more unclosed disk files. Use the HINT below to prevent this.

You can issue a CLOSE statement either by typing it in and pressing the RETURN key (immediate mode) or by including it in a BASIC program. When you CLOSE the command channel, you will not see any obvious effect unless some other disk files are also open. If one or more other files are open (the drive active light will be on), the drive motor will turn on briefly as the files are closed. After a few seconds, the drive motor will stop and the drive-active LED should go out. If the drive-active LED begins flashing, an error has occurred. Read the drive's error status report (see Sections 3.6 and 3.7) to find the cause of the error.

HINT:

Preventing improperly closed disk files. Have you ever had a program that aborted with a ?SYNTAX ERROR and left a disk file open? As long as you spot the red drive-active light glowing before you edit that offending line, everything is fine; the file is still open in both the computer and the disk drive. All you do is issue the appropriate CLOSE statement from immediate mode and the file will be closed properly. If you forget the file#, you can either LIST the program and find it or use the command channel fix below.

However, most of us are in such a rush to fix that offending line that we don't notice that the drive-active light is on until after we have edited the line. Once you do any editing, you have a problem. The computer will have closed the file automatically as soon as you did any editing, but the file is still open in the drive. Issuing a CLOSE command won't work because the file is already closed in the computer. The solution is to enter this line and press RETURN.

```
CLOSE15:OPEN15,8,15:CLOSE15
```

This works because of the special characteristics of the command channel. You can OPEN it without affecting any other active disk files. However, when you CLOSE it, any other active disk files are closed. The first CLOSE15 will close all the disk files if file# 15 happens to be open to the command channel. The rest of the command opens the command channel and then closes it immediately. The final CLOSE ensures that all active files will be properly closed.

DISKETTE HOUSEKEEPING

NOTE:

This chapter is designed for easy reference. As a result, each section must be independently readable and understandable. While this format may appear awkward and repetitious in a complete reading, users will rapidly discover that it saves much page flipping.

Unless you plan on only using commercially recorded software, you will have to do some housekeeping to maintain your collection of diskettes. As you saw in Chapter 1, you even have to do some housekeeping before you can save anything on a new, blank diskette; it must be formatted (newed) first. This chapter is designed to take some of the mystery out of diskette housekeeping. It not only tells you what to do, it also tells you what happens to your diskette when you issue a housekeeping command.

Diskette housekeeping involves sending commands to the disk drive over the command channel. You can either use the command channel directly (see Chapter 3) or use DOS 5.1 to make your job easier (see Chapter 2). In immediate mode you can use either method. If you will be building diskette housekeeping into a program, you will have to use the command channel directly.

There are a variety of tasks that are considered diskette housekeeping. They include the following:

1. Formatting a new diskette (full new).
2. Reusing a diskette (short new).
3. Initializing a diskette.
4. Scratching a file.
5. Renaming a file.
6. Copying a file.
7. Combining two or more files.
8. Validating a diskette.

This chapter explains how to do each of these tasks and describes what actually happens to your diskette as the command is carried out. If you feel somewhat lost after reading the chapter, don't panic! The chapter concludes with a listing of a menu-driven BASIC program that makes diskette housekeeping a breeze.

A few additional, non-standard diskette housekeeping tasks such as creating peculiar directory entries and changing a diskette's name are discussed in Section 13.8.

4.1 Formatting a New Diskette

When you purchase a new diskette there is nothing recorded on it. Before you can use it for storing programs or data files, the diskette must be formatted (newed). Despite what you may have heard from your Apple owning friends, this is *not* the same as initializing a diskette. In Commodore jargon, initializing a diskette means reading some directory information from the diskette and storing it in the disk drive's memory (see Section 4.3). Formatting or newing a diskette involves recording a pattern of information on each of 35 concentric tracks. This information allows the drive to tell which track, as well as which part of the track, it is on. The formatting process takes about 80 seconds to complete. Once formatting is completed, any information previously recorded on that diskette is permanently lost.

A NEW command is used to tell the disk drive to format a diskette. This is not the same as the NEW command in BASIC. This NEW command is a disk command and looks like this:

```
General form:
  NEW0:disk name,id

Alternate form:
  N:disk name,id

Examples:
  NEW0:GOOD GAMES #1,G1
  N:WORD PROCESSING,W1
```

WHERE:

NEW   = is the disk command. The command NEW may be abbreviated as N. The zero is the drive number. It is a holdover from Commodore's dual drives. Its use is optional on the 1541 disk drive.

disk name   = is the name that will appear on the first line of the directory listing. The name may be up to 16 characters long. Any letters, numbers, or graphics characters, except a comma (,), a question mark (?) or an asterisk (*) may be used. Using reverse-field characters in names is not recommended.

id   = is a two character disk ID. This appears following the disk name at the top of the directory listing. Any letters, numbers, or graphics characters may be used.

CAUTION:

Use a different ID for each diskette you format! It is a good idea to develop a systematic numbering system for your diskettes as soon as you buy your first box of diskettes. This will save a lot of renaming, renumbering and recopying later. For example, you might number your word processing diskettes W1, W2,..., your games diskettes G1, G2,..., etc..

Sending a NEW command using DOS 5.1:

```
SYNTAX:
  >NO:disk name,id

ALTERNATE:
  @NO:disk name,id

EXAMPLES:
  >NO:GOOD GAMES #1,G1
  @N:WORD PROCESSING,W1
```

Sending a NEW command using the command channel:

```
SYNTAX:
  OPEN 15,8,15
  PRINT#15,"NO:disk name,id"
  CLOSE 15

ALTERNATE:
  OPEN 15,8,15,"NO:disk name,id":CLOSE 15

EXAMPLE #1: (immediate mode)
  OPEN 15,8,15
  PRINT#15,"NO:C-64 PROGRAMS,64"
  CLOSE 15

EXAMPLE #2: (immediate mode)
  OPEN 15,8,15,"NO:SUPER STUFF,SS":CLOSE 15

EXAMPLE #3: (program mode)
  100 OPEN 15,8,15
  :   :   :   :   :
  360 PRINT#15,"N:CLUB MAIL LIST,C1"
  :   :   :   :   :
  500 CLOSE 15

EXAMPLE #4: (program mode)
  100 OPEN 15,8,15
  :   :   :   :   :
  350 FI$="NO:C-64 PROGRAMS,64"
  360 PRINT#15,FI$
  :   :   :   :   :
  500 CLOSE 15

EXAMPLE #5: (program mode)
  100 OPEN 15,8,15
  :   :   :   :   :
  250 INPUT"NEW DISK'S NAME";DN$
  260 INPUT"NEW DISK'S ID";DI$
  270 PRINT#15,"N:"+DN$+","+DI$
  :   :   :   :   :
  500 CLOSE 15
```

Examples 4 and 5 illustrate how you can use string variables to store either the entire disk command (4) or parts of a disk command (5). You can use this technique in either immediate or program mode as long as you use the command channel. You cannot use this technique when using DOS 5.1.

What Happens When You Issue a NEW Command?

When you send a NEW command to the disk drive, the disk operating system in the drive interprets (parses) the command. If the syntax is incorrect the command is rejected, the red drive-active light begins flashing and a SYNTAX ERROR report is generated (error number 30, 31, 32, 33, 34, or 39).

If the syntax is correct, formatting begins. The red drive-active LED turns on, the drive motor starts up and the drive's stepper motor moves the record/play head to the outer edge of the diskette (track 1). The head is moved outward a total of 45 tracks. When it reaches track 1 a cam on the drive pulley hits a mechanical stop. It is the cam hitting the stop that causes the clattering noise so familiar to 1541 owners. For rather obvious reasons this is known as doing a bump to track 1.

The record/play head is now stationary and the diskette is rotating at 300 rpm. As the diskette makes one complete rotation a circular strip of the diskette passes over the record/play head. This circular strip, about 1/64th of an inch wide, is called a track. First, any existing information recorded on this strip (track) is erased. Then a new pattern of information is recorded. This new information subdivides the track into a number of sectors. The diagram below shows how the tracks and sectors are arranged and numbered on a 1541 formatted diskette.

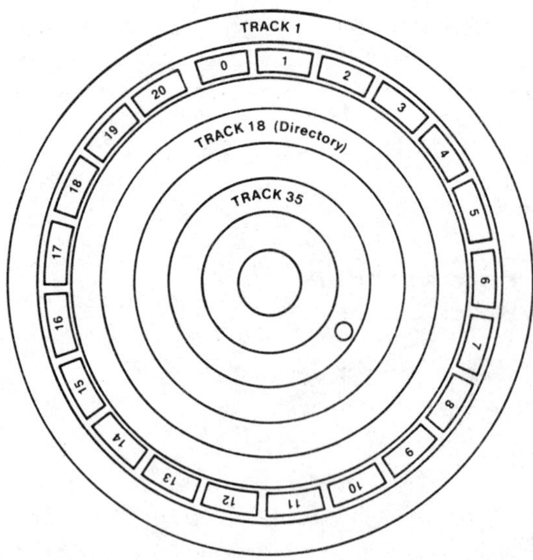

The number of sectors on a track is not constant. The tracks near the outer edge of the disk are longer and are divided into more sectors. The chart below shows how the number of sectors varies according to the track:

Zone	Track Numbers	Sector Numbers	Total Sectors
1	1 to 17	0 to 20	21
2	18 to 24	0 to 18	19
3	25 to 30	0 to 17	18
4	31 to 35	0 to 16	17

Each sector on a track consists of two parts, an identifying header and a data block containing 256 bytes (characters) of data. Here is an overview of what a short segment of a track looks like:

```
SYNC | Header of | Header | SYNC | Data block    | Tail | SYNC | Header of | Header | SYNC | Data
MARK | Sector #0 | Gap    | MARK | of Sector #0  | Gap  | MARK | Sector #1 | Gap    | MARK | Block
```

Note that both the header and the data block begin with a special character called a SYNC MARK and end with a gap. The SYNC MARK alerts the disk operating system that important information is coming up. The gap allows the drive some time to get ready for the next SYNC MARK. During formatting both the header information and a dummy data block are recorded for each of the sectors that make up a track. When you save a program or data file on the diskette, the original data blocks will be overwritten by the information to be saved. However, the header information is never altered unless you reformat the diskette.

Once all the headers and data blocks on the track have been recorded, they are read back and checked to make sure they have been recorded properly. If everything checks out, the head is moved inward one track (you'll hear a click as the stepper motor moves the head), and the process is repeated. If an error is detected, the disk operating system will try formatting that track again. You can get some idea of how many attempts it took by noting the time between clicks. If there is some flaw on the diskette that prevents formatting a track correctly, the disk operating system will eventually give up and report a 21, READ ERROR,00,00. Why on track 0, sector 0? Just because.

When all 35 tracks have been formatted, the stepper motor will move the head outward to track 18. The disk name, disk ID, and a blank Block Availability Map (BAM) will be recorded on track 18, sector 0. A blank directory will be recorded on track 18, sector 1. Once this has been done, formatting is complete. The drive-active LED and the drive motor are switched off.

4.2 Reusing a Diskette

Eventually you will want to erase everything off one of your diskettes and reuse it for something else. One way to do this is to format the entire diskette again as we did in Section 4.1 for a blank diskette. A quicker method is to simply erase the existing disk name, directory, and Block Availability Map (BAM) and leave the rest of the diskette alone. As this takes only a few seconds to do and you use a variation of the NEW command to do it, this is often referred to as a short NEW. Note that the command is very similar to an ordinary NEW, the only difference is that you omit the disk ID.

General form:
  NEWO:disk name

Alternate form:
  N:disk name

Examples:
  NO:GOOD GAMES #1
  N:WORD PROCESSING

WHERE:

NEW   = is the disk command. The command NEW may be abbre-
            viated as N. The zero is the drive number. It is a holdover
            from Commodore's dual drives. Its use is optional on the
            1541 disk drive.

disk name = is the name that will appear on the first line of the direc-
            tory listing. The name may be up to 16 characters long.
            Any letters, numbers or graphics characters, except a
            comma (,), a question mark (?) or an asterisk (*) may be
            used. Using reverse-field characters in names is not
            recommended.

Sending a short NEW command using DOS 5.1:

SYNTAX:
  >N:disk name

ALTERNATE:
  @NO:disk name

EXAMPLES:
  >NO:GOOD GAMES #1
  @N:WORD PROCESSING

Sending a short NEW command using the command channel:

SYNTAX:
  OPEN 15,8,15
  PRINT#15,"N:disk name"
  CLOSE 15

ALTERNATE:
  OPEN 15,8,15,"NO:disk name":CLOSE 15

EXAMPLE #1: (immediate mode)
  OPEN 15,8,15
  PRINT#15,"N:C-64 PROGRAMS"
  CLOSE 15

```
EXAMPLE #2: (immediate mode)
  OPEN 15,8,15,"NO:SUPER STUFF":CLOSE 15

EXAMPLE #3: (program mode)
  100 OPEN 15,8,15
  :   :   :   :   :
  360 PRINT#15,"N:CLUB MAIL LIST"
  :   :   :   :   :
  500 CLOSE 15

EXAMPLE #4: (program mode)
  100 OPEN 15,8,15
  :   :   :   :   :
  350 FI$="N:C-64 PROGRAMS"
  360 PRINT#15,FI$
  :   :   :   :   :
  500 CLOSE 15

EXAMPLE #5: (program mode)
  100 OPEN 15,8,15
  :   :   :   :   :
  250 INPUT"NEW DISK'S NAME";DN$
  270 PRINT#15,"N:"+DN$
  :   :   :   :   :
  500 CLOSE 15
```

Examples 4 and 5 illustrate how you can use string variables to store either the entire disk command (4) or a part of the disk command (5). You can use this technique in either immediate or program mode as long as you use the command channel. You cannot use this technique when using DOS 5.1.

What happens when you issue a short NEW command?

When you send a NEW command to the disk drive, the disk operating system in the drive interprets (parses) the command. If the syntax is incorrect, the command is rejected, the red drive-active light begins flashing and a SYNTAX ERROR report is generated (error number 30, 31, 32, 33, 34, or 39).

If the syntax is correct, the command is carried out. As always, the red drive-active LED turns on and the drive motor starts. This time, however, the head moves directly to track 18. The new disk name, the old disk ID (it hasn't been changed), and a blank Block Availabilty Map (BAM) will be recorded on track 18, sector 0. A blank directory will be recorded on track 18, sector 1. The remainder of the diskette is unaffected. Once these two sectors have been modified, the drive-active LED and the drive motor are switched off. Note that this is much different than what happens when a full reformatting takes place. In that case, all the sectors on the diskette were rewritten and any information previously stored on the diskette was permanently lost.

WARNING:

If you have been encountering disk errors when using a particular diskette, do not use a short NEW on it. If you do, the errors will remain. The only hope for a diskette that contains read errors is to copy as much information as possible onto another diskette and then reformat the entire error ridden diskette using a full NEW as described in Section 4.1.

NOTE:

Since only two sectors on the diskette are modified during a short NEW, it is possible to recover the information stored on the diskette if you issued a short NEW command by mistake. Section 11.4 explains how to do this.

4.3 Initializing a Diskette

In Commodore jargon, initializing a diskette means reading a copy of a diskette's Block Availability Map (BAM) from track 18, sector 0 into the disk drive's RAM memory. Normally the drive does this automatically whenever you insert a diskette and perform any disk operation. However, it is a good idea to initialize the diskette whenever you switch diskettes and *whenever a disk error occurs*. This ensures that the drive will correctly recognize the diskette. An initalize command looks like this:

```
General form:
  INITIALIZE0


Alternate form:
  I


Examples:
  I0
  I
```

WHERE:

INITIALIZE   = the disk command. The command INITIALIZE may
                   be abbreviated as I. The zero is the drive number. It
                   is a holdover from Commodore's dual drives. Its use
                   is optional on the 1541 disk drive.

Sending an INITIALIZE command using DOS 5.1:

```
SYNTAX:
  >I0


ALTERNATE:
  @I0


EXAMPLES:
  >I0
  @I
```

Sending an INITIALIZE command using the command channel:

```
SYNTAX:
  OPEN 15,8,15
  PRINT#15,"IO"
  CLOSE 15

ALTERNATE:
  OPEN 15,8,15,"IO":CLOSE 15

EXAMPLE #1: (immediate mode)
  OPEN 15,8,15
  PRINT#15,"IO"
  CLOSE 15

EXAMPLE #2: (immediate mode)
  OPEN 15,8,15,"IO":CLOSE 15

EXAMPLE #3: (program mode)
  100 OPEN 15,8,15
  :   :   :   :   :
  360 PRINT#15,"I"
  :   :   :   :   :
  500 CLOSE 15

EXAMPLE #4: (program mode)
  100 OPEN 15,8,15
  :   :   :   :   :
  350 FI$="IO"
  360 PRINT#15,FI$
  :   :   :   :   :
  500 CLOSE 15
```

Example 4 illustrates how you can use string variables to store the disk command.
You can use this technique in either immediate or program mode as long as you use
the command channel. You cannot use this technique when using DOS 5.1.

What happens when you issue an INITIALIZE command?

When you send an INITIALIZE command to the disk drive, the disk operating
system in the drive interprets (parses) the command. If the syntax is incorrect, the
command is rejected, the red drive-active light begins flashing and a SYNTAX
ERROR report is generated (error number 30, 31, 32, 33, 34, or 39).

If the syntax is correct, initialization begins. As always, the red drive-active LED
turns on and the drive motor starts. The head moves directly to track 18. The data
block of track 18, sector 0 is read into the disk drive's RAM memory (from $0700-
07FF). The disk drive's copy of the diskette's ID (in memory location $12/$13) is also
updated. Once this happens the drive-active LED and the drive motor are turned off.

NOTES:

Occasionally you may find that you get a 29, DISK ID MISMATCH,00,00 error when you initialize a diskette. Don't panic, just initialize the diskette again and the error should go away. If you get a 21, READ ERROR,18,00, you are probably trying to initialize a brand new, unformatted diskette. If you are sure the diskette is formatted and still get read errors, you have serious problems. See Section 11.5 for possible solutions.

4.4 Scratching a File

When you no longer need a program or data file, you can scratch it. This will eliminate the file's name from the directory and free the sectors (blocks) that were used to store the program or data file. This allows you to save new information there. A SCRATCH command looks like this:

```
General form:
  SCRATCHO:file name

Alternate form:
  S:file name

Examples:
  SO:OLD JUNK
  S:TEST ??.BAS
```

WHERE:

SCRATCH   = is the disk command. The command SCRATCH may be abbreviated as S. The zero is the drive number. It is a holdover from Commodore's dual drives. Its use is optional on the 1541 disk drive.

file name   = is the name of the file to be scratched. Wild cards (? and *) may be used in the name.

WARNINGS:

1. More than one file may be scratched. If you use wild cards in specifying the name of the file to be scratched, the resulting pattern may match more than one file name in the directory. If this happens, *all the files whose names match the pattern will be scratched.*

2. Do not scratch an unclosed file. You should *not* scratch a file that has an * beside its file type in the directory (e.g., *PRG, *SEQ, or *USR). The * indicates that this is a file that has not been closed properly. These files should be eliminated by using a VALIDATE command (see Section 4.8). If you accidentally SCRATCH an unclosed file, VALIDATE the diskette as soon as possible.

NOTE:

When you scratch a file, you create a vacancy in the directory file. The next time you save a program or store a data file on this diskette the new name will not be added to the end of the directory. It will fill the vacancy in the directory.

Sending a SCRATCH command using DOS 5.1:

```
SYNTAX:
  >S:file name

ALTERNATE:
  @SO:file name

EXAMPLES:
  >SO:TAXES 1981
  @S:WP/*
```

Sending a SCRATCH command using the command channel:

```
SYNTAX:
  OPEN 15,8,15
  PRINT#15,"SO:file name"
  CLOSE 15

ALTERNATE:
  OPEN 15,8,15,"SO:file name":CLOSE 15

EXAMPLE #1: (immediate mode)
  OPEN 15,8,15
  PRINT#15,"SO:GAME VERSION 1"
  CLOSE 15

EXAMPLE #2: (immediate mode)
  OPEN 15,8,15,"SO:BUNCHA*":CLOSE 15

EXAMPLE #3: (program mode)
  100 OPEN 15,8,15
  :   :   :   :   :
  360 PRINT#15,"SO:V?/GAME.P"
  :   :   :   :   :
  500 CLOSE 15

EXAMPLE #4: (program mode)
  100 OPEN 15,8,15
  :   :   :   :   :
  350 FI$="SO:UNPAID*"
  360 PRINT#15,FI$
  :   :   :   :   :
  500 CLOSE 15

EXAMPLE #5: (program mode)
  100 OPEN 15,8,15
  :   :   :   :   :
  250 INPUT"NAME OF FILE TO SCRATCH";DN$
  260 PRINT#15,"S:"+DN$
  :   :   :   :   :
  500 CLOSE 15
```

Examples 4 and 5 illustrate how you can use string variables to store either the entire disk command (4) or portions of the command (5). You can use this technique in either immediate or program mode as long as you use the command channel. You cannot use this technique when using DOS 5.1.

What happens when you issue a SCRATCH command?

When you send a SCRATCH command to the disk drive, the disk operating system in the drive interprets (parses) the command. If the syntax is incorrect, the command is rejected, the red drive-active light begins flashing and a SYNTAX ERROR report is generated (error number 30, 31, 32, 33, 34, or 39).

If the syntax is correct, the scratching process begins. As usual, the red drive-active LED turns on and the drive motor starts. The head moves directly to track 18 and begins reading the directory file (18-1, 18-4, and so on). When it finds a name that matches the one specified in the SCRATCH command, it checks the file type byte for this entry. What happens next depends on the value of the file type byte. If this is a normal SEQ, PRG, USR or REL file, the file type byte is set to $00 (this entry will no longer appear in a directory) and the DOS begins tracing the file across the surface of the diskette. The diskette's Block Availability Map (BAM) is modified to indicate that the sectors the file occupied are now free and may be reused. Once the end of the file is reached, the head returns to track 18 and continues reading the directory looking for names that match the file name specified. Once the end of the directory is reached, the revised BAM is written to track 18, sector 0. The operation is complete. The drive-active LED and the motor are switched off.

NOTE:

Since scratching a file does not erase the information from the diskette, it is possible to unscratch a file provided that you have not recorded any new information on the diskette after you scratched the file. If you scratch a file by accident, remove the diskette from the drive and read through Section 11.2.

Now that you know what normally happens, let's look at the more unusual situations. If the file is locked (bit six of the file type byte is a one), the scratch operation terminates. You can't scratch a locked file. If the file is unclosed (bit four of the file type byte is a zero), all that happens is that the file type byte is set to $00. An unclosed file is not traced across the diskette on a 1541 drive! As a result, the blocks that held the file will not be freed in the BAM. You must VALIDATE the diskette to free these blocks!

4.5 Renaming a File

You may change the name of any file that appears in a diskette's directory listing using the RENAME command. Only the name that appears in the directory is changed, the actual program or data file is unaffected. A RENAME command looks like this:

```
General form:
  RENAME0:new name=old name
```

```
Alternate form:
  R:new name=old name
```

```
Examples:
  R0:JUNK=TREASURES
  R:YESTERDAY=TODAY
```

WHERE:

RENAME = the disk command. The command RENAME may be abbreviated as R. The zero is the drive number. It is a holdover from Commodore's dual drives. Its use is optional on the 1541 disk drive.

new name = the revised name that you want to appear in the directory listing. The name may be up to 16 characters long. Any character except asterisks, colons, quotation marks, question marks or commas, may be used in the name. The use of reverse-field characters in names is not recommended.

old name = the name that currently appears in the directory listing. The old name must be spelled exactly as it appears. Wild cards (? and *) may not be used.

Sending a RENAME command using DOS 5.1:

```
SYNTAX:
  >R0:new name=old name
```

```
ALTERNATE:
  @R:new name=old name
```

```
EXAMPLES:
  >R0:PAST DUE=CURRENT BILLS
  @R:PAST AFFAIRS=LOVE LETTERS
```

Sending a RENAME command using the command channel:

```
SYNTAX:
  OPEN 15,8,15
  PRINT#15,"R:new name=old name"
  CLOSE 15
```

```
ALTERNATE:
  OPEN 15,8,15,"R0:new name=old name":CLOSE 15
```

```
EXAMPLE #1: (immediate mode)
   OPEN 15,8,15
   PRINT#15,"R:90 DAYS LATE=60 DAYS LATE"
   CLOSE 15

EXAMPLE #2: (immediate mode)
   OPEN 15,8,15,"RO:WIFE=GIRL FRIEND":CLOSE 15

EXAMPLE #3: (program mode)
   100 OPEN 15,8,15
   :   :   :   :   :
   360 PRINT#15,"R:FINAL GAME=VERSION 27"
   :   :   :   :   :
   500 CLOSE 15

EXAMPLE #4: (program mode)
   100 OPEN 15,8,15
   :   :   :   :   :
   350 FI$="RO:PAID BILLS=UNPAID BILLS"
   360 PRINT#15,FI$
   :   :   :   :   :
   500 CLOSE 15

EXAMPLE #5: (program mode)
   100 OPEN 15,8,15
   :   :   :   :   :
   250 INPUT"NAME OF FILE TO RENAME";ON$
   260 INPUT"NEW FILE NAME";NN$
   270 PRINT#15,"R:"+NN$+"="+ON$
   :   :   :   :   :
   500 CLOSE 15
```

Examples 4 and 5 illustrate how you can use string variables to store either the entire disk command (4) or portions of the command (5). You can use this technique in either immediate or program mode as long as you use the command channel. You cannot use this technique when using DOS 5.1.

What happens when you issue a RENAME command?

When you send a RENAME command to the disk drive, the disk operating system in the drive interprets (parses) the command. If the syntax is incorrect, the command is rejected, the red drive-active light begins flashing and a SYNTAX ERROR report is generated (error number 30, 31, 32, 33, 34, or 39).

If the syntax is correct, renaming begins. As usual, the red drive-active LED turns on and the drive motor starts. The head moves directly to track 18 and begins reading the directory file (18-1, 18-4, and so on). It reads through the entire directory checking for both the old name and the new name. If the old name is not found, the command is aborted and the drive reports a 62, FILE NOT FOUND,00,00 error. If the new name matches an existing name in the directory, the command is aborted and the drive reports a 63, FILE EXISTS,00,00 error. If everything looks OK, the old name in the directory is replaced by the new name. Once the modified directory sector is recorded on disk, the drive-active LED and the motor are switched off.

4.6 Copying a File

You may make a backup copy of any file, including a relative file, that appears in a diskette's directory listing using the COPY command. Unfortunately, this command is of little practical use because the backup copy must always be on the same diskette as the original file. If you want to make a copy onto another diskette, you must use the COPY/ALL program on the 1541TEST/DEMO diskette or the FAST COPY program at the end of Chapter 10. A COPY command looks like this:

```
General form:
  COPY0:backup name=0:original name


Alternate form:
  C:backup name=original name


Examples:
  C0:OLD JUNK/2=OLD JUNK
  C:BUNCHABACKUP=BUNCHASTUFF
```

WHERE:

COPY   = the disk command. The command COPY may be
                       abbreviated as C. The zero is the drive number. It is a
                       holdover from Commodore's dual drives. Its use is
                       optional on the 1541 disk drive.

backup name   = the name of the new backup copy as it should appear
                       in the directory. The name may be up to 16 characters
                       long. Any characters except asterisks, colons, quota-
                       tion marks, question marks or commas, may be used
                       in the name. The use of reverse-field characters in
                       names is not recommended.

original name   = the name that currently appears in the directory
                       listing. The original name must be spelled exactly as
                       it appears. Wild cards (? and *) may not be used.

Sending a COPY command using DOS 5.1:

```
SYNTAX:
  >C:backup name=original name


ALTERNATE:
  @C0:backup name=original name

EXAMPLES:
  >C0:BACKED UP BILLS=BILLS
  @C:LETTERS/BU=LOVE LETTERS
```

Sending a COPY command using the command channel:

```
SYNTAX:
  OPEN 15,8,15
  PRINT#15,"CO:backup name=original name"
  CLOSE 15


ALTERNATE:
  OPEN 15,8,15,"CO:backup name=original name"
  CLOSE 15


EXAMPLE #1: (immediate mode)
  OPEN 15,8,15
  PRINT#15,"CO:60 DAY COPY=60 DAYS LATE"
  CLOSE 15


EXAMPLE #2: (immediate mode)
  OPEN 15,8,15,"CO:TAX FORM COPY=TAX FORM":CLOSE 15


EXAMPLE #3: (program mode)
  100 OPEN 15,8,15
  :   :   :   :   :
  360 PRINT#15,"C:GAME AGAIN=GAME"
  :   :   :   :   :
  500 CLOSE 15


EXAMPLE #4: (program mode)
  100 OPEN 15,8,15
  :   :   :   :   :
  350 FI$="CO:RECEIPTS.C=RECEIPTS"
  360 PRINT#15,FI$
  :   :   :   :   :
  500 CLOSE 15


EXAMPLE #5:
  100 OPEN 15,8,15
  (program mode)
  :   :   :   :   :
  250 INPUT"NAME OF FILE TO COPY";ON$
  260 INPUT"NEW FILE NAME";NN$
  270 PRINT#15,"C:"+NN$+"="+ON$
  :   :   :   :   :
  500 CLOSE 15
```

Examples 4 and 5 illustrate how you can use string variables to store either the entire
disk command (4) or portions of the command (5). You can use this technique in either
immediate or program mode as long as you use the command channel. You cannot
use this technique when using DOS 5.1.

What happens when you issue a COPY command?

When you send a COPY command to the disk drive, the disk operating system in the drive interprets (parses) the command. If the syntax is incorrect, the command is rejected, the red drive-active light begins flashing and a SYNTAX ERROR report is generated (error number 30, 31, 32, 33, 34, or 39).

If the syntax is correct, the command is executed. As usual, the red drive-active LED turns on and the drive motor starts. The head moves directly to track 18 and begins reading the directory file (18-1, 18-4, and so on). First, it reads through the entire directory checking for both the original name and the backup name. If the original name is not found, the command is aborted and the drive reports a 62, FILE NOT FOUND,00,00 error. If the backup name matches an existing name in the directory, the command is aborted and the drive reports a 63, FILE EXISTS,00,00 error. If everything looks OK, the backup name is inserted in the directory and the drive begins to read the old file and make a duplicate copy. Once the copy is completed satisfactorily, the diskette's updated Block Availability Map (BAM) and the revised directory sector are recorded on the diskette, and the drive-active LED and the motor are switched off.

4.7 Combining Two or More Files

You may use a variation of the COPY command to combine two or more files into a single, new, larger file. The information will not be merged. The new file will consist of all the information from old file #1 followed by all the information from file #2, etc. The command will work with any combination of up to four sequential, program or user files. It does *not* work correctly with relative files.

In practice, this command is only used with sequential files. When two program files are used, the two programs are not linked together properly. If you want to merge two program segments together, check Section 7.7.

All the files, the new combined file and the old files, must be on the same diskette. If you need to combine two files that are on separate diskettes, copy them both onto a single diskette and then combine them. The COPY command that combines two or more files looks like this:

```
General form:
  COPY0:combofile=0:oldfile1,0:oldfile2

Alternate form:
  C:combofile=oldfile1,oldfile2

Examples:
  C0:ALL JUNK=0:OLD JUNK,0:NEW JUNK
  C:ALL MEMBERS=MALE MEMBERS,FEMALE MEMBERS
```

WHERE:

COPY   = the disk command. The command COPY may be
                  abbreviated as C. The zero is the drive number. It
                  is a holdover from Commodore's dual drives. Its use
                  is optional on the 1541 disk drive.

combofile   = the name of the new combined file as it should
                           appear in the directory. The name may be up to 16
                           characters long. Any characters except asterisks,
                           colons, quotation marks, question marks or commas,
                           may be used in the name. The use of reverse-field
                           characters in names is not recommended.

oldfile1, oldfile2,   = the names of the files to be combined. The names
oldfile3, oldfile4   must be spelled exactly as they appear in the
                           diskette directory. Wild cards (? and *) may not be
                           used. The files to be combined do not all have to be
                           of the same type. The combined file will be the
                           same file type as the first named oldfile. You may
                           combine up to four files at one time.

WARNING:

You cannot merge two relative files this way! If you try to use this command to
combine two relative files, the drive will accept the command and begin copying
information into the new combined file. The drive appears to copy all of the information from the first relative file correctly. However, part way through the second
file the drive becomes confused and aborts the job with a 66, ILLEGAL TRACK
AND SECTOR,73,01 error. The directory will show the correct name and file type
for the new combined file (you can't have an unclosed REL file), but the length of the
file will be given as zero blocks. However, the number of blocks free on the diskette
will have decreased indicating that the blocks that make up the new file have been
allocated in the diskette's BAM. The moral? This command just won't work with
relative files.

CAUTION:

The length of the combined file may be wrong! When the DOS creates the directory
entry for the new, combined file, the file length will be set to the sum of the lengths of
the files you have combined. In some cases the actual length will be one block less.
Let's look at an example to see how this can happen. Suppose we have two files,
FILE-A and FILE-B. The directory indicates that FILE-A is three blocks long and
FILE-B is five blocks long. However, a careful examination of what is actually stored
on the diskette using EDIT T&S (Appendix E) reveals that the last block in each file
is not full. FILE-A occupies two full blocks (254 bytes in each) and the first 50 bytes of
the third block. FILE-B occupies four full blocks and the first 132 bytes of the fifth
block. When we combine FILE-A and FILE-B to produce FILE-C, the directory will
indicate that FILE-C is (5+3)= 8 blocks long. However, the FILE-C will actually
occupy only seven blocks; (4+2)= 6 full blocks and the first (50+132)= 182 bytes of the
seventh block. Only when the sum of the number of bytes in the last blocks exceeds
254 will the block count be correct.

Sending a COPY command using DOS 5.1:

SYNTAX:

```
>C:combofile=oldfile1,oldfile2
```

```
ALTERNATE:
  @CO:combofile=0:oldfile1,0:oldfile2
```

```
EXAMPLES:
  >CO:ALL TAX=0:FED TAX,0:STATE TAX
  @C:OUR STUFF=MY STUFF,YOUR STUFF
```

Sending a COPY command using the command channel:

```
SYNTAX:
  OPEN 15,8,15
  PRINT#15,"CO:combofile=0:oldfile1,0:oldfile2"
  CLOSE 15
```

```
ALTERNATE:
  OPEN 15,8,15,"C:combofile=oldfile1,oldfile2"
  CLOSE 15
```

```
EXAMPLE #1: (immediate mode)
  OPEN 15,8,15
  PRINT#15,"C:JUNK=THIS,THAT,THE OTHER"
  CLOSE 15
```

```
EXAMPLE #2: (immediate mode)
  OPEN 15,8,15,"CO:GREEN=0:YELLOW,0:BLUE":CLOSE 15
```

```
EXAMPLE #3: (program mode)
  100 OPEN 15,8,15
  :   :   :   :   :
  360 PRINT#15,"C:SPEECH=INTRO,BODY,ENDING"
  :   :   :   :   :
  500 CLOSE 15
```

```
EXAMPLE #4: (program mode)
  100 OPEN 15,8,15
  :   :   :   :   :
  350 FI$="CO:EXPENSES=CAR EXP,HOUSE EXP,FOOD EXP"
  360 PRINT#15,FI$
  :   :   :   :   :
  500 CLOSE 15
```

```
EXAMPLE #5: (program mode)
  100 OPEN 15,8,15
  :   :   :   :   :
  250 INPUT"NAME OF COMBINED FILE";CF$
  260 INPUT"FIRST FILE NAME";N1$
  270 INPUT"SECOND FILE NAME";N2$
  280 PRINT#15,"C:"+CF$+"="+N1$+","+N2$
  :   :   :   :   :
  500 CLOSE 15
```

Examples 4 and 5 illustrate how you can use string variables to store either the entire disk command (4) or portions of the command (5). You can use this technique in either immediate or program mode as long as you use the command channel. You cannot use this technique when using DOS 5.1.

What happens when you issue this type of COPY command?

As usual, the disk operating system in the drive interprets (parses) the command. If the syntax is incorrect, the command is rejected, the red drive-active light begins flashing and a SYNTAX ERROR report is generated (error number 30, 31, 32, 33, 34, or 39).

If the syntax is correct, the command is executed. The red drive-active LED turns on and the drive motor starts. The head moves directly to track 18 and begins reading the directory file (18-1, 18-4, and so on). It reads through the entire directory checking for both the oldfile names and the combofile name. If any of the oldfile names are not found, the command is aborted and the drive reports a 62, FILE NOT FOUND,00,00 error. If the combofile name matches an existing name in the directory, the command is aborted and the drive reports a 63, FILE EXISTS,00,00 error. If everything looks OK, the combofile name is inserted into the directory and the drive begins to read the old files in sequence and copy them into the new combined file. Once the copy is completed satisfactorily, the updated BAM and the directory sector containing the combofile name are recorded on the diskette, and the drive-active LED and the motor are switched off.

4.8 Validating a Diskette

In Commodore jargon, validating a diskette means reading through all the files stored on a diskette and updating the map that indicates which sectors on the diskette are free (they are available for use) and which are allocated (they store part of a program or data file). This map is known as the diskette's Block Availability Map (BAM). It is stored on track 18, sector 0 of the diskette.

If the Block Availability Map is incorrect, one or more of the files on the diskette may be overwritten when you store new information on the diskette. When this happens all of the overwritten information is irretrievably lost. In addition, you will have crossed files. Two files are crossed when the one or more sectors on the diskette are part of two different files. You have crossed files if you load, or read, a file and get what appears to be the first part of one file followed by the last part of another file. Once you have crossed files on a diskette, the only solution is to copy the files onto another diskette and reformat the original.

The most common causes of errors in a diskette's BAM are scratching improperly closed files and using the save-and-replace command on an almost full diskette. You can prevent crossed files and other horrors by validating your working diskettes regularly. Read-only diskettes such as commercial programs do not need to be validated.

A VALIDATE command looks like this:

General form:
  VALIDATE0

Alternate form:
  V

Examples:
  V0
  V

WHERE:

VALIDATE   = the disk command. The command VALIDATE may be
              abbreviated as V. The zero is the drive number. It is a
              holdover from Commodore's dual drives. Its use is
              optional on the 1541 disk drive.

CAUTIONS:

1. Do *not* validate commercial games diskettes. Many commercial games are supplied
   on diskettes that have elaborate protection schemes to prevent you from making a
   backup copy of the diskette. Sometimes the diskette's BAM has been deliberately
   altered as part of the protection. If you remove the write protect tab and validate
   the diskette, the game may never work again. Don't do it!

2. Do *not* validate diskettes containing random access files. Some programs store
   data on a diskette in random access files. Note that a random access file is not a
   relative file. If you validate a diskette that contains a random access file, you may
   lose all the data stored in the file!

3. Validation may free deliberately allocated blocks. The CHECK DISK program on
   your 1541TEST/DEMO diskette scans a disk for bad sectors. If it finds one, that
   sector is deliberately allocated in the BAM so that the drive will not attempt to
   store any information in that sector. When you validate the diskette, that bad
   sector will be freed. When the drive attempts to store information there, you will
   get a disk error. If you use CHECK DISK to allow you to keep using a flawed
   diskette, you must rerun CHECK DISK after you validate the diskette. *It is a
   much better idea to junk any diskette that contains a flaw!*

Sending a VALIDATE command using DOS 5.1:

SYNTAX:
  >V

ALTERNATE:
  @V0

EXAMPLES:
  >V0
  @V

Sending a VALIDATE command using the command channel:

```
SYNTAX:
  OPEN 15,8,15
  PRINT#15,"V"
  CLOSE 15

ALTERNATE:
  OPEN 15,8,15,"V0":CLOSE 15

EXAMPLE #1: (immediate mode)
  OPEN 15,8,15
  PRINT#15,"V0"
  CLOSE 15

EXAMPLE #2: (immediate mode)
  OPEN 15,8,15,"V0":CLOSE 15

EXAMPLE #3: (program mode)
  100 OPEN 15,8,15
  :   :   :   :   :
  360 PRINT#15,"V"
  :   :   :   :   :
  500 CLOSE 15

EXAMPLE #4: (program mode)
  100 OPEN 15,8,15
  :   :   :   :   :
  350 FI$="V0"
  360 PRINT#15,FI$
  :   :   :   :   :
  500 CLOSE 15
```

Example 4 illustrates how you can use a string variable to store the disk command. You can use this technique in either immediate or program mode as long as you use the command channel. You cannot use this technique when using DOS 5.1.

What happens when you issue a VALIDATE command?

When you send a VALIDATE command to the disk drive, the disk operating system in the drive interprets (parses) the command. If the syntax is incorrect, the command is rejected, the red drive-active light begins flashing and a SYNTAX ERROR report is generated (error number 30, 31, 32, 33, 34, or 39).

If the syntax is correct, validation begins. As always, the red drive-active LED turns on and the drive motor starts. While the drive is getting up to speed, the disk operating system creates a new, blank Block Availability Map (BAM) in the disk drive's RAM memory. In this new map all sectors on the directory are free (available for use). Once the drive is up to speed, the head moves to track 18 and reads the first directory entry. This file is traced across the diskette by following the track and sector pointers. Each of the sectors (blocks) used to store the file is marked as in use (allocated) in the BAM. Each file in the directory is traced. Once all files in the directory have been traced, the revised BAM is recorded on track 18, sector 0 of the diskette and validation is complete.

If an improperly closed file is encountered in the directory, the file is not traced. All that happens is that the file type byte in the directory entry is changed to zero. This makes the file a scratched file. It will no longer appear in the directory. Since the file is not traced, any blocks that were used to store the file are freed in the BAM and become available for storage of new programs or data. Note that this is different from what happens when you SCRATCH an improperly closed file. In both cases the file is converted into a scratched file. However, with the SCRATCH command the sectors that had been allocated to the unclosed files are *not* freed in the BAM. These blocks can only be freed by use of the VALIDATE command. To avoid problems with the BAM, never scratch an improperly closed file.

NOTES:

If a disk error is encountered while reading any file, the entire validation process stops. No harm has been done because the diskette's original BAM is still intact. However, you can't validate the diskette either. The only solution is to copy the intact files one by one onto another diskette and then do a full NEW on the problem diskette to eliminate the errors.

Appendix E contains two programs that help you spot and localize problems on a diskette. The FULL DIRECTORY program allows you to do a quick check for BAM errors. It will point out any inconsistencies between the number of blocks free in the directory and in the BAM. The CONFIRM ALL FILES program does a much more comprehensive job of checking. It first checks the internal consistency of the BAM and then traces all files. Any problems, such as crossed files or inconsistencies between the actual length of the files and the length shown in the directory, are displayed. Full instructions for using these programs are given in Section 11.1.

4.9 Your BASIC Housekeeper

Doing diskette housekeeping is something like doing everyday household chores. Nobody really likes doing them, but they have to be done. To make your life a little more pleasant, let me introduce you to your BASIC housekeeper.

The BASIC housekeeper is a menu-driven BASIC program that makes doing diskette housekeeping a lot easier. When you RUN the program, you will be presented with a list of the housekeeping tasks and asked which you would like to do. After selecting the task you want, you will be prompted for all the necessary information to carry out the task. It should make your housekeeping chores less difficult.

```
********************
PROGRAM: HOUSE HELP
********************

0 REM 1541 USER'S GUIDE SECTION 4.9
1 REM  COPYRIGHT: G. NEUFELD, 1984
2 :
```

```
3 REM 1541 DISKETTE HOUSEKEEPING
4 :
100 POKE53280,15:POKE53281,15
110 PRINTCHR$(142)CHR$(8)CHR$(144)
120 Z$=CHR$(0)
130 PRINTCHR$(142)CHR$(8)CHR$(144)
140 D$="{HOME}{DOWN 22}"
150 DIM F$(144)
160 OPEN 15,8,15
170 PRINT"{CLR} 1541 DISKETTE HOUSEKEEPI
NG"
180 PRINT"{DOWN}{RVS}C{ROFF}OPY A FILE"
190 PRINT"{DOWN}{RVS}D{ROFF}ISPLAY DIREC
TORY"
200 PRINT"{DOWN}{RVS}I{ROFF}NITIALIZE DI
SKETTE"
210 PRINT"{DOWN}{RVS}N{ROFF}EW A DISKETT
E"
220 PRINT"{DOWN}{RVS}R{ROFF}ENAME A FILE
"
230 PRINT"{DOWN}{RVS}S{ROFF}CRATCH A FIL
E"
240 PRINT"{DOWN}{RVS}V{ROFF}ALIDATE A DI
SKETTE"
250 PRINT"{DOWN}{RVS}T{ROFF}ERMINATE PRO
GRAM"
260 PRINT"{DOWN} WHICH OPTION? ";
270 GET A$:IF A$="" GOTO 270
280 PRINTA$
290 IF A$="C" GOTO 410
300 IF A$="D" GOTO 680
310 IF A$="I" THEN PRINT#15,"I0":DF=0:GO
TO 170
320 IF A$="N" GOTO 890
330 IF A$="R" GOTO 1470
340 IF A$="S" GOTO 1690
350 IF A$="T" THEN CLOSE 15:PRINT"{CLR}"
:END
360 IF A$="V" GOTO 2230
370 GOTO 170
380 :
390 REM COPY A FILE
400 :
410 GOSUB 2380:IF FL<>0 GOTO 170
420 DF=0
430 PRINT"{CLR}COPY FILE"
440 PRINT"{DOWN}YOU CAN MAKE A BACKUP CO
PY OF ANY PRG,"
450 PRINT"SEQ, OR USR FILE ON THE SAME D
ISK."
```

```
460 PRINT"YOU CANNOT MAKE A COPY OF A RE
L FILE"
470 PRINT"OR COPY A FILE TO ANOTHER DISK
ETTE."
480 PRINT"USE COPY/ALL FROM THE 1541TEST
/DEMO"
490 PRINT"DISKETTE FOR THESE APPLICATION
S."
500 INPUT"{DOWN}OK TO CONTINUE (Y/N)   Y{
LEFT 3}";A$
510 IF (ASC(A$)AND127)<>89 GOTO 170
520 PRINT"{DOWN}FILE TO COPY (WILD CARDS
 ARE OK)"
530 F$="":INPUT" FILE NAME";F$
540 IF F$="" GOTO 430
550 GOSUB 2510:IF FL=1 GOTO430
560 PRINT"{DOWN}FOUND FILE NAMED: "F$"
  "
570 INPUT"{DOWN}IS THIS THE CORRECT FILE
 (Y/N)   Y{LEFT 3}";A$
580 IF (ASC(A$)AND127)<>89 GOTO 430
590 BF$=LEFT$(F$,13)+"/BU"
600 PRINT"{DOWN}BACKUP COPY NAME:   "BF$
610 PRINT"{UP}"TAB(17);:INPUT BF$
620 PRINT#15,"C:"+BF$+"="+F$
630 GOSUB 2420
640 GOTO 170
650 :
660 REM DISPLAY THE DIRECTORY
670 :
680 PRINT"{CLR}DISPLAY DISKETTE DIRECTOR
Y"
690 IF DF=1 GOTO 730
700 PRINT"{DOWN}ONE MOMENT PLEASE...."
710 GOSUB 2720:IF FL=1 GOTO 170
720 DF=1
730 T=0:PRINT"{CLR}    DISKETTE DIRECTORY
{DOWN}"
740 FOR K=1 TO NE
750 PRINTTAB(T)F$(K)
760 IF INT(K/20)<>K/20 GOTO 820
770 IF T=0 THEN PRINT"{HOME}{DOWN}":T=20
:GOTO 820
780 PRINT D$ "{DOWN}PRESS {RVS}RETURN{RO
FF} FOR MORE"
790 GET A$:IF A$<>"" GOTO 790
800 GET A$:IF A$<>CHR$(13) GOTO 800
810 T=0:PRINT"{CLR}    DISKETTE DIRECTORY
{DOWN}"
820 NEXT K
```

```
830 PRINT D$ "{DOWN}PRESS {RVS}RETURN{RO
FF} FOR MENU"
840 GET A$:IF A$<>"" GOTO 840
850 GET A$:IF A$<>CHR$(13) GOTO 850
860 GOTO 170
870 :
880 REM NEW A DISKETTE
890 TRY=0:DF=0
900 PRINT"{CLR} FORMAT A DISKETTE"
910 PRINT"{DOWN}ALLOWS YOU TO FORMAT A D
ISKETTE"
920 PRINT"{DOWN} FULL NEW = REFORMAT ENT
IRE DISKETTE"
930 PRINT"{DOWN} SHORT NEW = ERASE OLD D
IRECTORY & BAM"
940 INPUT"{DOWN}OK TO CONTINUE (Y/N)   Y{
LEFT 3}";A$
950 IF (ASC(A$)AND127)<>89 GOTO 170
960 PRINT"{UP}INSERT DISKETTE & PRESS {R
VS}RETURN{ROFF}"
970 GET A$:IF A$<>""GOTO 970
980 GET A$:IF A$<>CHR$(13)GOTO 980
990 PRINT#15,"M-W"CHR$(6)CHR$(0)CHR$(2)C
HR$(18)CHR$(0)
1000 PRINT#15,"M-W"CHR$(0)CHR$(0)CHR$(1)
CHR$(176)
1010 PRINT#15,"M-R"CHR$(0)CHR$(0)
1020 GET#15,A$:A=ASC(A$+Z$)
1030 IF A>127 GOTO 1010
1040 TRY=TRY+1
1050 IF A<>1 AND TRY<5 GOTO 990
1060 IF A>1 THEN FL=1:GOTO 1320
1070 PRINT#15,"M-R"CHR$(22)CHR$(0)CHR$(2
)
1080 GET#15,A$:IF A$=""THEN A$=Z$
1090 ID$=A$
1100 GET#15,A$:IF A$=""THEN A$=Z$
1110 ID$=ID$+A$
1120 OPEN1,8,4,"#"
1130 PRINT#15,"U1:4 0 18 0"
1140 PRINT#15,"B-P:4 144"
1150 DN$="":FOR K=1 TO 24
1160 GET#1,A$:IF A$=""THEN A$=Z$
1170 DN$=DN$+A$
1180 NEXT
1190 CLOSE1
1200 PRINT"{DOWN}THIS DISKETTE IS ALREAD
Y FORMATTED"
1210 PRINT"{DOWN}DISK NAME: "LEFT$(DN$,1
6)
```

```
1220 PRINT"COSMETIC ID: "MID$(DN$,19,2)
1230 PRINT"EMBEDDED ID: "CHR$(34)CHR$(20
)ID$
1240 INPUT"{DOWN}FULL NEW, SHORT NEW, OR
 QUIT(F/S/Q)";A$
1250 A$=LEFT$(A$,1)
1260 IF A$="F" THEN FL=1:GOTO 1320
1270 IF A$="S" THEN FL=0:GOTO 1320
1280 IF A$="Q" GOTO 170
1290 PRINT"{DOWN}ENTER ONLY 'F', 'S', OR
 'Q'"
1300 GOTO 1240
1310 :
1320 INPUT"{DOWN}NEW DISK NAME:";DN$
1330 IF FL=1 THEN ID$="":INPUT"{DOWN}FOR
MATTING ID";ID$
1340 IF LEN(ID$)<>2 THEN PRINT"{DOWN}ID
MUST BE 2 CHARACTERS LONG":GOTO1330
1350 IF FL=0 THEN PRINT"{DOWN}CAUTION: A
LL FILES WILL BE LOST"
1360 IF FL=1 THEN PRINT"{DOWN}CAUTION: A
NY OLD DATA WILL BE LOST"
1370 INPUT"{DOWN}OK TO CONTINUE (Y/N)  N
{LEFT 3}";A$
1380 IF (ASC(A$)AND127)<>89 GOTO 170
1390 PRINT"{DOWN}WORKING......."
1400 IF FL=1 THEN PRINT#15,"N:"+DN$+","+
ID$
1410 IF FL=0 THEN PRINT#15,"N:"+DN$
1420 GOSUB 2420:NE=0
1430 GOTO 170
1440 :
1450 REM RENAME A FILE
1460 :
1470 GOSUB 2380:IF FL<>0 GOTO 170
1480 DF=0
1490 PRINT"{CLR}RENAME A FILE"
1500 PRINT"{DOWN}ALLOWS YOU TO CHANGE TH
E NAME OF ANY"
1510 PRINT"FILE ON THE DISKETTE"
1520 INPUT"{DOWN}OK TO CONTINUE (Y/N)  Y
{LEFT 3}";A$
1530 IF (ASC(A$)AND127)<>89 GOTO 170
1540 PRINT"{DOWN}FILE TO RENAME (WILD CA
RDS ARE OK)"
1550 F$="":INPUT" FILE NAME";F$
1560 IF F$="" GOTO 1490
1570 GOSUB 2510:IF FL=1 GOTO 1490
1580 PRINT"{DOWN}FOUND FILE NAMED: "F$"
    "
```

```
1590 INPUT"{DOWN}IS THIS THE CORRECT FIL
E (Y/N)   Y{LEFT 3}";A$
1600 IF (ASC(A$)AND127)<>89 GOTO 1490
1610 PRINT"{DOWN}NEW FILE NAME:   "F$
1620 PRINT"{UP}"TAB(14);:INPUT NF$
1630 PRINT#15,"R:"+NF$+"="+F$
1640 GOSUB 2420
1650 GOTO 170
1660 :
1670 REM SCRATCH A FILE
1680 :
1690 PRINT"{CLR}SCRATCH A FILE"
1700 PRINT"{DOWN}ALLOWS YOU DELETE A FIL
E FROM THE"
1710 PRINT"DISKETTE'S DIRECTORY. YOU MAY
 NOT"
1720 PRINT"SCRATCH AN UNCLOSED FILE. USE
 THE"
1730 PRINT"VALIDATE OPTION FOR THESE."
1740 INPUT"{DOWN}OK TO CONTINUE (Y/N)  Y
{LEFT 3}";A$
1750 IF (ASC(A$)AND127)<>89 GOTO 170
1760 PRINT"{DOWN}FILE TO SCRATCH (WILD C
ARDS ARE OK)"
1770 F$="":INPUT" FILE NAME";F$
1780 IF F$="" GOTO 1690
1790 FOR K=LEN(F$) TO 1 STEP -1
1800 C$=MID$(F$,K,1)
1810 IF C$="*" OR C$="?" GOTO 1920:REM W
ILD CARDS
1820 NEXT
1830 GOSUB 2510:IF FL=1 GOTO 1690
1840 PRINT"{DOWN}FOUND FILE NAMED: "F$"
   "
1850 INPUT"{DOWN}SCRATCH THIS FILE (Y/N)
  Y{LEFT 3}";A$
1860 IF (ASC(A$)AND127)<>89 GOTO 1690
1870 PRINT#15,"S:"+F$
1880 DF=0
1890 GOSUB 2420
1900 GOTO 170
1910 :
1920 K=1:NEXT
1930 IF DF=1 GOTO 1970
1940 PRINT"{DOWN}ONE MOMENT PLEASE...."
1950 GOSUB 2720:IF FL=1 GOTO 170
1960 DF=1
1970 PRINT"{DOWN}THE FOLLOWING FILES WIL
L BE SCRATCHED{DOWN}"
1980 NS=0:LN=LEN(F$):FOR K=1 TO NE:FD=0
```

```
1990 FOR C=1 TO LN
2000 X$=MID$(F$,C,1):IF X$="?"GOTO 2030
2010 IF X$="*"THEN C=LN:FD=1:GOTO2030
2020 IF X$<>MID$(F$(K),C,1) THEN C=LN:FD
=-1
2030 NEXT C
2040 IF FD=-1 GOTO 2060
2050 PRINTF$(K):NS=NS+1:ND(NS)=K
2060 NEXT K
2070 IF NS=0 THEN PRINT "NO MATCHING NAM
ES FOUND":GOTO 2160
2080 PRINT "{DOWN}"NS"MATCHING NAMES FOU
ND"
2090 INPUT"{DOWN}OK TO CONTINUE (Y/N)  Y
{LEFT 3}";A$
2100 IF (ASC(A$)AND127)<>89 GOTO 170
2110 PRINT#15,"S:"+F$
2120 FOR K=1 TO NS
2130 F$(ND(K))="{RVS}"+F$(ND(K))
2140 NEXT
2150 GOSUB 2420
2160 PRINT"{DOWN}PRESS {RVS}RETURN{ROFF}
 FOR MENU"
2170 GET A$:IF A$<>"" GOTO 2170
2180 GET A$:IF A$<>CHR$(13) GOTO 2180
2190 GOTO 170
2200 :
2210 REM VALIDATE A DISKETTE
2220 :
2230 GOSUB 2380:IF FL<>0 GOTO 170
2240 PRINT"{CLR}VALIDATE A DISKETTE"
2250 PRINT"{DOWN}CREATES A NEW BAM THAT
MATCHES THE"
2260 PRINT"FILES LISTED IN THE DIRECTORY
."
2270 PRINT"IN ADDITION, ANY UNCLOSED FIL
ES IN THE"
2280 PRINT"DIRECTORY WILL BE ELIMINATED.
"
2290 INPUT"{DOWN}OK TO CONTINUE (Y/N)  Y
{LEFT 3}";A$
2300 IF (ASC(A$)AND127)<>89 GOTO 170
2310 PRINT"{DOWN}THIS CAN TAKE UP TO 2 M
INUTES..."
2320 PRINT#15,"V0"
2330 GOSUB 2420
2340 GOTO 170
2350 :
2360 REM INIT DISK & READ ERROR
2370 :
```

```
2380 PRINT#15,"IO"
2390 :
2400 REM READ ERROR STATUS
2410 :
2420 INPUT#15,EN,EM$,ET,ES
2430 IF EN<20 THEN FL=0:RETURN
2440 PRINT"{DOWN}{RVS}DISK ERROR{DOWN}"
2450 PRINT"   "EN;EM$;ET;ES
2460 PRINT"{DOWN}PRESS {RVS}RETURN{ROFF}
 TO CONTINUE"
2470 GET A$:IF A$<>""GOTO 2470
2480 GET A$:IF A$<>CHR$(13) GOTO 2480
2490 FL=1:RETURN
2500 :
2510 OPEN 1,8,4,"#"
2520 OPEN2,8,5,F$
2530 GOSUB 2420:IF FL=1 THEN CLOSE1:CLOS
E2:RETURN
2540 PRINT#15,"M-R"CHR$(144)CHR$(2)
2550 GET#15,A$:SE=ASC(A$+Z$)
2560 PRINT#15,"M-R"CHR$(148)CHR$(2)
2570 GET#15,A$:PT=ASC(A$+Z$)
2580 PRINT#15,"U1:4 0 18"SE
2590 PRINT#15,"B-P:4"PT+3
2600 F$=""
2610 FOR K=1TO16:GET#1,A$:IFA$=""THENA$=
Z$
2620 F$=F$+A$:NEXT
2630 FOR K=16TO1STEP-1
2640 IF ASC(MID$(F$,K))<>160 GOTO 2670
2650 NEXT
2660 F$=LEFT$(F$,K):GOTO 2690
2670 F$=LEFT$(F$,K):K=1:NEXT
2680 CLOSE1:CLOSE2
2690 FL=0:RETURN
2700 :
2710 REM READ THE DIRECTORY
2720 SE=1:NE=0
2730 OPEN1,8,4,"#"
2740 PRINT#15,"U1:4 0 18"SE
2750 GOSUB 2420:IF FL=1 THEN CLOSE1:RETU
RN
2760 FOR K=0 TO 7
2770 PRINT#15,"B-P:4"2+K*32
2780 GET#1,A$:FT=ASC(A$+Z$)
2790 GET#1,A$:TL=ASC(A$+Z$)
2800 GET#1,A$:SL=ASC(A$+Z$)
2810 IF SL=0 AND TL=0 GOTO 2940
2820 NE=NE+1
2830 F$(NE)=""
```

```
2840 IF FT=0 THEN F$(NE)="{RVS}"
2850 IF FT>0 AND FT<128 THEN F$(NE)="{RV
S}*{ROFF} "
2860 FOR L=1TO16
2870 GET#1,A$:IFA$=""THENA$=Z$
2880 F$(NE)=F$(NE)+A$
2890 NEXT L
2900 FOR P=LEN(F$(NE)) TO 1 STEP-1
2910 IF ASC(MID$(F$(NE),P))<>160 GOTO 29
30
2920 NEXT
2930 F$(NE)=LEFT$(F$(NE),P)
2940 NEXT K
2950 PRINT#15,"B-P:4"0
2960 GET#1,A$:TL=ASC(A$+Z$)
2970 GET#1,A$:SE=ASC(A$+Z$)
2980 IF TL=18 GOTO 2740
2990 CLOSE1
3000 FL=0:RETURN
```

CHAPTER 5

INTRODUCTION TO FILE HANDLING

This chapter is designed to introduce you to the main ideas and commands related to file handling. Each section includes several examples to help you learn how to make use of the excellent file-handling capabilities of your Commodore disk drive. You should read through this chapter before you read the chapters that deal with specific types of files.

5.1 Separating Data from a Program

Most people purchase a disk drive to enable them to load or save programs quickly and easily. However, the real power of your disk drive is not its speed in loading or saving programs. The real power lies in its ability to store and retrieve large amounts of information (data), independent of the program that produces or uses this information.

A program is a set of instructions to tell the computer how to do a task, such as how to set up and maintain a mailing list. The actual information, data, used by a program may or may not be part of the program. If it is part of the program, the information is usually stored in DATA statements. However, data is usually stored separately in a data file. The ability to separate the program (how to do a task) from the data (the information needed for a particular task) is very important. It allows you to write powerful, general purpose programs.

Most commercial programs store the data used or produced by the program in a data file stored on a diskette. Here are a few examples of types of programs that use this technique:

Program File	**Data File Produced**
Mailing list program	File of members' names & addresses
Grade book program	File of students' names & grades
Word processor	File of letters, documents, etc.
Accounting program	File of debit/credit transactions

Once the information used by the program is separated from the program itself, the program usually becomes more useful. A grade book program is a good example. Suppose you wrote a grade book program with the students' names and marks in DATA statements within the program. You would end up making many copies of the program, one for each class, subject or grade level you taught. If you had stored the names and marks in data files, you would need only one copy of the program. The same program would handle all your different classes, it would just access different data files.

5.2 What a Data File Is

A data file is a big, long string of information. We will use the file of information produced by a mailing list program to illustrate the structure of a data file. Here is the start of our data file.

NOTE:

* represents a carriage return character, CHR$(13)

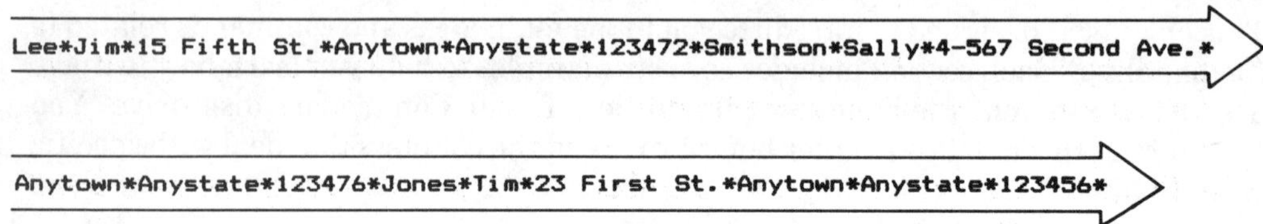

The information in a data file is divided up into clumps called records. Each record contains information about one particular person, place or thing. Records are usually separated from each other by a carriage return character, CHR$(13). One record in our mailing list file would probably contain the information about one member —his or her name, address and zip code.

The first part of the file (composed of three records):

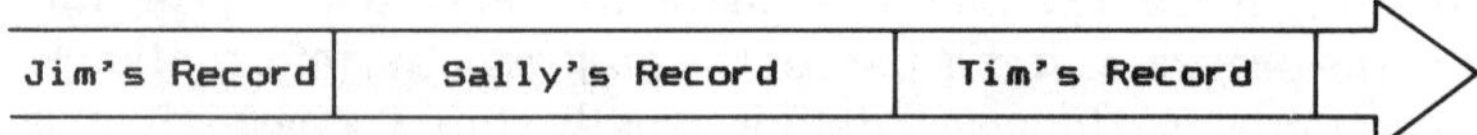

Within each record, the information is often divided into fields. Each field contains a specific piece of information about one person, place or thing. The fields within a record are usually separated from each other by a special character called a delimiter or separator. A carrige return character, CHR$(13), or a comma is often used as a delimiter.

Record #1 (45 characters grouped into seven fields):

NOTE:

* represents a carriage return character, CHR$(13)

Record #2 (57 characters grouped into seven fields):

```
Smithson*Sally*4-567 Second Ave.*Anytown*Anystate*123476*
```

Record #3 (47 characters grouped into seven fields):

```
Jones*Tim*23 First St.*Anytown*Anystate*123456*
```

Note that in this data file the records are not the same length. Record #2 is longer than either of the other records. This is simply because Sally Smithson's name and address contain more characters.

Since we will be using the terms file, record, field, and delimiter throughout this section, let's go over them one more time.

File: Contains information about all members of the group (e.g., information about Jim Lee, Sally Smith, etc.).

Record: Contains information about one member of the group (e.g., all information about Jim Lee).

Field: Contains one piece of information about one member; separated from other fields with a delimiter (e.g., Jim Lee's address: 15 Fifth Steet).

Delimiter: A special character that is used between records or fields as a separator. There are four characters that you can use as delimiters:

Delimiter Character	ASCII	For Use Between
a null character	CHR$(0)	not recommended
a carriage return	CHR$(13)	records or fields
a comma	CHR$(44)	fields only
a colon	CHR$(57)	fields only

5.3 Kinds of Files

There are four main types of files that you can use on your 1541 disk drive. They are program files, sequential files, relative files and user files. The file type abbreviations that appear in a directory listing and the main uses of these major types of files are summarized below:

File Type	Directory	Main Uses
Program files	PRG	Storing copies of RAM memory such as programs, routines and some data.
Sequential files	SEQ	Storing limited amounts of data or data that is rarely modified.

| Relative files | REL | Storing large amounts of data that needs frequent updating. |
| User files | USR | User designed files. For advanced programmers and special tasks only. |

Unclosed Files

Occasionally you may come across a file that has an * in front of its file type in the directory (e.g., *PRG, *SEQ, *REL or *USR). This is a file that has not been closed properly. This happens when you forget to close a file after you have written to it. Be sure to read the warning about unclosed files.

WARNING:

Do not scratch an unclosed file! If you want to eliminate an unclosed file from the directory, validate the diskette (see Section 4.8). If the data is very important, you can try to recover the file (see Section 11.3).

Locked Files

Occasionally you may run across a file that has a < following its file type in the directory (e.g., PRG<, SEQ<, REL< or USR<). This is a locked file. It cannot be scratched from the directory unless you first unlock it. You cannot lock or unlock a file easily. You have to change the file type byte in the diskette's directory using Block-Read (U1:) and Block-Write (U2:) commands. The MOD ENTRY program given in Section 13.8 makes this easy to do.

Unusual File Types

Once in a while you may encounter a file with a very odd looking file type (e.g., DEL, SR? or EL?). These strange file types are not very useful. They are used more for shock value than anything else. These unusual file types are produced by changing the file type byte in the directory entry to an abnormal value. The way to do this is described in Section 13.8.

5.4 Accessing a File

Using a data file on disk is very similar to using an ordinary filing cabinet. If you want to store or retrieve information in a filing cabinet you follow a three step procedure:

1. Open the drawer of the filing cabinet.
2. Remove or insert some information.
3. Close the drawer again.

To use a data file on disk, you follow a similar procedure:

1. Open the data file for access using an OPEN statement.
2. Read or write some information in the file.
3. Close the data file using a CLOSE statement.

CAUTION:

As with any filing system, careful attention to detail is important. If your filing habits are sloppy, you will misfile or even lose information.

Let's take a look at each of the steps in using a data file more closely.

5.5 Opening a File

Opening a data file is really establishing a data communication link between your program and some device. Your computer is a very sophisticated communications device that can communicate with many different devices in a variety of ways. As a result, we have to specify a number of different things when we establish our link:

1. A logical file number to identify this particular data communication link. This is necessary because several links can be in use at one time.

2. A device number to specify the device with which we want to communicate. This is necessary because your computer can communicate with a variety of devices (e.g., disk drive=8, tape recorder=1, screen=3 and printer=4).

3. A channel number to specify the nature of the communication. Its meaning depends on which device you are using. It is also called the secondary address.

4. File identification information to identify the specific file we wish to access and whether we want to read or write information. This is not necessary for devices that do not contain named files such as printers and keyboards.

All this information is specified in a single OPEN statement. Since there is a lot of information to be specified, let's go over the structure of an OPEN statement carefully.

NOTE:

Since this book deals with using your disk drive, we won't go into all the possible variations of the OPEN statement. Please consult your user's manual when using other devices.

```
SYNTAX:
  OPEN file#,device#,channel#,"fid"

EXAMPLES:
  OPEN 15,8,15
  OPEN 1,8,5,"HOME ACCOUNTS,SEQ,WRITE"
  OPEN 6,8,3,"FAST COPY,PRG,R"
  OPEN 2,8,12,"ARTICLES,L,"+CHR$(169)
```

WHERE:

file#   = logical file number (integer 1-127).

device#   = device number (eight for the disk drive).

channel#   = channel number (2-14 are data channels, 15 is the command
               channel).

fid   = file identification information (required for data files,
               optional for the command channel).

Before we examine each part in detail here are two typical OPEN statements:

ANNOTATED EXAMPLES:

```
OPEN 15,8,15
```

Opens file# 15 to the disk drive's command channel.

```
OPEN 3,8,4,"0:BUNCHADATA,S,R"
```

Opens file# 3 to device eight (drive) using channel# 4 to access the file on drive zero
named BUNCHADATA. It is a sequential file (S) and we want to read (R) it.

5.6 The Logical File Number (file#)

Your VIC-20 or Commodore 64 allows you to have several files open at once. For
example, at some point in your program you might be reading data from one disk file,
writing data to another disk file and sending information to a printer. As a result,
there has to be some simple way for you to indicate which file you want to access. This
is the function of the logical file number.

When you establish the communications channel using an OPEN statement, the file
you want is assigned the logical file number that you specified. Until you close down
the channel, you refer to it by its logical file number. For example, the logical file
number of this file is five.

```
OPEN 5,8,7,"BUNCHADATA,S,W"
PRINT#5,"HI MOM"
CLOSE 5
```

The OPEN statement establishes the association between the disk file, BUNCH-
ADATA, and the logical file number five. Subsequent statements that refer to this
file, refer to it by its logical file number five.

NOTES:

1. Use integers between one and 127 as logical file numbers. You can use any integer
   between one and 255 as a logical file number. However, the integers greater than
   127 act differently. These numbers cause your computer to send a line feed
   character, CHR$(10), as well as a carriage return character, CHR$(13), at the end
   of each line. This wastes disk space and makes it impossible for you to read the file
   using an INPUT# statement.

2. You can use different numbers for the same file. Many people are under the
   mistaken impression that you have to use the same file number to read a data file
   as you used to write the file. This is *not* true. Logical file numbers are only

temporarily associated with a particular file. Once a file has been closed, there is no longer any association between a number and a file.

3. All files open must have different logical file numbers. Since the logical file number is used to identify one particular file, you *must* use different logical file numbers for each of the files open simultaneously. Once you close a file, you are free to reuse that logical file number in your program.

5.7 The Device Number (device#)

This number specifies the device with which you want to communicate. Your 1541 disk drive is normally device number eight. As long as you are only using one drive, always use this number and ignore the rest of this section.

If you want to use two 1540 or 1541 disk drives simultaneously you will have to change the device number of one of the drives. You can change the device number of your disk drive either temporarily or permanently.

Permanently Changing a 1541's Device Number

If you own two or more disk drives, you may want to permanently change the device numbers on all but one of the disk drives. This way you will avoid the bother of changing the device numbers every time you fire up your system. Section 12.3 describes how to make this modification.

Temporarily Changing a 1541's Device Number

The procedure outlined below is useful when you have temporarily borrowed a second or third drive. The change of device number is temporary. When you turn the drive OFF and then ON again, the device number will be reset to eight.

1. Turn ON your computer and all your disk drives. Connect the drive, whose device number is to be changed, to the serial bus on the computer. Disconnect the other drive(s) from the serial bus (otherwise you will change the device number of all the drives).

2. Execute the following commands from either immediate mode or from within a program:

```
OPEN 15,8,15   (open the command channel)
PRINT#15,"M-W"CHR$(119)CHR$(0)CHR$(2)
   CHR$(dn+32)CHR$(dn+64)
CLOSE15
```

WHERE:

dn   = the device number desired (an integer 4-15; values greater than
          15 may cause problems).

For example, to change a 1541 to device number nine, you would use:

```
OPEN 15,8,15   (open the command channel)
PRINT#15,"M-W"CHR$(119)CHR$(0)CHR$(2)
   CHR$(41)CHR$(73)
CLOSE15
```

3. Connect one more disk drive to the serial bus. This newly attached drive will be
   device# 8. If you are only using two drives, you are now finished. If you are using
   three or more drives, repeat Steps 2 and 3 for each of the drives (be sure to give
   them all different device numbers). Note that you do not have to disconnect a drive
   once its device number has been changed. Since it is no longer device number
   eight, it will ignore the subsequent commands.

WARNING:

Be sure you use the commands *exactly* as indicated above. The format and examples
given on page 40 of the *1541 User's Manual* are incorrect. The correct syntax for a
Memory-Write command is "M-W" not "M-W:". If you include the colon, the 1541's
device number will *not* be changed!

HINT:

If you find it inconvenient to unplug the disk drives from the serial bus, you can turn
OFF a disk drive instead of disconnecting it as indicated in Step 1. Once you have
completed Step 2, turn the disk drive ON again.

5.8 The Channel Number (channel#)

The channel number is also known as the secondary address. It specifies the nature of
the communication desired. Its specific meaning depends on the device with which
you are communicating. Because its meaning varies so much, we will only consider
its meaning as it relates to the disk drive.

Channel#	Normal Use
0	Reserved by DOS for loading programs.
1	Reserved by DOS for saving programs.
2-14	Read or write to any type of disk file.
15	Disk drive command channel.
16-17	Reserved by DOS for internal use.
18+	Illegal values.

WARNING:

Every file that is open *must* have its own channel#. Once you have closed a file, you
are free to reuse that channel#.

The Command Channel

The 1541 disk drive can carry out a number of disk operations, such as formatting a
disk or scratching a file, without direct intervention by the computer. The command
channel is used to send commands to the disk drive when you want it to carry out
these types of operations. The housekeeping commands are described in detail in

Chapter 4. Appendix D contains a summary of all the diskette-housekeeping and direct-access commands. The command channel is also used by the disk drive to report disk errors.

Unusual Uses of Channel Numbers

Channel# 0 is normally reserved for use by the computer for loading programs. If you use a channel number of zero when opening a file to read it, you will get normal results unless you are trying to access the directory file, $. In this case, the DOS will convert the directory file into a pseudo program in the same way it does when you LOAD the directory. This is sometimes a useful approach to use when reading a diskette's directory from within a program. If you attempt to use a channel number of zero when opening a file in write mode, the file will not be opened and the drive will report a 62, FILE NOT FOUND, error message.

Channel# 1 is normally reserved for use by the computer for saving programs. If you use a channel number of one when opening a file to write to it, you will get normal results. If you attempt to use a channel number of one when opening a file in read mode, the file will not be opened and the drive will report a 63, FILE EXISTS, error message. The drive apparently overrides your read mode declaration and is attempting to prevent you from overwriting an existing file.

5.9 File Identification Information

The last part of an OPEN statement is used to identify the specific file you want to access.

```
OPEN file#,device#,channel#,"fid"
```

Program, Sequential and User Files

The "fid" syntax for program, sequential, and user files is:

```
SYNTAX:
  "drive#:filename,type,mode"        (for new or existing files)
  "drive#:filename"                  (for existing files only)


EXAMPLES:
  "O:BUNCHA STUFF,SEQ,READ"
  "O:ACCOUNTS,USR,W"
  "FAST COPY,PRG,WRITE"
  "BIGFILE"
```

WHERE:

drive#   = the drive number (always zero on the 1541); optional on all Commodore single disk drives.

filename   = the name of the file as given in the directory; may contain wild cards if file already exists.

type   = the file type (PRG, SEQ or USR); optional when reading or replacing an existing file.

mode   = type of operation (READ or WRITE); defaults to READ if
              not specified.

HINT:

Some or all of the information may be stored in variables. In many situations it is
convenient to store all or part of the file identification information in variables. This
makes it easy for you to write your program so that you can have the user input a file
name. You just store the name in a string variable and then concatenate (add on) the
pieces you need to complete the file identification information. Here are a few
examples of how you can concatenate pieces of information.

```
OPEN 1,8,5,"@0:MY DATA FILE,S,W"    (Original)

INPUT "FILE NAME DESIRED";FI$        (Name is variable)
OPEN 1,8,5,"@0:"+FI$+",S,W"

                                     (Name, file type and replace
INPUT "NAME OF FILE";NF$              are all variable)
INPUT "FILE TYPE (P/S/U)";FT$
INPUT "REPLACE EXISTING FILE (Y/N)";X$
R$="":IF X$="Y" THEN R$="@:"
OPEN 3,8,7,R$+NF$+","+FT$+",W"
```

NOTES:

1. To replace an existing file with a new version use @0 as the drive number. Be sure
   to read the warnings about replacing files (see Sections 6.6, 7.4 and 8.7).

2. When opening a file to read it, you may use the wild card characters (? and *) in
   the name. These are not allowed in write mode.

3. You may use S instead of SEQ, P instead of PRG, and U instead of USR when
   specifying the file type.

4. You may use R instead of READ and W instead of WRITE when specifying the
   mode of access.

5. There is a special APPEND (A) mode that is used for adding data to the end of an
   existing file.

6. There is also a special MODIFY (M) mode that is used for reading unclosed files
   (see Section 11.3).

ANNOTATED EXAMPLES:

```
OPEN 25,8,4,"0:BUNCHADATA,SEQ,READ"
```

Opens file# 25 to device# 8 (disk) using channel# 4 to access the file on drive zero
called BUNCHADATA. It is a sequential (SEQ) file and we want to read (READ) it.

```
OPEN 3,8,6,"0:PILAJUNK,SEQ,W"
```

Opens file# 3 to device# 8 (disk) using channel# 6 to access the file on drive zero called
PILAJUNK. It is a new sequential (SEQ) file and we want to write (W) it.

```
OPEN 1,8,5,"@0:DUMBNAME,P,W"
```

Opens file# 1 to device# 8 (disk) using channel# 5 to replace (@) the file on drive zero called DUMBNAME. It is a program (P) file and we want to write (W) it.

```
OPEN 2,8,9,"0:JUNK*,P,R"
```

Opens file# 2 to read (R) a program (P) file whose name begins with the letters JUNK on drive zero.

```
OPEN 3,8,6,"0:PILAJUNK"
```

Opens file# 3 to read an existing sequential file called PILAJUNK. NOTE: this same command can open an existing program or relative file called PILAJUNK.

Relative Files

The "fid" syntax for relative files is:

```
SYNTAX:
  "drive#:filename,L,"+CHR$(len)      (for new or existing files)
  "drive#:filename"                   (for existing files only)


EXAMPLES:
  OPEN 1,8,6,"PHONE LIST,L,"+CHR$(125)
  OPEN 7,8,3,"XMAS CARDS,L,"+CHR$(80)
  OPEN 9,8,12,"CUSTOMERS"
```

WHERE:

drive#   = the drive number (always zero on the 1541); optional on
              all Commodore single drives.
filename   = the name of the file as given in the directory; may contain
              wild cards if file already exists.
len   = the record length in characters (2 to 254).

WARNING:

There are three forbidden record lengths. You may not use record lengths of 42, 58, or 63. An OPEN command containing one of these record lengths will be rejected by the 1541 with a SYNTAX ERROR.

CAUTION:

The record length (an integer between two and 254) must be specified when a new relative file is created. Once you have created the file, its record length cannot be changed. If you try to specify a new record length for an existing file, your request will be ignored and the file will not be opened. The only way to change the record length is to open a new relative file using the new record size and copy the information into the new file one record at a time!

NOTES:

1. Do not bother trying to replace an existing relative file using @0 as the drive number. All that happens is a normal open of the file.

2. When accessing an existing file, you may use the wild card characters (? and *) in the name. These are not allowed when creating a new file.

3. You do not have to specify whether you want to read the file or write to a relative file. Any time you open a relative file you may read or write any record.

ANNOTATED EXAMPLES:

```
OPEN 5,8,4,"0:BIGFILE,L,"+CHR$(45)
```

Opens file# 5 to device# 8 (disk) using channel# 4 to access an existing relative file called BIGFILE with a record length of 45, or create a new relative file by this name if one does not exist.

```
OPEN 21,8,9,"0:BLACKHOLE,L,"+CHR$(254)
```

Opens file# 21 to device# 8 (disk) using channel# 9 to access an existing relative file called BLACKHOLE with a record length of 254, or create a new relative file by this name if one does not exist.

```
OPEN 6,8,5,"BLACKHOLE"
```

Opens file# 6 to device# 8 (disk) using channel# 5 to access an existing relative file called BLACKHOLE for read/write access. Note that this can also open a PRG, SEQ or USR file with this name for read access.

Direct-access Files

The "fid" syntax for direct-access files is:

```
SYNTAX:
  "#"


ALTERNATE:
  "#buffer"


EXAMPLES:
  OPEN 1,8,5,"#"
  OPEN 7,8,12,"#0"
```

WHERE:

buffer   = the buffer number desired (0-2 on the 1541).

NOTE:

The buffer number refers to which part of the disk's RAM you will use. Buffer #0 is the area $0300-03FF, buffer #1 is $0400-04FF, buffer #2 is $0500-05FF, and buffer #3 is $0600-06FF. If you do not specify a buffer number, you will be assigned an inactive buffer by the drive. If no buffer is available, you will get a 70, NO CHANNEL, error message. For most normal disk operations you don't need to specify a particular buffer.

ANNOTATED EXAMPLES:

```
OPEN 5,8,4,"#"
```

Opens file# 5 as a direct-access file using channel# 4. No buffer number is specified.

```
OPEN 1,8,6,"#2"
```

Opens file# 1 as a direct-access file using channel# 6. Buffer number two is specified.

Command Channel

The "fid" syntax for the command channel is:

```
SYNTAX:
  nothing

ALTERNATE:
  "command"

EXAMPLES:
  OPEN 15,8,15
  OPEN 15,8,15,"N:TEST DISK,T5"
```

WHERE:

command   = a disk command such as "I0" or "S0:JUNKFILE". See
Appendix D for a complete list of the direct-access
commands. Chapter 4 describes the diskette-
housekeeping commands in detail.

ANNOTATED EXAMPLES:

```
OPEN 15,8,15
```

Opens file# 15 as the command channel. No disk command is issued.

```
OPEN 15,8,15,"I0"
```

Opens file# 15 as the command channel and sends the disk command "I0" to tell the drive to read the BAM of the diskette in drive zero.

```
OPEN 3,8,15,"S0:JUNKYFILE"
```

Opens file# 3 as the command channel and sends the disk command "S0:JUNKYFILE" to tell the drive to scratch the file named JUNKYFILE from the directory of the diskette in drive zero.

5.10 Disk Drive Status

Whenever you perform a disk operation, such as opening a file, the 1541 DOS monitors the operation. When the operation is completed, the DOS generates a status report that indicates whether or not the operation was completed successfully. You should check the disk drive status after any disk operation.

The disk status report consists of four parts: an error code, an English language message, and the track number and sector number of the block where the error, if any, occurred. The table below lists the errors most frequently encountered during normal file handling. A complete listing of all the different error codes and messages is given in Appendix C.

Code	Message	Meaning
00*	OK	Everything went just fine.
01*	FILES SCRATCHED	Number of files scratched (not an error).
02-19*		Undocumented (ignore).
20	READ ERROR	Can't find header of sector.
21	READ ERROR	No sync mark on track requested.
22	READ ERROR	Can't find data block of sector.
23	READ ERROR	Checksum error in the data block.
26	WRITE PROTECT ON	Attempt write with write protect tab on.
27	READ ERROR	Checksum error in the header block.
29	DISK ID MISMATCH	Mismatch between BAM & disk ID.
30	SYNTAX ERROR	Bad command, general syntax error.
31	SYNTAX ERROR	Unrecognized command.
32	SYNTAX ERROR	Command longer than 58 characters.
33	SYNTAX ERROR	Incorrectly used wild card.
34	SYNTAX ERROR	File name omitted from command.
50*	RECORD NOT PRESENT	New relative file record being added.
51	OVERFLOW IN RECORD	Relative file record too long.
52	FILE TOO LARGE	Relative file too large for the disk.
60	WRITE FILE OPEN	Attempt to read a write file.
61	FILE NOT OPEN	File not open.
62	FILE NOT FOUND	File with that name does not exist.
63	FILE EXISTS	File by that name already exists.
64	FILE TYPE MISMATCH	File type mismatch.
66	ILLEGAL TRACK & SECTOR	Pointer to non-existent block.
70	NO CHANNEL	File did not open.
72	DISK FULL	Disk or directory is full.
74	DRIVE NOT READY	No diskette in drive.

* Not errors, therefore may be ignored.

You use the command channel (channel# 15) to check the disk status. It is a good idea to open the command channel early in your program and *leave it open* until just before your program terminates. This allows you to check the disk drive status at any point in your program.

WARNING:

Do *not* open and close the command channel each time you want to check the disk status. Whenever you close the command channel, all files are closed automatically. This can be used to close a disk file when your program aborts with a SYNTAX ERROR and you edited the line. See the HINT in Section 3.8 for more details.

To determine the disk drive status, use an INPUT# statement to read the four parts of the report like this:

```
10 OPEN 15,8,15:REM OPEN COMMAND CHANNEL
   :         :         :         :
230 INPUT#15,E,E$,T,S:REM CHECK DISK STATUS
240 IF E>19 THEN ?E;E$;T;S:CLOSE15:STOP
   :         :         :         :
```

In our example, line 230 inputs the disk status. The first variable, E, will contain the error code number. The second variable, E\$, will contain the error message. The remaining variables, T and S, will contain the track number (T) and the sector number (S) where the error, if any, occurred. Line 240 checks the error code number in E. Error codes less than 20 are ignored. If the error code is greater than 19, the entire report is printed on the screen, the files closed and execution halted.

5.11 Limitation on the Number of Files Open

If you check the manual for your Commodore 64 or VIC-20, you will find that you are allowed to have up to 10 files open simultaneously. For example, you could open one file to your printer, another one to your modem, another to your cassette tape recorder and a couple to your disk drive. With all these files open you might get confused, but your computer wouldn't.

Although your computer can handle 10 open files, the peripheral devices can't. Each peripheral has its own limitations. Your 1541 is limited by the amount of RAM memory that it contains. The following table indicates the maximum allowable number of disk files of various types that you can have open simultaneously.

SEQ or PRG Files	Relative Files	Direct Access Files	Total Disk Files Open
0	0	0 - 4	0 - 4
0	1	0 - 2	1 - 3
1	1	0 - 1	2 - 3
2	0	0 - 2	2 - 4
3	0	0 - 1	3 - 4

Note that you *cannot* have two relative files open at once.

5.12 Writing to a File

The PRINT# statement is used to write information into a file. A PRINT# statement can be used either within a program or in immediate mode. In general it looks like this:

```
SYNTAX:
  xxx PRINT# file#, var list
```

```
EXAMPLES:
  120 PRINT#3,N*3
  140 PRINT# 5,M$;
  250 PRINT#12,M$+N$",  EMPLOYEE#"W1
  300 PRINT# 6,NAM$;",";ADR$;",";CITY$
```

```
WHERE:

  xxx       = the line number.
  file#     = the file number used in the OPEN statement.
```

var list   = one or more numeric or string variable names or
              expressions; separated, where there may be ambiguity,
              by a space, comma or semicolon.

WARNING:

PRINT# does *not* output separators between values. When you use a BASIC command like X=3:Y=4:PRINT X;Y you see "3 4" on the screen, not "3,4". The PRINT# command works the same way. This means that when you output the values of several variables using a single PRINT# statement, there will be no separators between the values in the file. For example, if A=20, B=5, and C=12 and we use PRINT#xx,A,B,C, the file will contain 20 5 12 <cr>. This will be hard to read back correctly. If we use INPUT#xx,X to read this file, the blank spaces will be ignored and X will be assigned the value 20512. Field separators must be written out explicitly like this:

```
PRINT#xx,A","B","C      (Note the quotes around the commas.)
```

NOTES:

1. PRINT# is a single BASIC keyword. You may *not* leave a space between the word PRINT and the # sign. Spaces between the # sign and the file# or between the file# and the comma (,) are optional.

2. Do *not* use ?# as an abbreviation for PRINT#. The correct abbreviation for PRINT# is pR (press P and then hold the SHIFT key down while pressing R). If you do use ?#, the program will halt with a SYNTAX ERROR but when you list the line, *it will appear correct!*

3. PRINT# normally outputs a carriage return character following the value of the last variable named, unless you specifically suppress it by putting a semicolon at the end of the variable list.

4. PRINT# spaces the output just like a PRINT statement. The spacing of characters in the file will be the same as though you used a PRINT statement to print them on the video screen. This means that each numeric value is preceded by a space (for the + or - sign) and followed by another space. If you must pack a lot of numeric values into a file, use the STR$ function to convert them into strings and then use the MID$ function to delete the leading space like this:

```
PRINT#xx,MID$(STR$(AA),2)
```

This saves two bytes per number.

ANNOTATED EXAMPLES:

```
120 PRINT#3,A
```

Writes the value of the variable A followed by a carriage return character into file# 3.

```
470 PRINT#9,A","B","C$
```

Writes the value of the variable A, a comma, the value of the variable B, a comma, the value of the variable C$, and a carriage return character into file# 9.

```
235 PRINT#4,"THIS IS RECORD NUMBER"K
```

Writes the message THIS IS RECORD NUMBER followed by the value of the variable K and a carriage return character into file# 4.

```
125 PRINT#1,MX$(K);
```

Writes the value of the Kth element of the one dimensional array named MX$ into file# 1. No carriage return character is written.

5.13 Monitoring the Number of Blocks Free

Running out of space on a diskette can cause serious problems when you are writing to a file. You will lose some, if not all, of your data. As a result, it is a good idea to check the number of blocks free on your diskette whenever you want to write, save, replace or append new data to a file. This is easy to do if you are in immediate mode. Just load and list the directory. But how do you do this from within a program? It is actually quite easy. You can PEEK the value out of the 1541's RAM memory. Type in this short program and see how it's done.

```
*********************
PROGRAM: BLOCKS FREE
*********************

0 REM 1541 USER'S GUIDE SECTION 5.13
1 REM  COPYRIGHT: G. NEUFELD, 1984
2 :
3 REM READ BLOCKS FREE ON 1541
4 :
10 OPEN 15,8,15,"IO"
20 PRINT# 15,"M-R"CHR$(250)CHR$(2)CHR$(3
)
30 GET# 15,A$:BF=ASC(A$+CHR$(0))
40 GET# 15,A$
50 GET# 15,A$:BF=BF+256*ASC(A$+CHR$(0))
60 PRINT "THERE ARE";BF;"BLOCKS FREE"
70 CLOSE 15
```

Lines 20 to 50 are the ones that PEEK the value you want. You may want to include these lines as a subroutine in your file handling programs. Whenever you need to know how much space is left on the diskette, just GOSUB to this routine.

Here are a few suggestions about how to use this routine. When you know the approximate size of the file that is to be written, you can have your program check to see if there will be enough space. If there isn't enough space, you might display a message asking the user to change diskettes. When you don't have any idea about how much space will be needed, you can have your program monitor the amount of space left as the file is being written. If you run out of space, you might ask the user to switch diskettes and then rewrite the entire file. Remember though, when the user switches diskettes, all files in the 1541 will be closed!

5.14 Reading from a File

You can use either an INPUT# or a GET# statement to read information from a file.
In general, the INPUT# statement reads in several characters of information at once
while the GET# statement reads in one character of information at a time. Let's
examine the characteristics of these in some detail.

INPUT# Statement

The INPUT# statement can only be used within a program. It may not be given in
immediate mode. In general it looks like this:

```
SYNTAX:
  xxx INPUT# file#, var list


EXAMPLES:
  250  INPUT#1,X
  100  INPUT#7,NUM,NAM$,ADR$,CITY$,PROV$,PCODE$
  220  INPUT#12,N(K),M$(K+3)
```

WHERE:

xxx   = the line number.
file#   = the file number used in the OPEN statement.
var list   = one or more variable names separated from each other by
              commas. Any combination of numeric or string variables
              or arrays may be used.

WARNING:

INPUT# always reads as far as a carriage return character just like an INPUT
statement. Since many people are unaware of the problems this can cause, enter and
run this test program.

```
********************
PROGRAM: TEST INPUT#
********************

10  OPEN 1,8,5,"@0:NUMBERS,S,W"      Open file to write.
20  FOR K=1 TO 20                    Loop 20 times.
30  PRINT#1, K;",";K*K;","K*K*K      Write in the number,
40  NEXT                             its square and cube.
50  CLOSE 1                          Close file.
60  OPEN 2,8,6,"NUMBERS"             Reopen to read file.
70  INPUT#2,X                        Read value from file.
80  PRINT X                          Display what we read.
90  IF ST=0 GOTO 70                  Read to end (Section 5.15).
100 CLOSE 2:END                      Close file and quit.
```

The file contains 1, 1, 1 <cr> 2, 4, 8 <cr> 3, 9, 27.... However, when we read it back,
we only get 1, 2, 3, 4,.... The INPUT# statement in line 70 read as far as a carriage
return character each time. It assigned the first value it found to X. Since we did not

have any more variable names listed behind the INPUT#, the other two values were discarded. Notice that we were not warned that values were being discarded. This can happen whenever you use any delimiter other than a carriage return character as a field delimiter. *Beware!*

NOTES:

1. INPUT# is a single BASIC keyword. You may not leave a space between the word INPUT and the # sign. Spaces between the # sign and the file# or between the file# and the comma (,) are optional.

2. INPUT# can read past the first carriage return. If your INPUT# statement specifies several variable names (e.g., INPUT#5,X$,Y,Z) the file will be read until enough values are found to satisfy all the variables listed (e.g., TIM<cr>15, 29,37<cr>). In this example X$=TIM, Y=15, and Z=39; 37 is ignored (see WARNING above).

3. Do not read non-numeric characters into a numeric variable. If you specify a numeric variable name in the INPUT# statement and the computer encounters any non-numeric characters, the program aborts with a FILE DATA ERROR message.

4. INPUT# can only handle up to 88 characters. The INPUT# statement on the VIC-20 and Commodore 64 can handle up to 88 characters between delimiters. If there are more than 88 characters, the program will abort and report a STRING TOO LONG ERROR message. If you write programs for other machines, you should be aware that INPUT# on a 4032 or an 8032 only allows 80 characters between delimiters.

ANNOTATED EXAMPLES:

```
120 INPUT#3,A
```

Reads as far as the next carriage return character in file# 3. The first value read is stored as the value of the numeric variable A.

```
470 INPUT#9,A,B,C$
```

Reads at least as far as the next carriage return character in file# 1. The first value read is stored as the value of the numeric variable A, the second as B, and the third as C$. If carriage returns are encountered before all three values have been found, the file will be read as far as the first carriage return character that follows the value assigned to C$.

```
125 INPUT#1,MX$(K)
```

Reads as far as the next carriage return character in file# 1. The first value read is stored as the value of the Kth element in the one-dimensional array named MX$.

GET# Statement

The GET# statement inputs data one character at a time. It can only be used within a program. It may not be used in immediate mode. In general, it looks like this:

SYNTAX:
```
xxx GET# file#, var list
```

EXAMPLES:
```
120 GET#1,A$
350 GET#5,X$:IF X$="" THEN X$=CHR$(0)
230 GET#12,D$(K)
115 GET#6,A$,B$,C$,D$
```

WHERE:

xxx	= the line number.
file#	= the file number used in the OPEN statement.
var list	= one or more variable names separated from each other by commas. Generally only string variables or arrays are used.

NOTES:

1. GET# is a single BASIC keyword. You may not leave a space between the word GET and the # sign. Spaces between the # sign and the file# or between the file# and the comma (,) are optional.

2. Generally use only string variables with GET#. It is possible to use a numeric variable name in a GET# statement. If you do, the digits zero to nine will be read correctly, the plus sign (+), minus sign (-), colon (:), comma (,), period (.) and the letter E will be read as zero, and all other characters will cause a SYNTAX ERROR.

3. GET# reads a file one character at a time. Carriage return characters, CHR$(13), commas, colons, and other field or record delimiters are treated the same as any other character (except CHR$(0) —see below).

3. GET# is slow! Since the computer must send the disk drive a send-me-one-byte request each time you use GET#, it takes quite a while to read through a file. For example, when I first wrote the BACKUP program (Appendix E), I used GET# to fetch the bytes. It took about four hours to backup a diskette! Replacing the GET# with a short machine language routine cut the time to 25 minutes.

4. CHR$(0) is not read correctly. If your file contains a CHR$(0), it will not be read correctly. The value stored into the string variable is not CHR$(0). The null string (no characters) is stored there instead. This is the reason for the common GET# statement:

```
GET#1,X$:IF X$="" THEN X$=CHR$(0)
```

ANNOTATED EXAMPLES:

```
120 GET#3,A$
```

Reads one character from file# 3 and assigns its value to the string variable A$.

```
470 GET#9,A$,B$,C$
```

Reads three characters from file# 9. The value of the first is assigned to the string variable A$, the second assigned to B$ and the third to C$.

```
225 GET#5,A$: IF A$="" THEN A$=CHR$(0)
```

Reads one character from file# 5 and assigns its value to the string variable A$. If a null byte was read, it is corrected to CHR$(0).

5.15 Detecting the End of a File

Many people store a special end-of-file value, such as -99999, at the end of their data files so they can tell when they have reached the end of the file. This is not necessary with your Commodore computer. All you have to do is monitor the value stored in the special status variable, ST.

The status variable, ST, reflects the status of the most recent input or output (I/O) operation. Its normal value is zero. As you read the last value in a file, your computer will set ST to 64. This indicates an end-of-file condition. Type in and run this test program. The first time choose the W option to create the test file. Once the file has been stored on diskette, run the program again and choose the R option.

```
******************
PROGRAM: ST VALUE
******************

O REM 1541 USER'S GUIDE SECTION 5.15
1 REM   COPYRIGHT: G. NEUFELD, 1984
2 :
3 REM OBSERVE THE VALUE OF STATUS VARIAB
LE
4 :
10 INPUT "READ OR WRITE THE FILE (R/W)";
A$
20 OPEN 15,8,15,"IO"
30 IF A$="R" GOTO 110
40 OPEN 1,8,5,"@0:TEST FILE,S,W"
50 GOSUB 170:IF EN>19 THEN CLOSE 1:CLOSE
  15:STOP
60 FOR K=1 TO 15
70 PRINT#1,"THIS IS RECORD #";K
80 PRINT "WRITING RECORD #";K
90 NEXT
100 CLOSE 1:CLOSE 15:END
110 OPEN 3,8,5,"TEST FILE,S,R"
120 GOSUB 170:IF EN>19 THEN CLOSE 1:CLOS
E 15:STOP
130 INPUT#3,A$
140 PRINT A$;"THE VALUE OF ST ="ST
150 IF ST=0 GOTO 130
160 CLOSE 1:CLOSE 15:END
170 INPUT#15,EN,EM$,ET,ES
```

```
180 PRINT EN;EM$;ET;ES
190 RETURN
```

The example below illustrates the use of the status variable to locate the end-of-file when reading a file.

(File# 1 to disk opened previously.)

```
200 NUM=0
210 NUM=NUM+1
220 INPUT#1,NAM$(NUM),ADR$(NUM)
230 PRINT NAM$(NUM),ADR$(NUM)
240 IF ST<>64 GOTO 210
```

In our example above, we read data from the file, printed it to the screen and then checked the status variable, ST, to see if we were at the end of the file. Note that printing the data to the screen did not affect the value of ST. However, if we had printed the data to a printer using a PRINT# statement in line 230, we would be in trouble. The value of ST in line 240 would then indicate the status of the printing operation in 230 rather than the input operation in 220. When we reached the end of the file, we would never know it. In situations such as this, we have to save the value of ST before it is lost like this:

(File# 1 to disk and file# 4 to printer opened previously.)

```
200 NUM=0
210 NUM=NUM+1
220 INPUT#1,NAM$(NUM),ADR$(NUM)
225 S=ST:REM SAVE STATUS
230 PRINT#4,NAM$(NUM),ADR$(NUM)
240 IF S<>64 GOTO 210
```

CAUTION:

Even using INPUT# to read the disk drive error status (see Section 5.10) will change the value of ST.

5.16 Closing a File

The CLOSE statement is used to close a file when you are finished using it. It is very important to close a file, particularly if you have been writing to it. Otherwise you may create an unclosed file.

A CLOSE statement looks like this:

```
SYNTAX:
  xxx CLOSE file#
```

```
EXAMPLES:
  50 CLOSE 1
  200 CLOSE 5:CLOSE 15
  600 CLOSE CC
```

WHERE:

xxx   = the line number.
file#   = the file number used in the OPEN statement.

WARNINGS:

1. You will lose data if you don't close a write file! If you fail to close a sequential (SEQ), program (PRG) or user (USR) file that you have just written, you must use the techniques described in Section 11.3 to be able to access any of your data at all. Even using these techniques, *you will lose data!* If you fail to close a relative file after writing to it, some of the data will probably be lost. Be safe, not sorry! Close those files.

2. Closing the command channel will close all open files. Whenever you close the command channel, all the disk files that are open are closed automatically. This is the reason for the rule that the command channel should be opened first and closed last. See the HINT in Section 3.8 for a useful application of this.

ANNOTATED EXAMPLES:

```
120 CLOSE 3
```

Closes down file number three.

```
100 FL = 12
 :   :   :
470 CLOSE FL
```

Closes file number 12.

5.17 Conclusion

Now that you have learned some of the basic concepts of file handling and the commands you will need, it's time to get down to specifics. The next three chapters take a detailed look at program, sequential and relative files. Each chapter contains specific suggestions and examples to help you make more effective use of one type of file. Each of these chapters stands alone. You do not have to read and understand Chapter 6 to make use of Chapter 7 or 8.

PROGRAM FILES

This chapter takes a detailed look at program files and their contents. It includes an introduction to the inner structure of BASIC programs and concludes with a look at self-modifying programs. Each section includes several examples to help you learn how to make better use of this common, but underutilized, file type.

6.1 Introduction to Program Files

A program file is the most common type you will encounter. It is used to store a copy of the contents of some part of the computer's RAM or ROM memory. Usually it holds a copy of a BASIC or machine language program. Your Commodore 64 makes it very easy for you to create or read program files that contain BASIC programs. All you do is use a SAVE or LOAD command. When you do this the program is saved or loaded faster than any other file type.

Normally program files are not used for data storage. However some application programs, such as the word processing programs WordPro™ and PaperClip™, use a program file to store data. In these cases, the data (the text) always resides in a particular part of the computer's memory. When you want to memorize (save) the text you have typed in, the program sets some pointers and uses a SAVE command to save a copy of the appropriate part of the computer's RAM memory to the diskette. When you want to recall the text, the program uses a LOAD command to load the program file from diskette into the computer's memory. These programs use program files for data storage because loading or saving a program file is faster and easier than reading or writing a data file.

You are not limited to just saving or loading a program file. You can open the file and read or write to it as well. This is done to create a compacted program (all REM statements and unnecessary spaces are deleted), a cross reference (a list of the line numbers in which each variable is used), or a specialized program listing (such as was used to create the listings for this book).

The biggest difficulty in using program files in nonstandard ways is that you must have a thorough understanding of the way in which a BASIC program is structured and tokenized in your computer's memory. You must be sure to get all the pointers and tokens correct or your computer will hang.

When to use a program file:

1. To store BASIC or machine language programs in a form that can be loaded easily.
2. To store blocks of data that always occupy the same area of the Commodore 64's RAM memory (advanced users only).

The benefits from using program files are:

1. They are easy to access using SAVE or LOAD.
2. They are saved or loaded at maximum speed.

The drawbacks of using program files are:

1. The amount of information you can store in a program file is usually limited to the amount that can be held in the computer's memory at one time.
2. You must understand how a BASIC program is stored in memory to make sense of the contents of a program file or to create a new program file.

Some typical uses of program files are:

1. Storing BASIC programs.
2. Storing machine language programs.
3. Storing text by word processors.

6.2 Structure of a Program File

A program file has a simple structure. It is not divided into fields or records. The first two bytes in the file specify where the file is to start loading into memory (the load address). The rest of the file is a copy of what is to be loaded into memory. A program file that contains a BASIC program for the Commodore 64 would look like this:

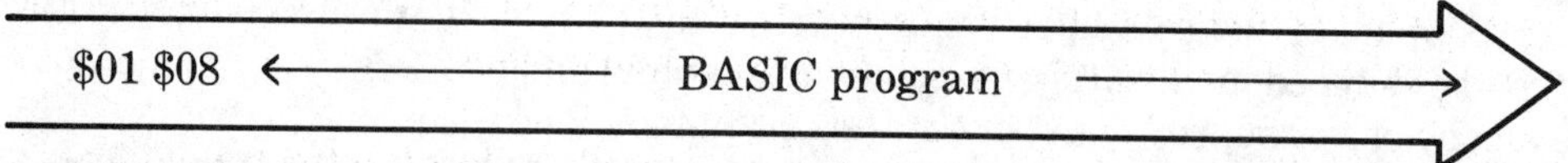

The load address consists of two bytes (in this file $01 and $08). The least significant byte is stored first (lo byte/hi byte). In this case the load address is $0801. You can convert this into decimal notation as follows:

load address = 256 * hi byte + lo byte
load address = 256 * 8 + 1 = 2049 ($0801)

A typical machine language routine looks like this:

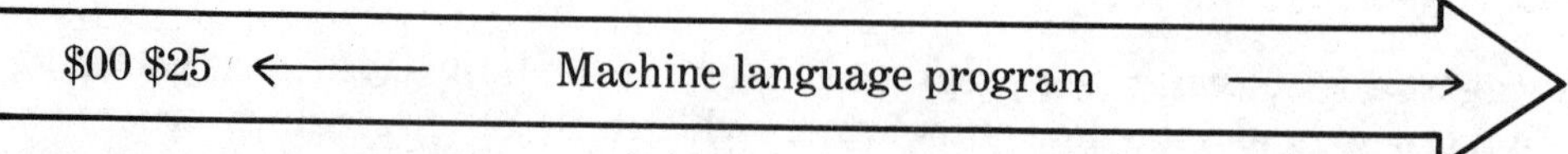

load address = 256 * (2*16 + 5) + 0 = 9472 ($2500)

6.3 Loading a Program File

You may load a copy of a program file into the Commodore 64's memory from immediate mode (i.e., you have a READY prompt and a flashing cursor),or from within a program.

Loading from Immediate Mode

Type in one of the following commands and press RETURN.

```
SYNTAX:
  LOAD "filename",device#            (program relocated)
  LOAD "filename",device#,channel#   (not relocated)


EXAMPLES:
  LOAD "GOOD GAME",8
  LOAD "ML SORT",8,1
  F$="SUPER FORCE"
  LOAD F$,8
```

WHERE:

filename = the name of the program file as it appears in a directory
            listing.
device#   = the device number of the 1541 (normally eight).
channel# = the channel number (secondary address). (Normally one
            for a non-relocating load; used when loading machine
            language programs.)

NOTES:

1. The file name may be stored as a string variable. If it is, use the string variable name instead of "filename."

2. The file name may contain one or more wild cards (? or *). If it does, the first file name that matches the pattern will be loaded into memory.

3. If a program file with the name given is not stored on the diskette, you will get a 63, FILE NOT FOUND, error message.

REMINDER:

If you do not specify ",1" after the device number (eight) in a LOAD command, the Commodore 64 will ignore the load address at the start of the file. The program will be loaded into memory starting at memory location 2049 (where a BASIC program normally starts in the Commodore 64).

ANNOTATED EXAMPLES:

```
LOAD"SPACE JUNK",8
```

Loads a copy of the program file, SPACE JUNK, into RAM memory starting at location 2049.

```
LOAD"$",8
```

Loads a copy of the directory file. The disk drive converts this into a pseudo program so you can list it. Do not use a ",1" when loading the directory. It has a load address of 1025 ($0401). If you use the ",1" form, the directory will be loaded into your Commodore 64's screen RAM and produce garbage on the screen.

```
FN$="UPPER CODE"
LOAD FN$,8,1
```

Loads a copy of the program file, UPPER CODE, into RAM memory starting at the load address specified at the start of the program file.

Loading from Within a Program

You can include a LOAD command within a BASIC program. When you do this, you do not have to RUN the incoming program. It is automatically run from the beginning as soon as the load is complete. This technique is often used:

1. To load one of several BASIC programs stored on a diskette in response to the user's selection from a menu.

2. To link or chain several program segments together when your program is too long to be held in memory at once.

3. To load one or more machine language routines (such as a fast sorting routine) needed by the BASIC program.

To have your program load another program or a machine language routine, simply include a line like this:

```
SYNTAX:
  xx LOAD "filename",device#                (program relocated)
  xx LOAD "filename",device#,channel#       (not relocated)

EXAMPLES:
  150 LOAD "GOOD GAME",8
  300 LOAD "ML SORT",8,1
  120 F$="SUPER FORCE"
  130 LOAD F$,8
```

WHERE:

xx   = the line number.
filename = the name of the program file as it appears in a directory
            listing.
device#   = the device number of the 1541 (normally eight).
channel# = the channel number (secondary address; normally one for a
            non-relocating load).

WARNING:

The first program must be the longest. Any BASIC program that you load from within another program *must not be longer* than the original program. The reason for this is that the variables are stored immediately following the program in RAM memory. If you were permitted to load in a longer program, the values of the variables would be destroyed. This can pose a problem if you want to create a short menu program that loads one of several long programs, unless you trick the Commodore 64 into believing that the menu program is very long by changing the end-of-program pointer like this:

```
10 REM MENU PROGRAM
20 POKE45,XX:REM SET LO BYTE OF POINTER
30 POKE46,YY:REM SET HI BYTE OF POINTER
40 CLR:REM RESET THE OTHER POINTERS
50 REM PROGRAM CONTINUES...
```

Get the XX and YY values by PEEKing memory locations 45 and 46 when the longest program is in memory.

NOTES:

1. The notes that apply to loading from immediate mode also apply to loading from program mode.

2. The values of variables are preserved. The values of any variables used in your program are not erased when you load in another BASIC program or machine language routine! The only time that values may be lost is when you have assigned a value to a string variable in your BASIC program like this: 5 A$="VALUE". In this situation, the value of A$ is not moved up into high RAM. The pointer to the value of A$ points at the word "VALUE" within the program. If you load in another program, the value of A$ will be lost. To prevent this, you must perform some string manipulation with A$ such as 5 A$="VALUE"+" ". This forces the value of A$ to be stored in high memory. Now your starting program will pass all its variables' values to subsequent programs.

3. After a LOAD, your program runs from the beginning. Whenever you load a program file, the BASIC program in memory will immediately begin to RUN from the beginning. This is exactly what you want if you just loaded a new BASIC program. However, if you load a character set or machine language routine into high memory, your BASIC loader program will be run again *from the beginning.* If you do not take steps to handle this, you'll end up in a loop that loads and reloads your routine endlessly.

(produces endless loop)

```
10 LOAD"MACHINE CODE",8,1
20 X=1:LOAD"MACHINE CODE",8,1
30 REM PROGRAM CONTINUES...
```

(prevents a loop)

```
10 IF X=1 GOTO 30
```

4. Loading machine code can cause your computer to hang. Whenever you load a program file, the end-of-program pointer (memory locations 45 & 46) in your Commodore 64 is reset to point to the end of the program or routine that you just loaded. When you load a routine into high memory, the end-of-program pointer will end up pointing to the end of memory. The first time that you try to store any values in memory, you will get an ?OUT OF MEMORY ERROR. The trick is to preserve the end-of-memory pointers before you LOAD and restore them immediately afterwards. Memory locations 1020-1023 are not used by BASIC and are very handy for temporary storage like this:

```
10 IF X=1 GOTO 50
20 POKE 1020,PEEK(45):REM SAVE LO BYTE
30 POKE 1021,PEEK(46):REM SAVE HI BYTE
40 X=1:LOAD"MACHINE CODE",8,1
50 POKE 45,PEEK(1020):REM FIX LO BYTE
60 POKE 46,PEEK(1021):REM FIX HI BYTE
```

ANNOTATED EXAMPLES:

```
15 IF A=1 THEN LOAD"SPACE JUNK",8
```

Loads a copy of the program file, SPACE JUNK, into RAM memory starting at location 2049 and runs it.

```
70 INPUT "FILE NAME";F$
80 LOAD F$,8,1
```

Loads a copy of the program whose name was input in line 70. The file is loaded into RAM memory starting at the load address specified at the start of the file. When the load is complete, the BASIC program in memory is run from the beginning.

6.4 Saving a Program File

You may save a copy of the contents of part of your computer's memory from immediate mode (i.e., if you have a READY prompt and a flashing cursor), or from within a program.

Saving from Immediate Mode

Type in the following command and press RETURN.

```
SYNTAX:
  SAVE "filename",device#
```

```
EXAMPLES:
  SAVE "NEW GAME",8
  F$="SUPER SOUND"
  SAVE F$,8
```

WHERE:

filename = the name of the program file as you want it to appear in a
           directory listing.
device# = the device number of the 1541 (normally eight).

WARNING:

The file name *must not contain* any of the following characters: asterisk (*), colon (:), question mark (?), quotation mark ("), or comma(,). Graphics characters, reverse-field characters and other special characters are permitted but their use is discouraged.

NOTES:

1. The file name may be stored in a string variable. If it is, use the string variable name instead of "filename."

2. The file name may be up to 16 characters long.

3. If a program file with the name given is already stored on the diskette, you will get a 62, FILE EXISTS, error message.

HINTS:

1. Choosing a name. You may save your program using any name you like. The disk drive does not care whether the name you select has any relationship to the nature of the program. But, to save you endless hours of frustration, choose a name you can remember. Otherwise as your collection of diskettes grows, you will be unable to find anything.

2. Saving machine language routines. The SAVE command stores a copy of RAM memory onto a diskette. The first byte that will be stored is one pointed to by the start-of-BASIC pointer (memory locations 43 and 44). The start-of-variables pointer (45 and 46) points to the last byte to be saved plus one. If you reset the pointers before you save, you can save a copy of any area of RAM. For example, to save a copy of the video screen RAM onto diskette type in:

```
POKE43,0:POKE44,4:POKE45,232:POKE46,7
SAVE"SCREEN",8
```

WARNING:

When the save is complete, either POKE these pointers with their original values or turn OFF your Commodore 64.

REMINDER:

Watch the error light on your drive. Occasionally a program will not be saved properly onto the diskette. When this happens, the red light on the drive will flash rapidly. Do not panic! Just try again using a different diskette. The most common causes for this are the diskette already has a file with the name that you chose, the diskette is full or the diskette is flawed. After your program has been saved correctly, be sure to check the directory of the diskette on which you had problems. If there is an unclosed file in the directory (*PRG), *don't scratch it,* VALIDATE the diskette (see Section 4.8).

ANNOTATED EXAMPLES:

```
SAVE"SPACE JUNK",8
```

Saves a copy of the program in memory onto diskette using the name SPACE JUNK.

```
A$="BUNCHASTUFF":SAVE A$,8
```

Saves a copy of the program in memory onto diskette using the name BUNCHASTUFF.

Saving from Within a Program

You can include a SAVE command within a BASIC program. This is not generally very useful because all you get on disk is a copy of the existing program. The only times this is useful are when you have a program that modifies itself as it runs (the MAIL LIST in Section 6.11 does this) or when you change the pointers and save a copy of something other than the program itself.

To have your program save a copy of itself at any point in the program, just include a line like this:

```
SYNTAX:
  xx SAVE "filename",8


EXAMPLES:
  125 SAVE "NEW GAME",8
  300 F$="SUPER SOUND"
  310 SAVE F$,8
```

WHERE:

xx   = the line number.
filename = the name of the program file as you want it to appear in a
              directory listing.

NOTE:

The same warnings, notes, and reminders that apply to saving from immediate mode also apply here.

HINT:

Saving machine language routines. Many people believe you must be in immediate mode and use a machine language monitor such as MICROMON or SUPERMON to save anything other than a BASIC program. *This is not true!* You can manipulate the start-of-BASIC and start-of-variables pointers so that you can save any part of memory you want. The part of memory to be saved might contain such things as a character set, a sprite character or a machine language routine. You can do this either in immediate mode or from within a BASIC program. To pull off this bit of magic in a program you have to be careful. Here's what to do:

1. Save the current values of the pointers to the start of BASIC (memory locations 43 & 44) and to the start of the variables (memory locations 45 & 46) by POKEing the values into some safe area of RAM (1020-1023 is just fine).

2. Set the start-of-BASIC pointer to point to the first byte you want saved (start-of-BASIC pointer = first byte saved).

3. Set the start-of-variables pointer to point to the last byte you want saved plus one (start-of-variables pointer = last byte saved + 1).

4. Issue a normal SAVE command.

5. Reset the pointers. WARNING: Do *not* use any variables for any purpose until the pointers have been reset!

ANNOTATED EXAMPLES:

```
15 IF A=1 THEN SAVE"SHOOT UP",8
```

Saves a copy of the program in memory onto diskette using the name SHOOT UP.

```
*********************
PROGRAM: SCREEN SAVE
*********************


0 REM 1541 USER'S GUIDE SECTION 6.4
1 REM  COPYRIGHT: G. NEUFELD, 1984
2 :
3 REM SAVE A COPY OF THE C-64'S SCREEN R
AM
4 :
10 REM SAVES A SCREEN IMAGE
20 PRINT"{CLR}":REM CLEAR THE SCREEN
30 FORK=1024TO2023:POKEK,INT(256*RND(1))
:NEXT
40 POKE 1020,PEEK(43):POKE 1021,PEEK(44)
:REM SAVE START
50 POKE 1022,PEEK(45):POKE 1023,PEEK(46)
:REM SAVE END
60 POKE 43,0:POKE 44,4:REM SET START TO
START OF SCREEN
70 POKE 45,233:POKE 46,7:REM SET END TO
END OF SCREEN
80 SAVE"SCREEN IMAGE",8
90 POKE 43,PEEK(1020):POKE 44,PEEK(1021)
:REM RESET START
100 POKE 45,PEEK(1022):POKE 45,PEEK(1023
):REM RESET END
```

6.5 Verifying a Program File

After you have saved or loaded a copy of a program you may check to see if the copy in RAM memory matches the copy on diskette by using the VERIFY command. Usually a program is verified from immediate mode (i.e., you have a READY prompt and a flashing cursor). You can do a verify from within a program but this has virtually no practical value.

Verifying from Immediate Mode

Type in one of the following commands and press RETURN.

```
SYNTAX:
  VERIFY "filename",device#               (program relocated)
  VERIFY "filename",device#,channel#      (not relocated)
```

If there is an exact match between the copy on diskette and the copy in RAM, the message OK will be displayed. If there is not an exact match, the message ? VERIFY ERROR will be displayed.

```
EXAMPLES:
  VERIFY "ADVENTURE",8
  VERIFY "SUPER SORT",8,1
  F$="INCOME TAX"
  VERIFY F$,8
```

WHERE:

filename   = the name of the program file as it appears in a directory listing. Wild cards may be used.

device#   = the device number of the 1541 (normally eight).

channel# = the channel number (secondary address; normally one for a non-relocating verify).

WARNING:

If you do not specify ",1" after the device number (eight) in a VERIFY command, the Commodore 64 will ignore the load address at the start of the file. The contents of the diskette file will be compared to the contents of memory starting at memory location 2049, where programs normally start on the Commodore 64.

NOTES:

1. The file name may be stored in a string variable. If it is, use the string variable name instead of "filename."

2. The file name may contain one or more wild cards (? or *). If it does, the first file name that matches the pattern will be used for verifying.

3. If a program file with the name given is not stored on the diskette, you will get a 63, FILE NOT FOUND, error message.

REMINDER:

If you have used the LOAD "filename",8 form of the LOAD command to load a BASIC program that was originally saved from a PET or a VIC-20, you will always get a VERIFY ERROR when you try to verify it. The reason is that during the load, the line links (see Section 6.7) have been changed so that the program will work correctly on your Commodore 64. There is no way to verify this kind of file!

```
VERIFY"SPACE JUNK",8
```

Compares the copy of the program, SPACE JUNK, on diskette with the program that starts at 2049 in RAM memory.

```
FI$="FANCY STUFF"
VERIFY FI$,8,1
```

Compares the copy of the program, FANCY STUFF, on diskette with the area of RAM memory starting at the load address specified at the start of the file.

Verifying from Within a Program

You can include a VERIFY command within a BASIC program. The only real use for this would be to check if a machine language routine or character set was loaded or saved properly. The syntax is the same as from immediate mode except for the line number. If the copies match, an OK message is printed on the screen and execution continues. If the copies don't match, the program aborts with a VERIFY ERROR message. If a copy of the named file is not on the diskette, the program aborts with a FILE NOT FOUND error.

6.6 Replacing a Program File

You may replace an existing copy of a program file on disk with a revised copy of the Commodore 64's memory from immediate mode (i.e., you have a READY prompt and a flashing cursor) or from within a program.

Replacing from Immediate Mode

Type in the following command and press RETURN.

```
SYNTAX:
  SAVE "@:filename",device#


ALTERNATE:
  SAVE "@0:filename",device#


EXAMPLES:
  SAVE "@:GOOD GAME",8
  F$="@0:NEW STUFF"
  SAVE F$,8
```

WHERE:

filename   = the name of the program file as it appears in a directory
               listing.

device#   = the device number of the 1541 (normally eight).

Be sure there is enough disk space to do a replace. When the file is opened for a replace, the old file is not deleted before the new file is written. This means that you must have enough free space on the disk for the new copy. If there is not enough space, the replace is aborted. The new file is incomplete and the old file is unrecoverable, unless you use the techniques given in Section 11.8. Be safe, not sorry! Check the number of blocks free on your disk before you try a replace (see Section 5.13).

NOTES:

1. The file name may be stored in a string variable. If it is, use the string variable name instead of "filename."

2. The file name may contain one or more wild cards (? or *). If it does, the first file name that matches the pattern will be replaced by the current memory contents.

3. If a program file with the name given is not stored on the diskette, you will get a 63, FILE NOT FOUND, error message.

REMINDER:

Do *not* replace an unclosed file! Be sure that the original program file you are going to replace has been properly closed. A file that has not been properly closed has an asterisk beside its file type in the directory (*PRG). Use the VALIDATE command (see Section 4.8) to eliminate these files! If you accidentally replace one of these files, VALIDATE the diskette as soon as possible.

ANNOTATED EXAMPLE:

```
SAVE"@0:SPACE  JUNK",8
```

Replaces the existing copy of the program, SPACE JUNK, with a copy of the current program in RAM memory.

Replacing from Within a Program

You can include a SAVE with replace command within a BASIC program. This works the same as a SAVE within a program. Use the techniques outlined in Section 6.4 but put an @: or @0: in front of the file name.

NOTES:

1. Unlike the ordinary SAVE command, the file name in the replace command may use one or more wild cards (? or *). If it does, the first file name that matches the pattern will be replaced by the current memory contents.

2. Program execution will continue with the next line.

6.7 The Internal Structure of a BASIC Program

To be able to use a program file for more than simply saving or loading programs you need to know how a BASIC program is put together. You may be surprised to discover that a program is not stored in memory the same way you typed it in or the way you see it when you LIST it. In general, one line of a BASIC program in memory looks like this:

Pointer to next line	Line Number	BASIC statement with keywords tokenized	Null byte	Next line follows

The first line of a BASIC program in your Commodore 64 begins at memory location 2049 ($0801). Its length is determined by what you typed in. It ends with a null byte ($00). The second line immediately follows the first. All the lines in a BASIC program are stored in this same manner.

HINT:

At this point you may want to let your computer help you. If you type in the program, PRG HEX DUMP (see Appendix E), it will help you understand how a program is organized. To use the program, save the program you want to analyze on diskette. Load and run PRG HEX DUMP. When you are asked for the name of the program you want analyzed, just type in the name you used to save it. PRG HEX DUMP will access the program file on diskette and produce a hex dump of the program with the important features highlighted. PRG HEX DUMP is fairly long but typing it in will be worth the time and effort it takes. You will have a utility that will allow you to scan any program. It flags any bad line numbers, line links or illegal bytes that it finds. If you don't want to type in PRG HEX DUMP, you can use a machine language monitor such as SUPERMON, TINYMON or MICROMON to follow along.

To see how this works in practice let's examine how a simple four line program is stored in the Commodore 64's memory. Here is our demonstration program.

```
10 REM SAMPLE PROGRAM
20 FOR K=1 TO 20
30 PRINT K;K*K
40 NEXT
```

Here is a dump of the Commodore 64's memory when the sample program shown above has been typed in.

```
.: 0800 00 16 08 0A 00 8F 20 53   10 REM SAMPLE PROGRAM
.: 0808 41 4D 50 4C 45 20 50 52
.: 0810 4F 47 52 41 4D 00 25 08
.: 0818 14 00 81 20 4B B2 31 20   20 FOR K=1 TO 20
.: 0820 A4 20 32 30 00 31 08 1E
.: 0828 00 99 20 4B 3B 4B AC 4B   30 PRINT K;K*K
.: 0830 00 37 08 28 00 82 00 00   40 NEXT
.: 0838 00 XX XX XX XX XX XX XX
```

Let's look at how the start of this program is organized.

1. The null byte just before the start of a BASIC program:

```
.: 0800 00 16 08 0A 00 8F 20 53   10 REM SAMPLE PROGRAM
.: 0808 41 4D 50 4C 45 20 50 52
.: 0810 4F 47 52 41 4D 00 25 08
```

The first byte shown in the hex dump of the Commodore 64's RAM memory, $0800 (2048), is not part of the BASIC program. However, it is important to the proper functioning of our program. Unless this memory location is $00, the program will list but *will not run*! Note that this byte is *not* saved when you save the program.

2. The pointer to the next line:

```
.: 0800 00 16 08 0A 00 8F 20 53    10 REM SAMPLE PROGRAM
.: 0808 41 4D 50 4C 45 20 50 52
.: 0810 4F 47 52 41 4D 00 25 08
                points to ____↑
```

The first two bytes in a line are a pointer that points to the first byte in the next program line. The pointer is in lo byte/hi byte form. In this case the pointer points to $0816. If you are more comfortable with decimal notation, you can find the memory location that it points to using this formula.

pointer value= 256 * hi byte + lo byte
pointer value= 256 * 08 + 22 = 2118

3. The line number:

```
.: 0800 00 16 08 0A 00 8F 20 53    10 REM SAMPLE PROGRAM
.: 0808 41 4D 50 4C 45 20 50 52
.: 0810 4F 47 52 41 4D 00 25 08
```

Bytes three and four in a line are the line number. They are stored in lo byte/hi byte form. In this case the line number is $000A. If you are more comfortable with decimal notation, you can find the line number using this formula.

line number= 256 * hi byte + lo byte
line number= 256 * 00 + 10 = 10

4. The BASIC statement with keywords tokenized.

```
.: 0800 00 16 08 0A 00 8F 20 53 10 REM SAMPLE PROGRAM
.: 0808 41 4D 50 4C 45 20 50 52
.: 0810 4F 47 52 41 4D 00 25 08
```

NOTE:

$8F = BASIC token for REM (more about tokens below).

To save space in memory the BASIC keywords such as REM, PRINT, etc. are represented by a single character called a BASIC token. BASIC tokens have numeric values between $80 and $DA (128 to 218). Numbers, letters and spaces within a line are represented by their ASCII codes. Graphics characters are not legal BASIC characters and may only appear between quotes. A list of all the BASIC tokens and ASCII codes is given in Appendix B.

5. The end-of-line null byte:

```
.: 0800 00 16 08 0A 00 8F 20 53
.: 0808 41 4D 50 4C 45 20 50 52
.: 0810 4F 47 52 41 4D 00 25 08
```

The last byte in a line of a BASIC program is always a null byte ($00).

Now that we've seen how the program is organized, let's take apart the program character by character to see how it is stored in the Commodore 64's memory.

HINT:

At this point you may want to let your computer help you. If you type in the program PRG ANALYZER, listed in Appendix E, you can use it to get a character by character analysis of any program. To use this program, save the program you want to analyze on disk. Then load and run PRG ANALYZER. It will ask you for the name of the program you want analyzed. It will then give you a complete character by character analysis of your program. This is quite a long program, but it is a very useful utility.

Here's the hex dump of our sample program again.

```
.: 0800 00 16 08 0A 00 8F 20 53    10 REM SAMPLE PROGRAM
.: 0808 41 4D 50 4C 45 20 50 52
.: 0810 4F 47 52 41 4D 00 25 08
.: 0818 14 00 81 20 4B B2 31 20    20 FOR K=1 TO 20
.: 0820 A4 20 32 30 00 31 08 1E
.: 0828 00 99 20 4B 3B 4B AC 4B    30 PRINT K;K*K
.: 0830 00 37 08 28 00 82 00 00    40 NEXT
.: 0838 00 xx xx xx xx xx xx xx
```

Remember that the first byte of our dump, $00, at $0800 (2048), is not actually part of the program. However, if this memory location is not $00, the program will LIST but will not RUN. If you try to run it, all you will get is a ?SYNTAX ERROR message.

The first line of our program is 10 REM SAMPLE PROGRAM. Our PRG ANALYZER indicates that it is stored from $0801 to $0815 like this:

$0801/2	$16 $08	pointer to $0816, the start of line 20
$0803/4	$0A $00	line number (10)
$0805	$8F	BASIC token for REM
$0806	$20	ASCII code for space
$0807	$53	ASCII code for S
$0808	$41	ASCII code for A
$0809	$4D	ASCII code for M
$080A	$50	ASCII code for P
$080B	$4C	ASCII code for L

$080C	$45	ASCII code for E
$080D	$20	ASCII code for space
$080E	$50	ASCII code for P
$080F	$52	ASCII code for R
$0810	$4F	ASCII code for O
$0811	$47	ASCII code for G
$0812	$52	ASCII code for R
$0813	$41	ASCII code for A
$0814	$4D	ASCII code for M
$0815	$00	end of line marker

The second line of our program is 20 FOR K=1 TO 20. It is stored from $0816 to $0824 like this:

$0816/7	$25 $08	pointer to $0825, the start of line 30
$0818/9	$14 $00	line number (1*16+4=20)
$081A	$81	BASIC token for FOR
$081B	$20	ASCII code for space
$081C	$4B	ASCII code for K
$081D	$B2	BASIC token for =
$081E	$31	ASCII code for 1
$081F	$20	ASCII code for space
$0820	$A4	BASIC token for TO
$0821	$20	ASCII code for space
$0822	$32	ASCII code for 2
$0823	$30	ASCII code for 0
$0824	$00	end of line marker

The third line of our program is 30 PRINT K;K*K. It is stored from $0825 to $0830 like this:

$0825/6	$31 $08	pointer to $0831, the start of line 40
$0827/8	$1E $00	line number (1*16+14=30)
$0829	$99	BASIC token for PRINT
$082A	$20	ASCII code for space
$082B	$4B	ASCII code for K
$082C	$3B	ASCII code for ;
$082D	$4B	ASCII code for K
$082E	$AC	BASIC token for *
$082F	$4B	ASCII code for K
$0830	$00	end of line marker

The fourth line of our program is 40 NEXT. It is stored from $0831 to $0836 like this:

$0831/2	$37 $08	pointer to $0837, the end of the program
$0833/4	$28 $00	line number (2*16+8=40)
$0835	$82	BASIC token for NEXT
$0836	$00	end of line marker

The last two bytes in our program are the two $00 bytes at $0837 and $0838. These two zeros are in the space normally occupied by the pointer to the start of the next line. This signals the end of your program.

Now that you understand how a BASIC program is put together, you will be able to create programs that read or even create other programs.

HINT:

Have you ever loaded a program, listed it, and found to your dismay that the line numbers or the line pointers have become jumbled? This can happen because of a bad load or POKEs to the wrong memory locations. Many people give up in disgust when this happens. Now that you understand how a BASIC program is put together, you can fix it using a monitor program. However, you still have to locate the problem. Here's how to do it.

Load and run your machine language monitor program. Exit from the monitor and load in the problem program. Now type in the following lines (no line numbers please).

```
S=2049

FORK=1TO1000:M=PEEK(S)+256*PEEK(S+1):L=P
EEK(S+2)+256*PEEK(S+3):?L;M:S=M:NEXT
```

You will get two lists of numbers like this.

```
10  2053
20  2096
30  2120
 :    :
```

The number on the left is the line number. The number on the right is the pointer to the start of the next line. When the numbers in either column are out of sequence, you have found your problem. The last number that is in the correct sequence in the second column will point to the problem area. Now that you have located the problem use your monitor and knowledge of how the BASIC pointers work to solve the problem.

6.8 Using a Program File

To be able to write programs that manipulate existing program files or even create new ones, you need to know how to read or write a program file. It is really quite easy. Follow these steps:

1. Open the program file.
2. Write information into the file using PRINT#.
3. Read information from the file using GET#.
4. Close the program file when you are finished using it.

Let's look at each of these steps in more detail.

Opening a Program File

An OPEN command is used to tell the disk drive the name of the file you wish to use. On the Commodore 64 or the VIC-20, the OPEN command to access a program file looks like this:

```
SYNTAX:
  OPEN file#,device#,channel#,"filename,PRG,mode"

EXAMPLES:
  OPEN 5,8,4,"COPY/ALL,PRG,R"
  OPEN 1,8,5,"BUNCHADATA,P,R"
  F$="SUPER FORCE"
  OPEN 2,8,12,F$+",P,W"
```

WHERE:

file#   = the logical file number (any integer 1-127).

device#   = the device number (normally eight on the 1541).

channel#   = the channel number (any integer 2-14).

filename   = the file name (up to 16 characters), may be contained in a string variable.

PRG   = file type, may be abbreviated with P.

mode   = R or W to indicate whether you want to read from a file or write to a file.

NOTES:

1. Part or all of the file identification information may be stored in a string variable.

2. The file type and mode are optional. If the file type is omitted, the file type will be determined from the directory entry for the file. If the mode is omitted, it defaults to READ mode unless the file is a relative file. In this case READ/WRITE mode is assumed.

3. You can open a program file in APPEND (A) mode to add new information to the end of the program file. The only possible use for this mode appears to be to append a machine language routine onto the end of a BASIC program. For more information about APPEND mode see Section 7.5.

4. There is a special MODIFY (M) mode for reading an unclosed file. See Section 11.3 for more details.

READ MODE:

5. The file name may contain one or more wild cards (? or *). If it does, the first file name that matches the pattern will be opened.

6. If there is no file with the name specified stored on the diskette, you will get a 63, FILE NOT FOUND, error message.

WRITE MODE:

7. The file name may not contain any wild cards (? or *).

8. If there already is a file with the specified name stored on the diskette, you will get a 62, FILE EXISTS, error message. To write over (replace) an existing file see below.

REMINDERS:

1. Monitor the error status of the disk drive. You should use the command channel to monitor the error status of the disk drive. Be sure to check the status whenever you open a file to make sure that the file has been opened properly. If the file is not open, your new data will be lost! See Section 5.10 for this procedure.

2. OPEN the command channel *first* and close it *last*. Do not open and close the command channel each time you want to check the error status. Open the command channel at the beginning of your program and leave it open until the end. When you CLOSE the command channel *all open files are closed automatically!*

3. All open files must have different logical file numbers. Since the logical file number is used to identify one particular file, you must use different logical file numbers for each of the files that are open simultaneously. Once you close a file, you are free to reuse that logical file number in your program.

4. All open files must have different channel numbers. Since the channel number (secondary address) identifies a particular data communication channel in the disk drive, each file that is open must have a unique channel number. Once you close a file, you are free to reuse that channel number in your program.

5. You can only have a few files open at once. Each sequential or program file that you have open takes up one of the buffers in the disk drive. Since the disk has only four buffers and one is reserved for internal use, you can only have three files open at once (not five as indicated on page 45 of your 1541 manual)! See Section 5.11 for the limits that apply for other file types.

ANNOTATED EXAMPLES:

```
OPEN 1,8,5,"BUNCHADATA,PRG,R"
```

Opens file# 1 to disk (eight) using channel# 5, to access the file on drive zero (default) named BUNCHADATA. It is a program (PRG) file and we want to read (R) it.

```
OPEN 3,8,9,"PILEAJUNK,P"
```

Opens file# 3 to disk (eight) using channel# 9, to access the file on drive zero (default) named PILEAJUNK. It is a program (PRG) file and we want to read it (defaults to R).

```
INPUT "NAME TO USE FOR NEW PROGRAM FILE";F$
OPEN 6,8,4,F$ + ",P,W"
```

Prepares to write (W) a new program (P) file with the name contained in the variable F$. Note how to combine the file name (F$), the file type (P) and the mode (W).

Replacing an Existing File

If you want to replace an existing program file with a new version, you can use one of two techniques. The first technique is to scratch the old file and then write out the revised file as though it were a new program file. The second technique is to open the program file for a replace by putting @0: in front of the file name in the OPEN statement. In some cases this method can cause serious problems (see WARNING in Section 6.6). The examples below illustrate these two methods:

1. Scratch old file and then open a new program file.

```
250 OPEN 15,8,15:REM
   OPEN COMMAND CHANNEL
260 PRINT#15,"S0:BUNCHAJUNK":REM
   SCRATCH OLD FILE
270 INPUT#15,E,E$,T,S:REM
   READ ERROR CHANNEL
280 IF E<20 GOTO 310:REM
   CHECK FOR DOS ERROR
290 PRINT E;E$;T;S:REM
   PRINT ERROR MESSAGE
300 CLOSE 15:STOP:REM
   ABORT ON ERROR
310 OPEN 3,8,5,"BUNCHAJUNK,P,W":REM
   OPEN FILE
320 REM PROGRAM CONTINUES...
```

2. Open file for a replace.

```
250 OPEN 3,8,5,"@0:BUNCHAJUNK,P,W"
```

NOTE:

Be sure to read the warnings about scratching or replacing existing files in Section 6.6 before attempting this.

Writing to a Program File

Once you have opened the file in write (W) mode, use a PRINT# statement to write information into the file. In this example, we begin by opening a new program file. Then we print in the load address followed by the main body of the file. Finally, we close the file.

```
200 REM OPEN FILE
210 OPEN 7,8,12,"FAKE PGM,P,W"
220 :
230 REM PRINT LOAD ADDRESS INTO FILE
240 PRINT#7,CHR$(1);:REM NOTE ';' AT END
 OF LINE!
250 PRINT#7,CHR$(8);
```

```
260 :
270 REM PRINT OUT THE FILE
280 FOR K=1 TO 85:READ X
290 PRINT#7,CHR$(X);
300 NEXT
310 CLOSE 7
320 DATA 15,8, ...    BASIC program to go into the file.
```

WARNING:

Be careful to always put a semicolon at the end of each PRINT# statement to suppress the printing of the carriage return character, CHR$(13). If you forget to do this, you will be in trouble when you try to LOAD the file.

NOTE:

The MAKE FAST COPY program listed in Appendix E is a practical example of how to write a program file.

Reading a Program File

Because a BASIC or machine language file is not broken up into records, you must read the file one character at a time using a GET# statement. Here is a short illustration of how to read a program file.

```
*******************
PROGRAM: LOAD ADDR
*******************

0 REM 1541 USER'S GUIDE SECTION 6.8
1 REM  COPYRIGHT: G. NEUFELD, 1984
2 :
10 REM READ LOAD ADDRESS OF PROGRAM FILE

20 INPUT"NAME OF FILE";F$
30 OPEN 15,8,15
40 OPEN 5,8,4,F$+",P,R"        ← Note how the file name, file
50 REM GET LOAD ADDRESS           type & mode are concatenated.
60 GET#5,A$:IF A$="" THEN A$=CHR$(0)
70 LO=ASC(A$)
80 GET#5,A$:IF A$="" THEN A$=CHR$(0)
90 HI=ASC(A$)
100 PRINT "THE LOAD ADDRESS OF "F$" IS"
256*HI + LO
110 CLOSE1:CLOSE15:END
```

REMINDER:

The GET# statement does not handle nulls correctly. When you use GET# (as in GET#5,X$) to get a $00 byte from a file, the string variable (X$) is not given the value CHR$(0). It becomes the null string (contains no characters). If you try to find the

ASCII value of a null string, you will get an ?ILLEGAL QUANTITY ERROR. That is the reason for the awkward statement:

```
GET#5,A$:IF A$="" THEN A$=CHR$(0)
```

NOTE:

The PRG HEX DUMP and PRG ANALYZER programs listed in Appendix E are practical examples of how to read and interpret a program file.

Closing a Program File

Once you have finished using a program file, you must close it. A CLOSE statement looks like this:

```
SYNTAX:
  CLOSE file#
```

```
EXAMPLES:
  CLOSE 1
  CLOSE 5:CLOSE 15
```

WHERE:

file#   = the logical file number you used when you opened the file.

NOTE:

Closing the file is particularly important when you have written to a file. Unless you close the file, the information you have sent to the disk drive may not even be recorded onto the diskette. See Section 11.3 for information about how to recover data from an unclosed file.

6.9 The Directory as a Program File

The diskette directory is a very special form of program file. Its name is $. It can be opened and read just like any other program file. However, you cannot open this file in write mode.

You can open this file in two different ways. You can open it using a normal data channel number (2-14) or with the reserved channel number zero. Surprisingly, the two different methods do not produce the same result! You may want to type in these short programs and see for yourself.

METHOD #1: Using a normal data channel.

```
********************
PROGRAM: DIR CH# 6
********************
O REM 1541 USER'S GUIDE SECTION 6.9
1 REM  COPYRIGHT: G. NEUFELD, 1984
2 :
3 REM READ DIRECTORY USING DATA CHANNEL
```

```
4 :
10 OPEN 1,8,6,"$,P,R"
20 K=K+1
30 GET#1,A$:IF A$=""THEN A$=CHR$(0)
40 A=ASC(A$)
50 PRINT K;A;
60 IF A>31 AND A<97 THEN PRINT A$;
70 PRINT,
80 IF ST=0 GOTO 20
90 CLOSE 1
```

This method allows you to read the entire directory file one byte at a time. The first
254 bytes in this file are the BAM, the diskette name, etc. from track 18, sector 0. The
bytes that follow are from the directory entries. This method allows you to see all the
bytes in the directory: the track and sector link, and the record size and side sector
link for a relative file. It also allows you to see the file name, length of the file, and the
file type that you see in a normal directory listing.

METHOD #2: Using data channel zero.

```
*******************
PROGRAM: DIR CH# 0
*******************

0 REM 1541 USER'S GUIDE SECTION 6.9
1 REM   COPYRIGHT: G. NEUFELD, 1984
2 :
3 REM READ DIRECTORY USING DATA CHANNEL
4 :
10 OPEN 1,8,0,"$"
20 K=K+1
30 GET#1,A$:IF A$=""THEN A$=CHR$(0)
40 A=ASC(A$)
50 PRINT K;A;
60 IF A>31 AND A<97 THEN PRINT A$;
70 PRINT,
80 IF ST=0 GOTO 20
90 CLOSE 1
```

This method produces different results. Because you have used the special channel# 0
that is normally reserved for loading programs, the disk drive thinks you are prepar-
ing to LOAD the directory. As a result, the drive assembles the directory into the
pseudo program (load address $0401) form that you get when you LOAD the directory.
In this form you only get the diskette name, cosmetic diskette ID, the lengths of the
file, the file names and the file type that you see in a normal directory listing.

The second technique is handy if you want your program to be able to call up and
display a directory quickly. The two sample programs listed below illustrate how to

do this. The first program displays the directory listing in the same form you would see if you loaded the directory and listed it. The second program suppresses the file lengths and the file types. Only the file names are displayed.

```
****************
PROGRAM: ALL DIR
****************
```

Displays directory as it appears in a normal listing.

```
0 REM 1541 USER'S GUIDE SECTION 6.9
1 REM   COPYRIGHT: G. NEUFELD, 1984
2 :
3 REM READ AND DISPLAY ALL OF DIRECTORY
4 :
100 REM ALL DIR
110 OPEN 15,8,15
120 OPEN 1,8,0,"$0"
130 GET#1,A$:GET#1,A$:BY=26
140 GET#1,A$:GET#1,A$
150 GET#1,A$:BL=ASC(A$+CHR$(0))
160 GET#1,A$:BL=BL+256*ASC(A$+CHR$(0))
170 N$="":FOR K=1 TO BY
180 GET#1,A$:IFST<>0 GOTO 220
190 N$=N$+A$:NEXT
200 PRINTBL;N$:BY=28
210 IF ST=0 GOTO 140
220 PRINTBL;N$
230 CLOSE 1:CLOSE 15
```

```
******************
PROGRAM: NAMES DIR
******************
```

Displays only the file names from the directory.

```
0 REM 1541 USER'S GUIDE SECTION 6.9
1 REM   COPYRIGHT: G. NEUFELD, 1984
2 :
3 REM READ AND DISPLAY NAMES FROM DIRECT
ORY
4 :
100 REM NAMES DIR
110 OPEN 15,8,15
120 OPEN 1,8,0,"$0"
130 FORK=1TO30:GET#1,A$:NEXT
140 GET#1,A$:IF ST<>0 GOTO 210
150 IF A$<>CHR$(34)GOTO 140
160 GET#1,A$:IF ST<>0 GOTO 210
170 IF A$<>CHR$(34)THENPRINTA$;:GOTO 160
```

```
180 N$="":FOR K=1 TO BY
190 PRINT:GOTO140
200 N$=N$+A$:NEXT
210 CLOSE1:CLOSE 15:END
```

In some cases you might like a more selective listing of the directory entries. You could use the brute force method; read all the directory entries into an array and then just display those that you want. However, there is a much easier way, just ask for a selective listing in your OPEN statement using wild cards. A request for a selective listing looks like this:

```
SYNTAX:
  OPEN 1,8,0,"$0:filename"
```

```
EXAMPLES:
  OPEN 1,8,0,"$0:PR*"
  OPEN 1,8,0,"$0:D*"
```

ANNOTATED EXAMPLE:

```
OPEN 1,8,0,"$0:D*"
```

The directory listing will consist of the diskette name and ID line, the entries for the files whose file names start with the letter D, and the BLOCKS FREE line.

NOTE:

For a practical example of this technique see the MOD ENTRY program in Section 13.8.

6.10 Self-modifying Programs

Programs that modify themselves have always fascinated computer buffs. Let's look at two different ways of doing this: direct POKEs into memory and automated editing.

Direct POKEs into Memory

The most obvious way to have a program modify itself is to have it POKE different values into that part of RAM memory that contains the program. For example, here is a very simple math drill program that becomes either an addition drill or a subtraction drill depending on your response to the input in line 10.

```
*****************
PROGRAM: ADD/SUBT
*****************
10 INPUT"ADD OR SUBTRACT (A/S)";A$
20 IFA$="A"THENPOKE2196,43:POKE2218,170
30 IFA$="S"THENPOKE2196,45:POKE2218,171
40 N1=INT(10*RND(1))
50 N2=INT(10*RND(1))
60 PRINT"WHAT IS"N1"+"N2;
```

```
70 INPUTA
80 AN=N1+N2
90 IFA=ANTHENPRINT"GOOD WORK"
100 IFA<>ANTHENPRINT"I GET"AN"AS AN ANSW
ER"
110 GOTO40
```

WARNING:

Do *not* make any changes in lines 10 to 80. Type in this ADD/SUBT DRILL program *exactly* as it appears above. Adding or subtracting even one character will make the program inoperative. Save a copy before you run it!

NOTE:

This program modifies line 60 by POKEing either a 43 (ASCII +) or 45 (ASCII -) into memory location 2196. It also modifies line 80 by POKEing either a 170 (+ token) or 171 (-token) into memory location 2218. The exact memory locations to use were determined by examining a hex dump of the program. If you are using a VIC, use locations 4244 and 4266.

If you want to add information to a program, such as adding new names to a mailing list, you would include some dummy DATA statements like this in your program:

```
2000 DATA:::::::::::::::::::::::::::::::::::::::::::::::::::::::
2010 DATA:::::::::::::::::::::::::::::::::::::::::::::::::::::::
2020 DATA:::::::::::::::::::::::::::::::::::::::::::::::::::::::
```

As more names were added, they would be POKEd into the appropriate memory locations and would replace the colons in these DATA statements.

The problem with this approach is that you *must never add or delete characters or lines* in your program. If you do, you will end up altering line numbers, line links or other important elements of your program when you POKE new information into memory. The only real benefit of this approach is that the changes that are made are internal to your program and do not affect the values of any variables that you are using.

Automated Editing

We all know how to edit a program. You just type out the line you want to add or modify on the screen and then press the RETURN key. What we are going to do is have the program edit itself. The basic process is rather simple. Here is what you have your program do:

1. Save the values of any important variables by POKEing them into a safe area of memory (e.g., cassette buffer 828-1019).

2. Clear the screen and print out the new program line, complete with line number, on line three of the screen.

3. Print RUN or GOTO xxx on the next line of the screen (xxx is the line number in your program where the rerun should start).

4. HOME the cursor and suppress a carriage return.

5. POKE two (up to 10 if needed) carriage return characters (ASCII 13) into the keyboard buffer (631 to 640). You need one for each new line plus one for the RUN or GOTO. The first one goes into 631, the second into 632, and so on.

6. POKE memory location 198 with the number of characters you have stuffed into the keyboard buffer and END the program.

7. On re-entry peek out the variable values.

This may sound a bit complicated but let's follow it through with an example. Here is a very simple self-editing program:

```
********************
PROGRAM: SELF-EDIT
********************

0 REM 1541 USER'S GUIDE SECTION 6.10
1 REM  COPYRIGHT: G. NEUFELD, 1984
2 :
3 REM SELF-EDIT FOR THE COMMODORE 64
4 :
100  INPUT"NEW LINE";A$          Input the new line.
110  PRINT"{CLR}{DOWN 3}"A$       Clear screen & print line.
120  PRINT"RUN"                   Print RUN so program will rerun.
130  PRINT"{HOME}"                Home the cursor.
140  POKE631,13:POKE632,13        POKE returns into buffer.
150  POKE198,2                    POKE # of characters in buffer.
160  END                          End the program.
```

Suppose you input the line 40 LIST in response to line 100. Just before the program ends, the top of the video screen will look like this:

```
line 1 | ■ ← cursor
line 2 |
line 3 | 40 LIST
line 4 | RUN
```

As soon as the program ends, the computer will print READY and be in immediate mode with the cursor flashing at the start of the line 40 LIST (you can see this if you add a line 135 END to the program). However, there are two carriage return characters in the keyboard buffer. The first one edits the program by entering the new line 40 just as though you had pressed the RETURN key. The second character forces a new RUN of the program. The mailing list program in the next section is a much more useful and sophisticated application of this technique.

6.11 Typical Application

For each of the chapters on file handling (Chapters 6, 7, 8 and 9), I have developed a mailing list program to illustrate a practical use for the techniques you have learned. Only those portions of the program that deal with data handling are changed from one chapter to the next. The portions relating to data entry, editing and printouts remain the same.

In this chapter, the mailing list program is a self-modifying program that stores the data about the club members in DATA statements.

Background information: You've just been elected secretary of a local civic organization. As secretary, you are responsible for making up mailing labels for the monthly newsletter that goes out to all 500 members. You would like to use your new computer to take some of the drudgery out of the task.

Analysis of the problem: You need a simple mailing list program to keep track of the names and addresses of the 500 members. The program should allow you to add new members, modify members' names and addresses, produce a list of members, and produce a set of mailing labels. Since you are interested in self-modifying programs, you've decided to try and write one.

Planning a record: The first step in planning the program is to decide what information we need about each member. You've checked over the club records and made up the following summary.

Field	Description	Typical Case	Worst Case
1	Last name	8 characters	14 characters
2	First name	6 characters	9 characters
3	Street address	18 characters	23 characters
4	City	8 characters	18 characters
5	State	2 characters	2 characters
6	Zip code	6 characters	6 characters
	Total	48 characters	72 characters

Data Statements: Since we are going to put the members' information into DATA statements in our program, we must decide how many statements to use for each member. We will enclose each field in quotation marks so that we can use both upper and lower case letters. This means that we will have a lot of extra characters to deal with. As a result, we had better use two DATA statements per member. We'll organize them like this:

```
5000 DATA"Last name","First name","Street address"
5005 DATA"City","State","Zip code"
```

Let's go over the main parts of the program to see how it works:

Line Range	Description
1020-1080	Loop to read and count the number of existing data items. When -999 is encountered, exit the loop and divide by six, the number of fields per member, to find the number of existing records. Convert this number into lo byte/hi byte form and POKE it into memory locations 1022 and 1023.
1120-1140	Reentry point after auto editing. PEEK memory locations 1022 and 1023 to recover the number of existing records (NR) and initialize variables.
1150-1250	Display main menu, input option chosen and branch to the appropriate part of the program.
1290-1460	Increment count of existing members, including the values in 1022/23. Determine line number for the new DATA lines. Input the data and assemble the statements in F1$ and F2$ and check their length. If the lines are too long, exit to edit routine.
1490-1550	Clear screen, print new DATA statements and GOTO 1120 on the screen, stuff the keyboard buffer and end the program. After the new lines are added, reenter at 1120.
1590-1710	Input the number of the record to edit and then position to the record.
1720-1850	Read and display the existing record. Input any changes to the record.
1870-1920	Calculate the line numbers for the revised DATA statements, assemble the lines and check length.
1940-1970	Clear screen, print revised DATA statements and GOTO 1120 on the screen, stuff keyboard buffer and end program. After the lines are edited, reenter at 1120.
2040-2190	Read the DATA statements and print a members list on the screen or printer.
2230-2540	Read the DATA statements and print mailing labels to the screen or printer. Pressing Q causes the printing to be suspended after the next label is printed and the user has the option of aborting the print job or restarting it at any point. This is very helpful when the paper jams!
2580-2590	Saves a new, revised copy of the program onto diskette and terminates the program.
5000-9995	DATA statements containing names and addresses.
10000	DATA statement with -999 as end of file indicator.

```
****************
PROGRAM: MAIL PRG
****************

0 REM 1541 USER'S GUIDE SECTION 6.11
1 REM   COPYRIGHT: G. NEUFELD, 1984
2 :
3 REM SELF-MODIFYING, MAIL-LIST PROGRAM
4 :
1000 REM* MAILING LIST PROGRAM
1010 :
1020 REM FIND NUMBER OF DATA ITEMS
1030 K=0
1040 K=K+1:READA$:IF A$="-999"GOTO1060
1050 GOTO1040
1060 NR=INT(K/6):REM 6 FIELDS PER PERSON

1070 RH=INT(NR/256):RL=NR-256*RH
1080 POKE 1023,RH:POKE1022,RL
1090 :
1100 REM* DISPLAY MENU
1110 :
1120 RH=PEEK(1023):RL=PEEK(1022):NR=RL+2
56*RH
1130 C$=CHR$(34)+CHR$(44)+CHR$(34):REM "
,"
1140 Q$=CHR$(34):REM "
1150 PRINTCHR$(14)"{CLR}{DOWN} MAILING L
IST MENU    "NR"RECORDS"
1160 PRINT"{DOWN}1. ENTER NEW MEMBER"
1170 PRINT"{DOWN}2. EDIT EXISTING RECORD
"
1180 PRINT"{DOWN}3. PRINT MEMBERS LIST"
1190 PRINT"{DOWN}4. PRINT MAILING LABELS
"
1200 PRINT"{DOWN}5. TERMINATE PROGRAM"
1210 PRINT"{DOWN}WHICH OPTION (1-5)"
1220 GETA$:IF A$=""GOTO 1220
1230 A=ASC(A$)-48
1240 IF A<1 OR A>5 GOTO 1220
1250 ON A GOTO 1290,1590,2040,2230,2550
1260 :
1270 REM: ENTER NEW MEMBER
1280 :
1290 RH=PEEK(1023):RL=PEEK(1022)
1300 RL=RL+1:IFRL>255 THEN RL=RL-256:RH=
RH+1
1310 POKE 1023,RH:POKE1022,RL
1320 NR=RL+256*RH
1330 L1$=MID$(STR$(4990+10*NR),2):REM LI
NE NUMBER
```

```
1340 L2$=MID$(STR$(4995+10*NR),2):REM LI
NE NUMBER
1350 PRINT"{CLR}{DOWN}  ENTER DATA FOR M
EMBER #"NR
1360 NL$="?":INPUT"{DOWN}LAST NAME:";NL$

1370 NF$="?":INPUT"{DOWN}FIRST NAME:";NF
$
1380 AD$="?":INPUT"{DOWN}STREET ADDRESS:
";AD$
1390 CI$="?":INPUT"{DOWN}CITY/TOWN:";CI$

1400 SA$="?":INPUT"{DOWN}STATE:";SA$
1410 ZP$="?":INPUT"{DOWN}ZIP CODE:";ZP$
1420 F1$=L1$+"DATA"+Q$+NL$+C$+NF$+C$+AD$
+Q$
1430 F2$=L2$+"DATA"+Q$+CI$+C$+SA$+C$+ZP$
+Q$
1440 IF LEN(F1$)<79 AND LEN(F2$)<79 GOTO
 1490
1450 PRINT"{DOWN}ERROR: RECORD IS TOO LO
NG":X=NR
1460 FOR K=1 TO 5000:NEXT:GOTO 1730
1470 :
1480 REM PRINT RECORD ON SCREEN
1490 PRINT"{CLR}{DOWN 3}"F1$:PRINTF2$
1500 PRINT"GOTO 1120{HOME}"
1510 :
1520 REM STUFF KEYBORD BUFFER WITH CARRI
AGE RETURNS
1530 POKE 631,13:POKE 632,13:POKE 633,13

1540 POKE 198,3
1550 END
1560 :
1570 REM* EDIT EXISTING MEMBER
1580 :
1590 PRINT"{CLR}{DOWN} EDIT EXISTING MEM
BER{DOWN}"
1600 M$="RECORD NUMBER (1-"+MID$(STR$(NR
),2)+")"
1610 PRINTM$;"  O"
1620 PRINT"{UP}"TAB(LEN(M$));:INPUT X$:X
=INT(VAL(X$))
1630 IF X<1 OR X>NR GOTO 1120
1640 :
1650 REM POSITION TO RECORD #X
1660 :
1670 RESTORE
1680 IF X=1 GOTO 1720
```

```
1690 FOR K=1TOX-1
1700 READ NL$,NF$,AD$,CI$,SA$,ZP$
1710 NEXT
1720 READ NL$,NF$,AD$,CI$,SA$,ZP$
1730 PRINT"{CLR}{DOWN} EXISTING DATA FOR
 MEMBER #"X
1740 PRINT"{DOWN}LAST NAME:   ";NL$
1750 PRINT"{DOWN}FIRST NAME:   ";NF$
1760 PRINT"{DOWN}STREET ADDRESS:   ";AD$
1770 PRINT"{DOWN}CITY/TOWN:   ";CI$
1780 PRINT"{DOWN}STATE:   ";SA$
1790 PRINT"{DOWN}ZIP CODE:   ";ZP$
1800 PRINT"{HOME}{DOWN 3}"TAB(10):INPUT
NL$
1810 PRINT"{DOWN}"TAB(11):INPUT NF$
1820 PRINT"{DOWN}"TAB(15):INPUT AD$
1830 PRINT"{DOWN}"TAB(10):INPUT CI$
1840 PRINT"{DOWN}"TAB(6):INPUT SA$
1850 PRINT"{DOWN}"TAB(9):INPUT ZP$
1860 REM FIND LINE NUMBER
1870 L1$=MID$(STR$(4990+10*X),2):REM LIN
E NUMBER
1880 L2$=MID$(STR$(4995+10*X),2):REM LIN
E NUMBER
1890 REM ASSEMBLE LINE
1900 F1$=L1$+"DATA"+Q$+NL$+C$+NF$+C$+AD$
+Q$
1910 F2$=L2$+"DATA"+Q$+CI$+C$+SA$+C$+ZP$
+Q$
1920 IF LEN(F1$)>79 OR LEN(F2$)>79 GOTO
1730
1930 REM PRINT RECORD ON SCREEN
1940 PRINT"{CLR}{DOWN 3}"F1$:PRINTF2$
1950 PRINT"GOTO 1120{HOME}"
1960 :
1970 REM STUFF KEYBOARD BUFFER WITH CARR
IAGE RETURNS
1980 POKE 631,13:POKE 632,13:POKE 633,13

1990 POKE 198,3
2000 END
2010 :
2020 REM* PRINT LIST OF MEMBERS
2030 :
2040 PRINT"{CLR}{DOWN} PRINT LIST OF MEM
BERS"
2050 INPUT"{DOWN}OUTPUT TO SCREEN OR PRI
NTER (S/P)  S{LEFT 3}";Z$
2060 PRINT:DN=3:IF LEFT$(Z$,1)="P" THEN
DN=4
```

```
2070 OPEN4,DN:RESTORE
2080 FOR K=1 TO NR
2090 REM POSITION TO RECORD #K
2100 READ NL$,NF$,AD$,CI$,SA$,ZP$
2110 PRINT#4,RIGHT$("    "+STR$(K),3);" "
NF$" "NL$
2120 PRINT#4,"     "AD$", "CI$", "SA$", "
ZP$
2130 NEXT
2140 CLOSE4
2150 IF DN=4 GOTO 1120
2160 PRINT"{DOWN}  PRESS {RVS}RETURN{ROF
F} FOR MENU"
2170 GET A$:IF A$<>"" GOTO 2150
2180 GET A$:IF A$<>CHR$(13) GOTO 2180
2190 GOTO 1120
2200 :
2210 REM* PRINT MAILING LABELS
2220 :
2230 PRINT"{CLR}{DOWN} PRINT MAILING LAB
ELS"
2240 INPUT"{DOWN}OUTPUT TO SCREEN OR PRI
NTER (S/P)   S{LEFT 3}";Z$
2250 PRINT"{DOWN}PRESS Q TO SUSPEND PRIN
TING"
2260 PRINT:DN=3:IF LEFT$(Z$,1)="P" THEN
DN=4
2270 OPEN4,DN:RESTORE
2280 FOR K=1 TO NR
2290 REM POSITION TO RECORD #X
2300 READ NL$,NF$,AD$,CI$,SA$,ZP$
2310 PRINT#4,NF$" "NL$","
2320 PRINT#4,AD$","
2330 PRINT#4,CI$", "SA$", "ZP$
2340 PRINT#4:PRINT#4
2350 GET A$:IF A$="Q" GOTO 2440
2360 NEXT
2370 CLOSE4
2380 IF DN=4 GOTO 1120
2390 PRINT"{DOWN}  PRESS {RVS}RETURN{ROF
F} FOR MENU"
2400 GET A$:IF A$<>"" GOTO 2400
2410 GET A$:IF A$<>CHR$(13) GOTO 2410
2420 GOTO 1120
2430 :
2440 PRINT"{DOWN}OUTPUT ABORTED"
2450 PRINT"{DOWN}COMMANDS:   A = ABORT"
2460 PRINT"               R = RESTART"
2470 GET A$:IF A$="A"THEN CLOSE4:GOTO 11
20
```

```
2480 IF A$<>"R" GOTO 2470
2490 PRINT"{DOWN}RECORD #"K"HAS JUST BEE
N PRINTED"
2500 PRINT"{DOWN}RESTART LIST AT RECORD
# "K+1
2510 PRINT"{UP}"TAB(24):INPUT K:PRINT
2520 RESTORE:IF K=1 GOTO 2540
2530 FORL=1TOK-1:READ NL$,NF$,AD$,CI$,SA
$,ZP$:NEXT
2540 GOTO 2380
2550 :
2560 REM* TERMINATE PROGRAM
2570 :
2580 SAVE"@0:MAIL PRG",8
2590 PRINT"{CLR}{DOWN} REVISED PROGRAM S
AVED"
5000 DATA"{SHIFT-S}MITH","{SHIFT-R}OBERT
","125 {SHIFT-M}AIN {SHIFT-S}TREET"
5005 DATA"{SHIFT-A}NYTOWN","{SHIFT-N}EW
{SHIFT-Y}ORK","12345"
5010 DATA"{SHIFT-J}ONES","{SHIFT-S}ALLY"
,"127 {SHIFT-F}IRST {SHIFT-S}T. {SHIFT-N
}{SHIFT-W}"
5015 DATA"{SHIFT-N}ORTHLAND","{SHIFT-M}{
SHIFT-N}","56024"
10000 DATA -999:REM DATA END FLAG
```

Possible modifications and improvements:

1. Have the new DATA lines and GOTO 1120 printed on the screen in the same color
   as the background. This way they would be less obvious.

2. Have the names sorted alphabetically. To do this you would have to devise a
   different method of determining the line numbers for the DATA statements. The
   line number would have some mathematical relationship to the characters that
   made up the name (this is called hashing).

Chapter 7

SEQUENTIAL FILES

In this chapter we will take a close look at sequential files, their structure and use. Several unique applications, such as using sequential files for merging program segments and hiding programs on a disk, are presented.

7.1 Introduction to Sequential Files

A sequential file is the most common type of data file. It is easy to use and makes very efficient use of diskette storage. Each record is just long enough to hold the information stored there. This type of file is particularly useful for storing relatively small amounts of data, up to about 20K. With this amount of data you can read all the data into the computer's memory, modify it in any way you want, and then rewrite the new version of the file. With a single disk drive, you can use a sequential file to hold up to a maximum of about 85K characters (half a disk full). But, if you use this large a file, you will find that updating or editing the data becomes quite tricky.

The biggest limitation of a sequential file is that you must access the file in a sequential manner. For example, if you want to read the address of the 100th person in your mailing list, you have to read through the first 99 records to get to the record you want. Another limitation is that you cannot modify individual records. You must read in the data, modify it and then rewrite the entire file, even if all you wanted to do was change one character in one record.

When to use a sequential file:

1. If you have a relatively small amount of data to store.
2. If you have up to 80K of data that rarely needs to be updated or modified.

The benefits from using sequential files are:

1. They are easy to use.
2. The data is stored very compactly.

The drawbacks in using sequential files are:

1. The amount of data you can store in a sequential file is usually limited to the amount of data that can be held in the computer's memory at one time.

2. You must read through all the preceding records to read a particular record.

3. You cannot modify just one record in the file, you must read in the whole file, modify the record(s), and then rewrite the entire file.

Some typical uses of sequential files are:

1. Grade book programs.
2. Phone book programs.
3. ASCII listings of programs that are to be merged (used by the programmer's aid program POWER™).
4. The management of small data bases.
5. As an index into a large relative file *.

* The use of a sequential file as an index into a large relative file is a very important and powerful technique. Chapter 9 on indexed relative files shows you how to do this.

7.2 Structure of a Sequential File

A sequential file is usually composed of many records. Each record stores all the information about a single person, place or thing. Since the length of a record is not fixed, the records are usually of varying lengths. A typical file might look like this:

```
| Record #1 |      Record #2      |   Record #3   | Record #4 \
```

Since each record occupies only as much space as it needs, the information is packed as tightly as possible on the diskette. This makes for efficient use of diskette storage space. However, it also means that there is no easy way to determine exactly where any given record starts or stops. The only way to read the Nth record is to start reading at the beginning of the file and read through N-1 records. The variable record size also makes revising a record difficult. You cannot rewrite an individual record in a sequential file. You must rewrite the entire file to revise a single record.

7.3 Using a Sequential File

Creating a program that reads or writes a sequential file is quite easy. Just follow these steps:

1. OPEN the sequential file.
2. Write information into the file using PRINT#.
3. Read information from the file using INPUT# or GET#.
4. CLOSE the sequential file when you are finished.

Let's look at each of these steps in more detail:

Opening a Sequential File

(See also Sections 7.4 and 7.5.)

An OPEN command is used to tell the disk drive the name of the file you wish to use. On the Commodore 64 or the VIC-20 the OPEN command to access a sequential file looks like this:

```
SYNTAX:
  OPEN file#,device#,channel#,"filename,SEQ,mode"

EXAMPLES:
  OPEN 5,8,4,"MEMBERS,SEQ,R"
  OPEN 1,8,5,"BUNCHADATA,S,R"
  F$="SUPER FILE"
  OPEN 2,8,12,F$+",S,W"
```

WHERE:

file#   = the logical file number (any integer 1-127).

channel#   = the channel number (any integer 2-14).

filename   = the file name (up to 16 characters).

SEQ   = file type, may be abbreviated with S.

mode   = R or W to indicate whether you want to read from a file or
                  write to a file.

NOTES:

1. Part or all of the file identification information may be stored in a string variable.

2. The file type and mode are optional. If the file type is omitted, the file type will be determined from the directory entry for the file. If the mode is omitted, it defaults to READ mode.

3. There is a special MODIFY (M) mode for reading an unclosed file. See Section 11.3 for more details.

READ MODE:

4. The file name may contain one or more wild cards (? or *). If it does, the first file name that matches the pattern will be opened.

5. If there is no file with the name specified stored on the diskette, you will get a 63, FILE NOT FOUND, error message.

WRITE MODE:

6. The file name may *not* contain any wild cards (? or *).

7. If there already is a file with the specified name stored on the diskette, you will get a 62, FILE EXISTS, error message. To write over (replace) an existing file see Section 7.4.

REMINDERS:

1. Monitor the error status of the disk drive.
   You should use the command channel to monitor the error status of the disk drive. Be sure to check the status whenever you open a file to make sure that the file has been opened properly. If the file is not open, your new data will be lost! See Section 5.10 about how to do this.

2. OPEN the command channel *first* and close it *last.*
   Do not open and close the command channel each time you want to check the error status. Open the command channel at the beginning of your program and leave it open until the end. When you CLOSE the command channel *all open files are closed automatically!*

3. All open files must have different logical file numbers.
   Since the logical file number is used to identify one particular file, you *must* use different logical file numbers for each of the files that are open simultaneously. Once you close a file, you are free to reuse that logical file number in your program.

4. All open files must have different channel numbers.
   Since the channel number (secondary address) identifies a particular data communication channel in the disk drive, each file that is open must have a unique channel number. Once you close a file, you are free to reuse that channel number in your program.

5. You can only have a few files open at once.
   Each sequential or program file that you have open takes up one of the buffers in the disk drive. Since the disk has only four buffers and one is reserved for internal use, you can only have three files open at once (not five as indicated on page 45 of your 1541 manual)! See Section 5.11 for the limits that apply for other file types.

ANNOTATED EXAMPLES:

```
35 OPEN 1,8,5,"OUTADATE,SEQ,READ"
```

Opens file# 1 to disk (eight) using channel# 5 to access the file on drive zero (default) with the name OUTADATE. It is a sequential (SEQ) file and we want to read (READ) it.

```
110 OPEN 3,8,12,"0:MISHMASH,S,R"
```

Opens file# 3 to disk (eight) using channel# 12 to access the file on drive zero with the name MISHMASH. This is a sequential (S) file and we want to read (R) it.

```
10 OPEN 9,8,6,"PILEAJUNK"
```

Opens file# 9 to disk (eight) using channel# 6 to access the file on drive zero (default) with the name PILEAJUNK. If it is a sequential, program or user file, it will be opened in READ mode. If it is a relative file, it will be opened in READ/WRITE mode.

```
100 F$="CONFUSION"
110 OPEN 7,8,2,"0:"+F$+",S,W"
```

Opens file# 7 to disk (eight) using channel# 2 to create a file on drive zero with the name CONFUSION. This is a new sequential (S) file and we want to write (W) to it. Note how to combine the drive#, file name, file type and mode using concatenation (+).

```
100 NL$="0:INCONSEQUENTIAL,SEQ,WRITE"
110 OPEN 2,8,5,NL$
```

Opens file# 2 to disk (eight) using channel# 5 to create a file on drive zero with the name INCONSEQUENTIAL. This is a new sequential (SEQ) file and we want to write (WRITE) it.

Writing to a Sequential File

Once you have opened a sequential file in write mode, you use a PRINT# statement to write information into the file. Be sure to plan the records so that they can be read back easily. I strongly recommend that you use carriage return characters as both field and record delimiters.

Here is a brief program that illustrates how to input data and how to write it to diskette immediately. Carriage return characters are used as both field and record delimiters:

```
********************
PROGRAM: PHONE/IMMED
********************

0 REM 1541 USER'S GUIDE SECTION 7.3
1 REM   COPYRIGHT: G. NEUFELD, 1984
2 :
3 REM WRITE AS SOON AS ENTERED
4 :
10 OPEN 15,8,15
20 OPEN 1,8,5,"@0:PHONE LIST,S,W"
30 INPUT#15,E,E$,T,S
40 IF E>19 THEN PRINT E;E$;T;S:CLOSE1:CL
OSE15:STOP
50 INPUT "ENTER NAME OR END TO QUIT";N$
60 IF N$="END" GOTO 110
70 INPUT "PHONE NUMBER";P$
80 PRINT#1,N$
90 PRINT#1,P$
100 GOTO 30
110 CLOSE 1:CLOSE 15:END
```

To change the above program to use commas as field delimiters and carriage returns as record delimiters, delete line 90 and change line 80 to read:

```
80 PRINT#1,N$ "," P$
```

In many cases, it is more convenient to input all the data into an array and, once all the data has been entered, write it to the diskette in one burst. This program illustrates this second technique.

```
*********************
PROGRAM: PHONE/ARRAY
*********************

0 REM 1541 USER'S GUIDE SECTION 7.3
1 REM   COPYRIGHT: G. NEUFELD, 1984
2 :
3 REM STORE IN ARRAY, THEN WRITE
4 :
10 DIM N$(100),P$(100)
20 K=0
30 INPUT "ENTER NAME OR END TO QUIT";N$(
K)
40 IF N$(K)="END" GOTO 70
50 INPUT "PHONE NUMBER";P$(K)
60 K=K+1:IF K<101 GOTO 30
70 OPEN 15,8,15
80 OPEN 1,8,5,"@0:PHONE LIST,S,W"
90 INPUT#15,E,E$,T,S
100 IF E>19 THEN PRINT E;E$;T;S:CLOSE1:C
LOSE15:STOP
110 FOR L=0 TO K-1
120 PRINT#1,N$(L)
130 PRINT#1,P$(L)
140 NEXT L
150 CLOSE 1:CLOSE 15:END
```

This second approach is often more useful because it allows you to sort or edit the list before the records are written into the sequential file. One disadvantage of this approach is that all the data must fit into the computer's RAM memory.

Reading a Sequential File

Whenever you open a sequential file in read mode you are automatically positioned to the start of the first record in the file. You may use either an INPUT# or GET# statement to read information from the file. In general, plan to use INPUT# rather than GET# because INPUT# reads more information at one time. However, there are some situations when you must use GET# to examine a file closely.

When to use GET#:

1. To check the contents of a file that won't read properly.
2. To read a file with more than 88 characters between delimiters.
3. To read a file that contains stray commas, colons or null bytes that cause problems for INPUT#.

Whether you use INPUT# or GET# you always start reading at the very beginning of the file. As you read records, fields or individual characters from the file the disk drive will keep track of where you are in the file. Note that you can only read forwards in the file. You cannot back up. If you have read past a piece of data that you need, you must close the file, reopen it and start from the beginning again.

There are two different approaches to reading a sequential file. One way is to read in the data piecemeal. When you need a particular record, you read through the file until you find it. You must use this approach when you have more data than can be held in memory at once. The other approach is to read the entire file into one or more arrays in memory in one burst. This is often a useful approach when your data may need to be edited or sorted.

Here is a brief program that illustrates the first approach reading the data as it is needed:

```
*******************
PROGRAM: READ/IMMED
*******************


0 REM 1541 USER'S GUIDE SECTION 7.3
1 REM   COPYRIGHT: G. NEUFELD, 1984
2 :
3 REM READ DATA FILE AS NEEDED
4 :
10 REM FIND PHONE NUMBER GIVEN THE NAME
20 OPEN 15,8,15:REM OPEN COMMAND CHANNEL

30 OPEN 1,8,5,"0:PHONE LIST":REM OPEN SE
Q FILE
40 INPUT#15,E,E$,T,S:REM CHECK DISK ERRO
R STATUS
50 IF E>19 THEN PRINT E;E$;T;S:CLOSE1:CL
OSE15:STOP
60 INPUT "ENTER NAME OR END TO QUIT";N$
70 IF N$="END" GOTO 150
80 :
90 INPUT#1,NAM$,PH$
100 IF N$=NAM$ THEN PRINT"NUMBER IS "PH$
:CLOSE1:GOTO 30
110 IF ST=0 GOTO 90:REM CHECK FOR END OF
 FILE
120 :
130 PRINT "NAME NOT FOUND IN FILE"
140 :
150 CLOSE 1:CLOSE 15:END
```

NOTE:

The status variable, ST, is used in line 110 to check for the end of the file. For more details see Section 5.15.

Here is the same program again but this time reading all the data into arrays at the start of the program:

```
********************
PROGRAM: READ/ARRAY
********************

0 REM 1541 USER'S GUIDE SECTION 7.3
1 REM   COPYRIGHT: G. NEUFELD, 1984
2 :
3 REM READ DATA FILE INTO ARRAY
4 :
10 REM FIND PHONE NUMBER GIVEN THE NAME
20 DIM NAM$(100),PH$(100)
30 OPEN 15,8,15:REM OPEN COMMAND CHANNEL

40 OPEN 1,8,5,"0:PHONE LIST":REM OPEN SE
Q FILE
50 INPUT#15,E,E$,T,S:REM CHECK DISK ERRO
R STATUS
60 IF E>19 THEN PRINT E;E$;T;S:CLOSE1:CL
OSE15:STOP
70 K=0
80 K=K+1
90 INPUT#1,NAM$(K),PH$(K)
100 IF ST<>64 GOTO 80:REM CHECK FOR END
OF FILE
110 CLOSE 1:CLOSE 15
120 :
130 INPUT "ENTER NAME OR END TO QUIT";N$

140 IF N$="END" THEN END
150 :
160 FOR C=1 TO K
170 IF N$=NAM$(C) THEN PRINT"NUMBER IS "
PH$(C):GOTO 130
180 NEXT
190 :
200 PRINT "NAME NOT FOUND IN FILE"
210 GOTO 130
```

NOTES:

1. The status variable, ST, is used in line 100 to check for the end of the file. For more details see Section 5.15.

2. The mailing list program at the end of this chapter is a good illustration of the use of this technique.

Let's take one last look at the first part of this same program again, but this time we will use GET# to read the sequential file.

```
******************
PROGRAM: READ/GET#
******************

0 REM 1541 USER'S GUIDE SECTION 7.3
1 REM   COPYRIGHT: G. NEUFELD, 1984
2 :
3 REM READ DATA FILE INTO ARRAY
4 :
10 REM FIND PHONE NUMBER GIVEN THE NAME
20 DIM NAM$(100),PH$(100)
30 OPEN 15,8,15:REM OPEN COMMAND CHANNEL

40 OPEN 1,8,5,"0:PHONE LIST":REM OPEN SE
Q FILE
50 INPUT#15,E,E$,T,S:REM CHECK DISK ERRO
R STATUS
60 IF E>19 THEN PRINT E;E$;T;S:CLOSE1:CL
OSE15:STOP
70 K=0
80 K=K+1
90 GET#1,A$:IF A$="" THEN A$=CHR$(0)
91 IF A$=CHR$(13) GOTO 95:REM CARRIAGE R
ETURN
92 NAM$(K)=NAM$(K)+A$
93 GOTO 90
94 :
95 GET#1,A$:IF A$="" THEN A$=CHR$(0)
96 IF A$=CHR$(13) GOTO 100:REM CARRIAGE
RETURN
97 PH$(K)=PH$(K)+A$
98 GOTO 95
100 IF ST<>64 GOTO 80:REM CHECK FOR END
OF FILE
110 CLOSE 1:CLOSE 15
120 :
130 INPUT "ENTER NAME OR END TO QUIT";N$

140 IF N$="END" THEN END
150 :
160 FOR C=1 TO K
170 IF N$=NAM$(C) THEN PRINT"NUMBER IS "
PH$(C):GOTO 130
180 NEXT
190 :
200 PRINT "NAME NOT FOUND IN FILE"
210 GOTO 130
```

(lines 100-210 as before)

1. The status variable, ST, is used in line 100 to check for the end of the file. For more details see Section 5.15.

2. When you use GET# to read the file like this, you must build up long strings using concatenation (X$=X$+A$). This can cause problems on a VIC-20 or Commodore 64 because you end up with a lot of unused string fragments in memory. For example, in building up the string NANCY, you create the following fragments: N, NA, NAN and NANC. These unused fragments gradually fill up the available RAM memory. Finally, you reach a point where the memory is full and the computer has to sort through the mess and discard all the strings not in use. The sorting process is called garbage collection and can take anywhere from five seconds to 20 minutes to complete. While garbage collection is taking place, the cursor goes away and nothing seems to be happening. If this happens to you, don't panic. Your computer is just busy sorting out the mess you have created! Don't turn off your machine. Take about a 30 minute coffee break. If your machine still appears to be hung up, your program may contain an infinite loop. Press RUN/STOP and do some snooping (you can always carry on with CONT). If this doesn't work, you may have to use RUN/STOP and RESTORE or even power down. Check for bad POKE statements.

Closing a Sequential File

Once you have finished using a sequential file, you must CLOSE it. Closing a file is particularly important after you have written to the file. A close statement looks like this:

```
SYNTAX:
  xx CLOSE file#
```

```
EXAMPLES:
  75 CLOSE 1
  600 CLOSE 5:CLOSE 15
```

WHERE:

xx   = the line number.
file#   = the logical file number you used when you opened the file.

WARNING:

Be sure to close a file which you opened in write mode. Closing the file is particularly important when you are writing to a file. Unless you close the file, the last block of data will not be recorded onto the diskette and you will have an unclosed file. You will be unable to access any of your data unless you use the techniques described in Section 11.3. Even if you do, some of your data will be lost!

7.4 Replacing an Existing Sequential File

Normally if you use the name of an existing file when you attempt to open a sequential file, you get a FILE EXISTS error and the file is not opened. However, there are times when you want to replace an existing file with a revised version. This is called

REPLACING the file. You can use either one of two techniques. The first technique
is to scratch the old file and then write out the revised file as though it were a new
sequential file. The second technique is to open the sequential file for a replace by
putting @0: in front of the file name in the open statement. In some cases this method
can cause serious problems (see WARNING below).

1. Scratch old file and then open a new sequential file.

```
250 OPEN 15,8,15:REM
   OPEN COMMAND CHANNEL
260 PRINT#15,"S0:BUNCHAJUNK":REM
   SCRATCH OLD FILE
270 INPUT#15,E,E$,T,S:REM
   READ ERROR CHANNEL
280 IF E<20 GOTO 310:REM
   CHECK FOR DOS ERROR
290 PRINT E;E$;T;S:REM
   PRINT ERROR MESSAGE
300 CLOSE 15:STOP:REM
   ABORT ON ERROR
310 OPEN 3,8,5,"BUNCHAJUNK,S,W":REM
   OPEN FILE
320 REM PROGRAM CONTINUES...
```

2. Open file for a replace.

Replacing a file is just like writing a file, except that you are replacing an existing file
with a newer version rather than creating a new file.

```
SYNTAX:
   OPEN file#,device#,channel#,"@:filename,
     SEQ,mode"

ALTERNATE:
   OPEN file#,device#,channel#,"@drive#:filename,
     SEQ,mode"

EXAMPLES:
   OPEN 5,8,4,"@:OLDSTUFF,SEQ,W"
   OPEN 1,8,5,"@0:LOTTADATA,S,W"
   F$="CURRENT MONTH"
   OPEN 2,8,12,"@:"+F$+",S,W"      <———
```

Note how the different
parts may be concatenated.

WHERE:

file#	= the logical file number (any integer 1-127).
channel#	= the channel number (any integer 2-14).
@drive#	= @ sign followed by the drive number; the drive# (zero) is optional on the 1541.
filename	= the file name (up to 16 characters); may be contained in a string variable.

SEQ   = file type, may be abbreviated with S.
W   = write mode required for replacement.

WARNINGS:

1. Do *not* scratch or replace improperly closed files. Be sure that the original program file you are going to replace has been properly closed. A file that has not been properly closed has an asterisk beside its file type in the directory (*SEQ). Do not scratch or replace an improperly closed file. Use the VALIDATE command (see Section 4.8) to eliminate these files! If you do scratch or replace one of these files by accident, VALIDATE the diskette as soon as possible, but certainly before writing to it again.

2. Be sure there is enough disk space to do a replace. When the file is opened for a replace, the old file is *not deleted* before the new file is written. This means that you must have enough free space on the diskette for the new copy. If there is not enough space, the replace is aborted. The new file is incomplete and the old file is unrecoverable unless you use the techniques given in Section 11.8. Be safe, not sorry! Check the number of blocks free on your diskette before you try a replace (see Section 5.13).

NOTES:

1. The file name may contain one or more wild cards (? or *). If it does, the first file name that matches the pattern will be replaced.

2. If there is no file with the name specified stored on the diskette, a new sequential file will be created.

REMINDER:

Part or all of the file identification information may be stored in a string variable.

ANNOTATED EXAMPLES:

```
20 OPEN 1,8,5,"@0:NEWSTUFF,SEQ,W"
```

Opens file# 1 to disk (eight) using channel# 5, to replace (@) the file on drive zero named NEWSTUFF. It is a sequential (SEQ) file and we want to write (W) it.

```
80 F$="TRIV*,W"
90 OPEN 3,8,7,"@0:"+F$
```

Opens file# 3 to disk (eight) using channel# 7, to replace (@) the first file on drive zero whose name begins with TRIV. The file type is determined from the directory entry. The file will be opened in write (W) mode.

7.5 Appending Data to a Sequential File

Normally when you open a sequential file in write mode you begin to write at the beginning of the file and write out the entire file. However, there are times when you want to add new information onto the end of an existing file without disturbing the data already in the file. This is called APPENDING data to the file. To do this you use a slightly different OPEN statement. It looks like this:

SYNTAX:
```
OPEN file#,device#,channel#,"filename,SEQ,A"
```

EXAMPLES:
```
OPEN 5,8,4,"MORESTUFF,SEQ,A"
OPEN 1,8,5,"BIGBUNCH,S,A"
F$="MORE EXPENSES"
OPEN 2,8,12,F$+",S,A"
```
⟵ Note how the different parts may be concatenated.

WHERE:

file#	= the logical file number (any integer 1-127).
channel#	= the channel number (any integer 2-14).
filename	= the file name (up to 16 characters); may be contained in a string variable.
SEQ	= file type, may be abbreviated with S.
A	= append mode.

WARNING:

Before you append more data to a file, check to be sure that you have enough free space on the diskette for the expanded file. If there is not enough space, the append job is aborted and you have produced an unclosed file. Both the old data and the new data are unrecoverable unless you use the techniques given in Section 11.3. Be safe, not sorry! Check the number of blocks free on your disk before you expand that file (see Section 5.13).

NOTES:

1. The file name may contain one or more wild cards (? or *). If it does, the first file name that matches the pattern will be opened.

2. If there is no file with the name specified stored on the diskette, you will get a 62, FILE NOT FOUND, error message.

REMINDER:

Part or all of the file identification information may be stored in a string variable.

ANNOTATED EXAMPLES:

```
20 OPEN 2,8,9,"0:BILLS PAID,SEQ,A"
```

Opens file# 2 to disk (eight) using channel# 9, to the file on drive zero named BILLS PAID. It is a sequential (SEQ) file and we want to append (A) data to it.

```
80 F$="EXP*,A"
90 OPEN 9,8,3,F$
```

Opens file# 9 to disk (eight) using channel# 3, to the first file on drive zero (default) whose name begins with EXP. The file type is determined from the directory entry. The file will be opened in append (A) mode.

Let's take a look at a short program that creates a sequential file, then appends some
more data to it. You may want to type in the example to see how appending works. In
lines 10-50 of the example, a new sequential file is created. Lines 70-110 append new
information to the end of our existing file. Lines 130-170 read back and display
the file.

```
****************
PROGRAM: APPENDER
****************

0 REM 1541 USER'S GUIDE SECTION 7.5
1 REM   COPYRIGHT: G. NEUFELD, 1984
2 :
3 REM   WRITE SEQ FILE, APPEND DATA, READ
  BACK
4 :
10 OPEN 2,8,5,"@0:TEST FILE,S,W"
20 FOR K=1 TO 15
30 PRINT#2,"ORIGINAL RECORD #";K
40 NEXT
50 CLOSE 2
60 :
70 OPEN 3,8,7,"TEST FILE,A"
80 FOR K=1 TO 10
90 PRINT#3,"APPENDED RECORD #";K
100 NEXT
110 CLOSE 3
120 :
130 OPEN 1,8,4,"TEST FILE"
140 INPUT#1,A$
150 PRINT A$
160 IF ST=0 GOTO 140:REM CHECK FOR END-O
F-FILE
170 CLOSE 1
```

Append mode is very much like write mode, except this time you begin writing data
at the end of an existing file rather than at the start of a new or replacement file.

7.6 Handling Very Large Sequential Files

For some applications it is necessary to use very large sequential files (over 30K of
data). In these cases there is simply too much data to be read into memory at once; you
have to read it piecemeal. This makes sorting or editing very difficult, particularly
with a single disk drive like the 1541. Here are some suggestions for handling this
type of situation.

Whenever you want to edit or add to your data file you will have to work with two
sequential files: your original data file and a new modified one. You read records one
at a time from your original file and, if nothing needs to be changed, you write them

out immediately to the new file. When you reach a record that you want to change, you modify it before you write it out to the new file. Diagrammaticall, the process looks like this:

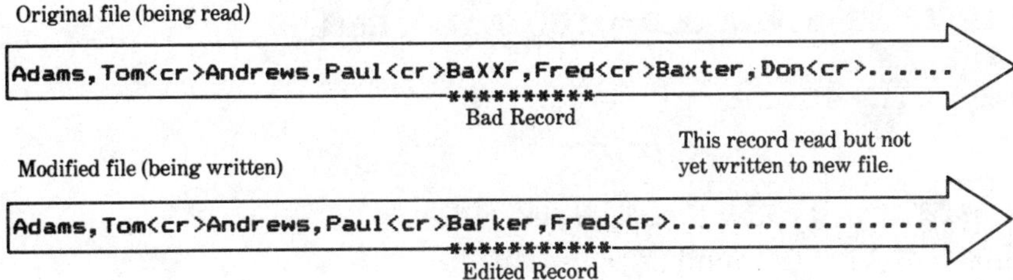

To add a new record you read records from the original file and write them into the new file. When you get to the position of the new record, you write it into the new file. Then you carry on with the read-old/write-new process. Adding a record looks like this:

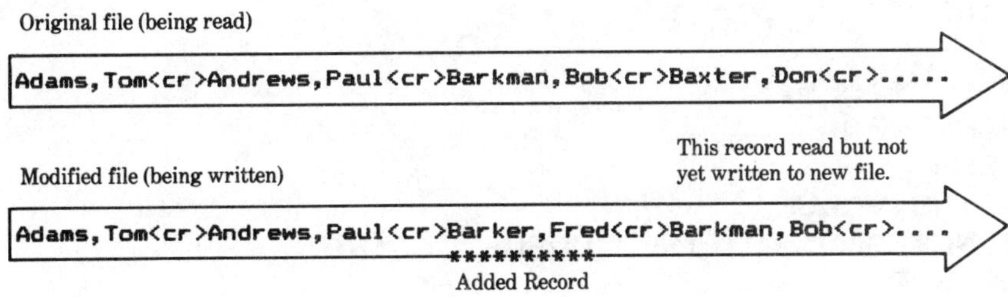

This is what is known as an insertion sort. The new record is inserted in its proper place among the old, sorted records. If you follow this procedure whenever the file is updated, the records will always be correctly sorted. The sample program shown below illustrates how to insert a single record into a large file.

```
*******************
PROGRAM: INSERTION
*******************

0 REM 1541 USER'S GUIDE SECTION 7.5
1 REM   COPYRIGHT: G. NEUFELD, 1984
2 :
3 REM   INSERTION SORT FOR SEQUENTIAL FIL
E
4 :
```

```
100 OPEN 15,8,15:REM
   OPEN COMMAND CHANNEL
110 OPEN 1,8,5,"0:OLD FILE,S,R":REM
   OPEN OLD FILE
120 INPUT#15,E,E$,T,S:REM
   CHECK DISK STATUS
130 OLD=1:IF E=62 THEN OLD=0:GOTO160:REM
   NO OLD FILE
140 IF E>19 GOTO 400:REM
   ABORT
150 :
160 OPEN 2,8,7,"@0:NEW FILE,S,W":REM
   OPEN NEW FILE
170 INPUT#15,E,E$,T,S:REM
   CHECK DISK STATUS
180 IF E>19 GOTO 400:REM
   ABORT
190 INPUT"NEW LAST NAME";NL$:REM
   RECORD TO INSERT
200 INPUT"NEW FIRST NAME";NF$
210 W=0:REM
   NEW RECORD WRITTEN
220 IF OLD=0 THEN GOSUB 360:GOTO 310:REM
   NO OLD FILE
230 :
240 INPUT#1,OL$,OF$:REM
   READ OLD RECORD
250 S=ST:REM
   STORE STATUS VALUE
260 IF OL$>NL$ AND W=0 THEN GOSUB 360:RE
M FOUND THE SPOT
270 PRINT#2,OL$",",OF$:REM
   WRITE OLD RECORD
280 IF S<>64 GOTO 240:REM
   MORE IN OLD FILE
290 IF W=0 THEN GOSUB 360:REM
   WRITE NEW IF LAST
300 :
310 CLOSE1:CLOSE2:REM
   CLOSE FILES
320 PRINT#15,"S0:OLD FILE":REM
   SCRATCH OLD FILE
330 PRINT#15,"R0:OLD FILE=NEW FILE":REM
   NEW BECOMES OLD
340 CLOSE15:END:REM
   FINISHED
350 :
360 PRINT#2,NL$",",NF$:REM
   WRITE NEW RECORD
370 W=1:REM
   SET FLAG
```

```
380 RETURN
390 :
400 PRINTE;E$;T;S:REM
   ABORT ON ERROR
410 CLOSE1:CLOSE2:CLOSE15:STOP
```

It is inefficient to read and rewrite a large file to modify just one record as we did in this example. You probably want to design your program so that all the changes you want to make are input first. Once they are all input, your program would sort them and then begin the read-old/write-new update sequence.

WARNING:

Be careful not to create too large a file. If you only have one 1541 drive, you must never create a sequential file that occupies more than 50 percent of the diskette. If you do, there won't be space on the diskette for both copies of the file, the old and the new, so you will be unable to edit or update the file. If you have two drives, you can use a complete diskette because you can always have the original in one drive and the updated version in the other drive.

7.7 Storing a Program as a Sequential File

Most Commodore users do not know that they can store a copy of a BASIC program in a sequential file. There are two ways to do this. One way produces an ASCII text file of the program while the other produces a sequential program file.

ASCII Text Files

In this type of file the BASIC keywords, such as PRINT and INPUT, are spelled out as they are in a program listing rather than tokenized as they are in a program in RAM memory or in a normal program file. Producing an ASCII text file of a program is very similar to producing a program listing on a printer. Here are the commands to enter in immediate mode:

```
OPEN 1,8,5,"filename,S,W"        Open sequential file in write mode.
CMD 1:LIST                       Divert output to file and list program.
```

The LIST command in the second line may be any one of the usual variations if you do not want the entire program listed. Once the flashing cursor returns, close the file like this:

```
PRINT#1                          Cancel CMD command.
CLOSE1                           Close diskette file.
```

Although the file contains a copy of your program, it cannot be loaded because the program is no longer in its tokenized form. The main use of this type of file is to merge subroutines you have stored on diskette into your current program. The excellent programmer's utility, POWER™, uses this technique.

HINT:

If you don't have access to POWER™, this four line BASIC routine is all you need to merge programs.

```
****************
PROGRAM: 64 MERGE
****************

0 OPEN 1,8,5,"TEST"
1 POKE 152,1:PRINT"{CLR}{DOWN}"
2 GET#1,A$:PRINTA$;:IFA$<>CHR$(13)GOTO2
3 PRINT"GOTO1{HOME}";:POKE631,13:POKE632
,13:POKE198,2:END
```

To use this routine follow these steps:

1. Check through a listing of the subroutine or program segment to be sure there are no lines more than 80 characters long. Lines more than 80 characters must be split into two shorter lines.
2. Save your subroutine as an ASCII file as described above.
3. LOAD your main program into memory.
4. Type in the routine as lines 0-3 of your program.
5. Insert the file name of the subroutine you want in line zero.
6. RUN the program to merge the subroutine.
7. When the merging stops, type CLOSE 1 and press RETURN.

WARNING:

Watch your line numbers! It is your responsibility to ensure that the line numbers of the incoming subroutine do not conflict with those in your program. If there is a conflict, the incoming line of the subroutine will replace the matching program line.

This little routine takes advantage of the auto-editing capabilities of your computer. Line two reads the next program line from the diskette file and displays it at the top of the screen. GET# rather than INPUT# is used to read the file to prevent colons and commas from causing us to lose parts of lines. Line three prints the message GOTO 1 below the program line, homes the cursor, stuffs two carriage return characters into the keyboard buffer and ends the program. The carriage returns in the buffer enter the new program line and cause the execution of the GOTO 1 line. When execution resumes on line one, the file has been closed in the computer but is still open in the drive. The POKE in line one reopens the file in the computer. Line two gets and displays the next line and so on. The last line in the ASCII file will be READY. This halts execution with either an OUT OF DATA ERROR or SYNTAX ERROR message. The merge is complete. Delete lines zero to three and you are all done.

Sequential Program Files

Mike Todd reported an interesting tidbit of information about Commodore computers in his DISK FILE column in the May 1983 issue of the *ICPUG Newsletter*. He reported that, because of the way Commodore computers interpret SAVE and LOAD commands, it is possible to SAVE a program as a sequential file. Not only can you SAVE it, you can even LOAD it again! Here are the commands to use:

```
SYNTAX:
  SAVE "filename,SEQ,W",device#
  LOAD "filename,SEQ,R",device#

EXAMPLES:
  SAVE "HIDDEN STUFF,SEQ,W",8
  LOAD "HIDDEN STUFF,S,R",8
  F$="SUPER FORCE,S,R"
  LOAD F$
```

WHERE:

filename	=	the file name (up to 16 characters); may be contained in a string variable.
SEQ	=	file type, may be abbreviated with S.
W	=	WRITE mode used to save hidden program file.
R	=	READ mode used to load hidden program file.
device#	=	the disk drive device number.

When you SAVE a program in this way, it appears in the directory as a SEQ file. However, this is not an ASCII text file. The program is in exactly the same form as it would be in a normal PRG file. That's why it can be loaded again. This appears to be a neat way of hiding programs on a diskette because everybody knows that you have to use GET# or INPUT# to read a sequential file.

7.8 Typical Application

For each of the chapters on file handling (Chapters 6, 7, 8 and 9), I have developed a mailing list program to illustrate a practical use for the techniques you have learned. Only those portions of the program that deal with data handling are changed from one chapter to the next. The portions relating to data entry, editing and printouts remain the same.

In this chapter, the mailing list program uses a sequential file for storing the data about the club members. The data is read into an array at the beginning of the program. A revised file is written just before the program terminates.

To illustrate the greater flexibility you have when the data is all held in memory, the program allows you to sort the list either alphabetically or by zip code. The Shell-Metzner sort used is a considerably modified adaptation of the one given by Raeto West in *Programming the PET/CBM*, p.134 (Compute! Books).

Background information:
You've just been elected secretary of a local civic organization. As secretary, you are responsible for making mailing labels for the monthly newsletter that goes out to all 500 members. You would like to use your new computer to take some of the drudgery out of the task.

Analysis of the problem:
You need a simple mailing list program to keep track of the names and addresses of the 500 members. The program should allow you to add new members, modify members' names and addresses, produce a list of members and produce a set of mailing labels.

Planning a record:
The first step in planning the program is to decide what information we need about each member. You've checked over the club records and made up the following summary.

Field	Description	Typical Case	Worst Case
1	Last name	8 characters	14 characters
2	First name	6 characters	9 characters
3	Street address	18 characters	23 characters
4	City	8 characters	18 characters
5	State	2 characters	2 characters
6	Zip code	6 characters	6 characters
	Total	48 characters	72 characters

Record organization:
Each record will consist of the six fields indicated above. The record size will vary. We will use carriage return characters as field delimiters in this application.

Let's go over the main parts of the program to see how it works:

Line Range	Description
1000-1110	Initialize variables and ask user to insert disk.
1130-1220	Open command channel and old data file. If there is no existing data file, branch to the menu.
1240-1360	Read the number of records in the old file and then loop to read the existing data into arrays. As data is read, check whether file is unsorted, sorted alphabetically or sorted by zip code.
1400-1550	Display main menu, input option chosen and branch to the appropriate part of the program.
1590-1680	Increment count of existing members, set flag to indicate an unsorted file, and input the data for the new member.
1720-1910	Input the number of the record to edit, set the flag to indicate an unsorted file, display the existing data and input any changes.
1950-2110	Print a list of members on the screen or printer.

2150-2470	Print mailing labels on the screen or printer. If the user presses Q, the printing is suspended after the next label is printed and the user has the option of aborting the print job or restarting it at any point. This is helpful for paper jams!
2510-2650	Replace the existing data file with a new updated file, close the files and end the program.
2700-2950	A Shell-Metzner sort of the mailing list data. Depending on the value of FL, the list is sorted alphabetically or by zip code.

```
*****************
PROGRAM: MAIL SEQ
*****************


0 REM 1541 USER'S GUIDE SECTION 7.8
1 REM  COPYRIGHT: G. NEUFELD, 1984
2 :
3 REM MAIL LIST PROGRAM USING SEQUENTIAL
 FILE
4 :
1000 REM* MAILING LIST PROGRAM (SEQ FILE
)
1005 DIM NL$(50),NF$(50),AD$(50),CI$(50)
,SA$(50),ZP$(50)
1010 PX$=CHR$(17):REM PRINTER UPPER/LOWE
R CASE
1020 FL=2:REM CURRENT SORT STATE
1030 SM$(0)="SORTED BY ZIP CODE"
1040 SM$(1)="SORTED ALPHABETICALLY"
1050 SM$(2)="UNSORTED"
1060 PRINT"{CLR} MAILING LIST PROGRAM"
1070 PRINT"{DOWN}INSERT DATA DISKETTE IN
 DISK DRIVE"
1080 PRINT"{DOWN}PRESS {RVS}RETURN{ROFF}
 WHEN READY"
1090 :
1100 GET A$:IF A$<>"" GOTO 1100
1110 GET A$:IF A$<>CHR$(13) GOTO 1110
1120 :
1130 REM OPEN COMMAND CHANNEL & INITIALI
ZE
1140 OPEN 15,8,15,"IO"
1150 INPUT#15,E,E$,T,S
1160 IF E>19 THEN PRINT E;E$;T;S:CLOSE15
:STOP
1170 :
1180 REM OPEN SEQUENTIAL FILE
1190 OPEN 1,8,7,"SEQ MAIL DATA,S,R"
1200 INPUT#15,E,E$,T,S
```

```
1210 IF E=62 THEN NR=0:CLOSE 1:GOTO 1400
:REM NO OLD FILE
1220 IF E>19 THEN PRINT E;E$;T;S:CLOSE15
:STOP
1230 :
1240 REM READ NUMBER OF RECORDS AT START
 OF FILE
1250 INPUT#1,NR
1260 :
1270 REM READ EXISTING RECORDS INTO ARRA
YS
1280 FOR K=1 TO NR
1290 : INPUT#1,NL$(K),NF$(K),AD$(K),CI$(
K),SA$(K),ZP$(K)
1300 IF NL$(K)<NL$(K-1)THEN AF=1
1310 IF ZP$(K)<ZP$(K-1)THEN ZF=1
1320 NEXT
1330 IF AF=1 AND ZF=1 THEN FL=2:REM UNSO
RTED
1340 IF ZF=0 THEN FL=0:REM SORTED BY ZIP

1350 IF AF=0 THEN FL=1:REM SORTED ALPHAB
ETICALLY

1360 CLOSE1
1370 :
1380 REM* DISPLAY MENU
1390 :
1400 PRINT"{CLR}{RVS}{DOWN} MAILING LIST
 MENU   "NR"{LEFT} RECORDS"
1410 PRINT"{DOWN}1. ENTER NEW MEMBER"
1420 PRINT"{DOWN}2. EDIT EXISTING RECORD
"
1430 PRINT"{DOWN}3. PRINT MEMBERS LIST"
1440 PRINT"{DOWN}4. PRINT MAILING LABELS
"
1450 PRINT"{DOWN}5. SORT ALPHABETICALLY"

1460 PRINT"{DOWN}6. SORT BY ZIP CODES"
1470 PRINT"{DOWN}7. TERMINATE PROGRAM"
1480 PRINT"{DOWN}  WHICH OPTION (1-7)"
1490 PRINT"{DOWN}{RVS} LIST IS "SM$(FL)"
"
1500 GETA$:IF A$=""GOTO 1500
1510 A=ASC(A$)-48
1520 IF A<1 OR A>7 GOTO 1500
1530 IF A=5 THEN FL=1
1540 IF A=6 THEN FL=0
1550 ON A GOTO 1590,1720,1950,2150,2700,
2700,2480
1560 :
```

```
1570 REM: ENTER NEW MEMBER
1580 :
1590 NR=NR+1:REM ADD 1 MEMBER
1600 FL=2:REM NO LONGER SORTED
1610 PRINT"{CLR}{DOWN}  ENTER DATA FOR M
EMBER #"NR
1620 NL$(NR)="?":INPUT"{DOWN}LAST NAME:"
;NL$(NR)
1630 NF$(NR)="?":INPUT"{DOWN}FIRST NAME:
";NF$(NR)
1640 AD$(NR)="?":INPUT"{DOWN}STREET ADDR
ESS:";AD$(NR)
1650 CI$(NR)="?":INPUT"{DOWN}CITY/TOWN:"
;CI$(NR)
1660 SA$(NR)="?":INPUT"{DOWN}STATE:";SA$
(NR)
1670 ZP$(NR)="?":INPUT"{DOWN}ZIP CODE:";
ZP$(NR)
1680 GOTO 1400
1690 :
1700 REM* EDIT EXISTING MEMBER
1710 :
1720 PRINT"{CLR}{DOWN} EDIT EXISTING MEM
BER{DOWN}"
1730 M$="RECORD NUMBER (1-"+MID$(STR$(NR
),2)+")"
1740 PRINTM$;"   0"
1750 PRINT"{UP}"TAB(LEN(M$));:INPUT X$:X
=INT(VAL(X$))
1760 IF X<1 OR X>NR GOTO 1400
1770 :
1780 PRINT"{CLR}{DOWN} EXISTING DATA FOR
 MEMBER #"X
1790 PRINT"{DOWN}LAST NAME:   ";NL$(X)
1800 PRINT"{DOWN}FIRST NAME:   ";NF$(X)
1810 PRINT"{DOWN}STREET ADDRESS:   ";AD$(
X)
1820 PRINT"{DOWN}CITY/TOWN:   ";CI$(X)
1830 PRINT"{DOWN}STATE:   ";SA$(X)
1840 PRINT"{DOWN}ZIP CODE:   ";ZP$(X)
1850 PRINT"{HOME}{DOWN 3}"TAB(10):INPUT
NL$(X)
1860 PRINT"{DOWN}"TAB(11):INPUT NF$(X)
1870 PRINT"{DOWN}"TAB(15):INPUT AD$(X)
1880 PRINT"{DOWN}"TAB(10):INPUT CI$(X)
1890 PRINT"{DOWN}"TAB(6):INPUT SA$(X)
1900 PRINT"{DOWN}"TAB(9):INPUT ZP$(X)
1910 GOTO 1400
1920 :
1930 REM* PRINT LIST OF MEMBERS
```

```
1940 :
1950 PRINT"{CLR}{DOWN} PRINT LIST OF MEM
BERS"
1960 INPUT"{DOWN}OUTPUT TO SCREEN OR PRI
NTER (S/P)  S{LEFT 3}";Z$
1970 PRINT"{CLR}{DOWN} LIST OF MEMBERS"
1980 PRINT:DN=3:IF LEFT$(Z$,1)="P" THEN
DN=4
1990 OPEN 4,DN
2000 FOR K=1 TO NR
2010 : IF DN=4 THEN PRINT#4,PX$;
2020 : PRINT#4,RIGHT$("    "+STR$(K),3);"
 "NF$(K)" "NL$(K)
2030 : IF DN=4 THEN PRINT#4,PX$;
2040 : PRINT#4,"      "AD$(K)", "CI$(K)",
"SA$(K)", "ZP$(K)
2050 NEXT
2060 CLOSE4
2070 IF DN=4 GOTO 1400
2080 PRINT"{DOWN}  PRESS {RVS}RETURN{ROF
F} FOR MENU"
2090 GET A$:IF A$<>"" GOTO 2070
2100 GET A$:IF A$<>CHR$(13) GOTO 2100
2110 GOTO 1400
2120 :
2130 REM* PRINT MAILING LABELS
2140 :
2150 PRINT"{CLR}{DOWN} PRINT MAILING LAB
ELS"
2160 INPUT"{DOWN}OUTPUT TO SCREEN OR PRI
NTER (S/P)  S{LEFT 3}";Z$
2170 PRINT"{CLR}{DOWN} PRINTING MAILING
LABELS"
2180 PRINT"{DOWN}PRESS Q TO SUSPEND PRIN
TING{DOWN}"
2190 PRINT:DN=3:IF LEFT$(Z$,1)="P" THEN
DN=4
2200 OPEN 4,DN
2210 FOR K=1 TO NR
2220 : IF DN=4 THEN PRINT#4,PX$;
2230 : PRINT#4,NF$(K)" "NL$(K)","
2240 : IF DN=4 THEN PRINT#4,PX$;
2250 : PRINT#4,AD$(K)","
2260 : IF DN=4 THEN PRINT#4,PX$;
2270 : PRINT#4,CI$(K)", "SA$(K)", "ZP$(K
)
2280 : IF DN=4 THEN PRINT#4,PX$;
2290 : PRINT#4:PRINT#4
2300 : GET A$:IF A$="Q" GOTO 2390
2310 NEXT
2320 CLOSE4
```

```
2330 IF DN=4 GOTO 1400
2340 PRINT"{DOWN}   PRESS {RVS}RETURN{ROF
F} FOR MENU"
2350 GET A$:IF A$<>"" GOTO 2350
2360 GET A$:IF A$<>CHR$(13) GOTO 2360
2370 GOTO 1400
2380 :
2390 PRINT"{DOWN}OUTPUT ABORTED"
2400 PRINT"{DOWN}COMMANDS:   A = ABORT"
2410 PRINT"              R = RESTART"
2420 GET A$:IF A$="A"THEN CLOSE4:GOTO 14
00
2430 IF A$<>"R" GOTO 2420
2440 PRINT"{DOWN}RECORD #"K"HAS JUST BEE
N PRINTED"
2450 PRINT"{DOWN}RESTART LIST AT RECORD
# "K+1
2460 PRINT"{UP}"TAB(24):INPUT K:PRINT
2470 GOTO 2230
2480 :
2490 REM* TERMINATE PROGRAM
2500 :
2510 REM OPEN SEQUENTIAL FILE FOR REPLAC
E
2520 OPEN 1,8,7,"@0:SEQ MAIL DATA,S,W"
2530 :
2540 PRINT#1,NR:REM NUMBER OF RECORDS
2550 :
2560 FOR K=1 TO NR
2570 : PRINT#1,NL$(K)
2580 : PRINT#1,NF$(K)
2590 : PRINT#1,AD$(K)
2600 : PRINT#1,CI$(K)
2610 : PRINT#1,SA$(K)
2620 : PRINT#1,ZP$(K)
2630 NEXT K
2640 :
2650 CLOSE1:END
2660 :
2670 REM SHELL-METZNER SORT - ALPHABETIC
ALLY
2680 REM FL=1 ALPHABETIC  FL=0 BY ZIP CO
DE
2690 :
2700 PRINT"{CLR}{DOWN 2}SORTING... PLEAS
E BE PATIENT"
2710 M=NR
2720 M=INT(M/2)
2730 IF M=0 GOTO 1400:REM SORT COMPLETED

2740 J=1:K=NR-M
```

```
2750 I=J
2760 L=I+M
2770 :
2780 IF FL=0 GOTO 2840
2790 :
2800 IF NL$(I)<NL$(L) GOTO 2940
2810 IF NL$(I)=NL$(L)ANDNF$(I)<=NF$(L) G
OTO 2940
2820 GOTO 2860
2830 :
2840 IF ZP$(I)<=ZP$(L) GOTO 2940
2850 :
2860 H$=NL$(I):NL$(I)=NL$(L):NL$(L)=H$
2870 H$=NF$(I):NF$(I)=NF$(L):NF$(L)=H$
2880 H$=AD$(I):AD$(I)=AD$(L):AD$(L)=H$
2890 H$=CI$(I):CI$(I)=CI$(L):CI$(L)=H$
2900 H$=SA$(I):SA$(I)=SA$(L):SA$(L)=H$
2910 H$=ZP$(I):ZP$(I)=ZP$(L):ZP$(L)=H$
2920 I=I-M
2930 IF I>0 GOTO 2760
2940 J=J+1:IF J>K GOTO 2720
2950 GOTO 2750
```

Possible improvements and modifications:

1. Provide retrieval of a record for editing by name rather than by the record number which changes when the file is resorted.

2. Provide selective printouts of lists or labels based on the contents of certain fields. For example, only those members who have zip codes between 60004 and 60120. Or, if your members live in Canada, those members with postal codes between S4K 3N2 and S6K 1L6.

RELATIVE FILES

Despite what you may have read in some popular magazines about problems with relative files on Commodore single disk drives, relative files are reliable. However, you must always specify the byte parameter in the position command and make sure that the disk drive has time to position to the record properly if you are writing or modifying records in a random sequence.

In this chapter we take a first look at relative files and their use. Relative files are somewhat more complex than program or sequential files but learning to use them is worth it. They are fast and quite reliable.

Chapter 9 takes a look at some more advanced applications of relative files. Section 13.13 describes how these files are stored on a diskette and explains just what those mysterious side sectors are all about.

8.1 Introduction to Relative Files

A relative file is a special type of data file. It is somewhat more complicated to use and understand than a sequential data file. However, it is a very useful file type because you can read or write any record in the file without disturbing the rest of the file. Relative files are particularly useful for storing information that needs to be changed or updated frequently.

One limitation of a relative file is that all the records must be the same length. When you create a relative file, you must specify the record length. All the records in the file will be this length whether or not all the space is needed. If the record length is large and the actual record is small, diskette storage space is wasted. If you make the record length small, you will inevitably end up with a record that won't fit. You must plan carefully to make sure that your longest record will fit. Many programmers feel that the ability to read and write individual records in the file more than compensates for this limitation.

When to use a relative file:

1. If your data must be revised or updated frequently.
2. You have more data than you can read into memory at once.

Unless your application meets both of these criteria, you would probably be better off using a sequential file.

The benefits of using relative files are:

1. Individual records within a file can be read or written.
2. Access to a record is fast provided you know the record number.

The drawbacks of using relative files are:

1. Storage space is wasted because the record length is fixed.
2. Usually you have to maintain one or more sequential files that hold a list of the record numbers in the order needed to access the records in alphabetical order or some other order. These are known as index files. Chapter 9 deals with indexed relative files.

Some typical uses of relative files are:

1. Mailing or membership lists.
2. Inventory control.
3. General data base management.

8.2 Structure of a Relative File

A relative file is composed of many records. Each record usually stores all the information about a single person, place or thing. The number of characters in each record is the same. This is called the record length and must be specified when the file is first created. A typical file might look like this:

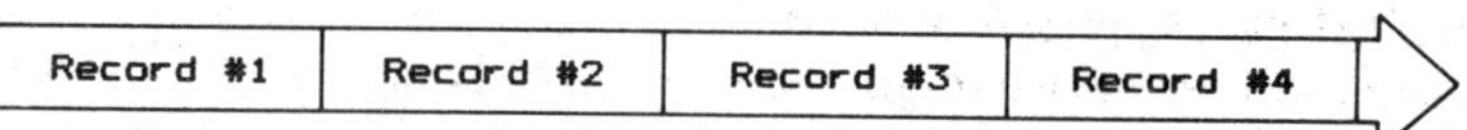

Since each record occupies the same amount of space, there may be a considerable amount of wasted space, particularly if the amount of actual data varies a great deal from record to record. However, the fixed record length makes it easy for the Disk Operating System (DOS) to determine exactly where any given record starts and stops. As a user of relative files you don't have to concern yourself about how this is done using side sectors and other pointers. All you have to do is specify the number of the record that you want to read or write and the disk drive takes care of all the messy details. If you are interested in the messy details, read through Section 13.13.

8.3 Planning a Record

Whenever you want to use a relative file in a program, you should spend some time preplanning the record length and layout. There are two general approaches to record layouts, fixed length fields and variable length fields.

Fixed length fields:
When a record is organized using fixed length fields, each field is always a particular

length and occupies the same position in a record. For example, suppose we used fixed length fields to store a last name, a first name, a street address, a city, a state and a zip code in a record for a mailing list program. We might decide that our record would be laid out this way:

Field	Field Contents	Field Length	Characters
#1	Last name + delimiter	14 characters	1 to 15
#2	First name + delimiter	9 characters	16 to 25
#3	Address + delimiter	22 characters	26 to 48
#4	City/town + delimiter	19 characters	49 to 68
#5	State/Prov.+ delimiter	2 characters	69 to 71
#6	Zip code + delimiter	6 characters	72 to 78

Diagrammatically our record would look like this:

* = carriage return character CHR$(13)

Variable length fields:
A second and usually better way to organize the record would be to use variable length fields. With this method the fields are not padded with blanks to make them any particular length. Only a field delimiter separates the fields. By using this approach, we can usually get away with a shorter record length. This is because the person with the longest last name usually does not have the longest first name and address. In the case of our mailing list we might well decide to use a record length of 66 (60 characters + 5 field delimiters + 1 record delimiter).

Diagrammatically our record would look like this:

Fields vary in length as needed   ⟵   Nulls at end   ⟶

Jones*Tim*23 First St.*Anytown*AS*123456*

* = carriage return character CHR$(13)

One limitation of this approach is that you have to be careful not to overfill the record. Always design your program so it checks the total length of the actual record before you write it.

When to use fixed length fields:

1. If the number of characters of actual data for each field does not vary much. A good example would be social security numbers that are always the same length.

2. If you need to read only selected portions of complex records. By using fixed length fields you can position within the record to the start of the field you want to read.

3. When convenience and speed of accessing parts of records is more important than conserving diskette storage space.

When to use variable length fields:

1. If the number of characters of actual data for each field varies considerably. A good example would be names or addresses in a mailing list.

2. When conserving diskette storage space is more important than convenience or speed of accessing parts of records.

Remember that any commas or carriage return characters you are using as separators (delimiters) between fields or records also count as characters in the record.

8.4 Deciding on the Record Length

Unfortunately, there is no magic formula for determining the optimum record length. You just have to make an intelligent guess after studying the data you want to store. If you make the record length large, you will never have to worry about overfilling a record but you will waste a great deal of diskette storage space. On the other hand, if you make the record length small, you may end up with some records that won't fit.

If you are using fixed length fields, you will have to determine the length of each field independently. In general, each field must be large enough to hold the worst case data for that field. For example, if the last names of the members of your organization vary in length from five (Smith) to 14 (Anadranastacki) characters, the last name field will have to be at least 15 characters long (remember that the delimiter counts). Once you have determined the worst case lengths for each field, add up the field lengths to get the record length.

If you are using variable length fields, you will have to make an intelligent guess. The optimum field length is somewhere between the sum of the typical field lengths and the sum of the worst case field lengths. Often the average of these two sums is a good guess.

WARNING:

When planning the record length for your file, you should be aware that there are three forbidden record lengths. These forbidden lengths are 42, 58 and 63 characters (see Section 8.5).

8.5 Using a Relative File

Using a relative file is quite easy. Just follow these steps:

1. Open the command channel.
2. Open the relative file.

3. Use the P command to position to the record you want.
4. Write information into the record using PRINT#.
5. Use INPUT# or GET# to read information from the record.
6. Close the relative file and the command channel when you are finished using the file.

Let's look at each of these steps in a bit more detail.

Opening the Command Channel

You *must* open the command channel so that you can specify the record you want to access using the P (position) command. You will also need the command channel open to check for disk errors (see Section 5.10 about how to do this). The statement that opens the command channel looks like this:

```
SYNTAX:
   OPEN file#,device#,cmd chnl#


ALTERNATE:
   OPEN file#,device#,cmd chnl#,"command"


EXAMPLES:
   OPEN 15,8,15
   OPEN 15,8,15,"IO"
   CN=7:DN=8:CC=15:C$="SO:OLD FILE"
   OPEN CN,DN,CC,C$
```

WHERE:

file#	= the logical file number (any integer 1-127; often 15 is used as the file#).
device#	= the device number (normally eight).
cmd chnl#	= 15; the command channel number.
command	= any disk command.

NOTE:

All examples use file# 15 for the command channel. The file# for the command channel may be any integer from one to 127. However, 15 is used in all examples because this makes it easier to remember which file# to use for disk commands.

Opening the Relative File

An OPEN command is used to tell the disk drive the name of the file you wish to use. On the Commodore 64 or the VIC-20, the OPEN command to access a relative file looks like this:

```
SYNTAX:
   OPEN file#,device#,channel#,"filename,L,"
     +CHR$(size)
   (may be used for either new or existing files)
```

```
ALTERNATE:
  OPEN file#,device#,channel#,"filename"
  (may be used for existing files only)

EXAMPLES:
  OPEN 5,8,4,"CUSTOMERS,L,"+CHR$(20)
  OPEN 1,8,5,"BUNCHASTUFF,L,"CHR$(125)
  OPEN 5,8,3,"OLD D*"
  F$="MEMBER DATA":RS=85
  OPEN 2,8,12,F$+",L,"+CHR$(RS)
```

WHERE:

file#	= the logical file number (any integer 1-127).
device#	= the device number (normally eight).
channel#	= the channel number (any integer 2-14).
filename	= the file name (up to 16 characters); may contain wild cards if file already exists.
L	= identifies that a record length follows; optional if the file already exists.
size	= the number of characters in a record. May be any integer 2-254 except 42, 58 or 63; optional if the file already exists.

WARNINGS:

1. Certain record lengths are forbidden. Although you are not warned about this in the *1541 User's Manual,* there are three forbidden record lengths. These forbidden record lengths are 42, 58 and 63.

2. An OPEN statement that specifies any of these forbidden lengths will be rejected by the DOS with a SYNTAX ERROR. The reason is that these lengths are the ASCII values of characters that have special meaning to the DOS (42 ="*", 58 = ":", and 63 = "?").

CAUTION:

The record length must be specified when a new relative file is created. Once you have created the file, its record length *cannot be changed.* If you try to specify a new record length for an existing file, your request will be ignored and the file will not be opened. The only way to change the record length is to open a new relative file using the new record size and copy the information into the new file one record at a time!

NOTES:

1. You do not have to specify whether you want to read or write to a relative file. Relative files are always opened in READ/WRITE mode.

2. Be very careful about punctuation. The comma that follows the L must be there if you are specifying the record length. If you are not going to specify the record length, close the quotes after the file name like this: "filename".

HINT:

If you are opening a new relative file, you should create the entire file at once. You do this by using the POSITION command to position to the highest record number you expect to have in the file. This forces the disk drive to create an entire file of blank records. You do not have to do this. However, it is good practice to do this because the file will be as compact as possible. This makes finding records faster and reduces the wear and tear on your drive.

REMINDERS:

1. Monitor the error status of the disk drive. You should use the command channel to monitor the error status of the disk drive. Be sure to check the status whenever you open a file to make sure that the file has been opened properly. If the file is not open, your data will be lost! See Section 5.10 about how to do this.

2. All open files must have different logical file numbers. Since the logical file number is used to identify one particular file, you must use different logical file numbers for each of the files that are open simultaneously. Once you close a file, you are free to reuse that logical file number in your program.

3. All open files must have different channel numbers. Since the channel number (secondary address) identifies a particular data communication channel in the disk drive, each file that is open must have a unique channel number. Once you close a file, you are free to reuse that channel number in your program.

4. You can only have a few files open at once. When you are using a relative file, you are very limited in the number of other disk files you can have open. The limits are:

   1 Relative + 1 Sequential, or
   1 Relative + 1 Sequential + 1 Direct-Access, or
   1 Relative + 2 Direct-Access

ANNOTATED EXAMPLES:

```
OPEN 1,8,5,"BUNCHADATA,L,"+CHR$(20)
```

Opens file# 1 to disk using channel# 5 to access or create a new relative file named BUNCHADATA. Each record is 20 characters long.

```
OPEN 3,8,9,"PILEAJUNK"
```

Opens file# 3 to disk using channel# 9 to access an existing file named LOTASTUFF. If this is a relative file, you will be in READ/WRITE mode. The record length will be the size specified in the OPEN statement used to create the file.

```
OPEN 7,8,12,"LOTASTUFF,L,"+CHR$(66)
```

Opens file# 7 to disk using channel# 12 to access or create a new relative file named LOTASTUFF. Each record is 66 characters long.

Positioning to a Record

Since you can read or write any record in the relative file, you must specify the number of the record you want. You do this using a P (position) command. Because the VIC-20 and the Commodore 64 have BASIC 2.0, you have to specify the record number in lo byte/hi byte form. You can calculate the lo byte and hi byte like this:

Hi byte = INT(Record Number/256)
Lo byte = Record Number -256 * Hi byte

NOTES:

1. INT stands for integer. The INT function on Commodore computers always rounds a number down to the next lower whole number. Here are a few examples of how it works:

INT(6.236) = 6   INT(0.3695) = 0   INT(53.589) = 53
INT(1.995) = 1   INT(-2.814) = -3   INT(-0.012) = -1

2. Be careful of the order of operations. The multiplication operation is performed before the addition operation.

Correct order   **Incorrect order**

LO = 675 -256 * 2   LO = 675 -256 * 2
LO = 675 -(256 * 2)   LO =(675 -256)* 2
LO = 675 -512   LO = 419 * 2
LO = 163   LO = 838

EXAMPLES:

Record number = 110
Hi byte   = INT(110/256)
          = INT(0.4296875)
          = 0

Lo byte   = 110 -0 * 256
          = 110 -0
          = 110

Record number = 725
Hi byte   = INT(725/256)
          = INT(2.83203125)
          = 2

Lo byte   = 725 -2 * 256
          = 725 -512
          = 213

Once you have calculated the lo and hi bytes of the record number, you use them in the P (position) command. On the Commodore 64 or the VIC-20 the command looks like this:

```
SYNTAX:
  PRINT#file#, "P";CHR$(channel#);CHR$(rl);CHR$(rh);
    CHR$(byte)

EXAMPLES:
  PRINT#15, "P";CHR$(5);CHR$(7);CHR$(0);CHR$(1)
  PRINT#15, "P";CHR$(9);CHR$(5);CHR$(1);CHR$(20)

  RH=INT(RN/256):RL=RN-256*RH:BY=24
  PRINT#15, "P";CHR$(3);CHR$(RL);CHR$(RH);CHR$(BY)
```

WHERE:

file#	= the file number of the command channel.
channel#	= the relative file's channel number.
rl	= the lo byte of the record number.
rh	= the hi byte of the record number.
byte	= the position within the record where you want the read or write operation to begin. Byte may be any integer between one and the record length.

WARNINGS:

1. The byte position must be specified! The byte parameter must always be present in a POSITION statement. It is *not optional* as indicated on page 35 of the *1541 User's Manual*. If this parameter is omitted, the carriage return character, CHR$(13), that is sent to the drive is sometimes assumed to be the position parameter and, if it is, you will be positioned to start reading or writing at position 13 in the record. Beware!

2. In some cases positioning may be inaccurate! When you position to a record in a relative file to write or rewrite the record, the position command may not work properly. This *only* occurs when you access files randomly and you write or rewrite the record. For more details and a fix see Section 8.6.

NOTE:

The P command is a direct command to the disk so it is issued over the command channel. As a result, you must have opened the command channel (OPEN 15,8,15) previously.

ANNOTATED EXAMPLES:

```
PRINT#15, "P";CHR$(7);CHR$(2);CHR$(0);CHR$(1)
```

In the relative file opened using channel# 7, position to record number 2 (2 + 0*256), byte number one.

```
RN=623
RH=INT(RN/256):REM HI BYTE OF RECORD NUMBER
RL=RN-256*RH   :REM LO BYTE OF RECORD NUMBER
PRINT#15,"P";CHR$(3);CHR$(RL);CHR$(RH);CHR$(1)
```

In the relative file opened using channel# 3, position to record number 623 (111 + 2*256), byte number one.

```
RN=1286
RH=INT(RN/256):REM HI BYTE OF RECORD NUMBER
RL=RN-256*RH   :REM LO BYTE OF RECORD NUMBER
PRINT#15,"P";CHR$(9);CHR$(RL);CHR$(RH);CHR$(27)
```

In the relative file opened using channel# 9, position to record number 1286 (6 + 5*256), byte number 27.

Writing a Record

Once you have positioned to the record you want, use a PRINT# statement to write the record. It is a good idea to write out the entire record using a single PRINT# statement (see WARNING below). You assemble all the parts of the record into one long string and then print out the string like this:

```
REM OPEN COMMAND CHANNEL AND FILE
OPEN 15,8,15
OPEN 7,8,12,"LOTASTUFF,L,"CHR$(66)
:
REM POSITION TO THE START (BYTE=1) OF RECORD #K
RH=INT(K/256):REM HI BYTE OF RECORD NUMBER
RL=K-256*RH   :REM LO BYTE OF RECORD NUMBER
PRINT#15,"P";CHR$(12);CHR$(RL);CHR$(RH);CHR$(1)
:
REM ASSEMBLE RECORD
C$=CHR$(13):REM FIELD SEPARATOR
S$=NAME$(K)+C$+ADDR$(K)+C$+CITY$(K)+C$+ZIP$(K)
:
REM WRITE OUT RECORD
PRINT#7,S$
```

WARNING:

The PRINT# statement always writes to a record from your current position in the record to the end of the record! This means that you cannot write out just the first part of a record and leave the last part untouched. Here is an example to show you what happens:

Suppose we wanted to change Charles' phone number.

```
Original      Smith      Charles      453-1248  Oct.15/47
              +---+-----+----+-------+--+----+----+----+--
Byte position 1   5   10   15        22 25  30   35   40
```

Position to byte #22 and PRINT# the new number 789-1238.

```
Final         Smith      Charles      789-1238 ///nulls///
              +---+-----+----+-------+--+----+----+----+--
Byte position 1   5   10   15        22 25  30   35   40
```

The end of our record has been wiped out with nulls!

CAUTION:

Be sure to check the length of your data before you write it to the file. If your data is longer than the record length, the data will be written into the file but will be truncated to the proper size to protect the following record. The drive will report a 51, OVERFLOW IN RECORD, error message. Remember that delimiters, including the final one at the end of the record, count as characters in the record.

NOTES:

1. The P command is a direct command to the disk so it is issued over the command channel. As a result, you must have opened the command channel (OPEN 15,8,15) previously.

2. You do not have to pad your data with blanks to make it the same length as the record length. The disk operating system will automatically fill the rest of the record with null characters, CHR$(0)'s. This can cause problems (see WARNING above).

Reading a Relative File

Whenever you open a relative file you are automatically positioned to the start of the first record in the file. The P command is used to position to the record you want. As noted above you *must always* specify the byte position within the record where you want to start reading. Once you have positioned to the record you want, you may use either an INPUT# or GET# statement to read information from the record. In general, plan to use INPUT# rather than GET# because INPUT# reads more information at one time. However, there are some situations when you must use GET# to examine a file closely.

When to Use GET#:

1. To check the contents of a file that won't read properly.
2. To read a file that contains stray commas, colons or null bytes that cause problems for INPUT#.

Whether you use INPUT# or GET# you always start reading at the position you specified in the P statement. As you read fields or individual characters from the record, the disk drive will keep track of where you are in the record. You can only read forward within a record. You cannot back up. If you have read past a piece of data that you need, you must reposition with another P command.

Normally data is read from a relative file as it is needed. Since any record may be accessed quickly, there is no need to read the data into an array.

Most programmers use an INPUT# statement since you get more information at once. If you used carriage return characters as field separators, you may use either a single INPUT# statement or a series of INPUT# statements, one for each field. If you used commas as field separators, you must use a single INPUT# statement to input all the information at once. Here's how to read the record we wrote earlier.

```
100 REM OPEN COMMAND CHANNEL AND FILE
110 OPEN 15,8,15
120 OPEN 7,8,4,"LOTASTUFF,L,"+CHR$(66)
130 REM POSITION TO START OF RECORD #K
140 RH=INT(K/256):REM HI BYTE OF RECORD
NUMBER
150 RL=K-256*RH   :REM LO BYTE OF RECORD
NUMBER
160 PRINT#15,"P";CHR$(4);CHR$(RL);CHR$(R
H);CHR$(1)
170 :
180 REM INPUT ALL INFORMATION AT ONCE          METHOD #1
190 INPUT#7,NAME$(K),ADDR$(K),CITY$(K),Z
IP$(K)


180 REM INPUT FIELDS SEPARATELY                METHOD #2
185 REM SEPARATOR IS CHR$(13)
190 INPUT#7,NAME$(K)
200 INPUT#7,ADDR$(K)
210 INPUT#7,CITY$(K)
220 INPUT#7,ZIP$(K)
```

WARNING:

You can read past the end of a record. When you attempt to write a record that is longer than the record size, you are warned (51, OVERFLOW IN RECORD) and the record is truncated to protect the next record. However, there is no similar mechanism to prevent you from reading past the end of a record. The only way to tell that you have reached the end of a record is by checking the status variable, ST (see NOTES below).

NOTES:

1. The position command works fine for reading a record. As long as you specify the byte parameter in the POSITION command, you will always be positioned to the correct record and be able to read it correctly.

2. You can use ST to check for the end of a record. Whether you use GET# or INPUT#, you may use the status variable, ST, to check for the last non-null

character in a record (see Section 5.15). When you have reached the end of the record, ST will have the value 64.

REMINDERS:

1. If your file contains a CHR$(0), it will not be read correctly. The value stored into the string variable is not CHR$(0). The null string (no characters) is stored there instead. This is the reason for the common GET# statement:

```
GET#1,X$:IF X$="" THEN X$=CHR$(0)
```

2. INPUT# always reads to a carriage return or null character. Since an INPUT# statement will always read as far as the next carriage return or null character, you must be careful not to skip over values and lose information (see Section 5.14).

3. Using GET# can cause garbage collection problems. If you use GET# for reading a relative file you have to build up long strings using concatenation (X$=X$+A$). This can cause problems on a VIC-20 or Commodore 64 because you store a lot of unused fragments of strings in memory. These slowly fill up RAM memory. When the memory is full, the computer has to sort through the mess and discard all the unused strings. This is called garbage collection. It takes from five seconds to 20 minutes to do. While garbage collection is taking place, the cursor goes away and nothing seems to happen.

Closing the File

Once you have finished using the relative file, you must close it. If you forget, you may lose data from the last few records you wrote and the BAM may be incorrect! A close statement looks like this:

```
SYNTAX:
  xx CLOSE file#

EXAMPLES:
  75 CLOSE 1
  600 CLOSE 5:CLOSE 15
```

WHERE:

xx   = the line number.
file#   = the logical file number you used when you opened the file.

CAUTION:

Be sure to close your relative file. Closing the file is important when you have been writing to your relative file. If you forget to close the file, the data block that contains the last record you wrote may not be recorded onto the diskette. However, failing to close a relative file is less disastrous than failing to close a program or sequential file. Because you are in read/write mode rather than write mode, you cannot create an unclosed relative file (*REL).

Although the following procedure does not appear to be necessary when closing a relative file on the 1541, following it guarantees that you will not have the problem of the last record never being recorded on the diskette.

1. Never CLOSE a relative file that is less than two full sectors (508 bytes) long. If necessary, create several empty records by positioning to the start of record number 1+(508/record size).

2. Just before closing the file, position to the start of the first record. Unless you have violated rule #1, this will force a write to disk and your file is safe.

8.6 The Problem with Relative Files and How to Fix It

Several articles have been published recently reporting problems with relative files on the 1541 and 2031 Commodore single disk drives. Various fixes were proposed. Since I had not encountered any problems when using relative files, I was interested in trying to duplicate the findings and possibly find a better fix. Unfortunately, most of the articles did not define the conditions under which the problems occurred (record size, record number, reading or writing or updating a record, etc.), nor did they provide listings of programs that produced errors. The articles just spoke in general terms about "problems with the POSITION command." This made it very difficult to localize the problem.

I began by writing a few simple test programs and found that the byte parameter was definitely *not optional* when using relative files on the 1541. Maybe that was the problem. I developed a comprehensive test program to check this out. The program systematically worked through all possible record sizes. For each record size it would create a test file. The number of records in the file was determined by the record size. As the record size increased, the number of records decreased so that each file contained about 20,000 characters (bytes) of data. The file was created by writing the records sequentially (record #1, #2,....#N). The records were designed so that you could identify where you were in the file by reading three consecutive bytes. The bytes were the record size (RS), the low byte of the record number (RN), and the byte position within the record (BY). For example, record #3 in a file with a record size of 12 would look like this:

RS	RN	BY	RS	RN	BY	RS	RN	BY	RS	RN	BY
12	3	3	12	3	6	12	3	9	12	3	12
$0C	$03	$03	$0C	$03	$06	$0C	$03	$09	$0C	$03	$0C

Once the file was written, 100 record numbers and byte positions were chosen at random. These records were accessed and read. If a positioning error occurred, a detailed report was printed. Once the program was written and checked, the test began. After 36 hours of steady running, the tests were completed.

The results? One very hot 1541 that was in desperate need of an alignment. My printout indicated the three forbidden record lengths. However, not a single positioning error was found. I was ready to conclude that any positioning problems were the result of programmers forgetting to specify the byte parameter in the POSITION command or alignment problems with their drives.

However, I decided to do some more testing and developed the program listed at the end of this section. This program makes it easy to do a wide variety of tests on relative files. You can create a new file of records, revise all the records, or read and check all the records. You can even choose the order in which the records are written, revised or read. They can be done normally (1, 2,..., N), in reverse order (N, N-1,..., 1), or in scrambled order (25, 2,...). Using this program I was finally able to generate the kind of errors described in the articles. I was also able to define the exact conditions under which problems do occur and try various fixes. Here are the results:

When do positioning problems occur?

The only time the POSITION command does not work with complete reliability is when you are writing or revising records in a scrambled order.

How frequently do errors occur?

The error rate is not consistent. Approximately one percent of the records will not be revised at all and another one percent will be revised incorrectly. Small files seem to have a higher error rate than large files.

Is there a pattern of errors?

The errors do not fall into an easily discernable pattern. However, a record that spans two blocks on a diskette rarely causes problems.

What seems to be the problem?

The Disk Operating System (DOS) uses two data buffers to hold records as they are being read from or written to the diskette. When a record that spans two sectors is being read or written, one buffer holds the start of the record and the other buffer holds the last part of the record. However, when records that are contained entirely within one block are being read or written, the DOS alternates between buffers (one active and the other inactive). It appears that during write operations the file manager side of the DOS may begin printing new information into the buffer before the disk controller side of DOS has finished reading in the sector that holds the appropriate record.

What is the fix?

By introducing a short time delay between the POSITION command and the PRINT# command the error rate can be reduced considerably. However, to ensure complete reliability you should issue the POSITION command twice and then delay for a short time before executing the PRINT# command that sends the revised data to the disk drive. The lines that you need are:

```
480 REM CONVERT RECORD # TO LO/HI FORM
490 RH=INT(N(K)/256):RL=N(K)-256*RH
```

```
500 :
510 REM POSITION ONCE
520 PRINT#15,"P"CHR$(5)CHR$(RL)CHR$(RH)C
HR$(1)
530 :
540 REM POSITION A SECOND TIME
550 PRINT#15,"P"CHR$(5)CHR$(RL)CHR$(RH)C
HR$(1)
560 :
570 REM PAUSE (30 JIFFIES = .5 SECONDS)
580 T2=TI+30
590 IF TI<T2 GOTO 590
600 :
610 REM PRINT TO THE FILE
620 PRINT#1,M$;CR$;N(K)
```

The two POSITION commands followed by the time delay seem to give the floppy disk controller side of the DOS enough time to read in the desired record from the diskette. With the test program the delay slows down the updating of the file by about 30 percent. With the delay it took about 15 minutes and 25 seconds for the computer to revise 600 records in scrambled order (1.54 sec/record) and there were no errors. Without the delay the same process took only 11 minutes and 25 seconds (1.14 sec/record), but there were three errors. In most practical applications the 0.4 second delay per record should be virtually undetectable because most of the time the computer is waiting for the operator to type in the revisions. The operator rarely waits for the computer.

Here is a listing of the test program that I used for checking the operation of relative files. You may want to use it to do a bit more testing on your own. Maybe you can come up with a better, and simpler, fix.

```
********************
PROGRAM: REL TESTER
********************
```

This program is designed to make the creation, revision and checking of test files easy. You may want to try various alternatives for the fix described. Just substitute your favorite fix for lines 780-810. To change the number of records or the record size, simply change lines 110 and 120.

```
0 REM 1541 USER'S GUIDE SECTION 8.6
1 REM  COPYRIGHT: G. NEUFELD, 1984
2 :
3 REM CREATE AND TEST RELATIVE FILES
4 :
100 REM REL TESTER
110 NR=30:REM NUMBER OF RECORDS
120 RS=25 :REM RECORD SIZE
130 M$(1)="ORIGINAL #"
140 M$(2)="MODIFIED #"
```

```
150 CR$=CHR$(13)
160 DIM N(NR)
170 :
180 PRINT"{CLR}REL FILE TESTER"
190 PRINT"{DOWN}INSERT TEST DISKETTE"
200 PRINT"{DOWN}OPTIONS:"
210 PRINT"{DOWN} 1. CREATE FILE"
220 PRINT" 2. MODIFY FILE"
230 PRINT" 3. READ FILE"
240 INPUT"{DOWN}YOUR CHOICE (1-3)   2{LEF
T 3}";X$
250 X=ASC(X$)-48
260 IF X<1 OR X>3 GOTO 180
270 :
280 OPEN 15,8,15,"IO"
290 INPUT#15,E,E$,T,S
300 IF E>19 THEN PRINTE;E$;T;S:STOP
310 IF X=1 THEN PRINT#15,"S:SHORT REL":P
RINT#15,"IO"
320 :
330 PRINT"{DOWN}NORMAL, REVERSE, OR SCRA
MBLED ORDER"
340 INPUT"{DOWN}(N/R/S)   S{LEFT 3}";O$
350 IF O$<>"N" AND O$<>"S" AND O$<>"R" G
OTO 330
360 :
370 IF O$="R"THEN FORL=1 TO NR:N(L)=NR-L
+1:NEXT:GOTO 490
380 :
390 PRINT"{DOWN}MAKING LIST OF RECORD NU
MBERS"
400 FORL=1 TO NR:N(L)=L:NEXT
410 IF O$="N" GOTO 490
420 :
430 PRINT" RANDOMIZING LIST"
440 FOR R=NR TO 1 STEP-1:REM SCRAMBLE SE
QUENCE
450 : RX=1+INT(RND(1)*R)
460 : H=N(R):N(R)=N(RX):N(RX)=H
470 NEXT
480 :
490 OPEN 1,8,5,"SHORT REL,L,"+CHR$(RS)
500 INPUT#15,E,E$,T,S:PRINT"{DOWN}REL FI
LE OPEN -"E;E$
510 IF E> 19 THEN PRINT"FATAL ERROR":STO
P
520 IF X=3 GOTO 890:REM TO READ FILE
530 :
540 IF X=2 GOTO 670
550 :
```

```
560 INPUT"{DOWN}POSITION TO END (Y/N)   Y
{LEFT 3}";W$
570 W=ASC(W$):IF W=78 GOTO 670
580 IF W<>89 GOTO 560
590 :
600 REM POSITION TO END TO CREATE ENTIRE
 FILE
610 RH=INT(NR/256):RL=NR-256*RH
620 PRINT#15,"P"CHR$(5)CHR$(RL)CHR$(RH)C
HR$(1)
630 INPUT#15,E,E$
640 PRINT"POSITION TO END -"E;E$
650 PRINT#1,"DUMMY RECORD"
660 :
670 INPUT"{DOWN}READ BEFORE WRITE (Y/N)
 Y{LEFT 3}";Y$
680 IF Y$<>"Y" AND Y$<>"N" GOTO 670
690 :
700 REM WRITE OR MODIFY RELATIVE RECORDS

710 PRINT"{DOWN}CONTENTS =   "M$(X)
720 PRINT"{UP}"TAB(10);:INPUT M$
730 FOR K=1 TO NR:PRINT M$;N(K)
740 RH=INT(N(K)/256):RL=N(K)-256*RH
750 PRINT#15,"P"CHR$(5)CHR$(RL)CHR$(RH)C
HR$(1)
760 IF Y$<>"Y" GOTO 820
770 :
780 REM POSITION AGAIN AND DELAY
790 PRINT#15,"P"CHR$(5)CHR$(RL)CHR$(RH)C
HR$(1)
800 T2=TI
810 IF TI<T2+30 GOTO 810
820 PRINT#1,M$;CR$;N(K)
830 NEXT
840 INPUT"{DOWN}READ BACK (Y/N)   Y{LEFT
3}";R$
850 IF R$="Y" THEN PRINT:GOTO 890
860 CLOSE 1:CLOSE 15:END
870 :
880 REM READ RELATIVE RECORDS
890 FOR K=1 TO NR
900 RH=INT(N(K)/256):RL=N(K)-256*RH
910 PRINT#15,"P"CHR$(5)CHR$(RL)CHR$(RH)C
HR$(1)
920 TH=INT(N(K)*RS/254):Z$=STR$(TH+1)
930 IF TH<>INT((1+N(K))*RS/254)THENZ$=Z$
+" SPAN"
940 INPUT#1,A$,B$:PRINT"#"N(K)"IS: ";A$;
B$;TAB(30);Z$
```

```
950 IF T$=A$ AND MID$(STR$(N(K)),2)+" "=
B$ GOTO 1000
960 :
970 PRINT"* BAD * PRESS RETURN":NE=NE+1
980 GET R$:IF R$<>CHR$(13) GOTO 980
990 PRINT"{UP}                        {UP}"

1000 NEXT
1010 CLOSE 1:CLOSE 15
1020 PRINT"THERE WERE"NE"ERRORS"
```

REMINDER:

The fix for the POSITION command is only needed when writing records in a
scrambled order. If you are reading the file or writing records in sequential order,
the fix is not required.

8.7 Replacing an Existing Relative File

Normally you would never want to replace an entire existing relative file with a
revised version. Instead, you would modify only those records that need changing.
The only way to eliminate an existing relative file is to scratch the entire file. Once the
old file is scratched, you are free to open a replacement file like this:


```
250 OPEN 15,8,15:REM
   OPEN COMMAND CHANNEL
260 PRINT#15,"S0:DATA":REM
   SCRATCH OLD FILE
270 INPUT#15,E,E$,T,S:REM
   READ ERROR CHANNEL
280 IF E<20 GOTO 310:REM
   CHECK FOR DOS ERROR
290 PRINT E;E$;T;S:REM
   PRINT ERROR MESSAGE
300 CLOSE 15:STOP:REM
   ABORT ON ERROR
310 OPEN 3,8,5,"DATA,L,"+CHR$(50):REM
   OPEN FILE
320 REM PROGRAM CONTINUES...
```


NOTE:

Replace does not work with relative files! The technique of replacing the file by
putting @0: in front of the file name in the OPEN statement does not work for a
relative file. If you try it, the @0: will be ignored and the file opened for normal
read/write access. You must SCRATCH a relative file.

8.8 Adding Data to a Relative File

Whenever you open a relative file you are free to position to any existing record in the file and read or write it. However, when you are adding information to the file, you may be positioning to records that don't exist yet. When you do this the 1541 disk operating system will report a 50, RECORD NOT PRESENT, error message. Surprisingly, you will not get this error for each new record you add. You only get this error when a new block (sector) must be added to the file. If you are adding new data to the file, this error is normal and can be ignored. It merely indicates that the file is being expanded to include the new record(s).

The only time to be concerned about a 50, RECORD NOT PRESENT, error message is if that record should really exist already. In this case, you should check for bugs in your program. If you get this error when trying to access the last few records in your file, you probably forgot to close the file the last time you used it and have lost the last few records.

CAUTION:

Before you append more data to a file, check to be sure that you have enough free space on the diskette to hold the longer file. If you run out of space, the last few records will not be written. However, with a relative file you do not lose your old data when this happens. See Section 5.13 for a method of checking the number of blocks free from within a program.

REMINDER:

It is good practice to create the entire file at once. You can improve the speed of accessing a relative file slightly if the data is stored on one area of the disk rather than being scattered around the disk surface. When it is stored in one area the read/write head doesn't have to move around as much. It is simple to reserve a block of space on disk for your file when you first create it. Simply position to the highest record number you expect to have in the file. This forces the disk drive to create all the records at one time, from #1 to the number you specified. Your file will be as compact as possible. As a bonus, you will never have to worry about whether your file is at least two blocks long (see NOTES about closing a relative file in Section 8.5), or about 50, RECORD NOT PRESENT, error messages.

8.9 Typical Application

For each of the chapters on file handling (Chapters 6, 7, 8 and 9), I have developed a mailing list program to illustrate a practical use for the techniques you have learned. Only those portions of the program that deal with data handling are changed from one chapter to the next. The portions relating to data entry, editing and printouts remain the same.

In this chapter, the mailing list program uses a relative file for storing the data about the club members. A record is read when the data is needed. Only the record currently being added, edited or printed is held in memory. This reduces the demands on RAM memory.

Records are stored in the relative file in the order in which they are entered. There is no provision for sorting the list either alphabetically or by zip code. To retrieve a record for editing, you must know its record number. The record numbers are given on the membership list printout.

Background information:
You've just been elected secretary of a local civic organization. As secretary, you are responsible for making up mailing labels for the monthly newsletter that goes out to all 500 members. You would like to use your new computer to take some of the drudgery out of the task.

Analysis of the problem:
You need a simple mailing list program to keep track of the names and addresses of the 500 members. The program should allow you to add new members, modify members' names and addresses, produce a list of members, and produce a set of mailing labels.

Planning a record:
The first step in planning the program is to decide what information we need about each member. You've checked over the club records and made up the following summary.

Field	Description	Typical Case		Worst Case	
1	Last name	8	characters	14	characters
2	First name	6	characters	9	characters
3	Street address	18	characters	23	characters
4	City	8	characters	18	characters
5	State	2	characters	2	characters
6	Zip code	6	characters	6	characters
	Total	48	characters	72	characters

Record organization:
Each record will consist of the six fields indicated above. We will use variable length fields. This allows us to use a somewhat shorter record. We anticipate that our longest record will contain about 60 characters (the average of 48 and 72). As a result, we will use a record size of 66 (60 characters + 5 field delimiters + 1 record delimiter). A typical record will look like this:

* = carriage return character

One limitation of using variable length fields is that we have to be careful not to overfill the record. The program must always check the total length of the actual record before we write it, to make sure we don't lose the end of the record.

Let's go over the main parts of the program to see how it works:

Note the fix is used only when records are being edited. It is not needed for initially writing the records (done sequentially) or reading the records.

Line Range	Description
1000-1070	Initialize variables and ask user to insert disk.
1100-1170	Open command channel and data file.
1200-1250	Position to record #1 and input the number of records in the file.
1290-1390	Display main menu, input option chosen and branch to the appropriate part of the program.
1430-1650	Increment count of existing members, input the data for the new member, assemble the record and check it for length. Position to record #1 to update the record count and then store new record in its place.
1690-2110	Input the number of the record to edit, position to the record and read it. Display the existing data, input any changes and rewrite the record. Note the fix when rewriting the record in lines 2000-2060.
2150-2330	Print a list of members on the screen or printer.
2370-2690	Print mailing labels on the screen or printer. If the user presses Q, the printing is suspended after the next label is printed and the user has the option of aborting the print job or restarting it at any point. This is helpful for paper jams!
2730-2790	Close the file and end the program.

```
*****************
PROGRAM: MAIL REL
*****************

0 REM 1541 USER'S GUIDE SECTION 8.9
1 REM  COPYRIGHT: G. NEUFELD, 1984
2 :
3 REM MAIL-LIST PROGRAM USING RELATIVE F
ILE
4 :
1000 REM* MAILING LIST (RELATIVE FILE)
1010 R$=CHR$(13):REM CARRIAGE RETURN CHA
RACTER
1020 PRINT"{CLR} MAILING LIST PROGRAM (R
EL)"
1030 PRINT"{DOWN}INSERT DATA DISKETTE IN
```

```
 DISK DRIVE"
1040 PRINT"{DOWN}PRESS {RVS}RETURN{ROFF}
 WHEN READY"
1050 :
1060 GET A$:IF A$<>"" GOTO 1060
1070 GET A$:IF A$<>CHR$(13) GOTO 1070
1080 :
1090 REM OPEN COMMAND CHANNEL & INITIALI
ZE
1100 OPEN 15,8,15,"IO"
1110 INPUT#15,E,E$,T,S
1120 IF E>19 THEN PRINT E;E$;T;S:CLOSE15
:STOP
1130 :
1140 REM OPEN RELATIVE FILE
1150 OPEN 1,8,7,"MAIL DATA,L,"+CHR$(66)
1160 INPUT#15,E,E$,T,S
1170 IF E>19 THEN PRINT E;E$;T;S:CLOSE15
:STOP
1180 :
1190 REM POSITION TO RECORD #1
1200 PRINT#15,"P"+CHR$(7)+CHR$(1)+CHR$(O
)+CHR$(1)
1210 INPUT#15,E,E$,T,S
1220 :
1230 REM INPUT NUMBER OF EXISTING RECORD
S
1240 INPUT#1,A$:IF A$=""THEN A$="O"
1250 NR=VAL(A$)
1260 :
1270 REM* DISPLAY MENU
1280 :
1290 PRINT"{CLR}{DOWN} MAILING LIST MENU
    "NR"RECORDS"
1300 PRINT"{DOWN}1. ENTER NEW MEMBER"
1310 PRINT"{DOWN}2. EDIT EXISTING RECORD
"
1320 PRINT"{DOWN}3. PRINT MEMBERS LIST"
1330 PRINT"{DOWN}4. PRINT MAILING LABELS
"
1340 PRINT"{DOWN}5. TERMINATE PROGRAM"
1350 PRINT"{DOWN}WHICH OPTION (1-5)"
1360 GETA$:IF A$=""GOTO 1360
1370 A=ASC(A$)-48
1380 IF A<1 OR A>5 GOTO 1360
1390 ON A GOTO 1430,1710,2150,2370,2700
1400 :
1410 REM: ENTER NEW MEMBER
1420 :
1430 NR=NR+1:REM ADD 1 MEMBER
```

```
1440 PRINT"{CLR}{DOWN}   ENTER DATA FOR M
EMBER #"NR
1450 NL$="?":INPUT"{DOWN}LAST NAME:";NL$

1460 NF$="?":INPUT"{DOWN}FIRST NAME:";NF
$
1470 AD$="?":INPUT"{DOWN}STREET ADDRESS:
";AD$
1480 CI$="?":INPUT"{DOWN}CITY/TOWN:";CI$

1490 SA$="?":INPUT"{DOWN}STATE:";SA$
1500 ZP$="?":INPUT"{DOWN}ZIP CODE:";ZP$
1510 F$=NL$+R$+NF$+R$+AD$+R$+CI$+R$+SA$+
R$+ZP$
1520 IF LEN(F$)<60 GOTO 1560
1530 PRINT"{DOWN}ERROR: RECORD IS TOO LO
NG":X=NR
1540 FOR K=1 TO 5000:NEXT:GOTO 2130
1550 :
1560 REM POSITION TO RECORD #1
1570 PRINT#15,"P"+CHR$(7)+CHR$(1)+CHR$(0
)+CHR$(1)
1580 PRINT#1,NR
1590 :
1600 REM POSITION TO RECORD # NR+1
1610 NH = INT((NR+1)/256)
1620 NL = (NR+1) - 256*NH
1630 PRINT#15,"P"+CHR$(7)+CHR$(NL)+CHR$(
NH)+CHR$(1)
1640 PRINT#1,F$
1650 INPUT#15,E,E$,T,S
1660 IF E>19 AND E<>50 THEN PRINT E;E$;T
;S:CLOSE15:STOP
1670 GOTO 1290
1680 :
1690 REM* EDIT EXISTING MEMBER
1700 :
1710 PRINT"{CLR}{DOWN} EDIT EXISTING MEM
BER{DOWN}"
1720 M$="RECORD NUMBER (1-"+MID$(STR$(NR
),2)+")"
1730 PRINTM$;"   0"
1740 PRINT"{UP}"TAB(LEN(M$));:INPUT X$:X
=INT(VAL(X$))
1750 IF X<1 OR X>NR GOTO 1290
1760 :
1770 REM POSITION TO RECORD #X
1780 :
1790 NH = INT((X+1)/256)
1800 NL = (X+1) - 256*NH
```

```
1810 PRINT#15,"P"+CHR$(7)+CHR$(NL)+CHR$(
NH)+CHR$(1)
1820 INPUT#1,NL$,NF$,AD$,CI$,SA$,ZP$
1830 PRINT"{CLR}{DOWN} EXISTING DATA FOR
 MEMBER #"X
1840 PRINT"{DOWN}LAST NAME:   ";NL$
1850 PRINT"{DOWN}FIRST NAME:   ";NF$
1860 PRINT"{DOWN}STREET ADDRESS:   ";AD$
1870 PRINT"{DOWN}CITY/TOWN:   ";CI$
1880 PRINT"{DOWN}STATE:   ";SA$
1890 PRINT"{DOWN}ZIP CODE:   ";ZP$
1900 PRINT"{HOME}{DOWN 3}"TAB(10):INPUT
NL$
1910 PRINT"{DOWN}"TAB(11):INPUT NF$
1920 PRINT"{DOWN}"TAB(15):INPUT AD$
1930 PRINT"{DOWN}"TAB(10):INPUT CI$
1940 PRINT"{DOWN}"TAB(6):INPUT SA$
1950 PRINT"{DOWN}"TAB(9):INPUT ZP$
1960 REM POSITION TO RECORD #X
1970 NH = INT((X+1)/256)
1980 NL = (X+1) - 256*NH
1990 :
2000 REM FIX FOR POSITION PROBLEM
2010 :
2020 PRINT#15,"P"+CHR$(7)+CHR$(NL)+CHR$(
NH)+CHR$(1)
2030 PRINT#15,"P"+CHR$(7)+CHR$(NL)+CHR$(
NH)+CHR$(1)
2040 :
2050 T2 = TI + 30
2060 IF TI<T2 GOTO 2060
2070 :
2080 F$=NL$+R$+NF$+R$+AD$+R$+CI$+R$+SA$+
R$+ZP$
2090 IF LEN(F$)>59 GOTO 1530
2100 PRINT#1,F$
2110 GOTO 1290
2120 :
2130 REM* PRINT LIST OF MEMBERS
2140 :
2150 PRINT"{CLR}{DOWN} PRINT LIST OF MEM
BERS"
2160 INPUT"{DOWN}OUTPUT TO SCREEN OR PRI
NTER (S/P)   S{LEFT 3}";Z$
2170 PRINT:DN=3:IF LEFT$(Z$,1)="P" THEN
DN=4
2180 OPEN 4,DN
2190 FOR K=1 TO NR
2200 REM POSITION TO RECORD #X
2210 NH = INT((K+1)/256)
```

```
2220 NL = (K+1) - 256*NH
2230 PRINT#15,"P"+CHR$(7)+CHR$(NL)+CHR$(
NH)+CHR$(1)
2240 INPUT#1,NL$,NF$,AD$,CI$,SA$,ZP$
2250 PRINT#4,RIGHT$("    "+STR$(K),3);" "
NF$" "NL$
2260 PRINT#4,"     "AD$", "CI$", "SA$", "
ZP$
2270 NEXT
2280 CLOSE4
2290 IF DN=4 GOTO 1290
2300 PRINT"{DOWN}  PRESS {RVS}RETURN{ROF
F} FOR MENU"
2310 GET A$:IF A$<>"" GOTO 2290
2320 GET A$:IF A$<>CHR$(13) GOTO 2320
2330 GOTO 1290
2340 :
2350 REM* PRINT MAILING LABELS
2360 :
2370 PRINT"{CLR}{DOWN} PRINT MAILING LAB
ELS"
2380 INPUT"{DOWN}OUTPUT TO SCREEN OR PRI
NTER (S/P)   S{LEFT 3}";Z$
2390 PRINT"{DOWN}PRESS Q TO SUSPEND PRIN
TING"
2400 PRINT:DN=3:IF LEFT$(Z$,1)="P" THEN
DN=4
2410 OPEN 4,DN
2420 FOR K=1 TO NR
2430 REM POSITION TO RECORD #X
2440 NH = INT((K+1)/256)
2450 NL = (K+1) - 256*NH
2460 PRINT#15,"P"+CHR$(7)+CHR$(NL)+CHR$(
NH)+CHR$(1)
2470 INPUT#1,NL$,NF$,AD$,CI$,SA$,ZP$
2480 PRINT#4,NF$" "NL$","
2490 PRINT#4,AD$","
2500 PRINT#4,CI$", "SA$", "ZP$
2510 PRINT#4:PRINT#4
2520 GET A$:IF A$="Q" GOTO 2610
2530 NEXT
2540 CLOSE4
2550 IF DN=4 GOTO 1290
2560 PRINT"{DOWN}  PRESS {RVS}RETURN{ROF
F} FOR MENU"
2570 GET A$:IF A$<>"" GOTO 2570
2580 GET A$:IF A$<>CHR$(13) GOTO 2580
2590 GOTO 1290
2600 :
2610 PRINT"{DOWN}OUTPUT ABORTED"
```

```
2620 PRINT"{DOWN}COMMANDS:   A = ABORT"
2630 PRINT"              R = RESTART"
2640 GET A$:IF A$="A"THEN CLOSE4:GOTO 12
90
2650 IF A$<>"R" GOTO 2640
2660 PRINT"{DOWN}RECORD #"K"HAS JUST BEE
N PRINTED"
2670 PRINT"{DOWN}RESTART LIST AT RECORD
# "K+1
2680 PRINT"{UP}"TAB(24):INPUT K:PRINT
2690 GOTO 2440
2700 :
2710 REM* TERMINATE PROGRAM
2720 :
2730 REM POSITION TO RECORD #20
2740 NH = 0
2750 NL = 20
2760 PRINT#15,"P"+CHR$(7)+CHR$(NL)+CHR$(
NH)+CHR$(1)
2770 INPUT#15,E,E$,T,S
2780 IF E>19 AND E<>50 THEN PRINT E;E$;T
;S:CLOSE15:STOP
2790 CLOSE1:CLOSE15
2800 :
```

Possible modifications and improvements:

1. Provide a means of recalling records by member's name or zip code rather than by record number.

2. Produce membership lists and mailing lists that are sorted alphabetically or by zip code.

3. Provide a way of deleting a member from the list. At present, the only way to delete a member is to call up his or her record for editing and enter the data for a new member.

INDEXED RELATIVE FILES

NOTE:

This chapter is not designed for beginners. The reader is assumed to be reasonably familiar with both sequential and relative files. The sections dealing with the binary chop should be useful for anyone who has to search ordered lists or arrays.

This chapter takes a more advanced approach to file handling. One or more sequential files are used as indices into a large data base held in a relative file. Many of the commercial data base management systems make use of the techniques discussed in this chapter.

9.1 Introduction to Indexed Relative Files

An indexed relative file is not a special type of data file. The term refers to a file-handling technique that uses a relative file to store data and one or more sequential files to store indices to the main relative file. This is one of the most powerful file-handling techniques available to micro users.

Programming for an application using indexed relative files is somewhat more complex than using either sequential or relative files by themselves. You must maintain a large, relative file that contains the data and one or more sequential files that index the information in the relative file in several ways. Unless these indices are carefully maintained, you will have a mess! However, careful attention to detail will pay off. This technique allows you to store large quantities of data and read or update it in a variety of ways quickly and easily. Some ambitious programmers have built systems that allow you to have several diskettes full of data. A few programmers have even produced programs that allow for variable length records in the main relative file. However, multi-diskette data banks and creating variable length records in a relative file are beyond the scope of this book, and are recommended only for those hackers with masochistic tendencies!

When to use an indexed relative file:

1. If you have very large amounts of data (over 30K).
2. The data must be revised or updated frequently.
3. You must be able to access the data in a variety of ways.

The benefits of using indexed relative files are:

1. They can provide very fast read/write access to any record.
2. They can handle very large amounts of data.
3. They can generate reports in a variety of ways such as by listing members either alphabetically or by zip codes.

The main drawback of using indexed relative files is the complexity of the programming required. Very careful attention to detail is required to program an application using this approach. It is very easy to ruin an index by failing to update it after some operation such as adding or editing a record. Extensive testing is required before you can be confident your program will work correctly.

Some typical uses of indexed relative files are:

1. Mailing or membership lists.
2. Bibliographies.
3. School or medical records.
4. General data base management.

9.2 Organization of the Files

The data is stored in a large, relative file composed of many records. One record usually stores all the information about a single person, place or thing. The records in the file are not sorted. They are simply entered one after another. A data file composed of last names and telephone numbers might look like this:

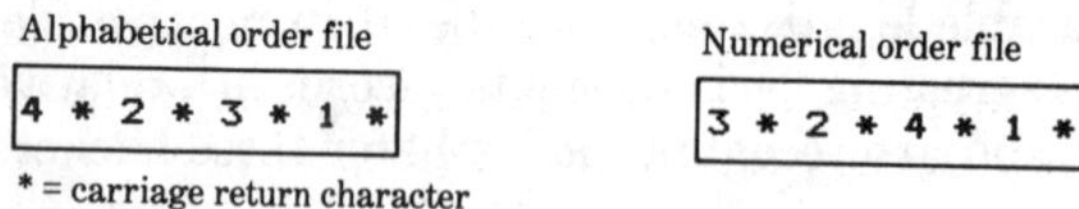

* = carriage return character

In this application there would probably be two sequential files that would serve as indices to the relative file. One file would contain the record numbers in the sequence required to list the records in alphabetic order by name. The second file would contain the record numbers in the sequence required to list the records in numeric order by telephone number. The two sequential, index files for our very simple four record relative file would look like this:

Alphabetical order file

    4 * 2 * 3 * 1 *

Numerical order file

    3 * 2 * 4 * 1 *

* = carriage return character

If we wanted to generate a list of the records in alphabetic order, we would read and print out the records from the relative file in the order specified in the alphabetical order file. If we wanted the list in numeric order, we would read and print out the records from the relative file in the order specified in the numerical order file.

9.3 Planning an Application of Indexed Relative Files

Whenever you want to use an indexed relative file in a program, you should spend some time preplanning both the main, relative file and the index files. It is much easier to fix mistakes before you begin programming than to patch your program later.

The Main Relative File

Since this is a normal relative file, you will have to consider record length and layout. You may use either fixed or variable length fields. In most cases, variable length fields are preferred because of the additional flexibility they provide (the worst case for a last name may really be 16 characters instead of the 14 you counted on). Be sure to make your records long enough!

If you have more than 254 characters of information about each individual, place or thing, it will not all fit into one record. In these situations you will have to decide whether to use two consecutive records in one file or two separate files. If you choose to use two consecutive records in a single file, you will have to program carefully. However, this approach keeps all the information together so that you don't have to access separate files to read all the information about one person, place or thing. If you choose the two file approach, you will have to close one to use the other, because on the 1541 you can have only one relative file open at a time.

The Sequential Index Files

The most important aspect of planning the index files is to decide how many different ways you want to be able to access the data in the main, relative file. In other words, how many different fields will be key fields and be indexed? The more different indices you have, the more ways you can list or scan your data. However, each additional index makes your program more complex. In general, plan on using at least two different indices.

Normally, you don't have to limit the number of index files because of space limitations on the diskette or in memory. These files are quite small, all you are storing in them is a list of numbers. If for some strange reason you do think you might run short of diskette space, you might want to convert the record numbers into lo byte/hi byte form and store CHR\$(lo) and CHR\$(hi) in the sequential file. This allows you to index up to 65,535 records using only two bytes for each. However, you will have to use GET# to retrieve these bytes from the sequential file.

The best tactic for handling the indices is to read them all into arrays in memory at the beginning of your program. This way they are always accessible for fast searching, sorting or scanning. Just before your program terminates, you should rewrite these index files so that you are always sure that they reflect any changes you have made in the relative file. You may want to include a flag that indicates whether or not any changes have been made and eliminate the rewriting of these files if no changes have been made. However, this is not usually necessary because the index files are small, and rewriting them does not take a long time.

An alternative approach would be to store both the record number and part or all of the key field in the sequential index file. With the key field in RAM memory you can search them without having to access the records on diskette. A memory search is faster and there won't be as much wear and tear on your disk drive. However, this technique uses more space both on the diskette and in RAM memory. As a result, this technique is not appropriate for very large data bases.

9.4 Keeping an Index

A significant portion of any program that uses indexed relative files is dedicated to updating the indices whenever a new record is added or a key field of an existing record is modified. To get a feeling for the problems involved, let's consider adding a new record to our four record name and phone number file.

The record we want to add is Brock,4532893.

Here are our existing files. The relative file will be on diskette while the two indices will be in RAM.

Record #1 | Record #2 | Record #3 | Record #4
| Smith,7281495* | Jones,4532659* | Pauls,4531875* | Adams,4533514* |

Alphabetical order file
| 4 * 2 * 3 * 1 * |

Numerical order file
| 3 * 2 * 4 * 1 * |

Our program will contain a record counter so it is easy to tell where to store the new record in the main relative file. It is stored as record #5 (4+1) like this:

Record #1 | Record #2 | Record #3 | Record #4 | Record #5
| Smith,7281495* | Jones,4532659* | Pauls,4531875* | Adams,4533514* | Brock,4532893* |

Storing the record in the relative file was easy. The tough part is updating the indices. How do we determine where Brock fits in among the other records? All we have in memory is a list of record numbers. Obviously, we will have to read some of the records in the relative file to find out.

The brute force method of determining Brock's position in the alphabetical order index would be to start at the beginning of the index and read each corresponding record and compare Brock with the name in the relative file. The process would go something like this:

- Position to record #4 (first in the alphabetic list).
- Read name from record #4 (Adams).
- Compare "Adams" and "Brock" (not far enough yet).

- Position to record #2 (second in the alphabetic list).
- Read name from record #2 (Jones).
- Compare "Jones" and "Brock" (Eureka! we're there).

Shift all numbers in the list up one position, from position #2 on.

Original list: 4 * 2 * 3 * 1 *

After shift: 4 * -* 2 * 3 * 1 *

Insert new record number into position #2 in the list.

Modified list: 4 * 5 * 2 * 3 * 1 *

Now that we have modified the alphabetic list, we have to repeat the process for the numeric list like this:

- Position to record #3 (first in the numeric list).
- Read phone number from record #3 (4531875).
- Compare "4531875" and "4532893" (not far enough yet).

- Position to record #2 (second in the numeric list).
- Read phone number from record #2 (4532659).
- Compare "4532659" and "4532893" (not far enough yet).

- Position to record #4 (third in the numeric list).
- Read phone number from record #4 (4533514).
- Compare "4533514" and "4532893" (Eureka! we're there).

Shift all numbers in the list up one position, from position #3 on.

Original list: 3 * 2 * 4 * 1 *

After shift: 3 * 2 * -* 4 * 1 *

Insert new record number into position #3 in the list.

Modified list: 3 * 2 * 5 * 4 * 1 *

This same process would be followed each time you add a new record. The main problem with this brute force method is that it is slow! The reason for this is the number of records we have to read from the relative file. Accessing the diskette is slow because we have to rely on the movement of mechanical parts. We could speed up our program a great deal if we could reduce the number of diskette accesses we need. The solution to our problem is the BINARY CHOP.

9.5 The Binary Chop

The binary chop is a very rapid way to scan a list. You may be familiar with it from kids' guessing games. Have you ever played the game where one person thinks of a number between one and 100, and the other person has to guess what it is? The way to guess the number in the minimum number of tries is to reduce the number of possibilities in half with each guess. Here's how it works with a number between one and 64.

<table>
<thead>
<tr><th>Player 1</th><th>Player 2</th></tr>
</thead>
<tbody>
<tr><td>Think of a number from 1 to 64.</td><td>Got one!</td></tr>
<tr><td>1 Is it larger than 32? (range=32)</td><td>No!</td></tr>
<tr><td>2 Is it larger than 16? (range=16)</td><td>Yes!</td></tr>
<tr><td>3 Is it larger than 24? (range=8)</td><td>No!</td></tr>
<tr><td>4 Is it larger than 20? (range=4)</td><td>No!</td></tr>
<tr><td>5 Is it larger than 18? (range=2)</td><td>Yes!</td></tr>
<tr><td>6 Is it larger than 19? (range=1)</td><td>Yes!</td></tr>
<tr><td>It must be 20!</td><td>Yes!</td></tr>
</tbody>
</table>

By using the binary chop technique as we did in this game, you can always locate an item in an ordered list very rapidly. The powers of two tell you the maximum number of guesses you'll need:

List length:	64	128	256	512	1024	2048	4096	8192
Max guesses:	6	7	8	9	10	11	12	13

As you can see, the maximum number of guesses needed increases very slowly in comparison to the size of the list. It is one of the most efficient ways of scanning a large, ordered list.

Let's apply the binary chop to scanning our relative file records. Consider the alphabetic list of record numbers. Here is our list:

Alphabetic list: 4 * 2 * 3 * 1 *

We first check to see if our new record fits someplace between the smallest and the largest values. In this case, record #4 is the smallest and record #1 is the largest. We have to check these end points because our new record might fit before the first existing record or after the last existing record.

- Look up first index number in alphabetic list (it's four).
- Position to record #4 (smallest).
- Read name from record #4 (Adams).
- Compare "Adams" and "Brock" (doesn't come before the first record).

- Look up last index number in alphabetic list (it's one).
- Position to record #1 (largest).
- Read name from record #1 (Smith).
- Compare "Smith" and "Brock" (doesn't come after the last record).

Since our new record fits somewhere between the first and the last, we have determined upper and lower limits on its position:

lower limit = position #1 in list = smallest record = record #4
upper limit = position #4 in list = largest record = record #1

To apply the binary chop method, we then split the range in half by finding the midpoint (average) between the positions of the records that are our upper and lower limits.

Average of positions of upper and lower limit
= (1 + 4)/2
= 2.5
= 2

In this case our average is not an integer. Since we can't position to record #2.5, we had better drop the fraction and settle on two. We would use the integer function (INT) to do this for us in a program.

- Look up the record# in position #2 of our alphabetic list (it's two).
- Position to record #2 (first average).
- Read name from record #2 (Jones).
- Compare "Jones" and "Brock" (too high).

The position of our new upper limit is two (since we were too high).
The position of our old lower limit is one (only changes if too low).

Split the range in half again by finding the midpoint (average) of the positions of our new upper and lower limits.

Average of positions of upper and lower limit
= (1 + 2)/2
= 1.5
= 1

At this point our average of the positions and the position of our lower limit are equal. This happens only when the positions of our upper and lower limits are one apart. This tells us that we have reached the end of our testing. The new value fits between our upper and lower limits!

We have found where the new value goes, so insert it into the alphabetic list.

Shift all numbers in the list up one, from position #2 on.

Original list: 4 * 2 * 3 * 1 *

After shift: 4 * -* 2 * 3 * 1 *

Insert new record number into the list.

Modified list: 4 * 5 * 2 * 3 * 1 *

In this situation, we didn't save any disk accesses by using the binary chop method. However, we used a very small relative file. As the file gets larger and larger, the binary chop begins to shine. Just take a look at this table:

Average Number of Disk Accesses to Scan an Ordered List

Length of List	8	16	32	64	128	256	512	1024	2048	4096
Binary Chop*	5	6	7	8	9	10	11	12	13	14
Brute Force**	4	8	16	32	64	128	256	512	1024	2048

* Assumes two end point accesses plus others.
** Average number of disk accesses.

The time and effort of programming the binary chop as illustrated in the typical application at the end of this chapter is well worth it.

9.6 Programming the Binary Chop

The binary chop makes a very useful subroutine that you can insert into any program in which you need to scan an ordered list. When you want to use it, you just pass it the search image you want, and the routine will find where it should fit in the list.

Definition of variables used: .

SI$	= Search image (the item to be inserted).
RN	= Record number (to be inserted into the index list).
IX()	= Index list (one dimensional array).
NR	= Number of items in old list (the starting upper limit).
FI$	= Image found in the file when we looked.
MAX	= Current upper limit.
MIN	= Current lower limit.
AVG	= Average of lower and upper limit.
R	= Record number to look up on disk (used by subroutine at line 6000).

```
5000 :                                           Check if new fits before first.
5010 R=IX(1)                                      Find record # offirst in list.
5020 GOSUB 6000                                   Read first record.
5030 IF SI$<FI$ THEN MAX=1 GOTO 5210              New fits before first.
5040 :                                            Check if new fits after last.
5050 R=IX(NR)                                      Find record # of last in list.
5060 GOSUB 6000                                   Read last record.
5070 IF SI$>FI$ THEN MAX=NR+1:GOTO 5240           New fits after last.
5080 :                                            We now know new fits somewhere
5090 :                                                between first and last.
5100 MIN=1:MAX=NR                                 Set lower & upper limits.
5110 AVG = INT((MAX+MIN)/2)                        Find average of upper & lower.
5120 IF AVG = MIN GOTO 5210                       We are done so jump out.
5130 R=IX(AVG)                                     Find record # of average.
5140 GOSUB 6000                                   Read average record.
5150 IF SI$<FI$ THEN MAX=AVG:GOTO 5110            New fits before average so set upper
5160 :                                                limit to average.
5170 IF SI$>FI$ THEN MIN=AVG:GOTO 5110            New fits after average so set lower
5180 :                                                limit to average.
5190 MIN=AVG:MAX=AVG+1                             New equals file value so we put new
5200 :                                                just after old.
5210 FOR K=NR TO MAX STEP -1                      Shift index numbers up one.
5220 : IX(K+1) = IX(K)
5230 NEXT
5240 IX(MAX) = RN                                 Insert new's record number.
5250 RETURN


6000 H=INT(R/256)                                 Find hi byte of record #.
6010 L=R-RH*256                                   Find lo byte of record #.
6020 PRINT#15, "P"CHR$(4)CHR$(L)CHR$(H)CH         Position to record.
R$(1)
6030 INPUT#1,FI$,B$,C$,C$                          Read record.
6040 RETURN
```

9.7 Alternate Uses for the Binary Chop

The binary chop is very versatile. Here are a few ways you might use it in different situations:

1. Searching for one particular item in the file.

This is a very common application. It would be useful to scan the file to locate the record# of an employee with a particular name, social security number or phone number. Let's see how we can modify our listing to adapt it to this application. In line 5150 we check if the search image, SI$, is less than the image from the file, FI$. In line 5170 we check if SI$ is greater than FI$. This means that in order for line 5180 to be executed, SI$ must equal FI$. To convert our listing into a search for a particular record, all we do is add a new line 5180 something like this:

```
5180 PRINT "RECORD #"R"IS THE ONE YOU WANT":RETURN
```

If the condition in 5120 is satisfied, AVG=MIN, we know that the item we were looking for is not in the file. To report this we could change line 5210 to read:

```
5210 PRINT "RECORD NOT FOUND IN THE FILE":RETURN
```

For this application, lines 5220 to 5250 are not required and should be deleted from the listing.

2. Searching for a range of values in the file.

This is another common application. For example, you might want to find the record numbers of all members having zip codes in the range of 60203 to 61258 or names between JONES and SMITH. For this application we really have two situations, one where we are looking for the top of our range, and the other for the bottom of our range. Rather than try to make our subroutine handle both jobs at once, we will use two calls to it and use a flag variable, FL, to indicate whether we want the upper limit (FL=1) or the lower limit (FL=0).

The main modification to our routine has to do with what happens when the file image, FI$, equals our search image, SI$. In this application, we may have several records that produce the match. For example, if we are looking for all those individuals having zip codes between 60000 and 61999, we will probably have several individuals in zip code area 60000 and several in 61999. This means we can't just quit when we find the first person with a particular zip code. We have to define the exact upper and lower boundaries. Here's how we do it.

Change lines 5180 and 5190 to read:

```
5180 IF FL=0 THEN MAX=AVG:GOTO 5110      Looking for lower.
5190 IF FL=1 THEN MIN=AVG:GOTO 5110      Looking for upper.
```

These two lines force the routine to find the exact lower limit when FL=0 and the exact upper limit when FL=1. Let's see how this works with a very simple example. This is a small part of a file with 48 records. Our search image, SI$, is 60000 and FL=0 (find lower limit).

#	FI\$	Pass	MAX	MIN	AVG	FI\$		SI\$	Result
31	60201	1	48	1	24	59589	<	60000	MIN = AVG
30	60000	2	48	24	36	?	>	60000	MAX=AVG
29	60000	3	36	24	30	60000	=	60000	MAX=AVG
28	60000	4	30	24	27	60000	=	60000	MAX=AVG
27	60000	5	27	24	25	59789	<	60000	MIN = AVG
26	60000	6	27	25	26	60000	=	60000	MAX=AVG
25	59789	7	26	25	25	Quit since MIN=AVG			
24	59589								

When our routine quits after looking for the lower limit (FL=0), MAX contains the number of the first record that we want. If we were looking for the upper limit (FL=1), MIN would contain the last record that we want. We can simplify our subroutine call slightly if we always return the boundary value in the same variable by adding these lines.

```
5210 IF FL=0 THEN LIMIT = MAX
5220 IF FL=1 THEN LIMIT = MIN
5230 RETURN
```

For this application lines 5240 and 5250 are not required and should be deleted from the listing.

9.8 Programming Considerations for Indexed Relative Files

There are several things that you should consider when programming an application that uses indexed relative files.

1. How large will the data base become?

Most data bases grow rapidly over time. If there is any possibility of your data base growing so large that it won't all fit on a single diskette, you should plan your program accordingly. One possible way to accomodate a large data base would be to plan to store the program and the index files on diskette #1, and the relative file(s) on diskettes #2, #3, etc. If you plan to use this approach, you must design your program so that all files are closed except when data is actually being read or written. This will allow you to swap diskettes. Be sure to remember to include the diskette number as well as the record number in the indices.

2. How many different indices will I need?

It is always difficult to foresee all the different ways you might want to access or scan your data. As a general rule, if you think that you might ever want your data indexed in a particular way, include it from the start! However, if you find that you do need to index your existing data base by a new field, you can do it. To create the new index file you will need to go through the entire relative file record by record reading the field of interest. The field followed by the record number is put into an array, the array is sorted, and then the new index file is written out like this:

```
100 DIM NI$(K)          Dimension temp array.
110 OPEN 15,8,15, "IO"  Open command channel.
120 OPEN 1,8,5, "REL DATA"  Open relative file.
```

```
130 FOR K=1 TO NR                          Loop for all records.
140 H=INT(K/256)                           Find lo & hi bytes of record number.
150 L=K-256*H
160 PRINT#15,"P"CHR$(5)CHR$(L)CHR$(H)CHR    Position to record.
$(1)
170 INPUT#1,A$,B$,C$,D$,E$,F$               Use D$ for new index.
180 NI$(K)=D$+RIGHT$("        "+STR$(K),4)  Store image + record #.
190 NEXT K
200 CLOSE 1
::::
Sort NI$ using your favorite sort
::::
300 OPEN 2,8,4,"NEW INDEX,S,W"             Open new index file.
310 FOR K=1 TO NR                          Loop for all records.
320 R=VAL(RIGHT$(NI$(K),4))                Extract record number.
330 PRINT#2,R                              Write index number.
340 NEXT K
350 CLOSE2:CLOSE15
```

3. What happens when your file is empty?

Don't get so involved in planning for your large data base that you forget to think about what happens when you first run your program. Remember that none of your files will even exist.

4. Have you covered all the possibilities?

Careful planning and extensive testing is required to make sure you have considered all possibilities. Often the possibilities of a new record coming at the very beginning or the very end of a file are overlooked.

5. How will you handle deletions from the file?

The easiest way to handle deletions is simply to use the edit record function to call up the record to be deleted, edit it to all blanks and delete that record number from the indices. If you decide to use this technique, you might change the printout routines to skip over blank records. The problem with this approach is that if you have many deletions, the file will gradually fill up with blank records. Another way of handling deletions is to use the edit function to insert the information for a new member into the record of the member to be deleted. This, however, assumes a relatively knowledgeable user. A more elegant approach would be to automatically blank the record to be deleted and save the record number in a file of deleted record numbers. When you want to add new information to the file, the program should first check to see if there were any deleted records where it could store the new information before it added a new record to the file. This is a nice, elegant solution but somewhat tricky to implement.

REMINDER:

You must always specify the byte position in a POSITION command.

Use the fix for the POSITION command (see Section 8.6) whenever your program calls for writing or reading records in the relative file in a non-sequential manner.

9.9 Typical Application

For each of the chapters on file handling (Chapters 6, 7, 8 and 9), I have developed a mailing list program to illustrate a practical use for the techniques you have learned. Only those portions of the program that deal with data handling are changed from one chapter to the next. The portions relating to data entry, editing and printouts remain the same.

In this chapter, the mailing list program uses an indexed relative file for storing the data about the club members. The records are stored in the relative file in the order in which they are entered. The relative file is indexed alphabetically by last name/first name and by zip codes. To retrieve a record for editing, you must know its record number. The record numbers are given on the membership list printout.

Background information:
You've just been elected secretary of a local civic organization. As secretary, you are responsible for making up mailing labels for the monthly newsletter that goes out to all 500 members. You would like to use your new computer to take some of the drudgery out of the task.

Analysis of the problem:
You need a simple mailing list program to keep track of the names and addresses of the 500 members. The program should allow you to add new members, modify members' names and addresses, and produce an alphabetized list of members or a set of mailing labels sorted by zip codes.

Planning a record:
The first step in planning the program is to decide what information we need about each member. You've checked over the club records and made up the following summary.

Field	Description	Typical Case	Worst Case
1	Last name	8 characters	14 characters
2	First name	6 characters	9 characters
3	Street address	18 characters	23 characters
4	City	8 characters	18 characters
5	State	2 characters	2 characters
6	Zip code	6 characters	6 characters
	Total	48 characters	72 characters

Record organization:
Each record in the relative file will consist of the six fields indicated above. We will use variable length fields. This allows us to use a somewhat shorter record. We anticipate that our longest record will contain about 60 characters (the average of 48 and 72). As a result, we will use a record size of 66 (60 characters + 5 field delimiters + 1 record delimiter). A typical record will look like this:

* = carriage return character

One limitation of using variable length fields is that we have to be careful not to overfill the record. The program must always check the total length of the actual record before we write it to make sure we don't lose the end of the record.

Indices:
Since we need to be able to produce an alphabetized list and a set of labels sorted by zip codes, we need to have two index files.

Let's go over the main parts of the program to see how it works:

Line Range	Description
1000-1100	Initialize variables and ask user to insert disk.
1120-1200	Open command channel and data file.
1220-1280	Position to record #1 and input the number of records in the file. If there are no records, branch to menu.
1300-1460	Open the alphabetic index file, read the index into an array, and then close the file. Repeat for the zip code index.
1500-1610	Display main menu, input option chosen and branch to the appropriate part of the program.
1650-1860	Increment count of existing members, input the data for the new member, assemble the record and check it for length. Position to record #1 to update to record count and then store new record in its place.
1880-1910	Call routines to sort the new record into the two indices.
1950-2390	Input the number of the record to edit, position to the record and read it. Display the existing data, input any changes, rewrite the record, and if any changes have been made in the key fields, re-sort the record into the indices.
2410-2650	Subroutines to delete the edited record's number from the indices and then re-sort the record into the indices again. This is needed because editing may have changed the record's position.
2690-2960	Print a list of members on the screen or printer. The list may be sorted alphabetically or by zip code.
3000-3370	Print mailing labels on the screen or printer. The labels may be sorted alphabetically or by zip code. If the user presses Q, the printing

is suspended after the next label is printed and the user has the option of aborting the print job or restarting it at any point. This is helpful for paper jams!

3410-3720	Close the main relative file, rewrite the two index files and end the program.
3740-3980	Subroutine to find a record's correct position in the alphabetic index and insert the record number into the index.
4010-4240	Subroutine to find a record's correct position in the zip code index and insert the record number into the index.
4260-4320	Subroutine to position to record number "k" in the main relative file and read the name field.
4350-4400	Subroutine to position to record number "k" in the main relative file and read the zip code field.

```
********************
PROGRAM: MAIL INDEX
********************

0 REM 1541 USER'S GUIDE SECTION 9.9
1 REM  COPYRIGHT: G. NEUFELD, 1984
2 :
3 REM MAIL-LIST PROGRAM USING INDEXED RE
LATIVE FILE
4 :
1000 REM* MAILING LIST (INDEXED RELATIVE
)
1010 DIM AX(500),ZX(500)
1020 R$=CHR$(13):REM CARRIAGE RETURN CHA
RACTER
1030 PRINTCHR$(14)CHR$(8)
1040 PRINT"{CLR} {RVS}        MAILING LIST
 PROGRAM        "
1050 PRINT"{DOWN}INSERT DATA DISKETTE IN
 DISK DRIVE"
1060 PRINT"{DOWN}        PRESS {RVS}RETURN{
ROFF} WHEN READY"
1070 :
1080 GET A$:IF A$<>"" GOTO 1080
1090 GET A$:IF A$<>CHR$(13) GOTO 1090
1100 PRINT"{UP} ONE MOMENT PLEASE WHILE
I SET UP"
1110 :
1120 REM OPEN COMMAND CHANNEL & INITIALI
ZE
1130 OPEN 15,8,15,"IO"
1140 INPUT#15,E,E$,T,S
```

```
1150 IF E>19 THEN PRINT E;E$;T;S:CLOSE15
:STOP
1160 :
1170 REM OPEN RELATIVE FILE
1180 OPEN 1,8,7,"INX MAIL DATA,L,"+CHR$(
66)
1190 INPUT#15,E,E$,T,S
1200 IF E>19 THEN PRINT E;E$;T;S:CLOSE15
:STOP
1210 :
1220 REM POSITION TO RECORD #1
1230 PRINT#15,"P"+CHR$(7)+CHR$(1)+CHR$(0
)+CHR$(1)
1240 INPUT#15,E,E$,T,S
1250 :
1260 REM INPUT NUMBER OF EXISTING RECORD
S
1270 INPUT#1,A$:IF A$="" OR A$=CHR$(255)
 THEN A$="0"
1280 NR=VAL(A$):IF NR=0 GOTO 1500
1290 :
1300 REM INPUT ALPHABETIC INDEX
1310 OPEN2,8,6,"ALPHA INDEX,S,R"
1320 INPUT#15,E,E$,T,S
1330 IF E>19 THEN PRINTE;E$;T;S:CLOSE2:C
LOSE1:CLOSE15:STOP
1340 FOR K=1 TO NR
1350 : INPUT#2, AX(K)
1360 NEXT
1370 CLOSE 2
1380 :
1390 REM INPUT ZIP CODE INDEX
1400 OPEN2,8,6,"ZIP INDEX,S,R"
1410 INPUT#15,E,E$,T,S
1420 IF E>19 THEN PRINTE;E$;T;S:CLOSE2:C
LOSE1:CLOSE15:STOP
1430 FOR K=1 TO NR
1440 : INPUT#2, ZX(K)
1450 NEXT
1460 CLOSE 2
1470 :
1480 REM* DISPLAY MENU
1490 :
1500 PRINT"{CLR}{DOWN}{RVS} MAILING LIST
 MENU    "NR"{LEFT} RECORDS {RVS}"
1510 PRINT"{DOWN}1. ENTER NEW MEMBER"
1520 PRINT"{DOWN}2. EDIT EXISTING RECORD
"
1530 PRINT"{DOWN}3. PRINT MEMBERS LIST"
1540 PRINT"{DOWN}4. PRINT MAILING LABELS
"
```

```
1550 PRINT"{DOWN}5. TERMINATE PROGRAM"
1560 PRINT"{DOWN}{RVS}   WHICH OPTION (1-
5) ";
1570 GETA$:IF A$=""GOTO 1570
1580 A=ASC(A$)-48
1590 IF A<1 OR A>5 GOTO 1570
1600 PRINTA$" "
1610 ON A GOTO 1650,1950,2690,3000,3420
1620 :
1630 REM: ENTER NEW MEMBER
1640 :
1650 NR=NR+1:REM ADD 1 MEMBER
1660 PRINT"{CLR}{RVS}   ENTER DATA FOR ME
MBER #"NR"{LEFT}   "
1670 NL$="?":INPUT"{DOWN}LAST NAME:";NL$

1680 NF$="?":INPUT"{DOWN}FIRST NAME:";NF
$
1690 AD$="?":INPUT"{DOWN}STREET ADDRESS:
";AD$
1700 CI$="?":INPUT"{DOWN}CITY/TOWN:";CI$

1710 SA$="?":INPUT"{DOWN}STATE:";SA$
1720 ZP$="?":INPUT"{DOWN}ZIP CODE:";ZP$
1730 F$=NL$+R$+NF$+R$+AD$+R$+CI$+R$+SA$+
R$+ZP$
1740 IF LEN(F$)<60 GOTO 1780
1750 PRINT"{DOWN}{RVS}ERROR: RECORD IS T
OO LONG":X=NR
1760 FOR K=1 TO 5000:NEXT:GOTO 2670
1770 :
1780 PRINT"{DOWN}{RVS}ONE MOMENT PLEASE
WHILE I UPDATE"
1790 :
1800 REM POSITION TO RECORD # NR+1
1810 NH = INT((NR+1)/256)
1820 NL = (NR+1) - 256*NH
1830 PRINT#15,"P"+CHR$(7)+CHR$(NL)+CHR$(
NH)+CHR$(1)
1840 PRINT#1,F$
1850 INPUT#15,E,E$,T,S
1860 IF E>19 AND E<>50 THEN PRINT E;E$;T
;S:CLOSE15:STOP
1870 :
1880 VX=NR
1890 GOSUB 3750: REM INSERT INTO ALPHABE
TIC INDEX
1900 GOSUB 4010: REM INSERT INTO ZIP COD
E INDEX
1910 GOTO 1500
1920 :
```

```
1930 REM* EDIT EXISTING MEMBER
1940 :
1950 PRINT"{CLR}{DOWN}{RVS} EDIT EXISTIN
G MEMBER {DOWN}"
1960 M$="RECORD NUMBER (1-"+MID$(STR$(NR
),2)+")"
1970 PRINTM$;"  0"
1980 PRINT"{UP}"TAB(LEN(M$));:INPUT X$:X
=INT(VAL(X$))
1990 IF X<1 OR X>NR GOTO 1500
2000 :
2010 REM POSITION TO RECORD #X
2020 :
2030 NH = INT((X+1)/256)
2040 NL = (X+1) - 256*NH
2050 PRINT#15,"P"+CHR$(7)+CHR$(NL)+CHR$(
NH)+CHR$(1)
2060 INPUT#1,NL$,NF$,AD$,CI$,SA$,ZP$
2070 PRINT"{CLR}{DOWN}{RVS} EXISTING DAT
A FOR MEMBER #"X"{LEFT}   "
2080 PRINT"{DOWN}LAST NAME:   ";NL$
2090 PRINT"{DOWN}FIRST NAME:   ";NF$
2100 PRINT"{DOWN}STREET ADDRESS:   ";AD$
2110 PRINT"{DOWN}CITY/TOWN:   ";CI$
2120 PRINT"{DOWN}STATE:   ";SA$
2130 PRINT"{DOWN}ZIP CODE:   ";ZP$
2140 PRINT"{HOME}{DOWN 3}"TAB(10):INPUT
TL$
2150 PRINT"{DOWN}"TAB(11):INPUT TF$
2160 PRINT"{DOWN}"TAB(15):INPUT AD$
2170 PRINT"{DOWN}"TAB(10):INPUT CI$
2180 PRINT"{DOWN}"TAB(6):INPUT SA$
2190 PRINT"{DOWN}"TAB(9):INPUT TP$
2200 PRINT"{DOWN}{RVS}ONE MOMENT PLEASE
WHILE I UPDATE"
2210 :
2220 REM POSITION TO RECORD #X
2230 NH = INT((X+1)/256)
2240 NL = (X+1) - 256*NH
2250 :
2260 REM  FIX FOR POSITION ERROR
2270 :
2280 PRINT#15,"P"+CHR$(7)+CHR$(NL)+CHR$(
NH)+CHR$(1)
2290 PRINT#15,"P"+CHR$(7)+CHR$(NL)+CHR$(
NH)+CHR$(1)
2300 :
2310 T2 = TI + 30
2320 IF TI<T2 GOTO 2320
2330 :
```

```
2340 F$=TL$+R$+TF$+R$+AD$+R$+CI$+R$+SA$+
R$+TP$
2350 IF LEN(F$)>59 GOTO 1750
2360 PRINT#1,F$
2370 IF TF$<>NF$ OR TL$<>NL$ THEN NF$=TF
$:NL$=TL$:GOSUB 2420
2380 IF TP$<>ZP$ THEN ZP$=TP$:GOSUB 2550

2390 GOTO 1500
2400 :
2410 REM* SQUEEZE OUT RECORD FROM ALPHA
INDEX
2420 FOR K=1 TO NR:REM FIND OLD POSITION

2430 : IF X=AX(K) GOTO 2450
2440 NEXT
2450 IF K>=NR GOTO 2490
2460 FOR L=K TO NR
2470 : AX(L)=AX(L+1)
2480 NEXT
2490 AX(NR)=0
2500 VX=X
2510 GOSUB 3750: REM INSERT INTO ALPHABE
TIC INDEX
2520 RETURN
2530 :
2540 REM* SQUEEZE OUT RECORD FROM ZIP IN
DEX
2550 FOR K=1 TO NR:REM FIND OLD POSITION

2560 : IF X=ZX(K) GOTO 2580
2570 NEXT
2580 IF K>=NR GOTO 2620
2590 FOR L=K TO NR
2600 : ZX(L)=ZX(L+1)
2610 NEXT
2620 ZX(NR)=0
2630 VX=X
2640 GOSUB 4010: REM INSERT INTO ZIP COD
E INDEX
2650 RETURN
2660 :
2670 REM* PRINT LIST OF MEMBERS
2680 :
2690 PRINT"{CLR}{DOWN}{RVS} PRINT LIST O
F MEMBERS "
2700 INPUT"{DOWN}OUTPUT TO SCREEN OR PRI
NTER (S/P)   S{LEFT 3}";Z$
2710 DN=3:IF LEFT$(Z$,1)="P" THEN DN=4
2720 INPUT"{DOWN}SORTED BY NAME OR ZIP C
ODE (N/Z)   N{LEFT 3}";Z$
```

```
2730 FL=0: IF LEFT$(Z$,1)="Z" THEN FL=1
2740 PRINT"{CLR}{RVS}REC#        LIST OF M
EMBERS     {DOWN}"
2750 OPEN 4,DN
2760 FOR K=1 TO NR
2770 IF FL=0 THEN X=AX(K)
2780 IF FL=1 THEN X=ZX(K)
2790 REM POSITION TO RECORD #X
2800 NH = INT((X+1)/256)
2810 NL = (X+1) - 256*NH
2820 PRINT#15,"P"+CHR$(7)+CHR$(NL)+CHR$(
NH)+CHR$(1)
2830 INPUT#1,NL$,NF$,AD$,CI$,SA$,ZP$
2840 PRINT#4,RIGHT$("      "+STR$(X),3);"
 "NF$" "NL$", "AD$
2850 PRINT#4,"         "CI$", "SA$", "ZP$
2860 IF INT(K/10)<>K/10 GOTO 2900
2870 PRINT"{DOWN}  PRESS {RVS}RETURN{ROF
F} FOR MORE"
2880 GET A$: IF A$<>CHR$(13) GOTO 2880
2890 PRINT"{CLR}{RVS}REC#        LIST OF M
EMBERS     {DOWN}"
2900 NEXT
2910 CLOSE4
2920 IF DN=4 GOTO 1500
2930 PRINT"{DOWN}  PRESS {RVS}RETURN{ROF
F} FOR MENU"
2940 GET A$: IF A$<>"" GOTO 2920
2950 GET A$: IF A$<>CHR$(13) GOTO 2950
2960 GOTO 1500
2970 :
2980 REM* PRINT MAILING LABELS
2990 :
3000 PRINT"{CLR}{DOWN}{RVS} PRINT MAILIN
G LABELS "
3010 INPUT"{DOWN}OUTPUT TO SCREEN OR PRI
NTER (S/P)  S{LEFT 3}";Z$
3020 :
3030 DN=3: IF LEFT$(Z$,1)="P" THEN DN=4
3040 INPUT"{DOWN}SORTED BY NAME OR ZIP C
ODE (N/Z)  N{LEFT 3}";Z$
3050 FL=0: IF LEFT$(Z$,1)="Z" THEN FL=1
3060 PRINT"{CLR}{DOWN}{RVS} PRINTING MAI
LING LABELS "
3070 PRINT"{DOWN}PRESS Q TO SUSPEND PRIN
TING{DOWN}"
3080 OPEN 4,DN
3090 FOR K=1 TO NR
3100 IF FL=0 THEN X=AX(K)
3110 IF FL=1 THEN X=ZX(K)
3120 NH = INT((X+1)/256)
```

```
3130 NL = (X+1) - 256*NH
3140 PRINT#15,"P"+CHR$(7)+CHR$(NL)+CHR$(
NH)+CHR$(1)
3150 INPUT#1,NL$,NF$,AD$,CI$,SA$,ZP$
3160 PRINT#4,NF$" "NL$","
3170 PRINT#4,AD$","
3180 PRINT#4,CI$", "SA$", "ZP$
3190 PRINT#4:PRINT#4
3200 GET A$:IF A$="Q" GOTO 3290
3210 NEXT
3220 CLOSE4
3230 IF DN=4 GOTO 1500
3240 PRINT"{DOWN}  PRESS {RVS}RETURN{ROF
F} FOR MENU"
3250 GET A$:IF A$<>"" GOTO 3250
3260 GET A$:IF A$<>CHR$(13) GOTO 3260
3270 GOTO 1500
3280 :
3290 PRINT"{DOWN}OUTPUT ABORTED"
3300 PRINT"{DOWN}COMMANDS:  A = ABORT"
3310 PRINT"              R = RESTART"
3320 GET A$:IF A$="A"THEN CLOSE4:GOTO 15
00
3330 IF A$<>"R" GOTO 3320
3340 PRINT"{DOWN}LABEL #"K"HAS JUST BEEN
 PRINTED"
3350 PRINT"{DOWN}RESTART LIST AT LABEL #
 "K+1
3360 PRINT"{UP}"TAB(23):INPUT K:PRINT
3370 GOTO 3100
3380 :
3390 REM* TERMINATE PROGRAM
3400 :
3410 REM POSITION TO RECORD #1 & STORE N
R
3420 PRINT"{DOWN}{RVS}ONE MOMENT PLEASE
WHILE I TIDY UP!"
3430 PRINT#15,"P"+CHR$(7)+CHR$(1)+CHR$(0
)+CHR$(1)
3440 PRINT#1,NR
3450 :
3460 REM POSITION TO RECORD #20
3470 NL = 20
3480 NH = 0
3490 PRINT#15,"P"+CHR$(7)+CHR$(NL)+CHR$(
NH)+CHR$(1)
3500 INPUT#15,E,E$,T,S
3510 IF E>19 AND E<>50 THEN PRINT E;E$;T
;S:CLOSE15:STOP
3520 CLOSE1
3530 :
```

```
3540 REM WRITE ALPHABETIC INDEX
3550 OPEN2,8,6,"@0:ALPHA INDEX,S,W"
3560 INPUT#15,E,E$,T,S
3570 IF E>19 THEN PRINTE;E$;T;S:CLOSE2:P
RINT#15,"IO":GOTO3550
3580 FOR K=1 TO NR
3590 : PRINT# 2, AX(K)
3600 NEXT
3610 CLOSE 2
3620 :
3630 REM WRITE ZIP CODE INDEX
3640 OPEN2,8,6,"@0:ZIP INDEX,S,W"
3650 INPUT#15,E,E$,T,S
3660 IF E>19 THEN PRINTE;E$;T;S:CLOSE2:P
RINT#15,"IO":GOTO3640
3670 FOR K=1 TO NR
3680 : PRINT# 2, ZX(K)
3690 NEXT
3700 CLOSE 2
3710 PRINTCHR$(9)CHR$(142)"{CLR}BYE"
3720 CLOSE15:END
3730 :
3740 REM* FIND CORRECT POSITION IN ALPHA
BETIC INDEX
3750 MX=NR:MN=1:OA=0:IF NR=1 GOTO 3970
3760 SI$=NL$+" "+NF$:REM MAKE SEARCH IMA
GE
3770 :
3780 K=AX(1):GOSUB4260:REM* LOWER LIMIT
IMAGE
3790 OU$=ZI$
3800 IF SI$<OU$ THEN MX=1:GOTO 3930:REM
BEFORE FIRST
3810 :
3820 K=AX(NR-1):GOSUB4260:REM* UPPER LIM
IT IMAGE
3830 UL$=ZI$
3840 IF SI$>UL$ THEN MX=NR:GOTO 3970:REM
 AFTER LAST
3850 :
3860 NA=INT((MX+MN)/2)
3870 IF NA=MN GOTO 3930:REM FOUND THE SP
OT
3880 K=AX(NA):GOSUB4260:REM* FIND AVERAG
E IMAGE
3890 IF SI$<ZI$THENUL$=ZI$:MX=NA:GOTO 38
60
3900 IF SI$=ZI$ THEN MN=NA:MX=NA+1:GOTO3
860
3910 IF SI$>ZI$THENOU$=ZI$:MN=NA:GOTO 38
60
```

```
3920 REM* SHIFT UP
3930 FOR K=NR TO MX STEP-1
3940 AX(K+1)=AX(K)
3950 NEXT
3960 :
3970 AX(MX)=VX:REM* INSERT INTO INDEX
3980 RETURN
3990 :
4000 REM* FIND CORRECT POSITION IN ZIP C
ODE INDEX
4010 MX=NR:MN=1:OA=0:IFNR=1 GOTO 4230
4020 SI$=ZP$:REM MAKE SEARCH IMAGE
4030 :
4040 K=ZX(1):GOSUB4340:REM* LOWER LIMIT
IMAGE
4050 OL$=ZI$
4060 IF SI$<OL$ THEN MX=1:GOTO 4190:REM
BEFORE FIRST
4070 :
4080 K=ZX(NR-1):GOSUB4340:REM* UPPER LIM
IT IMAGE
4090 OU$=ZI$
4100 IF SI$>OU$ THEN MX=NR:GOTO 4230:REM
 AFTER LAST
4110 :
4120 NA=INT((MX+MN)/2)
4130 IF NA=MN GOTO 4190:REM FOUND THE SP
OT
4140 K=ZX(NA):GOSUB4340:REM* FIND AVERAG
E IMAGE
4150 IF SI$<ZI$THENUL$=ZI$:MX=NA:GOTO 41
20
4160 IF SI$=ZI$ THEN MN=NA:MX=NA+1:GOTO
4120
4170 IF SI$>ZI$THENOU$=ZI$:MN=NA:GOTO 41
20
4180 REM* SHIFT UP
4190 FOR K=NR TO MX STEP -1
4200 ZX(K+1)=ZX(K)
4210 NEXT
4220 :
4230 ZX(MX)=VX:REM* INSERT INTO INDEX
4240 RETURN
4250 :
4260 REM FIND NAME IMAGE FOR RECORD #K
4270 NH = INT((K+1)/256)
4280 NL = (K+1) - 256*NH
4290 PRINT#15,"P"+CHR$(7)+CHR$(NL)+CHR$(
NH)+CHR$(1)
4300 INPUT#1,LZ$,FZ$,AZ$,CZ$,SZ$,ZZ$
4310 ZI$=LZ$+" "+FZ$
```

```
4320 RETURN
4330 :
4340 REM FIND ZIP CODE FOR RECORD #K
4350 NH = INT((K+1)/256)
4360 NL = (K+1) - 256*NH
4370 PRINT#15,"P"+CHR$(7)+CHR$(NL)+CHR$(
NH)+CHR$(1)
4380 INPUT#1,LZ$,FZ$,AZ$,CZ$,SZ$,ZZ$
4390 ZI$=ZZ$
4400 RETURN
```

Possible modifications and improvements:

1. Modify the editing routine to allow a record to be recalled by the member's name rather than by record number.

2. Allow the deletion of records and keep a file of deleted records that is scanned whenever a new member is added so that the new information displaces obsolete information in the file rather than expands the file.

3. Modify the label printout routine to provide for selective mailing to all individuals living within a certain geographic area (having a certain range of zip codes).

CHAPTER 10

MACHINE LANGUAGE FILE HANDLING

This chapter takes a look at accessing the disk drive from machine language programs. Each section includes several practical examples to help you understand the procedure. The reader is assumed to be relatively familiar with 6502 machine language programming and hexadecimal notation.

Only the Commodore KERNAL ROM routines are used for computer/disk drive communications. This ensures that the routines you develop will not become obsolete if a minor ROM change is made.

10.1 Introduction to Machine Language File Handling

For most file-handling applications a BASIC program is the quickest and easiest solution. However, there are some applications such as spelling checkers or programs that scan large data bases for keywords, where the speed of a machine language program is essential. This chapter explains how to open a file, read or write to it, and close it. In addition, it demonstrates how to send disk commands such as SCRATCH, VALIDATE and M-R to the 1541 disk drive and monitor the disk status. The routines in this chapter are given in PAL-64™ assembler format and are designed for use with the Commodore 64. In most cases, the routines will also work on a VIC-20 because the routines use the KERNAL routines that are common to both machines.

10.2 Opening a File

There are three KERNAL ROM routines that you must use when opening a file. They are SETNAM (sets pointers to the file name), SETLFS (sets the logical file), and OPEN (actually opens the file). Let's look at how to use them.

SETNAM ($FFBD)

This is the first routine to use. It sets the pointers to the file name for the OPEN routine.

Steps in using SETNAM:

1. Load .A with the length of the file name.
2. Load .X with the lo byte of the address of the file name.
3. Load .Y with the hi byte of the address of the file name.
4. JSR to SETNAM routine at $FFBD.

Registers affected: None

NOTE:

Even if you are not using a file name (as in OPEN 15,8,15), you still must use this routine. In this case, load .A with #$00 and JSR to the routine (.X and .Y can have any values).

EXAMPLE: File name is BUNCHADATA,S,W (len=14) stored at $033C.

```
LDA #$0E      ;LENGTH
LDX #$3C      ;LO BYTE POINTER
LDY #$03      ;HI BYTE POINTER
JSR $FFBD     ;CALL ROUTINE
```

SETLFS ($FFBA)

Use this routine second. It sets the file#, the device# and the channel# for use by the OPEN routine.

Steps in using SETLFS:

1. Load .A with the file# (logical file number).
2. Load .X with the device# (usually eight for disk).
3. Load .Y with the channel# (secondary address).
4. JSR to SETLFS routine at $FFBA.

Registers affected: None

EXAMPLE: We want to use file# 1, device# 8, channel# 5.

```
LDA #$01      ;FILE#
LDX #$08      ;DEVICE#
LDY #$05      ;CHANNEL#
JSR $FFBA     ;CALL ROUTINE
```

OPEN ($FFC0)

This last routine actually opens the file.

Steps in using OPEN:

1. Use SETNAM and SETLFS to set parameters.
2. JSR to OPEN routine at $FFC0.

Registers affected: .A, .X, and .Y

EXAMPLE:

```
JSR $FFC0     ;OPEN THE FILE
```

ANNOTATED EXAMPLES:

1. OPEN 15,8,15

```
        LDA #$00        ;LENGTH IS 0
        JSR $FFBD       ;CALL SETNAM
        LDA #$0F        ;FILE# 15
        LDX #$08        ;DEVICE# 8
        LDY #$0F        ;CHANNEL# 15
        JSR $FFBA       ;CALL SETLFS
        JSR $FFC0       ;CALL OPEN
```

2. OPEN 15,8,15,"IO"

```
        LDA #$02        ;LENGTH
        LDX #<IOMSG      ;LO BYTE POINTER
        LDY #>IOMSG      ;HI BYTE POINTER
        JSR $FFBD       ;CALL SETNAM
        LDA #$0F        ;FILE# 15
        LDX #$08        ;DEVICE# 8
        LDY #$0F        ;CHANNEL# 15
        JSR $FFBA       ;CALL SETLFS
        JSR $FFC0       ;CALL OPEN

IOMSG   .ASC "IO"
```

3. OPEN 1,8,5,"@0:BUNCHASTUFF,P,W"

```
        LDA #$12        ;LENGTH IS 18 CHR
        LDX #<FILNAM    ;LO BYTE POINTER
        LDY #>FILNAM    ;HI BYTE POINTER
        JSR $FFBD       ;CALL SETNAM
        LDA #$01        ;FILE# 1
        LDX #$08        ;DEVICE# 8
        LDY #$05        ;CHANNEL# 5
        JSR $FFBA       ;CALL SETLFS
        JSR $FFC0       ;CALL OPEN

FILNAM .ASC "@0:BUNCHASTUFF,P,W"
```

4. OPEN 1,8,5,"#2"

```
        LDA #$02        ;LENGTH IS 2 CHR
        LDX #<FILNAM    ;LO BYTE POINTER
        LDY #>FILNAM    ;HI BYTE POINTER
        JSR $FFBD       ;CALL SETNAM
        LDA #$01        ;FILE# 1
```

```
LDX #$08        ;DEVICE# 8
LDY #$05        ;CHANNEL# 5
JSR $FFBA       ;CALL SETLFS
JSR $FFCO       ;CALL OPEN

FILNAM .ASC "#2"
```

10.3 Reading a File

There are three KERNAL ROM routines which you use to read a file. They are
CHKIN (prepare channel for input), CHRIN (reads one character), and CLRCHN
(clears the I/O channel). Let's look at how to use them:

CHKIN ($FFC6)

This is the first routine you use. It designates the specified file# as the input file.

Steps in using CHKIN:

1. Load .X with the desired file#.
2. JSR to CHKIN routine at $FFC6.

Registers affected: .A and .X

EXAMPLE: Prepare to read from file# 1 (opened previously).

```
LDX #$01        ;FILE# 1
JSR $FFC6       ;CALL CHKIN
```

CHRIN ($FFCF)

Use this routine to actually read characters from the input file. If CHKIN has not
been used to specify an input file, data is expected from the keyboard. Note that the
value in .X is destroyed. As a result, you cannot use .X as a counter when reading
data.

Steps in using CHRIN:

1. JSR to CHRIN routine at $FFCF.
2. Byte appears in .A.

Registers affected: .A and .X

EXAMPLE: Read 256 bytes & store them starting at $2000.

```
        LDY #$00        ;SET POINTER
LOOP    JSR $FFCF       ;CALL CHRIN
        STA $2000,Y     ;STORE BYTE
        INY             ;INCREMENT POINTER
        BNE LOOP        ;READ NEXT
```

CLRCHN ($FFCC)

Use this routine once you have finished reading the file. It clears (deselects) the designated file# and restores I/O to normal (keyboard and screen). NOTE: CLRCHN does *not* close any files, it merely deselects the channel temporarily. Do not forget to use this routine. If you forget, you will have I/O problems.

How to use CLRCHN:

JSR to CLRCHN routine at $FFCC.

Registers affected: .A and .X

EXAMPLE:

```
JSR $FFCC       ;CALL CLRCHN TO RESTORE I/O
```

ANNOTATED EXAMPLES:

1. Read 256 bytes from file# 3 and store them starting at $4280.

```
        LDX #$03       ;FILE# 3
        JSR $FFC6      ;CALL CHKIN
        LDY #$00       ;SET POINTER
LOOP    JSR $FFCF      ;CALL CHRIN
        STA $4280,Y    ;STORE BYTE
        INY            ;INCREMENT POINTER
        BNE LOOP       ;READ NEXT
        JSR $FFCC      ;CALL CLRCHN TO RESTORE I/O
```

2. Read from file# 5 until carriage return and store them from $033C.

```
        LDX #$05       ;FILE# 5
        JSR $FFC6      ;CALL CHKIN
        LDY #$00       ;SET POINTER
LOOP    JSR $FFCF      ;CALL CHRIN
        CMP #$0D       ;CHECK FOR CARRIAGE RETURN
        BEQ DONE       ;BRANCH IF CARRIAGE RETURN
        STA $033C,Y    ;STORE BYTE
        INY            ;INCREMENT POINTER
        BNE LOOP       ;READ NEXT
DONE    JSR $FFCC      ;CALL CLRCHN TO RESTORE I/O
```

10.4 Writing a File

There are three KERNAL ROM routines that you use to write to a file. They are CHKOUT (prepare the channel for output), CHROUT (writes one character), and CLRCHN (clears the I/O channel). Let's look at how to use them:

CHKOUT (SFFC9)

This is the first routine you use. It designates the specified file# as the output file. Note that you *must* have opened the file previously.

Steps in using CHKOUT:

1. Load .X with the desired file#.
2. JSR to CHKOUT routine at $FFC9.

Registers affected: .A and .X

EXAMPLE: Prepare to write to file# 1 (opened previously).

```
LDX #$01        ;FILE# 1
JSR $FFC9       ;CALL CHKOUT
```

CHROUT (SFFD2)

Use this routine to actually write characters to the output file. If CHKOUT has not been used to specify an output file, data is sent to the screen. Note that the value in .X is destroyed. As a result, you cannot use .X as a counter when writing data.

Steps in using CHROUT:

1. Load .A with byte to output.
2. JSR to CHROUT routine at $FFD2.

Registers affected: .A and .X

EXAMPLE: Write out the 256 bytes starting at $2000.

```
        LDY #$00        ;SET POINTER
LOOP    LDA $2000,Y     ;LOAD BYTE
        JSR $FFD2       ;CALL CHROUT
        INY             ;INCREMENT POINTER
        BNE LOOP        ;READ NEXT
```

CLRCHN (SFFCC)

Use this routine once you have finished reading the file. It clears (deselects) the designated file# and restores I/O to normal (keyboard and screen). Remember, CLHCHN does *not* close any files, it merely deselects them temporarily. Do not forget to use this routine. If you forget, you will have I/O problems. When you are finished writing to the file, remember to close it.

Steps in using CLRCHN:

1. JSR to CLRCHN routine at $FFCC.

Registers affected: .A and .X

EXAMPLE:

```
JSR $FFCC      ;CALL CLRCHN TO RESTORE I/O
```

ANNOTATED EXAMPLES:

1. Write the 256 bytes starting at $4280 to file# 3.

```
            LDX #$03      ;FILE# 3
            JSR $FFC9     ;CALL CHKOUT
            LDY #$00      ;SET POINTER
LOOP        LDA $4280,Y   ;LOAD BYTE
            JSR $FFD2     ;CALL CHROUT
            INY           ;INCREMENT POINTER
            BNE LOOP      ;READ NEXT
            JSR $FFCC     ;CALL CLRCHN TO RESTORE I/O
```

2. Write bytes starting at $033C until $00 byte to file# 5.

```
            LDX #$05      ;FILE# 5
            JSR $FFC9     ;CALL CHKOUT
            LDY #$00      ;SET POINTER
LOOP        LDA $033C,Y   ;LOAD BYTE
            BEQ DONE      ;BRANCH IF $00 BYTE
            JSR $FFD2     ;CALL CHROUT
            INY           ;INCREMENT POINTER
            BNE LOOP      ;WRITE NEXT
DONE        JSR $FFCC     ;CALL CLRCHN TO RESTORE I/O
```

10.5 Closing a File

Once you have finished reading or writing a file, you must close it. Although there are two KERNAL ROM routines that appear to be associated with closing a file, CLALL (close all files) and CLOSE (close one file), you should *only use CLOSE*.

WARNING:

Do not use CLALL to close disk files. *The Commodore 64 Programmer's Reference Guide* seems to imply that this routine can be used to close all open files. However, it appears that this routine merely works internally. The files are shut down as far as the Commodore 64 is concerned, but the files are not closed properly on the 1541 disk drive. As a result, *do not use CLALL with disk files!*

CLOSE ($FFC3)

This is the routine to use. It closes the file whose file# you specify. Note that you *must* have used CLRCHN to clear the file# previously.

Steps in using CLOSE:

1. Load .A with the desired file#.
2. JSR to CLOSE routine at $FFC3.

Registers affected: .A, .X and .Y

EXAMPLE: Prepare to close to file# 1 (cleared previously).

```
LDX #$01       ;FILE# 1
JSR $FFC3      ;CALL CLOSE
```

ANNOTATED EXAMPLES:

1. File# 4 was designated output file. Clear and close it.

```
JSR $FFCC      ;CALL CLRCHN TO RESTORE I/O
LDA #$04       ;FILE# 4
JSR $FFC3      ;CALL CLOSE
```

2. Close command channel (file# 15).

```
LDA #$OF       ;FILE# 15
JSR $FFC3      ;CALL CLOSE
```

10.6 Monitoring I/O Status

You may want to monitor the I/O status when opening a file or reading it. Its main purpose is to detect a device not present or an end-of-file condition. In BASIC this is done by checking the ST variable. In a machine language program you use the KERNAL ROM routine READST to monitor the I/O status.

READST ($FFB7)

This is the routine to use. It returns the current I/O status in the accumulator. The meaning of the values returned are summarized below. They are the same as those for the ST variable in BASIC.

Value	Hex	Meaning
0	$00	Everything is OK.
1	$01	Time out on write.
2	$02	Time out on read.
64	$40	End of file.
-128	$80	Device not present.

Steps in using READST:

1. JSR to READST routine at $FFB7.
2. Interpret code and take action.

Registers affected: .A

EXAMPLE: Read current I/O status and branch if EOF.

```
JSR $FFB7      ;CALL READST
CMP #$40       ;COMPARE TO EOF
BEQ DONE       ;BRANCH IF EOF
```

ANNOTATED EXAMPLES:

1. Open command channel. Abort if device not present.

```
LDA #$00       ;LENGTH IS O
JSR $FFBD      ;CALL SETNAM
LDA #$OF       ;FILE# 15
LDX #$08       ;DEVICE# 8
LDY #$OF       ;CHANNEL# 15
JSR $FFBA      ;CALL SETLFS
JSR $FFCO      ;CALL OPEN
JSR $FFB7      ;CALL READST
CMP #$80       ;COMPARE TO DEVICE NOT PRESENT
BEQ ABORT      ;BRANCH IF DEVICE NOT PRESENT
```

2. Read file to memory starting at $2000. Quit at end of file.

```
       LDA #$11       ;LENGTH IS 17 CHR
       LDX #<FILNAM   ;LO BYTE POINTER
       LDY #>FILNAM   ;HI BYTE POINTER
       JSR $FFBD      ;CALL SETNAM
       LDA #$01       ;FILE# 1
       LDX #$08       ;DEVICE# 8
       LDY #$05       ;CHANNEL# 5
       JSR $FFBA      ;CALL SETLFS
       JSR $FFCO      ;CALL OPEN
       LDX #$03       ;FILE# 3
       JSR $FFC6      ;CALL CHKIN
       LDA #$20       ;HI BYTE OF WHERE TO STORE
       LDX #$00       ;LO BYTE OF WHERE TO STORE
       STX $FA        ;MAKE O PAGE INDIRECT POINTER
       STA $FB        ;
       LDY #$00       ;SET INDEX
LOOP   JSR $FFCF      ;CALL CHRIN
       STA ($FA),Y    ;STORE BYTE USING IND POINTER
       INY            ;INCREMENT INDEX
       BNE STATUS     ;NOT DONE PAGE
       INC $FB        ;INCREMENT HI BYTE OF POINTER
STATUS JSR $FFB7      ;READ STATUS
       CMP #$40       ;IS IT EOF
       BNE LOOP       ;NO, DO SOME MORE
       JSR $FFCC      ;CALL CLRCHN TO RESTORE I/O

FILNAM .ASC "O:BUNCHASTUFF,P,R"
```

NOTE:

Another way to monitor the I/O status is to monitor the value stored in ST ($0090) of the Commodore 64's RAM directly. The FAST COPY program at the end of this chapter uses this technique.

10.7 Monitoring the Disk Drive Status

You may want to monitor the disk drive's error status when sending direct disk commands, opening a file, reading from a file or writing to one. It allows you to check for a wide variety of disk errors. In BASIC this is done by inputting the disk status from the command channel. The process is similar in a machine language program. There is no special KERNAL ROM routine to do this job for you.

The steps you follow in reading the disk error status are:

1. OPEN the command channel (if not already open).
2. Use CHKIN to select the command channel for input.
3. Use CHRIN to read the error status and message.
4. Use CLRCHN to deselect the command channel.

CAUTION:

Be sure to input the entire disk status message and not just the error code. You don't want part of the message left in the drive's error buffer to fool you the next time you check the disk drive status. You can tell that you are at the end of the message when you reach a carriage return character.

HINT:

For a quick and dirty check, all you need to do is interpret the first character of the error code. Since error codes less than 20 can be ignored, just test if the first character is less than two. Remember that the codes are in ASCII format so that a two is really 50 ($32). If you use this technique, don't forget to dump the rest of the message as indicated above.

ANNOTATED EXAMPLES:

1. Quick and dirty check of first digit (command channel open).

```
        LDX #$OF      ;FILE# 15
        JSR $FFC6     ;CALL CHKIN TO SELECT CMD CHNL
        JSR $FFCF     ;CALL CHRIN TO GET FIRST DIGIT
        CMP #$32      ;COMPARE TO '2'
        BCS ABORT     ;ERROR CODE >= 20 SO ABORT
LOOP    JSR $FFCF     ;CALL CHRIN TO GET NEXT BYTE
        CMP #$OD      ;REACHED CARRIAGE RETURN YET
        BNE LOOP      ;STILL TO COME
        JSR $FFCC     ;CALL CLRCHN TO RESTORE I/O
```

2. Full interpretation of error code (stored in $FA).

```
        JSR $FFCC        ;CALL CLRCHN TO RESTORE I/O
        LDX #$OF         ;FILE# 15
        JSR $FFC6        ;CALL CHKIN TO SELECT CMD CHNL
        JSR $FFCF        ;CALL CHRIN TO GET 1ST DIGIT
        AND #$OF         ;CONVERT FROM ASCII TO HEX
        TAY              ;TEN'S PLACE
        JSR $FFCF        ;CALL CHRIN TO GET 2ND DIGIT
        AND #$OF         ;CONVERT FROM ASCII TO HEX
        CPY #$OO         ;IS TEN'S PLACE ZERO
        BEQ DONE         ;NO TEN'S PLACE, .A HAS ALL
LOOP1   CLC              ;CLEAR CARRY FOR ADD
        ADC #$OA         ;ADD IN ONE 10
        DEY              ;DECREMENT TEN'S PLACE
        BNE LOOP1        ;STILL MORE 10'S TO ADD IN
DONE    STA $FA          ;SAVE ERROR CODE
LOOP2   JSR $FFCF        ;CALL CHRIN TO GET NEXT BYTE
        CMP #$OD         ;REACHED CARRIAGE RETURN YET
        BNE LOOP2        ;STILL TO COME
        JSR $FFCC        ;CALL CLRCHN TO RESTORE I/O
```

NOTE:

See the FAST COPY program at the end of this chapter for a routine that does a quick and dirty check and, if a serious error has occurred, displays the error code and message on the screen.

10.8 Sending Disk Commands

As your machine language programs become more complex, you will find it necessary to send disk commands to the drive, such as NEW, SCRATCH, "M-R", and "U1:". This is similar to writing to a file except that you select the command channel file# as the output file#.

The steps you follow in sending disk commands are:

1. OPEN the command channel (if not already open).
2. Use CHKOUT to select the command channel for output.
3. Use CHROUT to send the disk command.
4. Use CLRCHN to deselect the command channel.

CAUTION:

You should check the disk error status after sending a disk command to be sure that the command has been executed properly (see Section 10.7).

ANNOTATED EXAMPLES:

1. Send disk command to NEW a diskette (command channel open). Equivalent to PRINT#15,"N0:DEVELOPMENT #3,D3".

```
                LDX  #$0F       ;FILE# 15
                JSR  $FFC9      ;CALL CHKOUT
                LDY  #$00       ;SET POINTER
        LOOP    LDA  NEWCMD,Y   ;LOAD BYTE OF COMMAND
                JSR  $FFD2      ;CALL CHROUT
                INY             ;INCREMENT POINTER
                CPY  #$14       ;HAVE WE FINISHED 20 BYTES YET
                BNE  LOOP       ;NO, MORE COMMAND TO COME
                JSR  $FFCC      ;CALL CLRCHN TO RESTORE I/O

        NEWCMD .ASC "N0:DEVELOPMENT #3,D3"
```

2. Send disk command to SCRATCH a file (command channel open). Equivalent to PRINT#15,"S0:BUNCHADATA".

```
                LDX  #$0F       ;FILE# 15
                JSR  $FFC9      ;CALL CHKOUT
                LDY  #$00       ;SET POINTER
        LOOP    LDA  SCRCMD,Y   ;LOAD BYTE OF COMMAND
                JSR  $FFD2      ;CALL CHROUT
                INY             ;INCREMENT POINTER
                CPY  #$0D       ;HAVE WE FINISHED 13 BYTES YET
                BNE  LOOP       ;NO, MORE COMMAND TO COME
                JSR  $FFCC      ;CALL CLRCHN TO RESTORE I/O

        SCRCMD .ASC "S0:BUNCHADATA"
```

3. Send disk command to position to record# 12 in relative file. Equivalent to PRINT#15,"P";CHR$(4);CHR$(0);CHR$(12);CHR$(1).

```
                LDX  #$0F       ;FILE# 15
                JSR  $FFC9      ;CALL CHKOUT
                LDY  #$00       ;SET POINTER
        LOOP    LDA  POSCMD,Y   ;LOAD BYTE OF COMMAND
                JSR  $FFD2      ;CALL CHROUT
                INY             ;INCREMENT POINTER
                CPY  #$05       ;HAVE WE FINISHED 5 BYTES YET
                BNE  LOOP       ;NO, MORE COMMAND TO COME
                JSR  $FFCC      ;CALL CLRCHN TO RESTORE I/O

        POSCMD .ASC "P"
               .BYTE $04,$00,$0C,$01
```

10.9 Typical Application

One of the most common complaints of 1541 disk drive owners is the length of time it takes to make a copy of an important disk file. Even some of the commercially available routines are quite slow. As a result, a file copy program is a prime candidate for conversion to machine language.

The FAST COPY program that serves as the culmination of this chapter illustrates the use of many of the routines we have developed. It includes routines to open files, read a file, write a file and check the disk status. The file to be copied is read into the Commodore 64's memory from $0B00 on. Since the entire RAM area from $0B00 to $9FFF can be used, files up to about 150 blocks long can be copied. Once the file has been read in and the copy diskette inserted, the contents of RAM are written into a new file.

The features of the FAST COPY program include:

1. High speed operation (less than 1.5 sec./block).
2. Copying of PRG or SEQ files.
3. Copying of files up to 150 blocks long.
4. Making multiple copies of a file.

Operating instructions:

1. Load and run to make one or more copies of a file.
2. Run the program again to copy other files.

The program listing is a slight modification of the printer output of the PAL™ assembler (line numbers have been added on comment lines). If you use a different assembler, you may have to make some minor changes. For example, PAL uses quotation marks around as ASCII string rather than the apostrophe used by the MAE™ and Commodore assemblers.

CAUTION:

Only the first three bytes of any ASCII message or hex BYTE string are shown in the 6502 CODE column. Be careful not to miss any characters as you type in the listing.

Since the assembler listing is well documented, no overview is provided. Readers who would like to make use of the FAST COPY program but do not have access to an assembler may use the MAKE FAST COPY program in Appendix E. This is a BASIC program that creates a working copy of the FAST COPY program on a diskette.


```
********************
PROGRAM: FAST CPY.P
********************

0 REM 1541 USER'S GUIDE SECTION 10.9
1 REM  COPYRIGHT: G. NEUFELD, 1984
2 :
3 REM MACHINE LANGUAGE FILE COPY FOR THE
  COMMODORE 64
4 REM              PAL ASSEMBLER FILE
5 :
1000 REM SAMPLE DISK HANDLING
1010 REM 1541 FILE 'COPY.P'
```

```
1020 :
1030 REM OPEN 4,4
1040 OPEN 1,8,4,"@0:COPY.B,P,W"
1050 :
1060 SYS 10*4096
1070 ;
1080 ;     SAMPLE DISK HANDLING - 1541 RE
AD.P
1090 ;
1100 ; ------------------------------------
----------
1110 ;   COPIES SEQ OR PRG FILES BY READ
ING THE
1120 ;   FILE INTO RAM ($0B00 UP) THEN W
RITING
1130 ;   OUT A NEW FILE ONTO ANOTHER DIS
KETTE.
1140 ;   FEATURES:
1150 ;        -FAST READ - ABOUT 2 SEC/BLO
CK
1160 ;        -FILES UP TO 150 BLOCKS LONG

1170 ;        -ALLOWS MULTIPLE COPIES
1180 ; ------------------------------------
----------
1190 ;
1200 ;
1210 *= $0801
1220 .OPT P,01
1230 ;
1240 ; 10 SYS2061
1250 ; -----------
1260 .BYTE $0B,$08,$0A,$00
1270 .BYTE $9E,$32,$30,$36
1280 .BYTE $31,$00,$00,$00
1290 ;
1300 ; START OF MACHINE LANGUAGE
1310 ; ----------------------------
1320 START JSR $FFCC ;CLEAR I/O CHANNELS

1330 JSR $FFE7 ;CLOSE ALL FILES
1340 ;
1350 ; PRINT REQUEST FOR FILE NAME
1360 ; ----------------------------
1370 LDY #$00
1380 ;
1390 LOOP1 LDA MSG,Y
1400 JSR $FFD2 ;CHROUT - OUTPUT A BYTE
1410 INY
1420 CPY #ENDMSG-MSG
```

```
1430 BNE LOOP1
1440 ;
1450 LDY #$00
1460 LOOP2 JSR $FFCF ;CHRIN - INPUT A BY
TE
1470 CMP ##$0D ;A CARRIAGE RETURN
1480 BEQ NAMEIN
1490 ;
1500 STA $033C,Y ;STORE IN TAPE BUFFER
1510 INY
1520 BNE LOOP2
1530 ;
1540 ;PRINT ERROR MESSAGE
1550 ;--------------------
1560 ERROR LDY #$00
1570 LOOP3 LDA ERRMSG,Y
1580 JSR $FFD2 ;CHROUT - OUTPUT A BYTE
1590 INY
1600 CPY #ENDERR-ERRMSG
1610 BNE LOOP3
1620 RTS
1630 ;
1640 NAMEIN STY $0334 ;SAVE NAME LENGTH
1650 CPY #$11
1660 BCS ERROR
1670 ;
1680 ; PRINT REQUEST FOR FILE TYPE
1690 ; ---------------------------
1700 AGAIN LDY #$00
1710 ;
1720 LOOP4 LDA MSG2,Y
1730 JSR $FFD2 ;CHROUT - OUTPUT A BYTE
1740 INY
1750 CPY #ENDMSG2-MSG2
1760 BNE LOOP4
1770 ;
1780 JSR $FFCF ;CHRIN - INPUT A BYTE
1790 STA $0335 ;STORE BELOW BUFFER
1800 CMP ##$53 ;IS IT 'S'
1810 BEQ OKTYPE
1820 CMP ##$50 ;IS IT 'P'
1830 BNE AGAIN
1840 ;
1850 OKTYPE LDY $0334 ;NAME LENGTH
1860 LDA #$2C ; ","
1870 STA $033C,Y
1880 INY
1890 LDA $0335 ; FILE TYPE (S/P)
1900 STA $033C,Y
1910 INY
```

```
1920 LDA #$2C ; ","
1930 STA $033C,Y
1940 INY
1950 LDA #$52 ; "R"
1960 STA $033C,Y
1970 INY
1980 STY $0334
1990 ;
2000 ; OPEN COMMAND CHANNEL
2010 ; --------------------
2020 JSR $FFCC ;CLRCHN - CLEAR I/O CHANN
ELS
2030 JSR OPEN15
2040 ;
2050 ; OPEN FILE TO READ (1,8,5)
2060 ; -------------------------
2070 JSR OPEN1
2080 ;
2090 JSR STATUS
2100 JSR $FFCC ;CLRCHN - CLEAR CHANNELS
2110 ;
2120 LDA $FB
2130 BEQ CONT
2140 ;
2150 ; ABORT ON BAD DISK STATUS
2160 ; ------------------------
2170 ABORT LDA #$01 ;CLOSE FILE# 1
2180 JSR $FFC3 ;CLOSE - CLOSE A FILE
2190 LDA #$0F ;CLOSE FILE# 15
2200 JSR $FFC3 ;CLOSE - CLOSE A FILE
2210 RTS
2220 ;
2230 ; SET UP INDIRECT POINTER
2240 ; -----------------------
2250 CONT LDA #$00 ;LO BYTE START
2260 STA $FC
2270 LDA #$0B ;HI BYTE START
2280 STA $FD
2290 ;
2300 ; PRINT LOADING MESSAGE
2310 ; ---------------------
2320 LDY #$00
2330 LOOP5 LDA RDMSG,Y
2340 JSR $FFD2 ;CHROUT - OUTPUT A BYTE
2350 INY
2360 CPY #ENDRD-RDMSG
2370 BNE LOOP5
2380 ;
2390 ; READ IN THE FILE
2400 ; ----------------
```

```
2410 LDX #$01 ;FILE#
2420 JSR $FFC6 ;CHKIN - PREPARE FOR INPU
T
2430 ;
2440 LDY #$00
2450 LOOP6 JSR $FFCF ;GET BYTE
2460 STA ($00FC),Y ;STORE IN
2470 ;
2480 LDA $90 ;KERNAL I/O STATUS FLAG
2490 BNE ENDLOAD
2500 ;
2510 INY
2520 BNE LOOP6
2530 INC $FD
2540 BNE LOOP6 ;ALWAYS
2550 ;
2560 ENDLOAD STY $FC ;LAST BYTE POINTER
2570 JSR $FFCC ;CLRCHN - CLEAR CHANNELS
2580 LDA #$01 ;CLOSE FILE# 1
2590 JSR $FFC3 ;CLOSE - CLOSE A FILE
2600 LDA #$0F ;CLOSE FILE# 15
2610 JSR $FFC3 ;CLOSE - CLOSE A FILE
2620 ;
2630 ; PRINT CHANGE DISK MESSAGE
2640 ; --------------------------
2650 CHANGE LDY #$00
2660 LOOP7 LDA CNGMSG,Y
2670 JSR $FFD2 ;CHROUT - OUTPUT A BYTE
2680 INY
2690 CPY #ENDCNG-CNGMSG
2700 BNE LOOP7
2710 ;
2720 ; WAIT FOR CARRIAGE RETURN
2730 ; --------------------------
2740 WAIT JSR $FFE4; GETIN - GET A CHR
2750 CMP #$0D
2760 BNE WAIT
2770 ;
2780 ; OPEN COMMAND CHANNEL
2790 ; --------------------
2800 JSR OPEN15
2810 ;
2820 ; OPEN FILE FOR WRITE
2830 ; -------------------
2840 LDY $0334 ;NAME LENGTH
2850 LDA #$57 ; "W"
2860 STA $033B,Y
2870 ;
2880 JSR OPEN1
2890 ;
```

```
2900 JSR STATUS
2910 JSR $FFCC ;CLRCHN - CLEAR CHANNELS
2920 ;
2930 ; ABORT ON BAD DISK STATUS
2940 ;
2950 LDA $FB
2960 BNE ABORT ;ABORT ON BAD STATUS
2970 ;
2980 ;
2990 ; SET UP INDIRECT POINTER
3000 ; ------------------------
3010 LDA #$00 ;LO BYTE START
3020 STA $FA
3030 LDA #$0B ;HI BYTE START
3040 STA $FB
3050 ;
3060 ; PRINT WRITING MESSAGE
3070 ; ---------------------
3080 LDY #$00
3090 LOOP8 LDA WRTMSG,Y
3100 JSR $FFD2 ;CHROUT - OUTPUT A BYTE
3110 INY
3120 CPY #ENDWRT-WRTMSG
3130 BNE LOOP8
3140 ;
3150 ; WRITE OUT THE FILE
3160 ; ------------------
3170 LDX #$01 ;FILE#
3180 JSR $FFC9 ;CHKOUT - PREPARE FOR OUT
PUT
3190 ;
3200 LDY #$00
3210 LOOP10 LDA ($FA),Y
3220 JSR $FFD2 ;CHROUT - OUTPUT A BYTE
3230 CPY $FC ;DOES .Y MATCH END COUNT
3240 BNE NOEND
3250 ;
3260 LDA $FB
3270 CMP $FD
3280 BEQ ALLDONE
3290 ;
3300 NOEND INY
3310 BNE LOOP10
3320 ;
3330 INC $FB
3340 BNE LOOP10 ;ALWAYS
3350 ;
3360 ALLDONE JSR $FFCC ;CLEAR I/O CHANNE
LS
3370 LDA #$01 ;CLOSE FILE# 1
```

```
3380 JSR $FFC3 ;CLOSE - CLOSE A FILE
3390 LDA #$0F ;CLOSE FILE# 15
3400 JSR $FFC3 ;CLOSE - CLOSE A FILE
3410 ;
3420 ; PRINT ANOTHER READ MESSAGE
3430 ; ------------------------
3440 LDY #$00
3450 LOOP11 LDA DUNMSG,Y
3460 JSR $FFD2 ;CHROUT - OUTPUT A BYTE
3470 INY
3480 CPY #ENDDUN-DUNMSG
3490 BNE LOOP11
3500 ;
3510 JSR $FFCC ;CLEAR I/O CHANNELS
3520 ;
3530 ; WAIT FOR Y/N RESPONSE
3540 ; --------------------
3550 WAIT2 JSR $FFE4; GETIN - GET A CHR
3560 CMP #$59 ; "Y"
3570 BEQ CNG
3580 CMP #$4E ; "N"
3590 BNE WAIT2
3600 ;
3610 JSR $FFCC ;CLEAR I/O CHANNELS
3620 RTS ;BACK TO BASIC
3630 ;
3640 CNG JMP CHANGE
3650 ;
3660 ;*==============================*
3670 ;*          SUBROUTINES         *
3680 ;*==============================*
3690 ;
3700 ; SUB TO CHECK DISK STATUS
3710 ; ------------------------
3720 STATUS JSR $FFCC ;CLRCHN - CLEAR CH
ANNELS
3730 ;
3740 LDX #$0F ;FILE#
3750 JSR $FFC6 ;CHKIN - PREPARE FOR INPU
T
3760 ;
3770 JSR $FFCF ;CHRIN - GET BYTE
3780 CMP #$32
3790 BCC DISKOK ;DS<20
3800 ;
3810 STA $FB ;TEMP STORAGE
3820 ;
3830 ;PRINT ERROR MESSAGE
3840 ;-------------------
3850 LDY #$00
```

```
3860 LOOP12 LDA DSKERR,Y
3870 JSR $FFD2 ;CHROUT - OUTPUT A BYTE
3880 INY
3890 CPY #ENDDSK-DSKERR
3900 BNE LOOP12
3910 ;
3920 LDA $FB ;RETRIEVE 1ST DIGIT
3930 JSR $FFD2 ;CHROUT - OUTPUT A BYTE
3940 ;
3950 LOOP13 JSR $FFCF ;CHRIN - GET BYTE
3960 CMP #$0D
3970 BEQ QUIT
3980 JSR $FFD2 ;CHROUT - OUTPUT A BYTE
3990 BNE LOOP13
4000 BEQ LOOP13
4010 ;
4020 QUIT LDA #$01 ;SET FLAG
4030 STA $FB
4040 RTS
4050 ;
4060 DISKOK JSR $FFCF ;CHRIN - GET BYTE
4070 CMP #$0D
4080 BEQ QUIT2
4090 BNE DISKOK
4100 BEQ DISKOK
4110 ;
4120 QUIT2 LDA #$00 ;SET FLAG
4130 STA $FB
4140 RTS
4150 ;
4160 ; OPEN COMMAND CHANNEL (OPEN 15,8,1
5,"IO")
4170 ; --------------------
4180 OPEN15 LDA $02 ;NAME LENGTH
4190 LDX #<IOMSG ;LO OF FILE NAME
4200 LDY #>IOMSG ;HI OF FILE NAME
4210 JSR $FFBD ;SETNAM - SET UP FILE NAM
E
4220 ;
4230 LDA #$0F ;FILE#
4240 LDX #$08 ;DEVICE#
4250 LDY #$0F ;CHANNEL#
4260 JSR $FFBA ;SETLFS - SET UP LOGICAL
FILE
4270 ;
4280 JSR $FFC0 ;OPEN COMMAND CHANNEL
4290 ;
4300 RTS
4310 ;
4320 ; OPEN FILE TO READ (1,8,5)
```

```
4330 ; ------------------
4340 OPEN1 LDA $0334 ;NAME LENGTH
4350 LDX #<$033C ;LO BYTE OF START
4360 LDY #>$033C ;HI BYTE OF START
4370 JSR $FFBD ;SETNAM - SET UP FILE NAM
E
4380 ;
4390 LDA #$01 ;FILE#
4400 LDX #$08 ;DEVICE#
4410 LDY #$05 ;CHANNEL#
4420 JSR $FFBA ;SETLFS - SET UP LOGICAL
FILE
4430 ;
4440 JSR $FFC0 ;OPEN FILE
4450 ;
4460 RTS
4470 ;
4480 ;  *===============================
====*
4490 ;  *              MESSAGES
    *
4500 ;  *===============================
====*
4510 ;
4520 MSG .BYTE $8E ;UPPER CASE
4530 .BYTE $93,$11 ;CLEAR SCR, DOWN
4540 .ASC "FILENAME TO COPY? "
4550 ENDMSG =*
4560 ;
4570 ERRMSG .BYTE $0D,$0D,$12
4580 .ASC "FILENAME TOO LONG"
4590 .BYTE $0D
4600 ENDERR =*
4610 ;
4620 MSG2 .BYTE $0D,$0D
4630 .ASC "FILE TYPE (S/P)? "
4640 ENDMSG2 =*
4650 ;
4660 DSKERR .BYTE $0D,$0D,$12
4670 .ASC "FATAL DISK ERROR"
4680 .BYTE $0D
4690 ENDDSK =*
4700 ;
4710 IOMSG .ASC "IO"
4720 ;
4730 RDMSG .BYTE $0D,$0D
4740 .ASC "READING DISK FILE"
4750 .BYTE $0D
4760 ENDRD =*
4770 ;
```

```
4780 CNGMSG .BYTE $0D
4790 .ASC "INSERT OTHER DISKETTE"
4800 .BYTE $0D,$0D
4810 .ASC "PRESS "
4820 .BYTE $12 ;RVS ON
4830 .ASC "RETURN"
4840 .BYTE $92 ;RVS OFF
4850 .ASC " WHEN READY"
4860 ENDCNG =*
4870 ;
4880 WRTMSG .BYTE $0D,$91
4890 .ASC "WRITING DISK FILE        "
4900 .BYTE $0D
4910 ENDWRT =*
4920 ;
4930 DUNMSG .BYTE $0D
4940 .ASC "ANOTHER COPY (Y/N)?"
4950 .BYTE $0D
4960 ENDDUN =*
```

Possible modifications and improvements:

1. To copy very long files (up to 154 blocks) assemble the machine code portion to begin at $C000 and modify the starting value of the indirect pointers to point to $0800.

2. To handle exceptionally long files (up to almost 200 blocks) incorporate the KERNAL routines into the copy program and then flip the BASIC ROM's out to provide a clear RAM area from the end of the extended routine to $CFFF.

CHAPTER 11

GETTING OUT OF TROUBLE

Despite your most careful efforts to follow proper operating procedures when using your 1541 disk drive, Murphy's Law will eventually catch up with you. This chapter is designed to help you localize and correct most of the common problems.

The chapter includes listings of several disk utility programs. In addition it makes extensive use of some of the utility programs listed in Appendix E.

11.1 Spotting and Diagnosing Problems

One of the difficulties of working with floppy diskettes is that errors can develop in the directory or BAM without your knowledge. If these errors are not found and corrected, they can precipitate other problems. In accordance with Murphy's Law, problems on a diskette will not become evident until you desperately need the programs or data stored on it. This section describes how to use two of the disk utility programs listed in Appendix E to check for and locate errors hidden on your diskettes.

The program FULL DIRECTORY, listed in Appendix E, provides a rapid, although incomplete, check for potential problems. The program is very easy to use. Load it, insert the diskette to be checked and run the program.

Here's an analysis of the 1541TEST/DEMO diskette.

```
DISK NAME: 1541TEST/DEMO
DOS TYPE:  65
COSMETIC DISK ID: ZX  ASCII = 90  88

BLKS    FILE NAME        TYPE  LINK   START
----   ----------------  ----  -- --  -----
  13   HOW TO USE        PRG   17  0  $0401
   5   HOW PART TWO      PRG   17  3  $0401
   4   VIC-20 WEDGE      PRG   17  9  $0401
   1   C-64 WEDGE        PRG   19  0  $0401
   4   DOS 5.1           PRG   19  1  $CC00
  11   COPY/ALL          PRG   19  3  $0401
   9   PRINTER TEST      PRG   19  9  $0401
```

```
 4   DISK ADDR CHANGE    PRG   16   0  $0401
 4   DIR                 PRG   16   1  $0401
 6   VIEW BAM            PRG   16   3  $0401
 4   CHECK DISK          PRG   16   7  $0401
14   DISPLAY T&S         PRG   16  15  $0401
 9   PERFORMANCE TEST    PRG   20   2  $0401
 5   SEQUENTIAL FILE     PRG   20   7  $0401
13   RANDOM FILE         PRG   15   1  $0401


BLOCKS FREE PER DIRECTORY = 558
BLOCKS FREE ACCORDING TO BAM= 558
SCRATCHED BLOCKS= 0
```

This is a much more detailed view of a diskette's directory than you get from an ordinary directory listing. An analysis is provided for all files, even scratched files.

Let's spend a moment going over the table of files and the meaning of the various entries. The first column of the table, BLKS, is the length of the file, in blocks, as recorded in the directory. The actual length of the file may be different. The second column lists the file name as recorded in the directory. The third column is the file type. Scratched file types have a reverse-field DEL in this column. Unclosed files have their file types in reverse-field. The next two columns are the track and sector numbers where the first block of the file is stored. The final column is the load address of the file expressed in hexadecimal notation. On the 1541TEST/DEMO diskette the load address for all the programs, except DOS 5.1, is $0401 (1025). This indicates that these programs were written on a PET. The normal load addresses for some Commodore computers are:

Commodore 64	$0801	(2049)
VIC-20 (unexpanded)	$1000	(4097)
VIC-20 (with 3K)	$0401	(1025)
VIC-20 (with 8/16K)	$1201	(4608)
4032 & 8032	$0401	(1025)

Although the expanded directory listing is interesting, the summary below the table is more important for spotting trouble. The first line, BLOCKS FREE PER DIRECTORY, shows 558, which is calculated by subtracting the sum of the first column of the table from the total number of usable blocks on the diskette (664). In our example, we would have SUM = 13+5+4+1+4+11+9+4+4+6+4+14+9+5+13 = 106. Thus our BLOCKS FREE PER DIRECTORY is 664 -106 = 558. (Note that we don't have to worry about the directory on track 18 in our calculations. The 19 sectors on this track have already been deducted, 683 -19 = 664.) The second summary line, BLOCKS FREE ACCORDING TO BAM, is the number that normally appears at the bottom of a directory listing. The third line, SCRATCHED BLOCKS, is the sum of the lengths of all the scratched files on the diskette. Since there are no scratched files on the 1541TEST/DEMO diskette, we have zero scratched blocks.

If the two independent calculations of the number of BLOCKS FREE agree, as above, no diagnostic message is printed. If the number of blocks free according to the

BAM is greater than the number calculated from the directory, something is wrong, and the diagnostic message, CROSSED FILES LIKELY, is printed. If the number of blocks free according to the BAM is less than the number calculated from the directory, the message, NON-FILE BLOCKS ALLOCATED, is printed and the number of such blocks is indicated. If you get either of these diagnostic messages, you should localize the problem using the CONFIRM ALL FILES program described below.

Although the FULL DIRECTORY program will not find all diskette problems, it provides a quick check of your diskette. It is a good idea to keep a printed copy of the output of this program for each of your diskettes. It makes recovery from problems such as a corrupted directory much easier.

A more thorough analysis of a diskette is produced by the utility program CONFIRM ALL FILES. This program is also easy to use. Simply load CONFIRM ALL FILES, insert the diskette to be analyzed, and run the program. You may direct the output either to the screen or a printer. You can also choose whether or not to display the file chains for the files or the SUPER BAM.

This program traces through all the active files stored on a diskette looking for errors. It even gives you the option of tracing scratched files. To see how this program works, let's look at the first part of an analysis of the 1541TEST/DEMO diskette.

```
CONFIRMING   1541TEST/DEMO        ZX  2A

CHECKING DISKETTE BAM
BAM IS INTERNALLY CONSISTENT

TRACING: HOW TO USE        ....PRG
17,00 17,10 17,20 17,08 17,18 17,06
17,16 17,04 17,14 17,02 17,12 17,01
17,11
 13 BLOCKS FOUND, 13 IN DIRECTORY

TRACING: HOW PART TWO      ....PRG
17,03 17,13 17,05 17,15 17,07
 5 BLOCKS FOUND, 5 IN DIRECTORY

TRACING: VIC-20 WEDGE      ....PRG
17,09 17,19 17,17 16,05
 4 BLOCKS FOUND, 4 IN DIRECTORY

TRACING: C-64 WEDGE        ....PRG
19,00
 1 BLOCKS FOUND, 1 IN DIRECTORY

TRACING: DOS 5.1           ....PRG
19,01 19,11 19,02 19,12
 4 BLOCKS FOUND, 4 IN DIRECTORY
```

Analysis of remaining programs

ALL FILES HAVE BEEN CHECKED

Let's examine what happens as a diskette is analyzed and what the printout means. When the analysis begins, the diskette's name and cosmetic diskette ID are printed out for identification purposes. The message, CHECKING DISKETTE BAM, indicates that the program is now reading and analyzing the diskette's Block Availability Map. This takes about 30 seconds. Any discrepancies found in the BAM (i.e., when the master count of blocks free on a track does not match the bit map) are printed out. If no errors are found, the message, BAM IS INTERNALLY CONSISTENT, is printed and the file analysis begins.

Let's use the first file on the diskette, HOW TO USE, as an example of how a file is analyzed.

```
TRACING: HOW TO USE        ....PRG
17,00 17,10 17,20 17,08 17,18 17,06
17,16 17,04 17,14 17,02 17,12 17,01
17,11
 13 BLOCKS FOUND, 13 IN DIRECTORY
```

The first line of the display is for identification purposes and reports the name and type of the file as given in the directory.

```
TRACING: HOW TO USE         ....PRG
        (file name)              (file type)
```

The file is then traced by following the track and sector links. If you have requested a display of the links, the track and sector numbers of each of the blocks that is used to store the file will be displayed like this:

```
17,00 17,10 17,20 17,08 17,18 17,06
17,16 17,04 17,14 17,02 17,12 17,01
17,11
```

In this case, the first block of the file is stored on track 17, sector 0. The second block is stored on track 17, sector 10, and so on....

As the file is traced the program checks that each block in the file:

1. Can be read without error.
2. Is properly allocated in the diskette's BAM.
3. Is not being used as part of a previously traced file.

If a block in the file cannot be read without error, the program reports the type and location of the error and goes on to the next file. If a block of the file is not allocated in the BAM, the track and sector numbers for that block are shown in reverse-field. If a block is also being used as part of a previously traced file, the name of the other file and the location of the collision are reported and the program goes on to the next file.

Once all the files have been traced, you have the option of displaying the SUPER BAM of the diskette. The SUPER BAM of the 1541TEST/DEMO diskette looks like this:

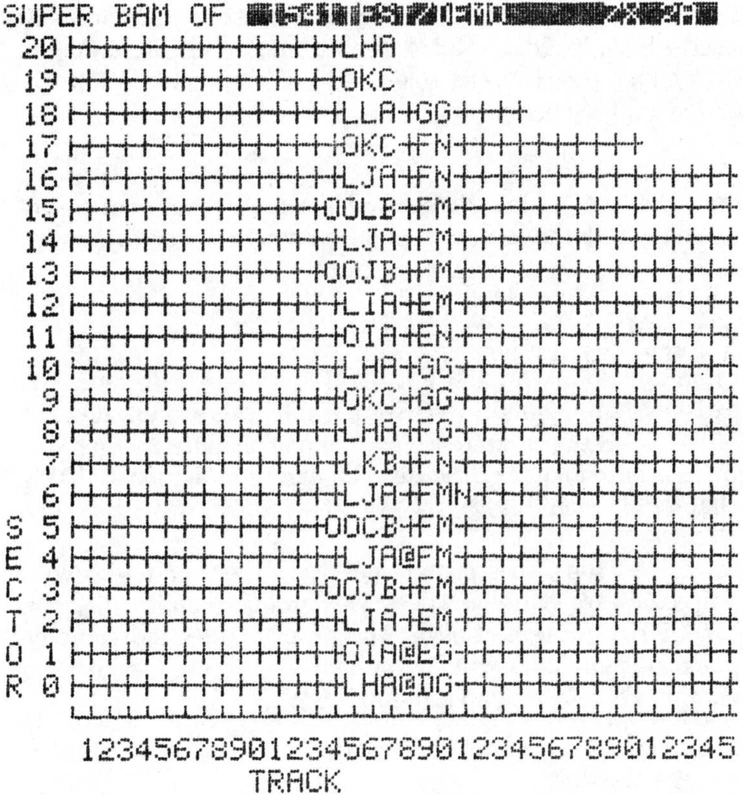


```
KEY TO SUPER BAM

@ = DIRECTORY (TRACK 18 ONLY)
A = HOW TO USE
B = HOW PART TWO
C = VIC-20 WEDGE
D = C-64 WEDGE
E = DOS 5.1
F = COPY/ALL
G = PRINTER TEST
H = DISK ADDR CHANGE
I = DIR
J = VIEW BAM
K = CHECK DISK
L = DISPLAY T&S
M = PERFORMANCE TEST
```

```
N = SEQUENTIAL FILE
O = RANDOM FIAL
```

The SUPER BAM is a map of the diskette. It shows in a compact form which blocks are being used to store the various files. For example, if we look at the vertical column that corresponds to track 17, we see several A's. Checking the key at the bottom of the SUPER BAM we find that an A represents a block being used to store part of the file HOW TO USE. If you compare the SUPER BAM with the printout of the file chain of HOW TO USE, you will see that they agree. Both indicate that the file is stored in sectors 0, 1, 2, 4, 6, 8, 10, 11, 12, 14, 16, 18, and 20 of track 17. However, the file chain also gives the sequence in which the sectors are used.

NOTE:

Unallocated blocks which are part of a file and allocated blocks which are not part of a file, are signs of trouble on the diskette. They are highlighted in reverse-field in the SUPER BAM printout.

Solving the Problems You Have Found

If any of the blocks are highlighted on the SUPER BAM of a normal diskette, you should VALIDATE the diskette immediately (see Section 4.8). This should solve the problem. If you can't VALIDATE the diskette because of one or more read errors, you will have to copy the files onto another diskette. You can use the FAST COPY program at the end of Chapter 10 to do this.

Other problems such as crossed files, files containing read errors and files with incorrect lengths in the directory are symptoms of serious problems on the diskette. Copy all the files onto another diskette and check the problem files individually. Hopefully, most of the programs and data will be usable. Do not reuse the problem diskette until you have completely reformatted it (a full NEW).

WARNING:

Do *not* remove the write protect tab from a commercially recorded diskette and validate it! A strange allocation of space on the diskette may be part of a disk protection scheme. If it is, the program may never run again!

11.2 Unscratching a File

At some point when you are doing diskette housekeeping you will get overzealous and scratch an important file by mistake. Don't panic. All is not lost. When you scratch a file, the file is not erased. All that happens is the file type byte in the directory entry for that file is changed to 00 and the blocks that were used to store the file are marked as free (available for use) in the diskette's BAM. As long as you have not stored any new files on that diskette, the original information is still intact.

As soon as you realize that you have scratched a file by mistake, label the diskette so that you won't use it inadvertently. Now, get out your copy of THE UNSCRATCHER disk utility program (listed in Appendix E). Load and run THE UNSCRATCHER program. When you do, you will see a display like this:

1541 FILE UNSCRATCHER

INSERT DISKETTE WITH SCRATCHED FILE

PRESS C TO CONTINUE
      Q TO QUIT

Insert the diskette with the scratched file and press C. The computer will respond with:

OK. READING DIRECTORY...

Once the diskette's directory has been read, the name of any scratched files will be displayed. If your diskette contained three scratched files named OLD STUFF, JUNK and BUNCHADATA, the display would look like this:

1541 FILE UNSCRATCHER

3 SCRATCHED FILES FOUND

1. OLD STUFF
2. JUNK
3. BUNCHADATA

WHICH FILE TO UNSCRATCH (1-3)? _

Suppose you wanted to recover BUNCHADATA. You would type the number three and press the RETURN key. Once you have selected the file to be unscratched, the BAM will be read and the file traced to be sure that all the blocks are still free. If everything is OK, you will be asked if the file is to be unscratched.

1541 FILE UNSCRATCHER

3 SCRATCHED FILES FOUND

1. OLD STUFF
2. JUNK
3. BUNCHADATA

WHICH FILE TO UNSCRATCH (1-3)? 3

READING THE BAM PRIOR TO CHECK....
CHECKING IF ALL BLOCKS ARE FREE...

FILE IS 24 BLOCKS LONG AND
CAN BE UNSCRATCHED

SHALL I UNSCRATCH IT (Y/N)? _

If you respond by typing Y and pressing the RETURN key, you will be asked for the
file type to use.

```
SHALL I UNSCRATCH IT (Y/N)? Y

FILE TYPE (P/S/U)? _
```

Enter P for a program file, S for a sequential file or U for a user file. The
UNSCRATCHER program also works with relative (REL) files. If the file you have
selected for unscratching is a relative file, you will not be asked for the file type. It
will be displayed automatically like this:

```
SHALL I UNSCRATCH IT (Y/N)? Y

THIS IS A RELATIVE FILE
RECORD SIZE = 40
```

Once the file type has been determined, the file will be unscratched by changing the
file type byte in the directory from zero to the appropriate value (SEQ=129=$81,
PRG=130=$82, USR=131=$83, REL=132=$84) and the diskette validated to allocate
the blocks that make up the file in the BAM.

```
NOW VALIDATING DISKETTE.....

ALL DONE!

PRESS RETURN TO CONTINUE
```

If any disk errors are encountered, the DOS error message will be displayed and the
unscratch job aborted. You may or may not be able to see the file in a directory
listing. However, the blocks of the unscratched file will not be allocated in the BAM
and there is still a danger of overwriting the file if new information is stored on the
diskette. If you can see the entry in a directory listing, all is not lost. Unscratch any
other files you want to recover from the problem diskette now. Once you can see all
the files you want to keep in a directory listing, copy them one at a time from the
problem diskette onto another diskette. Use a copy program such as FAST COPY at
the end of Chapter 10. Do not use a backup program. Do not reuse the problem
diskette until you have completely reformatted it with a full NEW.

11.3 Recovering Data from an Unclosed File

An unclosed file is one that shows up in a directory listing as being zero blocks long
and has an asterisk in front of its file type (*SEQ, *PRG or *USR). It is called an
unclosed file because the file was never closed properly. An unclosed file may be the
result of a power failure, a program that aborted before it finished writing a file, a
full diskette, a flawed diskette, removing the diskette from the 1541 while the file was
still open, or simply forgetting to close the file.

Some data will always be lost from an unclosed file because at least the last block is missing. It was never recorded on the diskette. To help you get a feel for what an unclosed file is like, let's try some experiments. Get out a test diskette and look at its directory. Be sure to write down the number of blocks free. Now type in this program and run it.

```
10 OPEN 15,8,15,"I"
20 OPEN 1,8,5,"UNCLOSED,S,W"
30 FOR K=10 TO 59
40 PRINT#1, "THIS IS RECORD #";K
50 NEXT
60 STOP
```

When the program stops, the red drive-active LED will still be on. Open the door of the drive and remove the test diskette. The LED will go out.

Now load the test diskette's directory again and list it. There will be a new directory entry that looks like this:

```
0    "UNCLOSED"             *SEQ
```

Notice that the number of blocks free on the diskette has decreased. Let's calculate how much space our file should take. Each of our records should occupy a total of 21 bytes of storage:

```
THIS IS RECORD # 10 *
+---+----+----+----+--
1   5   10   15   20
```

* = carriage return character

Since we have a total of 50 records, we should have used up 50 x 21 = 1050 bytes of disk storage space. Each block (sector) on the diskette can hold 254 bytes (two bytes are used for the forward pointer). Therefore our file should occupy a total of 1050/254 = 4.13385827 blocks.

Since the last block was never written to diskette, our file should have used up four full blocks on the diskette. Even if the next block has already been allocated in the BAM, we should only use five blocks. Did you find a difference of four or five in the number of blocks free? I'll bet you didn't! Surprisingly, the actual decrease in the number of blocks free depends on where the file is stored on the diskette. If you are using a blank diskette, the number of blocks free will decrease from 664 to 643 (21 blocks). The reason for the discrepancy is the strange way in which the 1541 allocates blocks. When a file is opened, all the blocks remaining on a track, or if a new track is needed, the blocks of an entire track, are allocated in the BAM and recorded on track 18, sector 0 of the diskette. The DOS maintains a separate BAM in the drive's RAM memory. Until the file is properly closed these two versions of the BAM will not be the same. The BAM in RAM will show the correct allocation of blocks while the BAM on diskette will show an over allocation of blocks. When the file is closed, the correct BAM is recorded on diskette.

This means that although the BAM of our diskette is incorrect, the blocks that were used to store the unclosed file are all allocated. As a result, storing new information on this diskette will not overwrite the unclosed file.

WARNING:

An unclosed program file that was produced by an aborted SAVE is not protected! In this case, none of the blocks in the file will have been allocated in the diskette's version of the BAM. Be sure to use the ALLOCATE program to allocate the blocks in such a file before you use the RECOVER UNCLOSED program.

Recovering the data stored in an unclosed file is a bit tricky. You cannot OPEN an unclosed file to read it using normal READ (R) mode. You have to use a special MODIFY (M) mode. Let's use a little test program to see how this works. Insert the test diskette in your drive, type in this short program and run it.

```
10 OPEN 15,8,15,"I"
20 OPEN 1,8,5,"UNCLOSED,S,M"
30 GET#1, A$:PRINT A$;
40 IF ST<>0 THEN PRINT "ST="ST
50 GET B$:IF B$="" GOTO 30
60 CLOSE 1: CLOSE 15
```

You should see something like this:

```
THIS IS RECORD #10
THIS IS RECORD #11
THIS IS RECORD #12
:   :   :   :   :   :
THIS IS RECORD #56
THIS IS RECORD #57
THIS IS
```

(garbage follows)   Press any key to stop!

The first part of the file can be read satisfactorily but the last part is lost. Note that the status variable, ST, is always zero. No end-of-file marker is present.

Since an unclosed file has no end-of-file marker and reading past the end of the data produces garbage, you must monitor what is being read and abort the reading process once the end of the file is reached. Here are two short programs to assist you in recovering the data from an unclosed file. The first program, RECOVER UNCLOSED, is used to recover the data from any type of unclosed file (note that it is impossible to have an unclosed REL file). Before you use this program to recover a program file, use the second program, ALLOCATE, to ensure that all the blocks in the file have been properly allocated.

```
********************
PROGRAM: RECOVER UN
********************
```

NOTE:

This program is used to recover the data from any type of unclosed file. The data is read from the unclosed file, displayed on the screen line by line and then stored in a new file. After each line of data you will be asked if you wish to abort the process. To bypass the question simply hold down the SHIFT key. To regain control at any point press the CTRL key.

CAUTION:

Be sure all blocks in the unclosed file are allocated in the BAM before using this program.

```
O REM 1541 USER'S GUIDE SECTION 11.3
1 REM   COPYRIGHT: G. NEUFELD, 1984
2 :
3 REM   RECOVER DATA FROM AN UNCLOSED FIL
E
4 :
100 REM READ UNCLOSED
110 B$="":Z$=CHR$(O):QT$=CHR$(34)+CHR$(2
O)
120 PRINT"{CLR}RECOVER UNCLOSED FILE"
130 INPUT"{DOWN}NAME OF UNCLOSED FILE";U
N$
140 INPUT"FILE TYPE OF UNCLOSED FILE (P/
S/U)";UT$
150 IF UT$="P" OR UT$="S" OR UT$="U" GOT
O 170
160 PRINT"{DOWN}ENTER ONLY 'P', 'S', OR
'U'":GOTO 140
170 OPEN 15,8,15,"IO"
180 OPEN 1,8,5,"O:"+UN$+","+UT$+",M"
190 GOSUB 490
200 IF FL=1 THEN CLOSE 1:CLOSE 15:END
210 INPUT"{DOWN}NAME FOR RECOVERED FILE"
;NF$
220 PRINT"FILE TYPE OF RECOVERED FILE (P
/S/U)   ";UT$
230 PRINT"{UP}"TAB(35);:INPUT NT$
240 IF NT$="P" OR NT$="S" OR NT$="U" GOT
O 260
250 PRINT"{DOWN}ENTER ONLY 'P', 'S', OR
'U'":GOTO 220
260 OPEN 2,8,6,"O:"+NF$+","+NT$+",W"
```

```
270 GOSUB 490
280 IF FL=1 THEN CLOSE 1:CLOSE 2:CLOSE 1
5:END
290 :
300 PRINT"{DOWN}PRESS [CTRL]  TO ABORT"
310 PRINT"        [SHIFT] FOR CONTINUOUS R
EAD{DOWN}"
320 PRINT QT$;
330 ZA$=""
340 GET#1,A$:IF A$=B$ THEN A$=Z$
350 ZA$=ZA$+A$
360 A=ASC(A$)
370 IF A<> 141 THEN PRINT A$;:IF A=34 TH
EN PRINT QT$;
380 P=PEEK(653)
390 IF P AND 4 GOTO 430
400 IF LEN(ZA$)=255 GOTO 430
410 IF A<>0 AND A<>13 GOTO 340
420 IF P AND 1 THEN PRINT:GOTO 460
430 PRINT:INPUT"ABORT NOW (Y/N)   N{LEFT
3}";X$
440 IF X$="Y" THEN CLOSE 1:CLOSE2:CLOSE1
5:END
450 PRINT"{UP}                        {UP}"
460 PRINT#2,ZA$;:ZZ=FRE(0)
470 PRINT QT$;
480 GOTO 330
490 INPUT#15,EN,EM$,ET,ES
500 IF EN<20 THEN FL=0:RETURN
510 PRINT"{DOWN}DISK ERROR"
520 PRINTEN;EM$;ET;ES
530 FL=1
540 RETURN
```

```
****************
PROGRAM: ALLOCATE
****************
```

NOTE:

This program is used to allocate all the blocks in an unclosed file before using the RECOVER UNCLOSED program to recover the data in it. To use this program, simply load and run it. You will need the name of the unclosed file (wild cards are OK) and its file type.

```
0 REM 1541 USER'S GUIDE SECTION 11.3
1 REM  COPYRIGHT: G. NEUFELD, 1984
```

```
2 :
3 REM   ALLOCATE ALL SECTORS IN A FILE
4 :
100 REM ALLOCATE UNCLOSED
110 B$="":Z$=CHR$(0):QT$=CHR$(34)+CHR$(2
0)
120 PRINT"{CLR}ALLOCATE UNCLOSED FILE"
130 INPUT"{DOWN}NAME OF UNCLOSED FILE";U
N$
140 INPUT"FILE TYPE OF UNCLOSED FILE (P/
S/U)";UT$
150 IF UT$="P" OR UT$="S" OR UT$="U" GOT
O 170
160 PRINT"{DOWN}ENTER ONLY 'P', 'S', OR
'U'":GOTO 140
170 OPEN 15,8,15,"IO"
180 GOSUB 410
190 OPEN 1,8,5,"0:"+UN$+","+UT$+",M"
200 GOSUB 410
210 OPEN 2,8,6,"#"
220 GOSUB 410
230 :
240 PRINT#15,"M-R"CHR$(144)CHR$(2)CHR$(1
)
250 GET#15,A$:SE=ASC(A$+Z$)
260 PRINT#15,"M-R"CHR$(148)CHR$(2)CHR$(1
)
270 GET#15,A$:PT=ASC(A$+Z$)
280 PRINT#15,"U1:6 0 18"SE
290 GOSUB 410
300 PRINT#15,"B-P:6"PT+1
310 GOSUB 410
320 GET#2,A$:T=ASC(A$+Z$)
330 GET#2,A$:S=ASC(A$+Z$)
340 NS=20+2*(T>17)+(T>24)+(T>30)
350 IF T<1OR T>35 OR S>NS THEN PRINT"DON
E":GOTO 450
360 PRINT#15,"B-A:0"T;S
370 INPUT#15,EN,EM$,ET,ES
380 IF EN>19 THEN PRINT"ALREADY ALLOCATE
D":GOTO 450
390 PRINT#15,"U1:6 0"T;S
400 GOTO 320
410 INPUT#15,EN,EM$,ET,ES
420 IF EN<20 THEN RETURN
430 PRINT"{DOWN}DISK ERROR"
440 PRINTEN;EM$;ET;ES
450 CLOSE 1:CLOSE 2:CLOSE 15
460 END
```

11.4 Recovering from a Short NEW

When you want to get rid of all the files on a diskette so that you can use it for storing new files, you can use a short NEW disk command. A short NEW command looks like this:

```
SYNTAX:
  NO:diskette name

EXAMPLES:
  OPEN 15,8,15,"NO:LOTTA DATA"
  PRINT#15,"N:NEW GAMES"
  >N:WORDPROCESSING 6
```

Note that no diskette ID is specified in the command. If a diskette ID is included in the command, the disk drive performs a full NEW and rewrites the entire diskette.

It is possible to recover from a short NEW because most of the information on the diskette is not erased. Only the diskette's BAM and the first directory block (track 18, sectors 0 and 1) are altered. The program FIX DIRECTORY listed in Appendix E will automatically recover all the files on your diskette.

To use the FIX DIRECTORY program to recover from a short NEW simply load and run the program. When you are asked which sector to fix, enter a 1 to signify that track 18, sector 1 is to be recovered. After this, everything is automatic. The file type for each file will be assigned as PRG or SEQ on the basis of the load address at the start of the file. The program also checks for possible REL files. If a file may be part of a REL file, you will be asked if this is possible. If you respond with a Y to this question, the program will attempt to reconstruct the relative file.

Once the program has run to completion, all the files on the diskette will have been recovered. The first eight entries in the directory will be named FILE # 1, FILE # 2, and so on, and will have to be renamed. However, this should be easy now that you can load or read the files.

NOTE:

In a few cases, such as the PRG files produced by WordPro™, PaperClip™ and Paint Magic™, you may have to use the EDIT T&S program (Appendix E) or the MOD ENTRY program (Section 13.8) to edit the file type byte to restore the correct file type.

11.5 Repairing a Damaged Directory

One of the most frustrating problems that you can encounter is a diskette with a damaged directory. You know that the files are there, but you can't get at them. Despite what you may have read, it is possible to recover a damaged directory. Here's what to do.

The first thing to do is eliminate your drive as a possible source of the error. If the problem occurs on just one diskette, your drive is probably OK. If you are having problems with most of your diskettes, your drive is probably out of alignment. Either have it aligned professionally or, if you are handy, read Chapter 12 and do it yourself.

Once you are sure the problem is caused by the diskette and not the disk drive, you must determine which directory sector is causing the problem. You can do this by attempting to load the directory and then reading the disk drive's error status, or you can use this short program:

```
********************
PROGRAM: FIND ERRORS
********************


O REM 1541 USER'S GUIDE SECTION 11.5
1 REM  COPYRIGHT: G. NEUFELD, 1984
2 :
3 REM  LOCATE READ ERRORS ON THE DIRECTO
RY TRACK
4 :
100 REM FIND ERRORS
110 PRINT"{CLR}FIND ERRORS IN THE DIRECT
ORY"
120 PRINT"{DOWN}INSERT DISKETTE"
130 PRINT"{DOWN}PRESS {RVS}RETURN{ROFF}
TO CONTINUE"
140 GET A$:IF A$<>CHR$(13) GOTO 140
150 PRINT"{CLR}ERROR ANALYSIS OF TRACK 1
8{DOWN}"
160 OPEN 15,8,15,"IO"
170 OPEN 1,8,5,"#"
180 DIM SE(20)
190 SE(1)=0:KT=1:NE=0
200 FOR K=2 TO 19
210 SE(K)=KT
220 KT=KT+3:IF KT>18 THEN KT=KT-17
230 NEXT
240 FOR K=1 TO 19
250 PRINT#15,"U1:5 0 18"SE(K)
260 INPUT#15,EN,EM$,ET,ES$
270 IF EN<20 GOTO 300
280 NE=NE+1
290 PRINT"SECTOR #"SE(K)"ERROR #"EN" - "
EM$
300 NEXT
310 CLOSE 1:CLOSE 15
320 IF NE=0 THEN PRINT"{DOWN}NO ERRORS F
OUND ON TRACK 18"
330 IF NE<>0 THEN PRINT"{DOWN}"NE"ERRORS
 ON TRACK 18"
```

Once you know which sector is causing problems, write down its sector number and the error code number. Now that you have this information, proceed to the appropriate section below.

Problems on Sector 0

If track 18, sector 0 has any read errors, you will be unable to initialize the diskette or access any files on it. This is the first sector in the directory file and contains the diskette's BAM, disk name and cosmetic ID.

If there is a 22, 23, or 24, READ ERROR on this sector, you can rewrite the sector using the program REDO 18/0 listed below. You can try using this program to recover from the less common 20, 21, or 27, READ ERROR as well, but you are unlikely to succeed. These errors are the result of problems in the header block. If you can't eliminate the problem with REDO 18/0, you will have to use the program BACKUP from Appendix E to make a duplicate of the problem diskette. Unlike most backup programs, this program will not abort when it encounters a read error. Once the backup is complete, validate the duplicate diskette and all your files should be intact.

```
********************
PROGRAM: REDO 18/0
********************

0 REM 1541 USER'S GUIDE SECTION 11.5
1 REM  COPYRIGHT: G. NEUFELD, 1984
2 :
3 REM RECOVER FROM ERRORS ON TRACK 18, S
ECTOR 0
4 :
100 REM REDO 18,0
110 FOR K=1TO16:B$=B$+CHR$(160):NEXT
120 PRINT"{CLR}REDO TRACK 18, SECTOR 0"
130 PRINT"{DOWN} INSERT DISKETTE INTO DR
IVE"
140 PRINT" PRESS {RVS}RETURN{ROFF} TO CO
NTINUE"
150 GET R$:IF R$<>CHR$(13) GOTO 150
160 OPEN 15,8,15
170 OPEN 1,8,5,"#"
180 PRINT#15,"U1:5 0 18 0"
190 INPUT#15,EN,EM$,ET,ES
200 PRINT"{CLR}REDO TRACK 18, SECTOR 0"
210 PRINT"{DOWN} DISK STATUS WHEN READIN
G 18/0 IS:"
220 PRINT"{DOWN}    "EN;EM$;ET;ES
230 CLOSE1
240 INPUT#15,EN,EM$,ET,ES
250 INPUT"{DOWN} CONTINUE (Y/N)  N{LEFT
3}";R$
260 IF R$<>"Y" THEN CLOSE15:END
270 PRINT"{CLR}REDO TRACK 18, SECTOR 0"
```

```
280 JOB=176:GOSUB 470
290 PRINT"{DOWN} EMBEDDED DISK ID IS:"ID
$
300 PRINT"{DOWN} DISK NAME DESIRED{DOWN}
   {COM-U 16}"
310 PRINT"{UP 2}"TAB(18);:INPUT DN$
320 DN$=LEFT$(DN$+B$,16)
330 PRINT"{DOWN 2} ONE MOMENT PLEASE....
"
340 PRINT#15,"M-W"CHR$(0)CHR$(3)CHR$(4)C
HR$(18)CHR$(4)CHR$(65)CHR$(0)
350 FOR K=4 TO 143:PRINT#15,"M-W"CHR$(K)
CHR$(3)CHR$(1)CHR$(0):NEXT
360 PRINT#15,"M-W"CHR$(144)CHR$(3)CHR$(2
0)DN$;CHR$(160)CHR$(160)ID$
370 PRINT#15,"M-W"CHR$(164)CHR$(3)CHR$(3
)CHR$(32)"2A"
380 FOR K=167 TO 170:PRINT#15,"M-W"CHR$(
K)CHR$(3)CHR$(1)CHR$(160):NEXT
390 FOR K=171 TO 179:PRINT#15,"M-W"CHR$(
K)CHR$(3)CHR$(1)CHR$(0):NEXT
400 PRINT#15,"M-W"CHR$(180)CHR$(3)CHR$(1
2)"BLOCKS FREE."
410 FOR K=192 TO 206:PRINT#15,"M-W"CHR$(
K)CHR$(3)CHR$(1)CHR$(32):NEXT
420 FOR K=207 TO 255:PRINT#15,"M-W"CHR$(
K)CHR$(3)CHR$(1)CHR$(0):NEXT
430 JOB=144:GOSUB 470
440 PRINT"{DOWN} VALIDATING DISKETTE TO
CORRECT BAM"
450 PRINT#15,"V":CLOSE 15:END
460 :
470 PRINT#15,"M-W"CHR$(6)CHR$(0)CHR$(2)C
HR$(18)CHR$(0)
480 PRINT#15,"M-W"CHR$(0)CHR$(0)CHR$(1)C
HR$(JOB)
490 PRINT#15,"M-R"CHR$(0)CHR$(0)
500 GET#15,A$:A=ASC(A$+CHR$(0))
510 IF A>127 GOTO 490
520 IF A=1 GOTO 570
530 TY=TY+1:IF TY<5 GOTO 470
540 IF JOB=176 THEN PRINT"{DOWN}CAN'T FI
ND TRACK 18":CLOSE15:END
550 PRINT"WILL NOT WRITE CLEANLY.":CLOSE
15:END
560 PRINT"SECTOR ZERO. ERROR #"A+18:CLOS
E15:END
570 PRINT#15,"M-R"CHR$(18)CHR$(0)CHR$(2)

580 GET#15,A$:ID$=A$
```

```
590 GET#15,A$:ID$=ID$+A$
600 RETURN
```

Problems on Sector 1

If track 18, sector 1 cannot be read without error, you will be unable to access any files on the diskette. This is the second block of the directory file and contains the directory entries for the first eight files on the diskette.

The FIX DIRECTORY program from Appendix E can recover the files if there is a 22, 23, or 24, READ ERROR on this sector. You can try using this same program to try to recover from the less common 20, 21, or 27, READ ERROR as well. You won't cause any harm, but you are unlikely to succeed in eliminating the error. These errors are the result of problems in the header block.

To use the FIX DIRECTORY program to recover from a read error on sector 1, simply load and run the program. When you are asked which sector to fix, enter a one. The program will then attempt to read the sector. If a read error is encountered, you will be informed of the type of error and presented with three choices:

1. Null out the sector.
2. Bridge over the damaged sector.
3. Terminate the program.

Always choose the null out the sector option at least once. If the sector contains a 22, 23, or 24, READ ERROR, this should repair the damaged sector. If the sector contains a 20, 21, or 27, READ ERROR, this attempt at repair may not work. If it doesn't, you must use the program BACKUP from Appendix E to make a duplicate of the problem diskette (you cannot bridge over errors in sector 1). Once the backup is complete (about 25 minutes), use the FIX DIRECTORY program with the backup diskette as indicated above.

Once sector 1 can be read without error, it is checked to make sure it is an empty sector. If any characters, other than nulls, are found, you will be asked if it is OK to continue. This is done so you have a chance to abort things if you gave the wrong sector number.

After this, everything is automatic. The file type for each file will be assigned as PRG or SEQ on the basis of the load address at the start of the file. The program also checks for possible REL files. If a file may be part of a REL file, you will be asked if this is possible. If you respond with a Y to this question, the program will attempt to reconstruct the relative file.

Once the program has run to completion, all the files will have been recovered. The first eight entries in the directory will be named FILE # 1, FILE # 2, and so on, and will have to be renamed. However, this should be easy since you can load or read the files.

NOTE:

In a few cases, such as the PRG files produced by WordPro™, PaperClip™ and Paint Magic™, you may have to use the EDIT T&S program (Appendix E) or the MOD ENTRY program (Section 13.8) to edit the file type byte to restore the correct file type.

Problems on Sectors 2 to 18

If any one of these blocks cannot be read without error *and* is being used as part of the directory file, you will be able to access some of the files on the diskette. However, any files whose entries are in the damaged block or in subsequent blocks of the directory file will not be accessible. Each block in the directory file can hold up to eight directory entries.

The FIX DIRECTORY program from Appendix E can recover the files regardless of the type of error on these sectors. To use the FIX DIRECTORY program to recover from a read error on one of these sectors, simply load and run the program. When you are asked which sector to fix, enter the sector number of the block to be recovered. The program will attempt to read the sector you specified. If a read error is encountered, you will be informed as to the type of error and presented with three choices:

1. Null out the sector.
2. Bridge over the damaged sector.
3. Terminate the program.

You should always choose the null out the sector option at least once. If the sector contains a 22, 23, or 24, READ ERROR, this should repair the damaged sector. If the sector contains a 20, 21, or 27, READ ERROR, this attempt at repair may not work. If it doesn't, choose the bridge over the damaged sector option. This causes the directory's file chain to be altered to bridge over the damaged sector. If you choose this option, your files will not be recovered immediately. The program will alter the directory file chain, trace it and tell you which sector number to specify when you rerun the program. To recover the lost files simply rerun the program and specify the sector number that was indicated.

Once the sector can be read without error, it is checked to make sure it is an empty sector. If any characters, other than nulls, are found, you will be asked if it is OK to continue. This check is made simply so you have a chance to abort things in case you specified the wrong sector number.

After this, everything is automatic. The file type for each file will be assigned as PRG or SEQ on the basis of the load address at the start of the file. The program also checks for possible REL files. If a file may be part of a REL file, you will be asked if this is possible. If you respond with a Y to this question, the program will attempt to reconstruct the relative file.

Once the program has run to completion, all the files will have been recovered. The recovered files will have to be renamed. However, this should be easy now that you can load or read the files.

NOTE:

In a few cases, such as the PRG files produced by WordPro™, PaperClip™ and Paint Magic™, you may have to use the EDIT T&S program (Appendix E) or the MOD ENTRY program (Section 13.8) to edit the file type byte to restore the correct file type.

11.6 Recovering from a Full NEW

If you are reading this section in a panic in hopes of gaining absolution for your past sins, relax; it's too late. However, if you are interested in learning how to avert a future catastrophy, read on.

When you want to prepare a brand new diskette for first use or erase everything from a previously used diskette, you use a full NEW disk command. A full NEW command looks like this:

```
SYNTAX:
  N0:diskette name,id

EXAMPLES:
  OPEN 15,8,15,"N0:LOTTA DATA,LD"
  PRINT#15,"N:NEW GAMES,G5"
  >N:WORDPROCESSING 6,W6
```

Note that a diskette ID is always specified in a full NEW. If the diskette ID is omitted, the disk drive performs a short NEW and just rewrites sectors 0 and 1 on track 18.

If you are busily making a backup copy of your favorite diskette and you realize you are standing there holding a blank diskette while your disk drive is merrily destroying your master copy, don't panic. Reach over, pop the door of your drive open *immediately*, and rescue your master diskette. At this point, you really don't care what the manual says about not opening the door while the red drive-active LED is on. You want that diskette now! A full track of data is being destroyed every two seconds starting at track 1.

Once you have rescued the diskette, it is time to assess the damage. Try to load and list the directory. If this works, use the CONFIRM ALL FILES program from Appendix E to check for any problems. If you were quick, you may be pleasantly surprised to find that all your files are safe. Copy all the intact files onto another diskette and do a full NEW on the partially formatted diskette.

The reason it is possible to recover from a full NEW is related to how space is utilized on the diskette. As you begin to store files on an empty diskette they are stored as close as possible to track 18 (the directory track). The first file is stored beginning on track 17. Once track 17 is full, the next file is stored beginning on track 19. As more and more files are added, the diskette gradually fills up. Tracks 1 and 35 are the last tracks to be filled. This means that a partially filled diskette may have nothing stored on tracks 1 to 10 and tracks 25 to 35. Since formatting begins on track 1 and progresses upwards, none of the files would be erased from such a diskette until formatting reached track 11. As long as you managed to pop the door before formatting reached your files, everything would be safe. The only problem is that tracks 1 to 10 would be formatted with a different embedded ID. Once the files were copied to another diskette, this two-ID diskette should be reformatted with a full NEW.

11.7 Recovering a Damaged File

If one of the sectors used to store a file contains a read error, you will be unable to read the entire file. You can use the RECOVER UNCLOSED program from Section 11.3 to recover the file as far as the damaged block. Trying to reclaim the rest of the file is a bigger problem. Here are some suggestions.

The first thing to do is to trace the file. You can use the CONFIRM ALL FILES program from Appendix E to print out the file chain for you. You want to specify the printer output, trace file chains and print SUPER BAM options. Once you have these printouts in hand, it is time for a bit of detective work.

The printout of the file chain for the program will list all the blocks in the file up to, and including, the block containing the error. You want to make note of the track and sector numbers of the last block before the error. Write these numbers down, you'll need them in a minute.

Now look at the printout of the SUPER BAM. You should see several allocated blocks that are not part of any file. These blocks will be highlighted in reverse field in the printout. Your task is to determine which of these is the block that follows the damaged block in the file chain. If you study the pattern of the numbers in the file chain you should be able to make a pretty good guess. Let's look at an example.

Existing file chain:
17,00 17,10 17,20 17,08 17,18 17,06

Damaged block:
17,16

Allocated blocks not part of any file (from SUPER BAM):
17,01 17,02 17,04 17,12 17,14

The sector sequence seems to alternate between a low number and a high number with a difference of 10 between them (0-10-20; 8-18; 6-16). Since the damaged block has a high sector number, we would expect the next block to have a low sector number. If we study the low numbers, we find that they seem to be decreasing by two each time (10 -8 -6). As a result, we would expect the next sector in this file chain to be track 17, sector 4.

Once you have determined the most likely next sector in the file chain, you can check it using the TRACE CHAIN program listed below. Given a starting track and sector, this program will trace the file chain to completion and display the file chain on the screen. You can try several of the allocated blocks that are not part of any file as starting points to see which produces the longest file chain.

```
*********************
PROGRAM: TRACE CHAIN
*********************

0 REM 1541 USER'S GUIDE SECTION 11.7
1 REM   COPYRIGHT: G. NEUFELD, 1984
2 :
3 REM   TRACE & DISPLAY FILE CHAIN
4 REM   INCLUDING THE SIDE SECTOR FILE
5 :
100 REM TRACE FILE CHAIN
110 PRINT"{CLR}TRACE FILE CHAIN"
120 INPUT"{DOWN}START AT (TRACK,SECTOR)"
;T,S
130 Z$=CHR$(0)
140 OPEN 15,8,15,"IO"
150 GOSUB 370
160 OPEN 1,8,5,"#"
170 GOSUB 370
180 PRINT"{DOWN}FILE CHAIN{DOWN}"
190 NX=0
200 NX=NX+1
210 IF NX=7 THEN PRINT:NX=1
220 FC$=RIGHT$(STR$(T),2)+","+RIGHT$("0"
+MID$(STR$(S),2),2)+" "
230 PRINTFC$;
240 PRINT#15,"U1:5 0"T;S
250 GOSUB 370
260 PRINT#15,"B-P:5 0"
270 GOSUB 370
280 GET#1,A$:T=ASC(A$+Z$)
290 GET#1,A$:S=ASC(A$+Z$)
300 IF T=0 AND S>0 THEN PRINT:PRINT"{DOW
N}END OF CHAIN":GOTO 420
310 IF T=0 AND S=0 THEN PRINT:PRINT"{DOW
N}VIRGIN SECTOR"T;S:GOTO 420
320 IF T=75 AND S=1 THEN PRINT:PRINT"{DO
WN}VIRGIN SECTOR"T;S:GOTO 420
330 NS=20+2*(T>17)+(T>24)+(T>30)
340 IF T>35 OR S>NS THEN PRINT:PRINT"{DO
WN}BAD LINK"T;S:GOTO 420
350 GOTO 200
360 :
370 INPUT#15,EN,EM$,ET,ES
380 IF EN<20 THEN RETURN
390 PRINT:PRINT"{DOWN}DISK ERROR"
```

```
400 PRINTEN;EM$;ET;ES
410 :
420 CLOSE 1:CLOSE 15:END
```

When you are certain that you know the track and sector numbers of the block that
follows the damaged one, you are ready to alter the file chain. You will use the EDIT
T&S program from Appendix E to do this. Here's the procedure:

Step 1: Load and run the EDIT T&S program.

Step 2: Insert the damaged diskette and ask to edit the last block before the damaged
one.

Step 3: Press F1 to switch to hex edit mode.

Step 4: Edit the first two bytes on the top line of the display. These two bytes currently
are the track and sector numbers of the damaged block. Change them so that they are
the track and sector numbers of the block immediately following the damaged block
in the file chain. Remember, the numbers are in hexadecimal notation. Check the
table in Appendix B if you need help converting from decimal to hex.

Step 5: Press F6 to write out the revised sector to diskette.

Step 6: Press F5 to exit from the program.

You have now bridged over the damaged sector. One block of your file will be
missing, but now you can get at the rest of the file. Hopefully, you will be able to
reconstruct the missing data or program lines.

HINT:

If the file you have just recovered is a program file, it may cause your computer to
hang if you load it and try to edit it. However, you should be able to list it. If this
happens to you, read over Section 7.7 carefully. You should be able to create an ASCII
text file of your program. If you can, do so. Then, turn your computer OFF and ON,
type in the little merge routine from Section 7.7, and merge the ASCII copy of your
program back into memory. You should now be able to edit your program normally.
Naturally, with one whole block of lines missing, it won't run properly until you
reconstruct those missing lines.

11.8 Recovering from a Bad Replacement

Despite what you may have read, the save with replacement (SAVE "@0:name",8)
and the open for replacement (OPEN 1,8,5,"@0:name,type,W") commands usually
work fine. As long as no disk errors are encountered during the writing of the
replacement file, everything works perfectly. However, if any disk error occurs and
the file is closed (this happens automatically with the SAVE with replacement
command), the new file will be incomplete and the old file appears to be lost.

Actually the old file is not really lost, it can be recovered, as we will see shortly. It is still recorded on the diskette like a scratched file, but this time there is no corresponding directory entry to assist us in recovering the file. The old directory entry has been modified so that the track and sector link now points to the replacement file. This means that we cannot use our UNSCRATCHER program to recover it. We need a program that creates a new directory entry and finds the correct track and sector link for us.

The program, RECOVER FILE, listed below will recover any program, sequential or user file stored on a diskette. It recovers scratched files as well as those lost by an aborted replacement command. The only restriction is that the blocks used to store the file must not be allocated in the BAM. You may have to VALIDATE the diskette to free the blocks used to store the file.

The RECOVER FILE program is not as elegant as the FIX DIRECTORY program, but it uses the same basic technique. Since this technique has never been documented before, let me explain it. Line 230 of the program opens the specified file. When the 1541 receives this command, it checks the BAM for the first block available for use on the diskette, and creates a new directory entry with a track and sector link that points to this block. Since this is the same process it went through when the file to be recovered was first opened, the new track and sector link inevitably points to the first block in the file to be recovered! Lines 260-300 dig out the directory sector containing the new entry and its location in that sector. (You could read through the directory file to find the new entry but this is much more elegant.) In line 330 we issue an initialize command. This automatically aborts (not closes) any active disk files. (We don't want to close the file normally because this would overwrite the first block in the file we want to recover.) We have now created a new directory entry that points to the file we want to recover. However, it has the wrong file type; it is an unclosed file. Lines 370-430 read in the directory sector containing the entry and correct the file type byte. The only job left is to validate the diskette to correct the BAM. Line 460 does this.

The resurrected file will show up in a directory listing as having a length of zero blocks. This is a cosmetic problem. The entire file has been recovered and all blocks have been allocated in the BAM and are protected. If you copy the file onto another diskette, the new file will show the correct length. However, if you don't want to copy the file onto another diskette and this cosmetic problem bothers you, here's how to solve it. First, use the CONFIRM ALL FILES program (Appendix E) to find out the file's actual length. Then use the MOD ENTRY program (Section 13.8) to change the directory entry so that it indicates the proper length.

```
****************
PROGRAM: RECOVER
****************
```

NOTES:

1. The RECOVER FILE program recovers any stray files on the diskette. If your diskette contains any scratched files, you may have to run the program several times until you recover the file you want.

2. Be sure to use a new file name for the recovered file. Otherwise you will get a 63,
   FILE EXISTS, error and the program will abort.

```
0 REM 1541 USER'S GUIDE SECTION 11.8
1 REM   COPYRIGHT: G. NEUFELD, 1984
2 :
3 REM   RECOVER FILE WITHOUT DIRECTORY EN
TRY
4 :
100 REM RECOVER FILE FOR C-64/V-20 & 154
1
110 QT$=CHR$(34)
120 PRINT"{CLR}        RECOVER FILE"
130 INPUT"{DOWN}NAME FOR RECOVERED FILE"
;RN$
140 INPUT"FILE TYPE (P/S/U)";RT$
150 IF RT$="S" THEN FT=129:GOTO 200
160 IF RT$="P" THEN FT=130:GOTO 200
170 IF RT$="U" THEN FT=131:GOTO 200
180 PRINT"{DOWN}ENTER ONLY 'P', 'S', OR
'U'":GOTO 140
190 :
200 DEF FN A(X)=PEEK(57)+256*PEEK(58)
210 OPEN 15,8,15,"I0"
220 LN=FN A(X):GOSUB 520
230 OPEN 1,8,5,"0:"+UN$+","+UT$+",W"
240 LN=FN A(X):GOSUB 520
250 :
260 REM DIG OUT POINTER TO DIRECTORY ENT
RY
270 PRINT#15,"M-R"CHR$(144)CHR$(2)CHR$(1
)
280 GET#15,A$:SE=ASC(A$+CHR$(0))
290 PRINT#15,"M-R"CHR$(148)CHR$(2)CHR$(1
)
300 GET#15,A$:PT=ASC(A$+CHR$(0))
310 :
320 REM INITIALIZE TO CREATE UNCLOSED FI
LE
330 PRINT#15,"I0"
340 CLOSE 1
350 :
360 REM CHANGE ENTRY TO CORRECT FILE TYP
E
370 OPEN 2,8,6,"#"
380 PRINT#15,"U1:6 0 18"SE
390 LN=FN A(X):GOSUB 520
400 PRINT#15,"B-P:6"PT
410 PRINT#2,CHR$(FT);
420 PRINT#15,"U2:6 0 18"SE
```

```
430 LN=FN A(X):GOSUB 520
440 :
450 REM VALIDATE DISKETTE TO ALLOCATE BL
OCKS
460 PRINT#15,"VO"
470 INPUT#15,EN,EM$,ET,ES
480 IF EN<20 THEN PRINT"{DOWN}FILE "QT$;
RN$;QT$" HAS BEEN RECOVERED":GOTO 560
490 PRINT"{DOWN}WARNING: BAM IS NOT CORR
ECT"
500 PRINT"{DOWN}FILE RECOVERED BUT NOT P
ROTECTED":GOTO 560
510 :
520 INPUT#15,EN,EM$,ET,ES:PRINTLN
530 IF EN<20 THEN RETURN
540 PRINT"{DOWN}DISK ERROR AT LINE"LN
550 PRINTEN;EM$;ET;ES
560 CLOSE 2:CLOSE 15
570 END
```

11.9 Recovering a Physically Damaged Diskette

Despite all the warnings you have heard and read, you probably still like to sip a cup of coffee or a soft drink while using your computer. Eventually the inevitable happens. You end up with a very wet and soggy diskette. Of course, this diskette is the one with all your current work on it and there is no backup. Why else would it be lying around so conveniently?

Well, now that the inevitable has happened, what do you do about it? You treat it somewhat like a kid that just fell in a puddle. You take off its wet clothes, wash it up a bit, and put it in dry clothes.

The first step is to remove the mylar disk from its protective jacket. Use a sharp knife to pry up the flaps that hold the two sides of the jacket together and open it up. Remove the mylar disk carefully (try to remember which side is up). Do not touch the recording surface with your skin as you do this (a pair of gloves makes this easier).

Now rinse off the disk with clean water. If you have hard water, a little wetting agent (like photographers' PHOTO FLO) will help prevent streaking and mineral deposits. Set the disk on a soft, lint free surface to dry.

Now for the dry clothes. You can sacrifice a new diskette to get a clean, dry jacket. Or, if you have a floppy disk type head cleaner (see Section 12.2), you can use its permanent jacket as a temporary home for your freshly cleaned diskette. Insert the diskette into its new jacket. Try loading a directory. You may be pleasantly surprised to find that everything is back to normal. If it is, how about a backup, or maybe two?

If you can't load the directory, you may have put the diskette in the jacket upside down. Try putting the diskette in the drive upside down. Still no luck? Too bad!

11.10 Conclusion

This chapter has described how to recover from most types of diskette problems. As you may have noticed, recovery is usually possible but can be difficult. The disk utility programs listed in this chapter and in Appendix E are very powerful tools and represent the current state of the art in file recovery. They allow automated recovery of files from almost any kind of problem, even from problems that eminent authorities have claimed make the files completely unrecoverable! However, any powerful tool can be misused. You should always practice using a program with a test diskette before you operate on one that is important or valuable.

Despite these powerful utilities, it is always easier to dig out your archival copy of a program or data file than to recover a damaged diskette. Be safe, not sorry! *Backup your diskettes regularly!* If you don't have a backup program, you can use the BACKUP program from Appendix E. It is not the fastest backup program available (it takes about 25 minutes to backup a diskette), but it does a reasonable job and does not abort if it encounters a read or write error.

CHAPTER 12

CARE AND MAINTENANCE

This chapter describes how to care for your 1541 disk drive and keep it in top shape. Included are such topics as cleaning the record/play head, permanently changing the device number and preventing drive wheel slippage. This chapter also includes a listing of a disk utility program that allows you to align your 1541 disk drive without using an oscilloscope or other expensive equipment.

12.1 General Operating Hints

Many of the problems that people encounter with their disk drives are the result of a poor operating environment. Dust, smoke particles and stray magnetic fields all cause problems. Keep your working environment clean and smoke free. Be sure to keep your diskettes away from sources of magnetic fields such as TV sets (this includes your monitor) and electric motors. These simple steps will eliminate many potential errors.

Another source of problems is switching your disk drive ON or OFF with a diskette in it. The resulting sudden surge of current through the record/play head may produce a magnetic spike on the diskette surface. If the spike occurs in the wrong place, you will make one block of information on the diskette unreadable. Since the record/play head spends much of its time on track 18, you are likely to destroy the diskette's directory. This is the most common cause of a 23, READ ERROR.

Heat buildup is also a cause of problems with the 1541 drive. The case is not well ventilated. As a result, the temperature inside the case gradually rises, over a 30 minute period, until it reaches a stable value. At this point, the temperature inside the case may be high enough to exceed the maximum design operating temperature of some of the integrated circuit chips. This can cause a chip to fail. The high temperature can also cause alignment problems as indicated in Section 12.4. To minimize the temperature problem follow these operating rules:

1. Always place the drive on a hard, clean surface. If it is placed on a soft surface, the bottom air vents may be restricted or blocked.

2. Turn off your 1541 when it is not in use.

3. Do not place papers, diskette envelopes or diskettes on top of the drive. You may restrict or block the upper vents.

If you have a severe heat problem, you may have to install a fan or cut larger vents in the case.

12.2 Cleaning the Record/Play Head

There are a lot of conflicting opinions about how often you should clean a disk drive's record/play head. Some experts claim you should clean it once a month while others suggest less frequent cleaning. I have worked with disk drives for several years, and tend to favor yearly cleaning. One disk drive that I use regularly has not been cleaned for three years and there is no noticeable buildup of residue on the head. However, I always use medium grade diskettes. If you use inexpensive off-brands, you may get a more rapid buildup.

The easiest way to clean the record/play head is to use a commercial head cleaner. They look somewhat like a floppy diskette but instead of having a plastic disk inside the jacket, they have a slightly abrasive disk impregnated with a cleaning solvent. To use one of these cleaners simply insert the cleaning diskette in the drive and attempt to load a directory several times. This causes the drive motor to switch on. The rotating disk cleans the head.

You can also clean the head using a cotton swab moistened with denatured alcohol (*not rubbing alcohol!*). However, you must disassemble the 1541 to gain suitable access to the record/play head, so this procedure is not recommended for the novice.

12.3 Permanently Changing the Device Number

The procedure outlined below is useful when you own two or more disk drives. By permanently altering the device numbers you avoid the bother of changing the device numbers every time you turn on your system. The procedure involves using a knife to cut one or two jumpers on the printed circuit board inside the disk drive. You will need a small Phillips (+) screwdriver and a sharp knife. If you feel uncomfortable about tinkering around with things electronic, have your dealer do it for you.

Note that there are two types of 1541 disk drives: the long board and the short board versions. The location of the jumpers mentioned in Step 5 is different for the two versions, so you will have to know which version you have. In most cases you can tell by the color of the exterior case. Most, if not all, of the original, long board versions have ivory colored cases. If your drive has a brown case, it is probably the newer, short board version. Once you open the case you will be able to tell for sure. The printed circuit board on a long board version is about 12.5 inches (31 cm) long. It is only about 9.5 inches (24 cm) long on the short board version.

1. Remove all connecting cables, including the power cable, from your drive.

2. Turn your disk drive upside down on a flat, level, stable surface and remove the four small Phillips screws that hold the case together. They are recessed into the bottom — two at the front and two at the rear of the drive.

3. Carefully turn the drive upright and remove the top cover.

4. There may be a metal plate that covers the printed circuit board. This must be removed. It is held in place by two small screws. Both are on the left-hand side as you face the front of the drive. If you have a long board version, be careful of the two wires that lead to the green power light at the front of the drive. These wires are attached to a plug that plugs into the circuit board. You can unplug them but make a diagram showing how and where they are attached.

5. Locate the device number jumpers. They look like two semicircles joined by a narrow strip. The diagram below indicates the location of the jumpers on the two versions of the 1541.

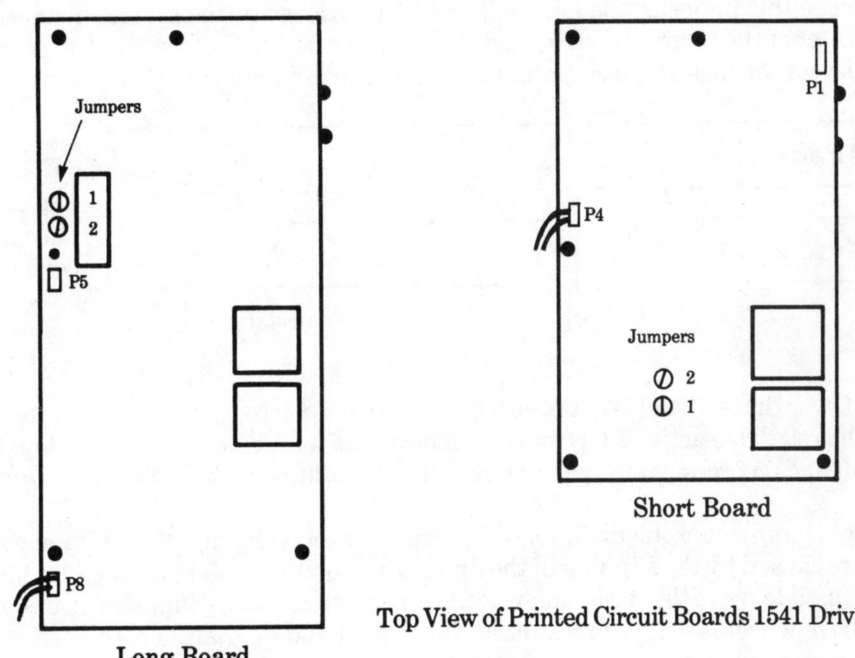

Top View of Printed Circuit Boards 1541 Drive

On the long board version the two jumpers are labeled one and two. They are not labeled on the short board version. On the short board version jumper one is the one closest to the front of the drive near the transistor marked Q3. Jumper two is the one near the capacitor marked C46.

6. Use a knife to cut through the narrow trace connecting the two semicircles for one or both of the jumpers. Use the following table to determine which jumpers to cut.

Device #	#8	#9	#10	#11
Jumper 1	intact	cut	intact	cut
Jumper 2	intact	intact	cut	cut

EXAMPLE: For a 1541 drive to be device# 9, cut jumper one and leave jumper two intact.

7. Replace the metal cover and fasten it in place with the two small screws. If you have a long board version, be sure to reconnect the power light wires.

8. Replace the top of the case and fasten it in place with the four screws. Now reconnect the power cord and cables.

Since this procedure is recommended in your *1541 User's Manual* (page 40), it should not affect your warranty. To convert a drive back to device# 8, bridge the jumper you cut with solder.

12.4 The Alignment Problem

The most common problem with the 1541 disk drive is head alignment. The mechanism that positions the record/play head tends to shift out of alignment easily. When this happens, the head will not be positioned at the correct distance from the center of the rotating disk to read the tracks and sectors correctly. A greatly enlarged view of the disk and head might look something like this:

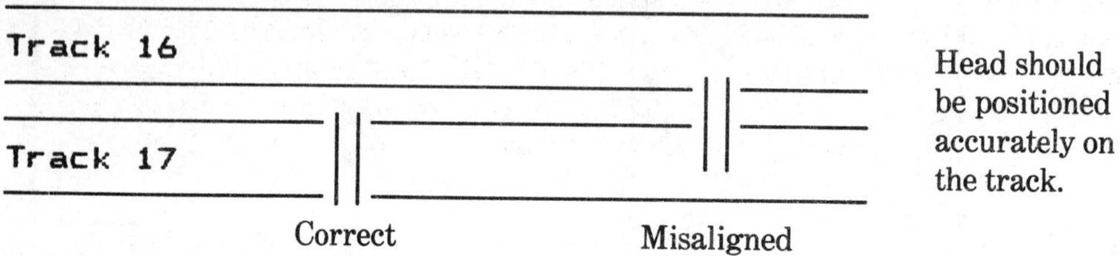

If your drive's head is not properly aligned, read errors will occur frequently. Watch the red drive-active LED on your drive while a long program is loading. If it blinks off and on occasionally, your drive is having trouble reading the diskette.

An alignment problem may develop gradually or suddenly. Most alignment problems are caused by the slipping of the drive wheel on the shaft of the stepper motor which is used to move the record/play head from track to track. Slippage occurs because the drive wheel is only a press fit on the stepper motor shaft. There is no set screw or keyway to maintain the correct alignment. When the 1541 has been operating for a long time, it gets hot inside, the metal parts expand and the drive wheel may slip if stress is applied. Normal accessing of files does not produce enough stress to cause problems. However, slippage will occur if there is a bump to track 1. When the drive does a bump, the stepper motor attempts to move the head outward a total of 45 tracks. This is done to ensure that the head is positioned over track 1. A lobe on the stepper motor drive wheel hits a mechanical stop to prevent the head from moving past track 1. It is the hammering of this lobe against the mechanical stop that causes the clatter each time you format a diskette or when the drive is attempting to recover from an error. If a bump occurs when your drive is hot, some slippage is likely.

You can minimize the possibility of slippage by following these general operating rules:

1. Turn off your 1541 disk drive when it is not in use. This minimizes the heating problem.

2. Do not format a diskette when your disk drive is hot.

3. Do not load any DOS protected diskette that causes the drive to err out when your disk drive is warm. Many disk drives have been thrown out of alignment by the use of such programs. A DOS protection scheme does not have to hammer your drive to death to be effective. You should return as defective any commercial diskette that causes a bump each time the program loads. Don't take chances. It's your drive that will be damaged!

If you follow these rules, you will minimize, but not eliminate, the alignment problem. When your drive finally does go out of alignment, you can realign it yourself using the procedure described in Section 12.6.

12.5 Checking the Alignment of your 1541

Normally you need an oscilloscope and a special alignment diskette to align a disk drive. However, the program listed below can be used to check the alignment of your drive and even realign it (see Section 12.6). All you need is your Commodore 64 computer, your 1541 drive, a copy of the ALIGN 1541 program and a standard diskette. You can use any formatted diskette as your standard. However, we'll use your 1541TEST/DEMO diskette in our examples.

Here's what to do:

1. Load and run the ALIGN 1541 program. If your drive is very badly out of alignment, you may have to load the program from cassette or borrow a friend's drive.

2. Insert your 1541TEST/DEMO or other standard diskette.

If your drive is reasonably well aligned, you should see a display like the one shown below. If your drive is not aligned, the track numbers and head position message may be different.

```
    ALIGN THE 1541 DRIVE

TRACK # FROM STEPPER: 18

HEAD POSITION:CLEAN READ OF TRACK

TRACK # AS READ:   18
SECTOR # AS READ:   4
ID OF TRACK READ: ZX


COMMANDS:

   F1 = MOVE HEAD OUT (LOWER TRACK #)
   F3 = MOVE HEAD IN (HIGHER TRACK #)
   F7 = TERMINATE PROGRAM
    I = INITIALIZE (TO TRACK 18)
```

Let's analyze this display line by line.

`TRACK # FROM STEPPER: 18`

This tells us that the stepper motor has positioned the 1541's read/write head to the position where it expects to find track 18. As the diskette rotates past the record/play head a special machine language routine (that the ALIGN 1541 program stored in the disk drive's RAM memory) attempts to read the header blocks of the sectors as they move past.

`HEAD POSITION:CLEAN READ OF TRACK`

This line of the display tells us whether our routine was successful in reading and interpreting a header. There are three possible messages that can be displayed:

`CLEAN READ OF TRACK` — indicates that a header was read successfully.
`CLOSE TO HALFWAY POINT` — found a header but it was junk (high tone).
`EXACTLY HALFWAY BETWEEN` — couldn't even find a sync mark (low tone).

At this point you should be getting the CLEAN READ OF TRACK message. You can force a display of the third message by opening the drive door and removing the diskette. This will not harm your drive or diskette. You can even switch diskettes and try a different standard. The program doesn't mind!

```
TRACK # AS READ:   18
SECTOR # AS READ:   4
ID OF TRACK READ: ZX
```

These three lines of the display tell us the contents of the header if we managed to read one successfully. If you watch the display, you will see the sector number change as the sectors flip past. Since we are only reading a header about once a second, we don't get to see the sectors in sequence.

`COMMANDS:`

```
F1 = MOVE HEAD OUT (LOWER TRACK #)
F3 = MOVE HEAD IN (HIGHER TRACK #)
F7 = TERMINATE PROGRAM
 I = INITIALIZE (TO TRACK 18)
```

The last part of the display shows us our options. Each time you press F1, the head moves outward half a track. Yes, you read that correctly — half a track. Try it and see what happens. The line that gives the track number from the stepper motor should now indicate that you are on track 17.5! Depending on the alignment of your drive, the track number as read may be either 17, 18 or ??. If you are getting ?? as the track number, you should be hearing either a low or a high-pitched chime and have either a CLOSE TO HALFWAY POINT or EXACTLY HALFWAY BETWEEN message on the screen.

Now that you know what the screen display means, practice moving the record/play head around. Remember, you press:

F1 to move half a track outwards (towards track 1).
F3 to move half a track inwards (towards track 35).
I to return to track 18.
F7 to terminate the program.

If your drive is reasonably well aligned, you should be able to read all the tracks cleanly. On the half tracks you may read the upper track, the lower track, or something in between.

Now that you know how to move the head around, let's take a look at the amount of hysteresis (his-tur-e-sis) in the head positioning mechanism. This is a fancy way of talking about the amount of play there is in the mechanism. Here's what to do:

1. Use F3 to move the head to track 19 (stepper motor).
2. Use F1 to move the head out to track 17.5.
3. Write down the information about what is being read.
4. Use F1 to move the head out to track 16.
5. Use F3 to move the head in to track 17.5.
6. Write down the information about what is being read.

The difference between what you found in Steps 3 and 6 gives you an indication of the amount of play in the head-positioning mechanism. On an optimally aligned drive you should get the message, CLOSE TO HALFWAY POINT whether you approach track 17.5 from a lower or higher track number. If you always get a large discrepancy (a clean read of 17 from one direction and a clean read of 18 from the other) with several different standard diskettes, there is an excessive amount of play or friction in the head-positioning mechanism. You should take your drive to a competent technician or at least lubricate the rods that the head carriage slides on (see Step 11 in Section 12.7).

The reason we chose track 17.5 as the place to make our hysteresis check was that 1541 drives are normally aligned using track 17. However, there is nothing particularly sacred about this track. If you decide to use some other point as your standard reference point, make sure it is near the middle of the recording area of the diskette.

By now you should have a pretty good idea whether your drive should be realigned. It should be realigned if you found:

1. That any track could not be read cleanly (i.e., you received either the CLOSE TO HALFWAY POINT or EXACTLY HALFWAY BETWEEN message when the stepper motor track number was a whole number).

2. That there were any tracks where the track number, as read, did not agree with the track number from the stepper motor.

You don't really have to worry about what happens between tracks unless you are in the process of realigning your drive. In that case you would like to adjust the drive so you get the message, CLOSE TO HALFWAY POINT, whether you approach track 17.5 from a lower or higher track number.

```
********************
PROGRAM: ALIGN 1541
********************

0 REM 1541 USER'S GUIDE SECTION 12.5
1 REM   COPYRIGHT: G. NEUFELD, 1984
2 :
3 REM   CHECK ALIGNMENT AND/OR RE-ALIGN A
  1541
4 :
100 PRINT"{CLR}{DOWN}     1541 ALIGNMENT"
110 PRINT"{DOWN 2}INSERT STANDARD DISK"
120 PRINT"{DOWN 2}PRESS {RVS}RETURN{ROFF
} WHEN READY"
130 :
140 REM   MACHINE CODE ROUTINE TO READ A
HEADER
150 REM   RESIDES AT $0300 (BUFFER #0)
160 :
170 DATA 169,48:       :REM LDA #$30
180 DATA 133,69:       :REM STA $45
190 DATA 169,00:       :REM LDA #$00
200 DATA 133,63:       :REM STA $3F
210 DATA 76,177,243 :REM JMP $F3B1
220 :
230 D$(0)="00":D$(1)="01":D$(2)="10":D$(
3)="11"
240 SID = 54272
250 DIM FD$(16)
260 FD$(0)="                            "
270 FD$(1)="CLEAN READ OF TRACK        "
280 FD$(2)="CLOSE TO HALFWAY POINT     "
290 FD$(3)="EXACTLY HALFWAY BETWEEN    "
300 FD$(9)="CLOSE TO HALFWAY POINT     "
310 T=18:N1$="?":N2$="?":TR=255
320 GET A$:IF A$<>CHR$(13) GOTO 320
330 :
340 OPEN 15,8,15,"I"
350 PRINT"{CLR}"
360 :
370 REM READ THE DISK CONTROLLER PORT
380 :
390 PRINT#15,"M-R"CHR$(0)CHR$(28)
400 GET#15,A$:IF A$=""THEN A$=CHR$(0)
410 A=ASC(A$)
420 CV=3 AND A
430 A=(159ANDA)OR(96+32*((T>17)+(T>24)+(
T>30)))
440 PRINT#15,"M-W"CHR$(0)CHR$(28)CHR$(1)
CHR$(A OR 4)
450 :
```

```
460 REM DISPLAY VALUES
470 :
480 PRINT"{HOME}{DOWN}    ALIGN THE 1541
DRIVE"
490 PRINT"{DOWN}TRACK # FROM STEPPER:"T"
{LEFT}    "
500 PRINT"{DOWN}HEAD POSITION:"FD$(E)
510 T$=STR$(TR):S$=STR$(SE):IF E<>1 THEN
  T$="??":N1$="?":N2$="?":S$="??"
520 PRINT"{DOWN}TRACK # AS READ:   "RIGHT
$(T$,2)
530 PRINT"SECTOR # AS READ: "RIGHT$(S$,2
)
540 PRINT"ID OF TRACK READ:  "N1$;N2$
550 PRINT"{DOWN 2}COMMANDS:"
560 PRINT"{DOWN}  F1 = MOVE HEAD OUT (LO
WER TRACK #)
570 PRINT"  F3 = MOVE HEAD IN (HIGHER TR
ACK #)
580 PRINT"  F7 = TERMINATE PROGRAM"
590 PRINT"   I = INITIALIZE (TO TRACK 18
)"
600 GET A$:A=ASC(A$+CHR$(0))
610 IF A=136 GOTO 800
620 IF A=133 AND T>1 THEN C=-1:GOTO 690
630 IF A=134 AND T<35 THEN C=1:GOTO 690
640 IF A=73 THEN PRINT#15,"I":T=18:E=0:A
=214:GOTO420
650 GOTO 890
660 :
670 REM MOVE HEAD ONE HALF-TRACK IN OR O
UT
680 :
690 CV=(CV + C)AND3
700 T=T+C*.5:IFT<1 THENT=1
710 IFT>36THENT=36
720 B=A AND 252
730 C=B+CV
740 PRINT#15,"M-W"CHR$(0)CHR$(28)CHR$(1)
CHR$(C)
750 E=0
760 GOTO 390
770 :
780 REM TERMINATE PROGRAM (DRIVE OFF)
790 :
800 PRINT#15,"M-W"CHR$(0)CHR$(28)CHR$(1)
CHR$(240)
810 FOR I=SID TO SID+23:POKE I,0:NEXT
820 FOR K=1TO10:GETA$:NEXT
830 CLOSE 15:END
840 :
```

```
850 REM ATTEMPT TO READ ANY HEADER
860 :
870 REM READ & SEND MACHINE CODE ROUTINE

880 :
890 RESTORE:C$=""
900 FOR K=1 TO 11:READ X:C$=C$+CHR$(X):N
EXT
910 PRINT#15,"M-W"CHR$(0)CHR$(3)CHR$(11)
C$
920 :
930 REM PUT JMP JOB IN THE JOB QUEUE
940 :
950 PRINT#15,"M-W"CHR$(0)CHR$(0)CHR$(1)C
HR$(208)
960 :
970 REM WAIT FOR JOB TO FINISH
980 :
990 PRINT#15,"M-R"CHR$(0)CHR$(0)
1000 GET#15,E$:E=ASC(E$+CHR$(0))
1010 IF E>127 GOTO 680
1020 :
1030 REM "E" IS FDC ERROR CODE RETURNED
1040 IF E=3 THEN HZ=1000:GOSUB 1190
1050 IF E=2 OR E=9 THEN HZ=1500:GOSUB 11
90
1060 IF E<>1 GOTO 390
1070 :
1080 REM CLEAN READ SO DIG OUT ID, TRAK
& SECT
1090 :
1100 PRINT#15,"M-R"CHR$(22)CHR$(0)CHR$(4
)
1110 GET#15,N1$
1120 GET#15,N2$
1130 GET#15,X$:TR=ASC(X$+CHR$(0))
1140 GET#15,X$:SE=ASC(X$+CHR$(0))
1150 GOTO 390
1160 :
1170 REM BLEEP IF NO SYNC
1180 :
1190 FOR I=SID TO SID+23:POKE I,0:NEXT
1200 POKE SID+5,9
1210 POKE SID+6,9
1220 POKE SID+24,15
1230 POKE SID+1,E+20
1240 POKE SID,177
1250 POKE SID+4,17:FOR I=1TO50:NEXT
1260 REM POKE SID+24,0
1270 RETURN
```

```
1280 POKE A1,85:POKE S1,150:POKE W1,65
1290 REM FOR K=1 TO 1000:NEXT
1300 RETURN
```

12.6 Realigning Your 1541

When you have your 1541 professionally realigned, the service technician uses an oscilloscope, an alignment program and a special alignment diskette. You probably don't have access to equipment like this. However, that doesn't mean you can't realign your drive. The utility program listed in Section 12.5 makes it possible for you to check the alignment of your 1541 and realign it without the use of any expensive equipment.

> *Know what you are doing!* Mistakes can be costly.

Don't attempt to realign your drive unless you have practiced using the ALIGN 1541 program to check your drive's alignment. Read the instructions below *and* those given in Section 12.5 several times before you start on this procedure. If you are a novice in things electronic, you may not want to realign the drive yourself.

It should take you less than an hour to disassemble your drive, adjust the alignment and reassemble everything. To disassemble your drive and realign it you will need the following tools:

1. #1 and #2 Phillips (+) screwdrivers.
2. A previously formatted diskette to use as your standard.
3. A copy of the ALIGN 1541 utility program.

To adjust the drive speed you will also need:

4. A fluorescent light.
5. A very small, flat (-) jeweler's screwdriver.

Here's what to do:

1. Load and run the ALIGN 1541 program listed in Section 12.5. Check the screen display. The head should be positioned on track 18 and should be reading the headers for track 18 cleanly. If you are not getting the head-position message, CLEAN READ OF TRACK, press the F1 key to move the head to track 17.5. Once you can see which track is being read, compare it to the stepper motor track position. If the difference between these is greater than one (e.g., you are reading track 16 while positioned over track 18), the drive is so far out of alignment that you should have it professionally realigned. It is beyond the normal adjustment range.

2. Once you are satisfied that your drive can be aligned, remove all connecting cables, including the power cable, from your drive.

3. Turn your disk drive upside down on a flat, level, stable surface and use your #1 Phillips screwdriver to remove the four small screws that hold the case together. They are recessed into the bottom, two at the front and two at the rear of the drive.

4. Carefully turn the drive upright and remove the top cover.

5. Use your #1 Phillips screwdriver to remove the six small screws that hold the drive and the bottom of the case together. They are down inside the edge of the case at the bottom, three on each side of the drive.

6. Carefully lift the drive out of the bottom of the case and turn it upside down on a piece of foam to the left of the case. Be careful that you don't tear off the wires leading to the green power-on LED.

7. Use the diagram below to locate the two screws that hold the stepper motor, the strobe disk and the speed adjustment access hole.

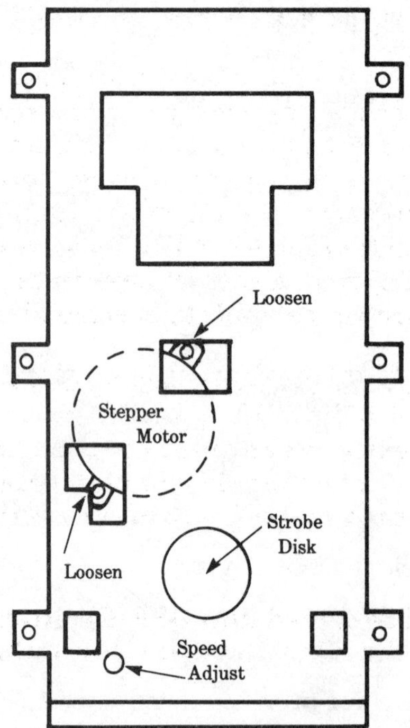

Bottom View Case Removed — Short and Long Board Versions 1541 Drive

8. Leaving the drive upside down, carefully reconnect the power cord and serial bus cable and switch ON the drive.

9. With the drive still upside down, run the ALIGN 1541 program and insert your standard diskette into the drive. Although you can use any formatted diskette as a standard, you may want to use the 1541TEST/DEMO diskette that came with your drive.

10. Use your #2 Phillips screwdriver to loosen the two screws holding the stepper motor in place. The motor should not be loose but you should be able to turn it by hand.

11. Look at the video display. It should indicate that the head is positioned above track 18 and that the head is reading track 18 cleanly. If you don't get this result, turn the stepper motor case slightly clockwise or counterclockwise until you do get this display. If you are unable to adjust the motor to get this display, there has been a great deal of slipping and you should let a professional realign your drive.

12. Use the F3 key to move the record/play head to track 19 and then use F1 to bring it back out to track 17.5. Turn the stepper motor case clockwise or counter-clockwise until the display indicates that you are near the midpoint between tracks 17 and 18. A slight turn one way should allow you to read track 17 and a slight turn the other way should give you track 18.

13. Use the F1 key to move the record/play head out to track 16 and then use F3 to bring it back in to track 17.5. Turn the stepper motor case clockwise or counter-clockwise slightly until the display indicates that you are near the midpoint.

14. Since there is some play (hysteresis) in the head-positioning mechanism you will have to repeat Steps 12 and 13 making smaller and smaller adjustments each time until the head is about equally close to the midpoint between the two tracks whether the head approaches from lower or higher track numbers. Remember that on an optimally aligned drive you will be able to read all tracks cleanly and should get the CLOSE TO HALFWAY POINT message (high tone) whether the head approaches track 17.5 from higher or lower track numbers. Once you are satisfied with the head position, carefully tighten the adjustment screws.

15. Since the drive is apart, you may as well adjust the drive speed. The outer ring of the strobe disk (marked 60) should appear stationary when viewed under fluorescent light. Use the fine screwdriver to turn the small screw clockwise or counterclockwise to adjust the drive speed. Be careful not to short out any traces on the printed circuit board as you insert the screwdriver through the small access hole.

16. Remove your standard diskette and turn OFF the drive. Disconnect the power cord and serial bus cable. Reassemble the drive. Your realignment job is complete.

12.7 Preventing Drive Wheel Slippage

Since alignment problems on the 1541 are common and are usually the result of slippage of the drive wheel on the shaft of the stepper motor, various ways have been suggested to lock the shaft and drive wheel together. Epoxy or crazy glue by themselves do not solve the problem permanently! There must be a solid mechanical connection if the fix is to last. The modification described below is fairly easy to do, requires relatively simple tools, and locks the stepper motor shaft and the drive wheel together permanently so there is no possibility of any slippage.

Know what you are doing! Mistakes can be costly.

The modification described below will definitely void any warranty on your disk drive. If your disk drive is still under warranty, you should not modify it. Do not attempt this modification if your drive is badly out of alignment! Make sure you read all the instructions and *understand them* before you begin. This modification requires careful work. If you are not comfortable with things mechanical, you should have your dealer make the modification for you.

You will need the following tools to carry out this modification.

1. #1 and #2 Phillips (+) screwdrivers.
2. A Dremel™ tool or other hand grinder.
3. A thin (1/32 inch), metal cutting wheel for the grinder.
4. Some five-minute epoxy cement.
5. A steel dressmaker's pin.
6. Wire cutters.

Here's what to do:

1. Load and run the alignment program listed in Section 12.5. Follow the procedure described in that section for checking the head alignment and hysteresis. If you are not able to read the correct tracks cleanly, you should realign your drive before proceeding any further. You do not want to permanently misalign your drive!

2. Once you are satisfied that your drive is reasonably well aligned, remove all connecting cables, including the power cable, from your drive.

3. Turn your disk drive upside down on a flat, level, stable surface and remove the four small Phillips screws that hold the case together. They are recessed into the bottom, two at the front and two at the rear of the drive.

4. Carefully turn the drive upright and remove the top cover.

5. There may be a metal plate that covers the printed circuit board. This must be removed. It is held in place by two small screws. Both are on the left-hand side as you face the front of the drive. If you have a long board version, be careful of the two wires that lead to the green power light at the front of the drive. These wires are attached to a plug that plugs into the circuit board. You can unplug them but make a diagram showing how they are attached.

6. Using your #1 Phillips screwdriver, remove the seven screws that hold the printed circuit board in place. There are five screws that go through the board itself. There are two more screws through the right-hand side of the case that hold the heat sink on.

7. Tip the printed circuit board to one side so you can get at the drive mechanism beneath it. You may have to unplug one or more cables from the board to do this. Be sure to make a sketch of the position of any plugs before you unplug them.

8. With the help of the diagram below, locate the stepper motor's drive wheel.

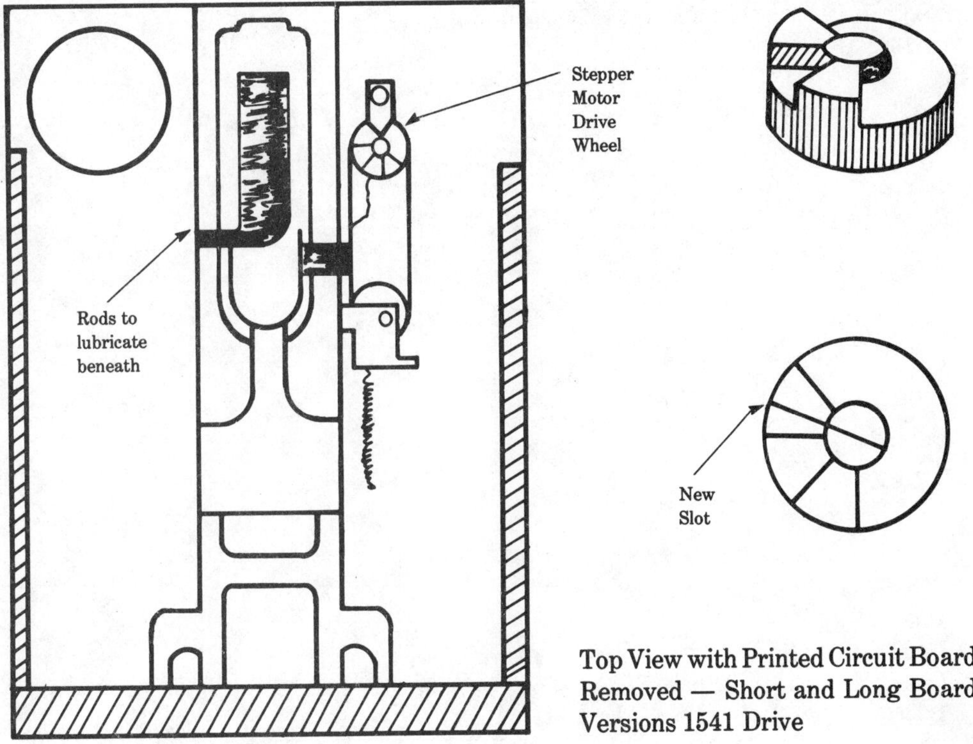

Top View with Printed Circuit Board Removed — Short and Long Board Versions 1541 Drive

9. Use the Dremel™ tool to cut a narrow slot across the top of the stepper shaft and one of the lobes on the drive wheel as indicated above. The dressmaker's pin should just fit into the slot when you are done. Take your time and use a very light touch. Too much heat may cause the drive wheel to shift on the shaft. You may want to mask off the work area to keep flecks of metal out of the drive mechanism. When you are finished, use a vacuum to clean up the area.

10. Trim the dressmaker's pin to the correct length and epoxy it in place. Once the glue is dry, partially reassemble the drive and check the alignment. You may want to touch up the alignment and drive speed before final reassembly.

11. If you found a fair bit of play in the head-positioning mechanism when you checked the alignment, you may want to lubricate the two round bars that the head-positioning mechanism slides on. Use a *very small amount* of a high grade oil (such as clock oil) or a lightweight grease (such as a lithium based bicycle grease) on a cotton swab to lubricate them *sparingly.*

Once you have made this modification, you should realign your drive (see Section 12.6). This time it should stay in alignment!

A BIT OF BACKGROUND

This chapter is designed to take some of the mystery out of the actual operation of your 1541. You don't need to know about the inner workings of your car to be able to drive it. However, if you run into trouble on the road, it helps to know a bit about spark plugs, distributors and carburetors. Similarly, you do not need to know about the inner workings of your disk drive to use it effectively. But, a bit of background comes in handy when you start having problems. Topics discussed in this chapter include the recording process, how the directory is organized, and how sequential, program, user and relative files are stored.

13.1 Inside a Floppy Diskette

A floppy diskette consists of three parts: a plasticized outer protective jacket, an inner liner and a circular disk of thin mylar with a magnetic coating.

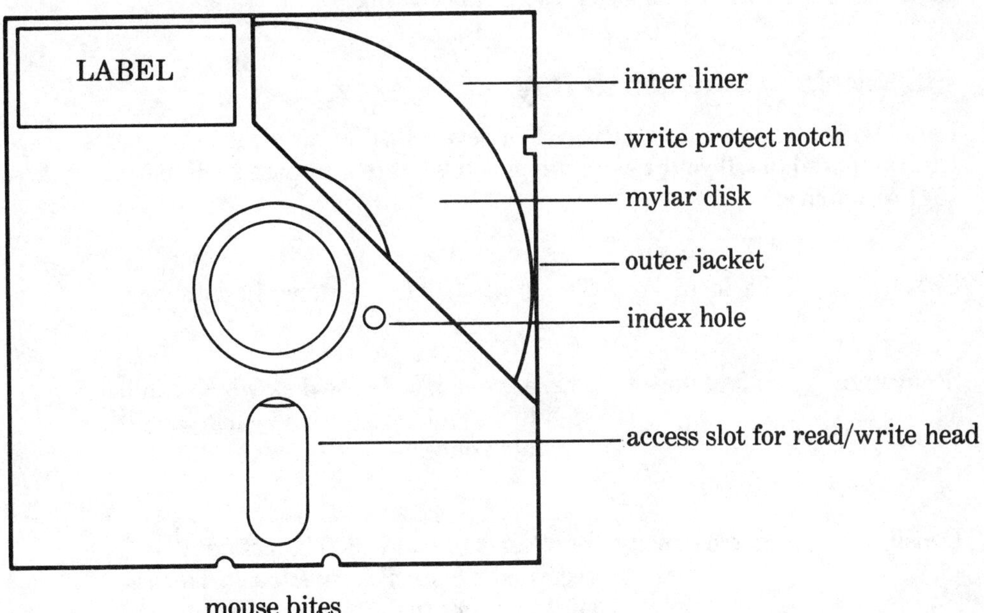

Outer Protective Jacket

The outer protective jacket is made of a relatively stiff plasticized material. Its job is to protect the fragile disk inside. There are several holes and notches in the outer jacket. The large central hole allows the wedge-shaped central hub in the drive to grip the inner disk and turn it. The large elongated slot allows the drive's read/write head to contact the disk so it can read or write information. The write protect notch can be used to protect information stored on a diskette. If the write protect notch is covered with an opaque tab, the drive will not write (record) onto the diskette. The mouse bites on the edge of the jacket near the access slot are strain relief notches to prevent the plastic disk from binding. The index hole is not used on any Commodore drives. It is used on some brands of drives to determine the position of the mylar disk. If you rotate the inner disk carefully you will see one or more holes in the disk that become visible as the disk is turned.

Inner Liner

The inner liner is a loosely woven, slippery material. Its main job is to reduce friction between the jacket and the rotating disk. Since the material is fibrous, it also cleans the surface of the disk as it turns. Small particles of dust, smoke and grit are collected from the disk and become embedded among the fibers.

Mylar Disk

The inner disk is a circular piece of mylar. Better quality diskettes have a ring of reinforcing material around the large central hole. This is known as a hub ring. It helps prevent the disk from being bent or warped in this area of maximum stress. During the manufacturing process the disk is coated on both sides with a magnetic material similar to that used on cassette tapes. The coating is burnished in the read/write area to create a smooth surface. After burnishing, the diskette is tested to ensure that there are no serious flaws in the coating.

13.2 Which Diskettes to Buy

Floppy diskettes are manufactured in several different sizes and grades. Here is what you need to tell your dealer when you want to purchase some for use with your 1541 disk drive:

Size:	5 ¼ inch	The inner disk is 5 ¼ inches in diameter.
Sectoring:	Soft sectored	There is one hole in the disk which can be seen through the index hole when the disk is rotated once.
Density:	Single density	Between 4100 and 5800 bits of data are recorded per inch along a track. This is slightly more than the normal rating for a single density diskette but usually single density diskettes work adequately.

Sidedness: Single-sided   Data is recorded only on one side of the
                                  diskette (the back side!).

You can use virtually any 5 ¼ inch diskette in your 1541. The sectoring, density and
sidedness of the diskette are not critical. Note that using a premium quality diskette
will not increase the speed or storage capacity of your drive. As a result, use double-
sided/double density diskettes only if you can get a bargain. Do not pay a premium
for these diskettes!

Most major brands of diskettes will provide adequate service. In general, you get
what you pay for. The magnetic coating on cheap off-brands may be too soft and gum
up your drive's read/write head, or too hard and wear the head away. You are not
really interested in having your valuable programs or data lost!

13.3 The Back Side Controversy

If you cut a new write protect notch on the other edge of the diskette and insert the
diskette into the drive upside down, you can use the second side of the diskette for
storing programs or data. A floppy diskette that has been modified this way is often
called a flippy.

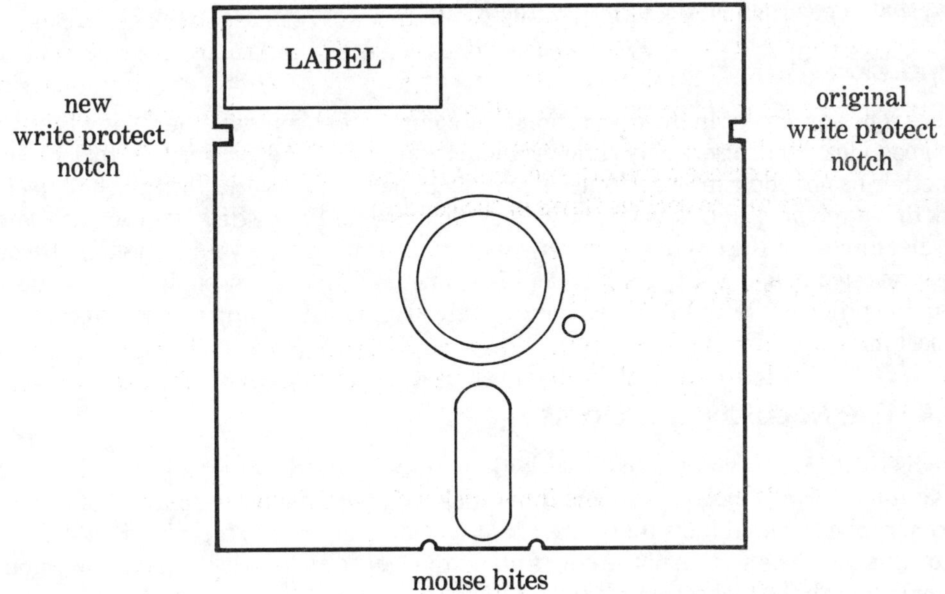

Some companies even sell (for an exorbitant price) a special punch for converting
floppies into flippies. You don't need any special equipment to do this job. Use another
diskette turned upside down and a pencil to mark where the notch should go. Then
use a one-hole paper punch or a pair of scissors to cut out the new notch.

Although you may save some money by using flippies, you may be in for some
long-term problems. Problems can occur for at least three different reasons:

1.   Flawed surfaces: Most manufacturers of single-sided diskettes guarantee that the designated recording surface (the back side) is free of any manufacturing defects. The other side is untested. It may be perfectly OK or it may contain flaws. Before you store any data on the reverse side of a diskette you should format it and then check it for flaws using the CHECK DISK program on your 1541TEST/DEMO diskette.

2.   Premature wear: Sometimes a flippy will wear out rapidly. One source of wear is the pressure pad that presses against the non-recording surface of the disk to hold the disk tightly against the record/play head. The pressure pad is made of a felt-like material. If it gets contaminated with dirt or grit it can abrade the non-recording surface. Normally this causes no problems. However, when you start recording on both sides, it can wear away your data.

Another source of wear is the inner liner. It normally traps dust, smoke, and grit and removes them from the disk surface. However, when you insert a diskette upside down, the disk now turns in the opposite direction. The dust, smoke and grit tend to be redeposited onto the disk where they can cause premature wear. Note that even double-sided diskettes are designed to rotate in only one direction.

3.   Print through: When data is being recorded onto the disk surface, the record/play head is magnetized by an electric current. On a disk drive that is designed to record data on only one side of the diskette, the magnetic field may be strong enough to affect data that is recorded on the other magnetic surface.

Conclusion

There is no agreement in the microcomputer community about whether using flippies is a good idea. Some users report no problems while others report serious difficulties. Whether or not you can use flippies probably depends on several things: the type of disk drive you have and how it is adjusted, the brand of floppy diskettes you use, and the cleanliness of the environment in which you use and store your diskettes. If you are interested in using flippies, do a lot of experimenting and testing before you store valuable programs or data on them, and, as always, keep a backup copy of everything important.

13.4 The Recording Process

Data is read from or written to the diskette surface by the drive's read/write head. In its simplest form, a read/write head is a C-shaped piece of steel with a coil of copper wire wrapped around it, as illustrated below. The break in the steel ring is called the recording gap. The section of the ring around the recording gap is the part that comes in contact with the diskette surface.

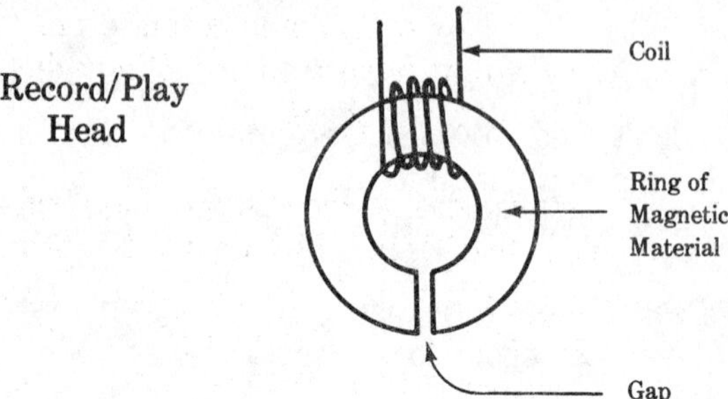

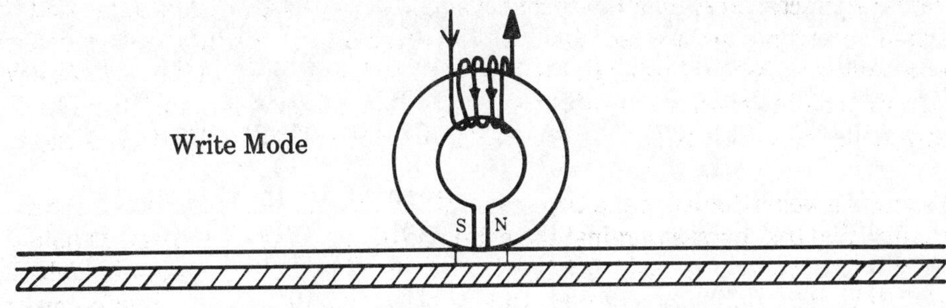

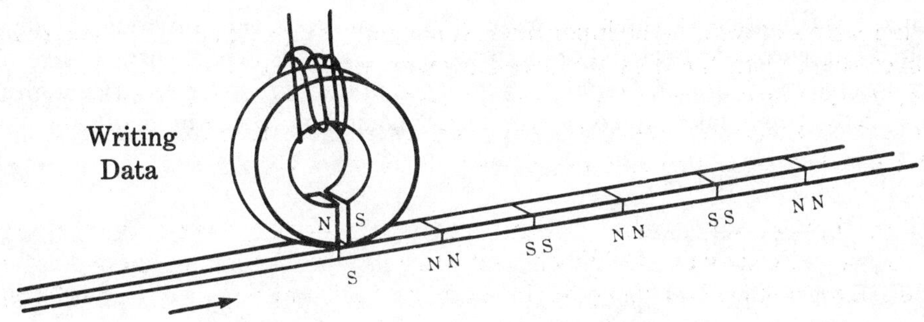

When an electric current passes through the coil, the read/write head becomes an electromagnet. The gap in the ring causes a strong localized magnetic field. Since this area of the ring is in contact with the diskette, the diskette becomes magnetized. As the diskette rotates past the head a strip of the surface becomes magnetized. To record data on the diskette we change the direction of the current through the coil. This changes the direction of the magnetization of the magnetic strip. If we let the diskette make one complete rotation without moving the head, we would find that the magnetized strip has become a circle. We would have recorded one track of information on the diskette.

Since computers work in binary (any character is represented by a string of 1's and 0's) and there are two possible directions of magnetization (N-S and S-N), you might expect that data is recorded on the diskette in a relatively straight forward manner, one direction of magnetization representing a zero bit and the other direction of magnetization representing a one bit. Unfortunately, life is not that simple. Suppose we wanted to record 256 null bytes (00000...) in a row. This would produce a very long strip with no change in the direction of magnetization. Since the speed of the drive is not absolutely constant, we might have trouble telling whether there were supposed to be 254, 256 or even 258 null bytes there.

Commodore gets around the timing problem by encoding the data before it is recorded on the diskette surface. Each 8-bit byte of data is broken into two 4-bit nybbles. Each 4-bit nybble is converted into a 5-bit code. The codes are designed so that no combination of encoded characters can ever contain more than two consecutive zero bits. This is called GCR (Group Code Recording). It solves the timing problem.

Hex	Nybble	GCR Code	Hex	Nybble	GCR Code
$0	0000	01010	$8	1000	01001
$1	0001	01011	$9	1001	11001
$2	0010	10010	$A	1010	11010
$3	0011	10011	$B	1011	11011
$4	0100	01110	$C	1100	01101
$5	0101	01111	$D	1101	11101
$6	0110	10110	$E	1110	11110
$7	0111	10100	$F	1111	10101

Bits of encoded data are sent to the write circuitry at about 250,000 bits per second (the actual rate depends on which track is being recorded). The write circuitry makes one final modification to the data before it is recorded. The direction of current through the record/play head only changes when a one bit is to be recorded. A zero bit is represented by a lack of change in the direction of magnetization. Although this sounds pretty complicated, the example below should help clear things up.

Original Byte ($91): 10010001

Two 4-bit nybbles: 1001 0001

After GCR encoding: 11001 01011

As recorded:

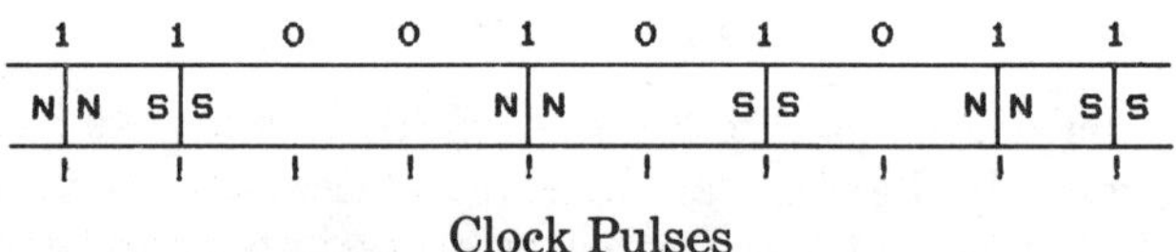

Clock Pulses

When the data is read back later, every change in the direction of magnetization is interpreted as a one bit. If there is no change at the next tick of the clock, a zero bit is assumed. To keep things synchronized the clock is reset each time a one bit is detected. Actually, you never have to know about how the data is encoded and recorded on disk. The DOS takes care of all the picky details. However, you are now in a better position to understand what happens when you turn your drive OFF or ON with a diskette in it. The magnetic spike can introduce an extra one bit into the bit stream and throw off the entire decoding process!

13.5 The Sync Mark

Data is recorded on a track as a continuous bit stream. There are no blank unmagnetized areas to indicate the beginning or end of a sector. To enable the drive to locate where it is on a track, special characters called sync marks are used. A sync mark is simply eleven or more one bits in a row. Most typical sync marks consist of at least 30 consecutive one bits. The magnetic pattern recorded for a sync mark looks like this:

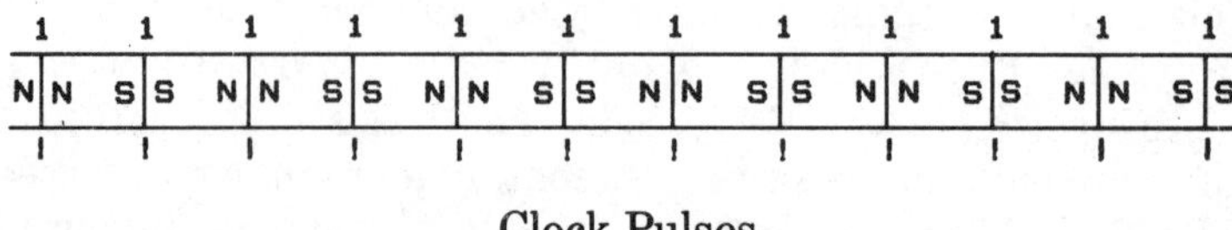

Clock Pulses

The sync mark is unique because there is no combination of five-bit codes that can produce more than eight consecutive one bits. The internal electronics of the 1541 are designed so that whenever a sync mark is read, the 1541's microprocessor is alerted.

Each sector has two sync marks. One at the start of the header block and another at the start of the data block.

13.6 How a Sector is Organized

Each sector consists of two parts, a header block and a data block. The header block contains identifying information. The data block holds the 256 bytes of data that are stored in this sector. The general layout of a sector is indicated below:

SYNC MARK	Header Block Information	Header Gap	SYNC MARK	Data Block Information	Tail Gap	SYNC MARK	Header of next sector

The header block begins with a sync mark. The sync mark warns the drive that there is important information coming. Next comes the actual header block information. It includes the track number, sector number and the two-character disk ID. This allows the drive to identify which of the 683 sectors on the diskette is being read. The final part of the header block is the header gap. This consists of nine non-sync characters. These characters are never read and interpreted by the drive. They are there to allow the drive a bit of time to interpret the header information and get ready to read the data block.

The data block also begins with a sync mark. It is followed by the data block information. This includes the 256 data bytes that are stored in the sector. The final part of the data block is the tail gap. The length of this gap varies but tends to be from eight to 20 bytes long. Like the characters in the header gap these characters are never read and interpreted by the drive. They simply allow a bit of breathing space between sectors.

When you issue a full NEW command, the disk operating system creates and records a new header block and a dummy data block for each of the 683 sectors on the diskette. This erases any information that was previously stored on the diskette. Once these header blocks and dummy data blocks have been recorded, the diskette is said to be formatted. As you store new files on the diskette, the dummy data blocks (including the starting sync marks) are overwritten. The header blocks, however, are never rewritten. They are permanent markers on the diskette until such time as you reformat the diskette.

Now that you have a general idea of how the parts of a sector are arranged and used, let's examine the parts in a bit more detail. We'll start with the header block. The characters that make up a header block are arranged as follows (*not* as indicated on page 54 of your *1541 User's Manual*):

SYNC MARK	Header Block Identifier	Header Checksum	Sector Number	Track Number	Disk ID Byte #2	Disk ID Byte #1	Header Gap

Header block identifier: The sync mark that begins a header block is always followed by a $08 character. This indicates that this is a header block and not a data block. If this character is not $08, the drive will report a 20, READ ERROR, when you try to access this sector.

Header checksum: This character is used for error checking. The ASCII value of this character may be found by EORing the sector number, the track number and the ASCII values of the two disk ID characters. To EOR two numbers convert them to their eight-bit binary form. Now combine them bit by bit according to the following rules: 0+0=0, 1+0=1, 0+1=1, and 1+1=0. This is *not* the same as adding, as there is no carry; 1+1=0, not 1+1=10. The result may then be combined with the next number. Let's look at an example:

Find the header checksum for:

Track = 18
Sector = 1
ID = AB (65)(66)

```
            Track = 18 = $12 =  00010010
            Sector = 1 = $01 =  00000001
                                --------
            EOR of 18 & 1 =     00010011
      ID #1 (A) = 65 = $41 =    01000001
                                --------
      EOR of 18, 1 & 65 =       01010010
      ID #2 (B) = 66 = $42 =    01000010
                                --------
  EOR of 18, 1, 65 & 66 =       00010000 = $10
```

When a header block is read, a new checksum is computed and compared with the checksum read from the diskette. If they don't match, you get a 27, READ ERROR.

Sector number: Sectors are numbered sequentially from zero to the maximum number for that track. The maximum sector number for the various tracks are:

Track Range	Sector Numbers
1 to 17	0 to 20
18 to 24	0 to 18
25 to 30	0 to 17
31 to 35	0 to 16

Track number: Tracks are numbered sequentially from one to 35. Track 1 is the outermost track (farthest from the center). Track 35 is the innermost.

Disk ID: This is the two-character disk ID that you specified when the diskette was formatted. However, their order is reversed. If you specify an ID of AB in a full NEW command, the headers will contain BA. Since these two characters are recorded as part of each sector header on the diskette, they are often called the embedded disk ID. The disk ID characters that you see when you list a diskette's directory are only a cosmetic ID that is stored on track 18, sector 0. DOS protected diskettes may have different cosmetic and embedded ID's. On some commercial diskettes different tracks have different embedded ID's.

Now that you have an idea of how a header block is arranged, let's examine a data block. It is arranged as follows:

SYNC MARK	Data Block Identifier	256 Bytes of Data	Data Checksum	Tail Gap

Data block identifier: The sync mark that begins a data block is always followed by a $07 character. This indicates that this is a data block and not a header block. If this character is not $07, the drive will report a 22, READ ERROR, when you try to access this sector.

Data bytes: Each sector stores 256 bytes of data. In a normal file, the first two bytes are used to store the track and sector numbers of the next block in the file (a forward pointer; see Section 13.9). As a result, only 254 bytes of actual data are stored in each sector of a file.

Data checksum: This character is used for error checking. The ASCII value of this character may be found by EORing the ASCII values of all 256 data bytes together. When the data block is read, a new checksum is computed and compared with the checksum read from the diskette. If they don't match, you get a 23, READ ERROR.

Now that you have an idea of how the various parts that make up a sector are arranged, let's take a look at a diskette's directory.

13.7 How the Directory Is Organized

The directory is the most important part of any diskette. It is stored on track 18. It consists of the diskette's Block Availability Map (BAM) on track 18, sector 0 and a file of directory entries, one for each file stored on the diskette.

In this section we will be examining the directory entries of the 1541TEST/DEMO diskette. It will be instructive for you to use your computer to follow along. So get out your copy of the 1541TEST/DEMO diskette. You can use either the DISPLAY T&S program (from the 1541TEST/DEMO diskette) or the EDIT T&S program (from Appendix E) to view the various sectors we will be discussing. Turn on your system and let's get going.

NOTE:

If you have a Commodore 64, you may want to modify the DISPLAY T&S program on your 1541TEST/DEMO diskette to take advantage of your 40 column screen. To modify the program, list lines 438 to 448 and make the changes indicated below. *Do not* change or delete lines 442 and 446.

```
438 FOR J=0 TO 31:IF J=16 THEN GOSUB 710
:IF Z$="N"THEN J=80:GOTO 458
440 FOR I=K TO 7
444 IF K=1 AND I<6 THEN NB(2)=ASC(A$(I))
448 A$="":B$=":":N=J*8:GOSUB 790:A$=A$+"
:"
```

Let's begin by looking at track 18, sector 0. This sector contains the diskette's BAM, name and cosmetic ID. Here is what you will see when you display this sector. Note that when you display this sector on your video screen you can only see half the sector at a time.

```
             TRACK 18    SECTOR 0

.  00:  12 01 41 00 15 FF FF 1F   ..A.....   Link, DOS type, BAM track 1
.  08:  15 FF FF 1F 15 FF FF 1F   ........   BAM tracks 2 and 3
.  10:  15 FF FF 1F 15 FF FF 1F   ........   BAM tracks 4 and 5
.  18:  15 FF FF 1F 15 FF FF 1F   ........   BAM tracks 6 and 7
.  20:  15 FF FF 1F 15 FF FF 1F   ........   BAM tracks 8 and 9
.  28:  15 FF FF 1F 15 FF FF 1F   ........   BAM tracks 10 and 11
.  30:  15 FF FF 1F 15 FF FF 1F   ........   BAM tracks 12 and 13
.  38:  11 D7 5F 1F 00 00 00 00   ........   BAM tracks 14 and 15
.  40:  00 00 00 00 00 00 00 00   ........   BAM tracks 16 and 17
.  48:  10 EC FF 07 00 00 00 00   ........   BAM tracks 18 and 19
.  50:  00 00 00 00 12 BF FF 07   ........   BAM tracks 20 and 21
.  58:  13 FF FF 07 13 FF FF 07   ........   BAM tracks 22 and 23
.  60:  13 FF FF 07 12 FF FF 03   ........   BAM tracks 24 and 25
.  68:  12 FF FF 03 12 FF FF 03   ........   BAM tracks 26 and 27
.  70:  12 FF FF 03 12 FF FF 03   ........   BAM tracks 28 and 29
.  78:  12 FF FF 03 11 FF FF 01   ........   BAM tracks 30 and 31
.  80:  11 FF FF 01 11 FF FF 01   ........   BAM tracks 32 and 33
.  88:  11 FF FF 01 11 FF FF 01   ........   BAM tracks 34 and 35
.  90:  31 35 34 31 54 45 53 54   1541TEST   Disk name
.  98:  2F 44 45 4D 4F A0 A0 A0   /DEMO...
.  A0:  A0 A0 5A 58 A0 32 41 A0   ..ZX.2A.   Cosmetic disk ID and
.  A8:  A0 A0 A0 00 00 00 00 00   ........   DOS type
.  B0:  00 00 00 00 00 00 00 00   ........
.  B8:  00 00 00 00 00 00 00 00   ........
.  C0:  00 00 00 00 00 00 00 00   ........
.  C8:  00 00 00 00 00 00 00 00   ........   Garbage ($AB-$FF)
.  D0:  00 00 00 00 00 00 00 00   ........
.  D8:  00 00 00 00 00 00 00 00   ........
.  E0:  00 00 00 00 00 00 00 00   ........
.  E8:  00 00 00 00 00 00 00 00   ........
.  F0:  00 00 00 00 00 00 00 00   ........
.  F8:  00 00 00 00 00 00 00 00   ........
```

Although the annotations down the side of the display point out the major features, let's examine the display carefully:

```
Byte#  00 01 02 03 04 05 06 07
       -- -- -- -- -- -- -- --
.  00: 12 01 41 00 15 FF FF 1F   ..A..... Link to next directory sector
```

Bytes zero and one are the track ($12=18) and sector ($01=1) numbers of the next sector in the directory file. These two bytes are ignored when you load a directory, but are used to locate the next sector when you open the directory file to read it.

```
Byte#  00 01 02 03 04 05 06 07
       -- -- -- -- -- -- -- --
.  00: 12 01 41 00 15 FF FF 1F   ..A..... DOS type
```

Byte two is the DOS type ($41=65="A"). If this byte is changed, you will no longer be able to write to the diskette. You will always get a 73, DOS MISMATCH, error. If you have a dual disk drive you will find that you can no longer duplicate or backup the diskette either. Some early, simple protection schemes simply modified this byte to prevent you from copying the diskette.

```
Byte# 00 01 02 03 04 05 06 07
      -- -- -- -- -- -- -- --
. 00: 12 01 41 00 15 FF FF 1F  ..A..... Unused byte
```

Byte $03 is not used by the DOS. It is normally $00 but may be any value.

```
Byte# 00 01 02 03 04 05 06 07
      -- -- -- -- -- -- -- --
. 00: 12 01 41 00 15 FF FF 1F  ..A..... BAM for track 1
```

Bytes $04 to $07 are the BAM for track 1. Since the BAM entry for each track has the same form, let's examine these bytes in some detail. The BAM entry for a track consists of a master count of the blocks free for that track and a bit map showing the status of the individual sectors.

```
Byte# 00 01 02 03 04 05 06 07
      -- -- -- -- -- -- -- --
. 00: 12 01 41 00 15 FF FF 1F  ..A..... Blocks free on track 1
```

Byte $04 gives the number of blocks free on track 1. In this case we have $15 or 21 blocks free. None of the blocks on track 1 are in use.

```
Byte# 00 01 02 03 04 05 06 07
      -- -- -- -- -- -- -- --
. 00: 12 01 41 00 15 FF FF 1F  ..A..... Bit map showing sector status
```

Bytes $05 to $07 indicate which sectors are in use. Each bit represents the status of one sector. If the bit that corresponds to a particular sector is one, that sector is free. If the bit is zero, the sector is in use. The diagram below indicates which bit represents which sector:

Byte#	$05	$06	$07
Bit position	76543210	76543210	76543210
Sector number		111111	21111
	76543210	54321098	---09876
Value for track 1	$FF	$FF	$1F
Binary value	11111111	11111111	00011111
Sector status	FFFFFFFF	FFFFFFFF	---FFFFF
(F=Free, A=Allocated)			(no sectors 21-23)

An example should help make things clear. What is the current status of sector 12 of track 1? From the diagram we see that sector 12 is represented by bit four of byte $06. The value stored in byte $06 is $FF (11111111). Bit four is a one; therefore track 1, sector 12 is free.

To be sure that you understand how things work, let's work through another example for track 14. What is the present status of sector 15 on track 14? From the annotations down the side of our listing we see that bytes $38 to $3B represent the BAM entry for track 14.

```
Byte# 38 39 3A 3B 3C 3D 3E 3F
      -- -- -- -- -- -- -- --
. 38: 11 D7 5F 1F 00 00 00 00  .. ...... Blocks free on track 14
```

Byte $38 gives the number of blocks free on track 14. In this case we have $11 or 17 blocks free. Some of the blocks/sectors on track 14 are in use. Let's check sector 15.

Byte#	$39	$3A	$3B
Bit position	76543210	76543210	76543210
		111111	21111
Sector number	76543210	54321098	----09876
Value for track 14	$D7	$5F	$1F
Binary value	11010111	01011111	00011111
Sector status	FFAFAFFF	AFAFFFFF	----FFFFF
(F=Free, A=Allocated)			

Since the bit that corresponds to sector 15 on track 14 is a zero, this sector is in use.

The next part of track 18, sector 0 contains the diskette name.

```
. 90: 31 35 34 31 54 45 53 54  1541TEST
. 98: 2F 44 45 4D 4F A0 A0 A0  /DEMO... Diskette name
```

This is the name specified in the NEW command when the diskette was formatted. Note the three $A0 characters that follow 1541TEST/DEMO. These are shifted blanks. They are used to pad out the diskette name to 16 characters. You can use either the EDIT T&S program (Appendix E) or the MOD DISK NAME program (Appendix E) to change the name stored here.

The cosmetic diskette ID is stored at location $A2 and $A3.

```
Byte# A0 A1 A2 A3 A4 A5 A6 A7
      -- -- -- -- -- -- -- --
. A0: A0 A0 5A 58 A0 32 41 A0  ..ZX.2A. Cosmetic diskette ID
```

This is the two-character diskette ID you specified when the diskette was formatted. This is known as the cosmetic ID because it is only used to generate a directory listing. The DOS uses the ID embedded in the header blocks to identify a diskette.

The cosmetic DOS type (2A) is stored at location $A5 and $A6.

```
Byte# A0 A1 A2 A3 A4 A5 A6 A7
      -- -- -- -- -- -- -- --
. A0: A0 A0 5A 58 A0 32 41 A0  ..ZX.2A.  Cosmetic DOS type
```

This is known as the cosmetic DOS type because it is only used to generate a directory listing. The DOS uses the byte $02 of track 18, sector 0 to identify the diskette's DOS type.

The remainder of track 18, sector 0 is essentially garbage. Some disk protection schemes have even used this area for storing machine language programs!

This completes our tour of track 18, sector 0. Now let's take a look at the actual directory entries themselves. They begin on track 18, sector 1.

Track 18, sector 1 is the start of the file of directory entries. Since the file entries are the key to finding our way around the diskette, let's take a look at them in some detail.

```
          TRACK 18     SECTOR 1

. 00: 12 04 82 11 00 48 4F 57  .....HOW       Entry 1: file type = $82 (130)
. 08: 20 54 4F 20 55 53 45 A0  .TO.USE.       First block on $11/$00 (17/0)
. 10: A0 A0 A0 A0 A0 00 00 00  ........       File name = HOW TO USE
. 18: 00 00 00 00 00 00 0D 00  ........       Length = $0D (13) blocks
. 20: 00 00 82 11 03 48 4F 57  .....HOW       Entry 2: file type = $82 (130)
. 28: 20 50 41 52 54 20 54 57  .PART.TW       First block on $11/$03 (17/3)
. 30: 4F A0 A0 A0 A0 00 00 00  O.......       File name = HOW PART TWO
. 38: 00 00 00 00 00 00 05 00  ........       Length = $05 (5) blocks
. 40: 00 00 82 11 09 56 49 43  .....VIC       Entry 3: file type = $82 (130)
. 48: 2D 32 30 20 57 45 44 47  -20.WEDG       First block on $11/$09 (17/9)
. 50: 45 A0 A0 A0 A0 00 00 00  E.......       File name = VIC-20 WEDGE
. 58: 00 00 00 00 00 00 04 00  ........       Length = $04 (4) blocks
. 60: 00 00 82 13 00 43 2D 36  .....C-6       Entry 4: file type = $82 (130)
. 68: 34 20 57 45 44 47 45 A0  4.WEDGE.       First block on $13/$00 (19/0)
. 70: A0 A0 A0 A0 A0 00 00 00  ........       File name = C-64 WEDGE
. 78: 00 00 00 00 00 00 01 00  ........       Length = $01 (1) block
. 80: 00 00 82 13 01 44 4F 53  .....DOS       Entry 5: file type = $82 (130)
. 88: 20 35 2E 31 A0 A0 A0 A0  .5.1....       First block on $13/$01 (19/1)
. 90: A0 A0 A0 A0 A0 00 00 00  ........       File name = DOS 5.1
. 98: 00 00 00 00 00 00 04 00  ........       Length = $04 (4) blocks
. A0: 00 00 82 13 03 43 4F 50  .....COP       Entry 6: file type = $82 (130)
. A8: 59 2F 41 4C 4C A0 A0 A0  Y/ALL...       First block on $13/$03 (19/3)
. B0: A0 A0 A0 A0 A0 00 00 00  ........       File name = COPY/ALL
. B8: 00 00 00 00 00 00 0B 00  ........       Length = $0B (11) blocks
. C0: 00 00 82 13 09 50 52 49  .....PRI       Entry 7: file type = $82 (130)
```

```
. C8: 4E 54 45 52 20 54 45 53  NTER.TES    First block on $13/$09 (19/9)
. D0: 54 A0 A0 A0 A0 00 00 00  T.......    File name = PRINTER TEST
. D8: 00 00 00 00 00 00 09 00  ........    Length = $09 (9) blocks
. E0: 00 00 82 10 00 44 49 53  .....DIS    Entry 8: file type = $82 (130)
. E8: 4B 20 41 44 44 52 20 43  K.ADDR.C    First block on $10/$00 (16/0)
. F0: 48 41 4E 47 45 00 00 00  HANGE...    File name = DISK ADDR CHANGE
. F8: 00 00 00 00 00 00 04 00  ........    Length = $04 (4) blocks
```

The annotations down the side of the listing point out the major features of the eight entries. Let's examine the first part of the listing in some detail.

```
Byte# 00 01 02 03 04 05 06 07
      -- -- -- -- -- -- -- --
. 00: 12 04 82 11 00 48 4F 57  .....HOW  Link to next directory sector
```

Bytes $00 and $01 of this sector ($12=18; $04=4) are not really part of any entry. They are the track and sector numbers of the next sector in the directory (18/4). Note that the other seven entries in this sector have $00/$00 in this position.

Byte $02 is really the start of the first directory entry.

```
Byte# 00 01 02 03 04 05 06 07
      -- -- -- -- -- -- -- --
. 00: 12 04 82 11 00 48 4F 57  .....HOW  Entry 1: file type = $82 (130)
```

This is the file type byte. The value of this byte determines the file type. The table below summarizes the major file types:

Hex	Decimal	File Type	Comment
$00	0	Scratched	Not shown in a directory listing.
$01	1	*SEQ	An unclosed sequential file.
$02	2	*PRG	An unclosed program file.
$03	3	*USR	An unclosed user file.
$80	128	DEL	An unusual, but legal, file type.
$81	129	SEQ	A normal sequential file.
$82	130	PRG	A normal program file.
$83	131	USR	A normal user file.
$84	132	REL	A normal relative file.
$C0	192	DEL<	A locked unusual file type.
$C1	193	SEQ<	A locked sequential file.
$C2	194	PRG<	A locked program file.
$C3	195	USR<	A locked user file.
$C4	196	REL<	A locked relative file.

NOTES:

1. Locked files cannot be scratched. The file type byte must be changed back to a normal value before the file can be scratched. See Section 13.8.

2. By editing the file type byte, unusual file types can be produced (see Section 13.8).

```
Byte#  00 01 02 03 04 05 06 07
       -- -- -- -- -- -- -- --
. 00:  12 04 82 11 00 48 4F 57  .....HOW   First block on $11/$00 (17/0)
```

Bytes $03 and $04 give the track and sector numbers of the sector where the first block of the file is stored. In this case the first block of the file is on track 17, sector 0.

```
Byte#  00 01 02 03 04 05 06 07
       -- -- -- -- -- -- -- --
. 00:  12 04 82 11 00 48 4F 57  .....HOW   File name = HOW TO USE
```

```
Byte#  08 09 0A 0B 0C 0D 0E 0F
       -- -- -- -- -- -- -- --
. 08:  20 54 4F 20 55 53 45 A0  .TO.USE.
```

```
Byte#  10 11 12 13 14 15 16 17
       -- -- -- -- -- -- -- --
. 10:  A0 A0 A0 A0 A0 00 00 00  ........
```

Bytes $05 to $14 contain the file name. Note that the name is padded with shifted blanks ($A0=160) so that the name is always 16 characters long.

```
Byte#  10 11 12 13 14 15 16 17
       -- -- -- -- -- -- -- --
. 10:  A0 A0 A0 A0 A0 00 00 00  ........   REL files only
```

Bytes $15 to $17 are only used with relative file entries. They are always $00 for other file types. Bytes $15 and $16 hold the track and sector numbers of the side-sector file for the relative file. Byte $17 holds the record size. More details about these bytes may be found in Section 13.13 on relative file storage.

```
Byte#  18 19 1A 1B 1C 1D 1E 1F
       -- -- -- -- -- -- -- --
. 18:  00 00 00 00 00 00 0D 00  ........   Unused bytes
```

Bytes $18 to $1B are unused. They are always $00.

```
Byte#  18 19 1A 1B 1C 1D 1E 1F
       -- -- -- -- -- -- -- --
. 18:  00 00 00 00 00 00 0D 00  .......   Used during replacement only
```

Bytes $1C and $1D are used only temporarily during a replace operation (SAVE replacement or OPEN to replace). During these operations they hold the track and sector numbers of the first block in the new replacement file. Otherwise they are always $00.

```
Byte#  18  19  1A  1B  1C  1D  1E  1F
       --  --  --  --  --  --  --  --
. 18:  00  00  00  00  00  00  0D  00  ........  Length = $0D (13) blocks
```

The final two bytes in a directory entry $1E and $1F give the length of the file in blocks. The file length is in lo byte/hi byte form. To find the length of the file, multiply the value of byte $1F by 256 and add the value of byte $1E like this:

Length of file = 256 x ($1F value) + ($1E value)
           = 256 x (0) + (13)
           = 13 blocks

All the other file entries in the directory have this same form. To acquire facility in reading the directory, you should spend some time identifying the parts of the other entries.

To locate the next sector of directory entries simply follow the pointer in bytes $00 and $01. In this case the next sector will be $12/$04, track 18 sector 4. Let's take a brief look at this sector.

```
            TRACK 18    SECTOR 4

. 00:  00 FF 82 10 01 44 49 52  .....DIR        Entry 1: file type = $82 (130)
. 08:  A0 A0 A0 A0 A0 A0 A0 A0  ........        First block on $10/$01 (16/1)
. 10:  A0 A0 A0 A0 A0 00 00 00  ........        File name = DIR
. 18:  00 00 00 00 00 00 04 00  ........        Length = $04 (4) blocks
. 20:  00 00 82 10 03 56 49 45  .....VIE        Entry 2: file type = $82 (130)
. 28:  57 20 42 41 4D A0 A0 A0  W.BAM...        First block on $10/$03 (16/3)
. 30:  A0 A0 A0 A0 A0 00 00 00  ........        File name = VIEW BAM
. 38:  00 00 00 00 00 00 06 00  ........        Length = $06 (6) blocks
. 40:  00 00 82 10 07 43 48 45  .....CHE        Entry 3: file type = $82 (130)
. 48:  43 4B 20 44 49 53 4B A0  CK.DISK.        First block on $10/$07 (16/7)
. 50:  A0 A0 A0 A0 A0 00 00 00  ........        File name = CHECK DISK
. 58:  00 00 00 00 00 00 04 00  ........        Length = $04 (4) blocks
. 60:  00 00 82 10 0F 44 49 53  .....DIS        Entry 4: file type = $82 (130)
. 68:  50 4C 41 59 20 54 26 53  PLAY.T&S        First block on $10/$0F (16/15)
. 70:  A0 A0 A0 A0 A0 00 00 00  ........        File name = DISPLAY T&S
. 78:  00 00 00 00 00 00 0E 00  ........        Length = $0E (14) blocks
. 80:  00 00 82 14 02 50 45 52  .....PER        Entry 5: file type = $82 (130)
. 88:  46 4F 52 4D 41 4E 43 45  FORMANCE        First block on $14/$02 (20/2)
. 90:  20 54 45 53 54 00 00 00  .TEST...        File name = PERFORMANCE TEST
. 98:  00 00 00 00 00 00 09 00  ........        Length = $09 (9) blocks
. A0:  00 00 82 14 07 53 45 51  .....SEQ        Entry 6: file type = $82 (130)
. A8:  55 45 4E 54 49 41 4C 20  UENTIAL.        First block on $14/$07 (20/7)
. B0:  46 49 4C 45 A0 00 00 00  FILE....        File name = SEQUENTIAL FILE
. B8:  00 00 00 00 00 00 05 00  ........        Length = $05 (5) blocks
. C0:  00 00 82 0F 01 52 41 4E  .....RAN        Entry 7: file type = $82 (130)
. C8:  44 4F 4D 20 46 49 4C 45  DOM.FILE        First block on $0F/$01 (15/1)
. D0:  A0 A0 A0 A0 A0 00 00 00  ........        File name = RANDOM FILE
. D8:  00 00 00 00 00 00 0D 00  ........        Length = $0D (13) blocks
. E0:  00 00 00 00 00 00 00 00  ........
. E8:  00 00 00 00 00 00 00 00  ........
. F0:  00 00 00 00 00 00 00 00  ........
. F8:  00 00 00 00 00 00 00 00  ........
```

Although this display is similar to the one for sector 1, there are two things to notice. The most obvious difference is that this sector of the directory is not full. It contains only seven file entries. The last entry is blank. When a new file is stored on this diskette its directory entry will be stored from $E0 to $FF. The second thing to notice is the pointer to the next directory sector (bytes $00 and $01). The pointer says that the next sector of the directory is on track 0 ($00), sector 255 ($FF). This seems strange. There is no track 0, sector 255! Actually, it means that this is the last sector in the directory. Whenever you see a pointer to track 0 it means that you have reached the end of the file you have been tracing.

This concludes our tour of the directory. Now that we know what the various parts of the directory do, let's create some non-standard directory entries.

13.8 Modifying the Directory

Now that you understand how the directory is organized, you are in a position to be able to modify the directory. By editing track 18, sector 0 you can change a diskette's name. By editing a file's directory entry you can lock or unlock the file, create a strange file name or an unusual file type. You can even change the length of the file so that it appears to be thousands of blocks long.

There are three programs listed in this book that you can use to modify a diskette's directory: EDIT T&S (Appendix E), MOD DISK NAME (Appendix E), and MOD ENTRY (listed below). The EDIT T&S program is the most powerful program. It allows you to edit any part of the directory. However, you *must* understand the structure of the directory thoroughly to use this program! Don't practice on your only copy of a diskette! The MOD DISK NAME is a short, special purpose utility that allows you to change a diskette's name quickly and easily. The MOD ENTRY program makes it very easy to change a directory entry's file type, file name and length. It also shows you what effect the change has had on a directory listing. The MOD DISK NAME and MOD ENTRY programs do not allow you to create names that contain special characters (nulls, clear screen characters, etc.). You will have to use the EDIT T&S program to do this.

The MOD DISK NAME program is easy to use. Insert the diskette whose name is to be changed and RUN the program. The existing diskette name will be displayed. Make any changes you like. The new name will then be recorded on the diskette.

When you load and run the MOD ENTRY program, you will be asked if you want to work with file names or directory positions. If you choose the name option, you will be asked for the name of the file entry you want to modify. Just type in the name (wild cards are OK) and press RETURN. If you choose the position option you will be asked for the number of the directory sector that contains the entry (1, 4, 7,...) and the entry's position in the sector (0-7). This option is provided so that you can rescue a file which no longer appears in a directory listing. If you are using a 1541 drive, you can use either option. If you are using a 4040 drive you can only use the position option.

Once you have identified which file you want, the directory entry for that file will be displayed. The display of the entry for the HOW TO USE file on your 1541TEST/DEMO diskette looks like this:

```
MODIFY DIRECTORY ENTRY

FILE NAME =  HOW TO USE

FILE TYPE BYTE =  130

TYPE   NORMAL LOCKED UNCLOSED
 DEL    128    192      0
 SEQ    129    193      1
 PRG    130    194      2
 USR    131    195      3
 REL    132    196      4


FILE LENGTH =  13

DIRECTORY ENTRY

 0  "1541TEST/DEMO    " ZX   2A
 13    "HOW TO USE"           PRG
 558 BLOCKS FREE

EDIT THIS ENTRY (Y/N)?  _
```

If you type N and press RETURN, the program will terminate (to edit a different entry, simply rerun the program). However, if you respond with a Y, editing begins. A question mark will appear on the screen right next to the name field like this:

```
FILE NAME =? HOW TO USE
```

When you have finished making changes to the file's name, press RETURN. You will then have a chance to edit the file type and length. If you don't want to make any changes to a particular field, simply press RETURN.

Once all three fields have been entered, you will be asked whether you want to re-edit the entry.

```
RE-EDIT THIS ENTRY (Y/N)?  _
```

If you respond with a Y, you have another chance to make changes. Once you are satisfied with the entry, respond with an N.

You will then be asked if you want to have this entry recorded in the directory.

```
CHANGE ON DISKETTE (Y/N)?  _
```

If you type N and press RETURN, the program will terminate. However, if you respond with a Y, the modified entry will be recorded in the diskette's directory. In a few moments, the entry will be redisplayed and you will get to see what the entry will look like in the directory listing.

CAUTION:

Modifying directory entries can be fun and interesting. However, you may manage to make some or all of the files inaccessible. Use a test diskette for practice and experimentation.

Now that you know how to use the MOD ENTRY program, try some experiments. What happens when you try to SCRATCH a locked file? What file type bytes give you the file types SR?, EQ? and G? Can you load or open any of these strange file types?

Here are a few more things you can try:

1. What happens to the directory when you include a null character in the file name like this?

```
SAVE CHR$(0)+"filename",8
```

2. What happens if you put a shifted blank in the file name?

```
SAVE "GOOD"+CHR$(160)+"STUFF",8
```

3. Here's another one to try. But be sure to remember the hidden letter if you ever want to load it again.

```
SAVE "H"+CHR$(20)+"filename",8
```

4. Here's a good way to disguise a program. Change it from a PRG file into a DEL file by editing the file type byte. Now try this:

```
LOAD "filename,DEL,R",8
```

5. Have you ever thought of time-stamping the various versions of the program you are working on? Try this:

```
SAVE "filename "+TI$,8
```

The possibilities for playing with the directory are endless. Enjoy!

NOTE:

If you are a programmer, you may want to study some of the techniques used in the MOD ENTRY program. The techniques which are used for editing, accessing a directory entry and reading a selective directory listing may be of interest.

```
******************
PROGRAM: MOD ENTRY
******************

0 REM 1541 USER'S GUIDE SECTION 13.8
1 REM  COPYRIGHT: G. NEUFELD, 1984
2 :
```

```
3 REM   MODIFY FILE'S NAME, TYPE OR LENGT
H
4 :
100 REM MOD ENTRY
110 PRINT"{CLR}MODIFY DIRECTORY ENTRY"
120 GET A$:IF A$<>"" GOTO 120
130 INPUT"{DOWN}USE NAME OR POSITION (N/
P)  N{LEFT 3}";X$
140 IF LEFT$(X$,1)<>"P" THEN ZF=0:GOTO 2
80
150 :
160 REM WORK FROM SECTOR# AND ENTRY NUMB
ER
170 ZF=1
180 INPUT"{DOWN}DIRECTORY SECTOR NUMBER
 1{LEFT 3}";X$
190 SE=VAL(X$):IF SE<1 OR SE>18 GOTO 180

200 INPUT"{DOWN}POSITION IN SECTOR (0-7)
  0{LEFT 3}";X$
210 P=INT(VAL(X$)):IF P<0 OR P>7 GOTO 20
0
220 PT=2 + 32*P
230 OPEN 15,8,15,"IO"
240 OPEN 2,8,4,"#0"
250 GOTO 500
260 :
270 REM WORK FROM NAME
280 PRINT"{CLR}MODIFY DIRECTORY ENTRY"
290 PRINT"{DOWN}FILE NAME   "F$
300 PRINT"{UP}"TAB(11);:INPUT F$
310 :
320 OPEN 15,8,15,"IO"
330 OPEN 1,8,5,F$+",M"
340 INPUT#15,EN,EM$,ET,ES
350 IF EN<20 GOTO 400
360 PRINT"{DOWN}DISK ERROR"
370 PRINTEN;EM$;ET;ES
380 CLOSE 1:CLOSE 15:END
390 :
400 OPEN 2,8,4,"#0"
410 IF ZF=1 GOTO 500
420 :
430 REM DIG OUT SECTOR & POINTER TO ENTR
Y
440 PRINT#15,"M-R"CHR$(144)CHR$(2)
450 GET#15,A$:SE=ASC(A$+CHR$(0))
460 PRINT#15,"M-R"CHR$(148)CHR$(2)
470 GET#15,A$:PT=ASC(A$+CHR$(0))
480 :
```

```
490 REM READ SECTOR AND DIG OUT ENTRY
500 PRINT#15,"U1:4 0 18"SE
510 PRINT#15,"B-P:4"PT
520 GET#2,A$:FT=ASC(A$+CHR$(O))
530 GET#2,TL$,SL$
540 F$=""
550 FOR K=1 TO 16
560 GET#2,A$:IFA$=""THENA$=CHR$(O)
570 F$=F$+A$
580 NEXT
590 PRINT#15,"B-P:4"PT+28
600 GET#2,A$:FL=ASC(A$+CHR$(O))
610 GET#2,A$:FL=FL+256*ASC(A$+CHR$(O))
620 CLOSE 1:CLOSE 2
630 :
640 REM DISPLAY ENTRY
650 PRINT"{CLR}MODIFY DIRECTORY ENTRY"
660 PRINT"{DOWN}FILE NAME =   ";F$
670 PRINT"{DOWN}FILE-TYPE BYTE = ";FT
680 PRINT"{DOWN}{RVS}TYPE   NORMAL LOCKED
 UNCLOSED"
690 PRINT" DEL     128     192        O"
700 PRINT" SEQ     129     193        1"
710 PRINT" PRG     130     194        2"
720 PRINT" USR     131     195        3"
730 PRINT" REL     132     196        4"
740 PRINT"{DOWN}FILE LENGTH = "FL
750 PRINT"{DOWN}DIRECTORY ENTRY{DOWN}"
760 :
770 REM DISPLAY WHAT IT LOOKS LIKE IN DI
RECTORY LIST
780 TRY=0
790 OPEN 1,8,0,"$0:"+F$+",P,R"
800 INPUT#15,EN,EM$,ET,ES
810 IF EN<20 GOTO 840
820 TRY=TRY+1:IFTRY<5 THEN CLOSE1:PRINT#
15,"I":GOTO790
830 PRINT"{DOWN}DISK ERROR":PRINTEN;EM$;
ET;ES:CLOSE15:STOP
840 GET#1,A$:GET#1,A$:FOR K=1 TO 3
850 GET#1,A$:GET#1,A$:IFK=3 THEN GET#1,A
$:GET#1,A$
860 GET#1,A$:L=ASC(A$+CHR$(O))
870 GET#1,A$:L=L+256*ASC(A$+CHR$(O)):PRI
NTL;
880 FORM=1TO25:GET#1,A$:PRINTA$;:NEXTM
890 GET#1,A$:IF A$<>"" AND K=2 THEN PRIN
TA$;
900 PRINT:NEXT:CLOSE 1
910 :
```

```
920 REM EDIT ENTRY
930 INPUT"{DOWN}EDIT THIS ENTRY (Y/N)   N
{LEFT 3}";X$
940 IF X$<>"Y" THEN CLOSE 15:END
950 PRINT"{UP}
"
960 PRINT"{HOME}{DOWN 2}"TAB(11);:INPUT
F$
970 IF LEN(F$)>16 THEN PRINT"{UP}"TAB(29
)"          ":GOTO 960
980 PRINT"{DOWN}"TAB(16);:INPUT NT
990 IF NT>=0 AND NT<256 AND NT=INT(NT) T
HEN FT=NT:GOTO 1040
1000 IF NT>255 THEN PRINT "{UP}"TAB(25)"
MAX IS 255"
1010 IF NT<0 THEN PRINT "{UP}"TAB(25)"MI
N IS 0"
1020 IF NT<>INT(NT) THEN PRINT "{UP}"TAB
(25)"INTEGERS ONLY"
1030 FOR K=1 TO 2000:NEXT:GOTO 650
1040 PRINT"{DOWN 8}"TAB(13);:INPUT NL
1050 IF NL>=0 AND NL<65536 AND NL=INT(NL
) THEN FL=NL:GOTO 1100
1060 IF NL>65535 THEN PRINT "{UP}"TAB(25
)"MAX IS 65535"
1070 IF NL<0 THEN PRINT "{UP}"TAB(25)"MI
N IS 0"
1080 IF NL<>INT(NL) THEN PRINT "{UP}"TAB
(25)"INTEGERS ONLY"
1090 FOR K=1 TO 2000:NEXT:GOTO 650
1100 PRINT"{DOWN 6}"
1110 INPUT"RE-EDIT THIS ENTRY (Y/N)   N{L
EFT 3}";X$
1120 IF LEFT$(X$,1)<>"N" GOTO 950
1130 INPUT"{UP}CHANGE ON DISKETTE (Y/N)
  Y  {LEFT 5}";X$
1140 IF LEFT$(X$,1)<>"Y" THEN CLOSE 15:E
ND
1150 :
1160 REM MODIFY ENTRY ON DISKETTE
1170 IF LEN(F$)<16 THEN F$=F$+CHR$(160):
GOTO 1170
1180 PRINT"{UP}WRITING TO DISKETTE......
   "
1190 OPEN 2,8,4,"#"
1200 PRINT#15,"U1:4 0 18"SE
1210 PRINT#15,"B-P:4"PT
1220 PRINT#2,CHR$(FT);
1230 PRINT#15,"B-P:4"PT+3
1240 PRINT#2,F$;
```

```
1250 PRINT#15,"B-P:4"PT+28
1260 H=INT(FL/256):L=FL-256*H
1270 PRINT#2,CHR$(L)CHR$(H);
1280 PRINT#15,"U2:4 0 18"SE
1290 CLOSE 2
1300 ZF=1:REM DON'T LOSE OUR PLACE
1310 GOTO 400
```

NOTE:

Sections 13.9 through 13.14 deal with how files are stored on a diskette. If you are an average user of disk files, you do not have to be concerned about the way in which files are stored. All you have to do is open a file, read or write data, and when you are done, close it again. You will never see a forward pointer or side sector and you don't have to worry about how your files are stored. The Disk Operating System (DOS) takes care of all those details for you.

However, if you are interested or having troubles, read on. You can learn the inner mysteries of your disk drive.

13.9 How Forward Pointers Work

The key to understanding Commodore file storage is the idea of forward pointers. Each part of a file contains a pointer that points ahead to the next part. We saw some forward pointers when we explored the file of directory entries in Section 13.7. The values stored in bytes $00 and $01 of any block in the directory were the track and sector numbers of the next block in the file. The table below summarizes the pointers in the directory file of the 1541TEST/DEMO diskette.

Dir Block	Track/ Sector	Value in $00	Value in $01	Points forward to the next block at
#1	18/0	$12(18)	$00(1)	Track 18, sector 1
#2	18/1	$12(18)	$04(4)	Track 18, sector 4
#3	18/4	$00(00)	$FF(255)	Last block in file

All Commodore disk files use forward pointers like this. They make it easy to trace a file, just find the first block and follow the pointers stored in bytes $00 and $01. When you find a track link of $00 (zero), you've reached the end of the file. But how do you find that first block? It's in the directory entry!

Let's do a bit of exploring and see what we can find. We'll trace through the program HOW PART TWO. Here is the directory entry:

```
          TRACK 18    SECTOR 1

. 20: 00 00 82 11 03 48 4F 57 .....HOW
. 28: 20 50 41 52 54 20 54 57 .PART.TW
```

```
. 30:  4F A0 A0 A0 A0 00 00 00  O.......
. 38:  00 00 00 00 00 00 05 00  ........
```

The pointer to the first block in the file is in bytes $23 and $24. The first part of the program is stored on track $11 (17), sector $03 (3). Let's take a look.

```
             TRACK  17     SECTOR  3

. 00:  11 0D 01 04 0A 04 0C 03  ........
. 08:  99 22 93 22 00 2D 04 16  ."."._..
. 10:  03 99 22 20 20 20 20 20  ..".....
. 18:  20 20 20 20 20 20 50 45  ......PE
. 20:  52 46 4F 52 4D 41 4E 43  RFORMANC
. 28:  45 20 54 45 53 54 22 00  E.TEST".
. 30:  36 04 20 03 99 22 20 22  6...."."
. 38:  00 62 04 2A 03 99 22 20  ...*..".
. 40:  54 48 45 20 50 45 52 46  THE.PERF
. 48:  4F 52 4D 41 4E 43 45 20  ORMANCE.
. 50:  54 45 53 54 20 50 52 4F  TEST.PRO
. 58:  47 52 41 4D 20 41 4C 4C  GRAM.ALL
. 60:  4F 57 53 22 00 8C 04 34  OWS"...4
. 68:  03 99 22 41 4E 59 4F 4E  .."ANYON
. 70:  45 20 54 4F 20 54 45 53  E.TO.TES
. 78:  54 20 54 48 45 20 45 4C  T.THE.EL
. 80:  45 43 54 52 4F 4E 49 43  ECTRONIC
. 88:  20 41 4E 44 20 22 00 B8  .AND."..
. 90:  04 3E 03 99 22 4D 45 43  .>.."MEC
. 98:  48 41 4E 49 43 41 4C 20  HANICAL.
. A0:  43 41 50 41 42 49 4C 49  CAPABILI
. A8:  54 49 45 53 20 4F 46 20  TIES.OF.
. B0:  54 48 45 20 44 49 53 4B  THE.DISK
. B8:  20 22 00 DA 04 48 03 99  ."...H..
. C0:  22 44 52 49 56 45 20 57  "DRIVE.W
. C8:  48 45 4E 45 56 45 52 20  HENEVER.
. D0:  4E 45 43 45 53 53 41 52  NECESSAR
. D8:  59 2E 20 22 00 08 05 52  Y.."...R
. E0:  03 99 22 55 53 45 20 54  .."USE.T
. E8:  48 49 53 20 50 52 4F 47  HIS.PROG
. F0:  52 41 4D 20 57 48 45 4E  RAM.WHEN
. F8:  45 56 45 52 20 59 4F 55  EVER.YOU
```

This may not look like the program listings you are familiar with, but it is a program just the same. The BASIC words like PRINT, GOTO and FOR are all tokenized. If you worked through Section 6.7, you may recognize some familiar landmarks such as line pointers, line numbers, null bytes marking the ends of lines, etc. However, this time only the first two bytes are of interest.

```
. 00:  11 0D 01 04 0A 04 0C 03  ........
```

Bytes $00 and $01 are the pointer to the next block in the file. In this case they point to track 17 ($11), sector 13 ($0D). Let's follow this forward pointer to the next block on track 17, sector 13. We'll only look at the first few lines of the display because we are primarily interested in following the file chain pointers.

```
          TRACK  17      SECTOR  13

. 00:  11 05 20 53 55 53 50 45  ...SUSPE
. 08:  43 54 20 22 00 36 05 5C  CT.".6.
. 10:  03 99 22 54 48 41 54 20  .."THAT.
```

This time the forward pointer (bytes $00 and $01) indicate that the next block is on track 17 ($11), sector 5 ($05). Let's take a look.

```
          TRACK  17      SECTOR  5

. 00:  11 0F 20 41 4E 44 20 43  ...AND.C
. 08:  41 4E 22 00 30 06 AC 03  AN".O...
. 10:  99 22 42 45 20 55 53 45  ."BE.USE
```

Nothing of interest here. Let's follow the pointer to track 17 ($11), sector 15 ($0F).

```
          TRACK  17      SECTOR  15

. 00:  11 07 4E 44 4F 4D 20 46  ..NDOM.F
. 08:  49 4C 45 20 42 4F 54 48  ILE.BOTH
. 10:  22 00 33 07 F2 03 99 22  ".3...."
```

Again, nothing new here. Onwards, to track 17 ($11), sector 7 ($07).

```
          TRACK  17      SECTOR  7

. 00:  00 52 2E 22 00 04 08 2E  .R."....
. 08:  04 8D 39 30 30 30 00 0A  ..9000..
. 10:  08 40 1F 80 00 26 08 28  . ...&.(
. 18:  23 99 22 20 3C 3C 50 52  #.".<<PR
. 20:  45 53 53 20 53 50 41 43  ESS.SPAC
. 28:  45 20 42 41 52 3E 3E 22  E.BAR>>"
. 30:  00 3A 08 32 23 A1 41 24  .:.2#.A$
. 38:  3A 8B 41 24 B2 22 22 A7  :.A$."".
. 40:  39 30 31 30 00 46 08 3C  9010.F.<
. 48:  23 99 22 93 22 3B 3A 8E  #."."; :.
. 50:  00 00 00 45 59 20 41 4C  ...EY.AL
. 58:  53 4F 20 22 00 81 06 C0  SO."....
. 60:  03 99 22 49 4C 4C 55 53  .."ILLUS
. 68:  54 52 41 54 45 20 54 48  TRATE.TH
```

```
. 70:  45 20 49 4D 50 4F 52 54   E.IMPORT
. 78:  41 4E 54 20 54 45 43 48   ANT.TECH
. 80:  4E 49 51 55 45 20 22 00   NIQUE.".
. 88:  AC 06 CA 03 99 22 4F 46   ....."OF
. 90:  20 43 48 45 43 4B 49 4E   .CHECKIN
. 98:  47 20 54 48 45 20 45 52   G.THE.ER
. A0:  52 4F 52 20 43 48 41 4E   ROR.CHAN
. A8:  4E 45 4C 20 41 46 54 45   NEL.AFTE
. B0:  52 22 00 D3 06 D4 03 99   R"......
. B8:  22 45 41 43 48 20 41 43   "EACH.AC
. C0:  43 45 53 53 20 54 4F 20   CESS.TO.
. C8:  54 48 45 20 44 49 53 4B   THE.DISK
. D0:  20 44 52 49 56 45 2E 20   .DRIVE..
. D8:  22 00 DD 06 D9 03 8D 39   "......9
. E0:  30 30 30 00 09 07 E8 03   000.....
. E8:  99 22 53 45 51 55 45 4E   ."SEQUEN
. F0:  54 49 41 4C 20 46 49 4C   TIAL.FIL
. F8:  45 20 41 4E 44 20 52 41   E.AND.RA
```

Ah ha! Finally something different. A track link of zero ($00). We've reached the end
of our file! However, this time we don't have a sector link of 255 ($FF) like we had
with the last block in the directory file. This time we have a sector link of 82 ($52).
What does that mean? Let's take a look around byte $52 and see if we can figure it out.

```
. 40:  39 30 31 30 00 46 08 3C   9010.F.<
. 48:  23 99 22 93 22 3B 3A 8E   #.".";:.
. 50:  00 00 00 45 59 20 41 4C   ...EY.AL
. 58:  53 4F 20 22 00 81 06 C0   SO."....
. 60:  03 99 22 49 4C 4C 55 53   .."ILLUS
```

The only thing that looks peculiar is that bytes $50, $51 and $52 all have the value
$00. If you have read through Section 6.7, you should remember that a BASIC
program always ends with three $00 bytes. One to end the last line, and another two
to indicate that there are no more lines. Now we know the meaning of the sector link
in the last block of a file. It points to the last byte in the sector that is part of the file.

NOTE:

Only BASIC program files end with three null bytes. Don't expect to find null bytes
on the end of other types of files.

But what about all the rest of that stuff in the sector from bytes $53 to $FF? It sure
looks like part of a BASIC program. It may well be. However, it is not part of this file.
It's junk. As the program was being saved each block of the file was built up in the
disk drive's RAM before it was encoded and recorded onto the diskette. This time
there wasn't enough program to completely fill the last block so the drive took the end
of the program and whatever else happened to be in that 256 bytes of RAM, encoded
it, and recorded it on the diskette. You'll find many strange things in the last blocks of
files.

Here is a program that you can use to trace any file on a diskette. The program is very easy to use. Just run it and enter the name of the file to be traced (wild cards are OK). You will see a listing of the entire file chain, including bytes $00 and $01 of the final block. The program even lists the side-sector file chain for relative files.

```
********************
PROGRAM: TRACE FILE
********************


0 REM 1541 USER'S GUIDE SECTION 13.9
1 REM   COPYRIGHT: G. NEUFELD, 1984
2 :
3 REM   TRACE & DISPLAY FILE CHAIN FOR NA
MED FILE
4 :
100 REM TRACE FILE
110 PRINT"{CLR} TRACE FILE 1541"
120 INPUT"{DOWN}FILE NAME";F$
130 PRINT"{DOWN}FILE CHAIN{DOWN}"
140 OPEN 15,8,15,"IO"
150 OPEN 1,8,4,"#"
160 OPEN2,8,5,F$
170 GOSUB 600
180 :
190 REM DIG OUT POINTER TO DIRECTORY ENT
RY
200 PRINT#15,"M-R"CHR$(144)CHR$(2)
210 GET#15,A$:SE=ASC(A$+Z$)
220 PRINT#15,"M-R"CHR$(148)CHR$(2)
230 GET#15,A$:PT=ASC(A$+Z$)
240 :
250 REM DIG OUT FILE TYPE & POINTER TO M
AIN FILE
260 PRINT#15,"U1:4 0 18"SE
270 PRINT#15,"B-P:4"PT
280 GET#1,A$:FT=ASC(A$+CHR$(0))
290 GET#1,A$:TL=ASC(A$+CHR$(0))
300 GET#1,A$:SL=ASC(A$+CHR$(0))
310 REM DIG OUT POINTER TO SIDE SECTOR F
ILE
320 PRINT#15,"B-P:4"PT+19
330 GET#1,A$:RT=ASC(A$+CHR$(0))
340 GET#1,A$:RS=ASC(A$+CHR$(0))
350 PRINT"{DOWN}MAIN FILE":GOSUB 430:PRI
NT:PRINTM$
360 IF FT<>132 GOTO 390
370 TL=RT:SL=RS
380 PRINT"{DOWN}SIDE SECTOR FILE":GOSUB
430:PRINT:PRINTM$
390 PRINT"{DOWN}ALL DONE"
```

```
400 CLOSE 1:CLOSE 2:CLOSE 15:END
410 :
420 REM PRINT LINK AND CHECK IF OK
430 NB=0
440 PRINT RIGHT$(STR$(TL),2)","RIGHT$("0
"+MID$(STR$(SL),2),2)" ";
450 NB=NB+1:IF NB/6 = INT(NB/6) THEN PRI
NT
460 IF TL=0 THEN M$="END OF FILE":RETURN

470 IF TL>35 THEN M$="BAD TRACK LINK":RE
TURN
480 NS = 20+2*(TL>17)+(TL>24)+(TL>30)
490 IF SL>NS THEN M$="BAD SECTOR LINK":R
ETURN
500 :
510 REM READ IN NEXT BLOCK AND GET NEW L
INK
520 PRINT#15,"U1:4 0"TL;SL
530 GOSUB 600
540 PRINT#15,"B-P:4 0"
550 GOSUB 600
560 GET#1,A$:TL=ASC(A$+CHR$(0))
570 GET#1,A$:SL=ASC(A$+CHR$(0))
580 GOTO 440
590 :
600 INPUT#15,EN,EN$,ET,ES
610 IF EN<20 THEN RETURN
620 PRINT"{DOWN}DISK ERROR"
630 PRINTEN;EM$;ET;ES
640 CLOSE 1:CLOSE 2:CLOSE 15
```

Now that you understand how the file pointers work, let's look briefly at how the various types of files are stored.

13.10 How Sequential Files Are Stored

The directory entry of a sequential file has a file type byte of $81 (129) and the track and sector pointer points to the first block of the file. A sequential file has a very simple structure. All the blocks in the file, except the last one, look like this:

Track Link	Sector Link	254 bytes of the sequential file

When we find a block in a sequential file with a track link of zero ($00), we know we have come to the last block in the file. Normally the second byte in the block would be the sector link. However, in the last block this byte is a pointer. It points to the last byte in the sector that is part of the file. Any bytes beyond this point are garbage. Diagrammatically the last block looks like this:

$00 Link	Pointer to final byte	Remaining bytes of the sequential file	Garbage

13.11 How Program Files Are Stored

The directory entry of a program file has a file type byte of $82 (130) and the track and sector pointer points to the first block of the file. The first block of a program file is somewhat unusual because it contains the load address for the file. The first block looks like this:

Track Link	Sector Link	Load Address (lo byte)	Load Address (hi byte)	The first 252 bytes of the program

Let's take another look at the start of the program HOW PART TWO.

```
. 00: 11 0D 01 04 0A 04 0C 03 ........
```

Bytes $00 and $01 are the pointer to the next block in the file. In this case they point to track 17 ($11), sector 13 ($0D).

```
. 00: 11 0D 01 04 0A 04 0C 03 ........
```

Bytes $02 and $03 are the load address of the file. The load address is in lo byte/hi byte form. In this case the load address is $0401. If you are more comfortable with decimal numbers, you can convert to decimal by multiplying the hi byte by 256 and adding the lo byte like this:

$$
\begin{aligned}
\text{Load Address} &= 256 \times (\text{Value of hi byte}) + (\text{Value of lo byte}) \\
&= 256 \times (4) + (1) \\
&= 1024 + 1 \\
&= 1025
\end{aligned}
$$

The remaining 252 bytes in this block are the first 252 bytes of our program.

All the other blocks in a program file, except the last one, have the same basic structure as a sequential file.

Track Link	Sector Link	254 bytes of the program

When we find a block in a program file with a track link of zero ($00), we know we have come to the last block in the file. The second byte in the sector points to the last byte in the sector that is part of the file. Any bytes beyond this point are garbage. Diagrammatically the last block looks like this:

$00 Link	Pointer to final byte	Remaining bytes of the program	Garbage

13.12 How User Files Are Stored

A user file does not have any specific form. Apparently Commodore included the user file type to give programmers a file type that they could use for special purpose files that were neither program nor sequential files. An example might be a true random access file. The need for such files was almost entirely eliminated when Commodore introduced relative files. As a result, very few programs were ever produced that made use of user files. At present, a user file is used mainly for showmanship and to intimidate the uninitiated.

If you are planning to create user files, they must have the normal track and sector links. Otherwise all the blocks in the file will be marked as free in the BAM the first time you validate the diskette.

13.13 How Relative Files Are Stored

Although relative files are easy to use, their structure is quite complex. A relative file actually consists of two separate files; a main data file that holds the records and a separate side-sector file for storing the track and sector numbers of the blocks that make up the main file.

In order to understand the structure of a relative file, we need one to explore. Unfortunately, there is no prerecorded relative file on the 1541TEST/DEMO diskette. We will have to create one. So get your system fired up, we've got some work to do.

INSTRUCTIONS:

If you want your files to be just like the ones shown in the diagrams, follow these instructions carefully.

1. Start with a diskette that has no files stored on it. A newly formatted diskette will do just fine.

2. Type in the program listed below.

3. SAVE the program onto the diskette.

4. RUN the program. It will create a simple relative file on your diskette.

```
*****************
PROGRAM: MAKE REL
*****************
```

```
100 REM MAKE TEST RELATIVE FILE
110 NR=50:REM NUMBER OF RECORDS IN FILE
120 PRINT"{CLR} MAKING RELATIVE FILE"
130 OPEN 15,8,15,"IO"
140 GOSUB 320:REM CHECK STATUS
150 OPEN 1,8,5,"TEST REL FILE,L,"+CHR$(2
0)
160 GOSUB 320:REM CHECK STATUS
170 RH=INT(NR/256):RL=NR-256*RH
180 PRINT"{DOWN}CREATING FILE OF EMPTY R
ECORDS"
190 PRINT#15,"P"CHR$(5)CHR$(RL)CHR$(RH)C
HR$(1)
200 PRINT#1,"LAST RECORD"
210 FOR R=1 TO NR
230 : RH=INT(R/256):RL=R-256*RH
240 : PRINT#15,"P"CHR$(5)CHR$(RL)CHR$(RH
)CHR$(1)
250 : PRINT"FILLING RECORD #"R
260 : PRINT#1,"TEST RECORD #"R
270 NEXT R
280 PRINT#15,"P"CHR$(5)CHR$(1)CHR$(0)CHR
$(1)
290 CLOSE 1: CLOSE 15
300 PRINT"{DOWN}ALL DONE":END
310 :
320 INPUT#15,EN,EM$,ET,ES
330 IF EN<20 OR EN=50 THEN RETURN
340 PRINT"{DOWN}DISK ERROR"
350 PRINTEN;EM$;ET;ES
360 CLOSE 1:CLOSE15:END
```

Once you have created the test file you may want to use the TRACE FILE program
from Section 13.8 to trace the file. If you followed the instructions, you should see
something like this when you run the TRACE FILE program.

```
 TRACE FILE 1541

FILE NAME? TEST REL FILE

FILE CHAIN

MAIN FILE
17,01 17,12 17,02 17,13  0,239
END OF FILE

SIDE SECTOR FILE
```

```
17,11   0,23
END OF FILE

ALL DONE
```

Notice that we seem to have two separate files. A main file that is four blocks long and a side-sector file that is only one block long.

Let's begin our investigation of how relative files are stored by looking at the directory entry for our relative file. It should be on track 18, sector 1.

```
            TRACK 18    SECTOR 1

. 00:  00 FF 82 11 00 4D 41 4B  .....MAK
. 08:  45 20 54 45 53 54 20 52  E.TEST.R
. 10:  45 4C A0 A0 A0 00 00 00  EL......
. 18:  00 00 00 00 00 00 03 00  ........
. 20:  00 00 84 11 01 54 45 53  .....TES
. 28:  54 20 52 45 4C 20 46 49  T.REL.FI
. 30:  4C 45 A0 A0 A0 11 0B 14  LE......
. 38:  00 00 00 00 00 00 05 00  ........
```

There it is, the second entry in the directory. Let's look at it carefully.

```
. 20:  00 00 84 11 01 54 45 53  .....TES
```

The entry begins with the file type byte (byte $22). The file type is $84 (134) which indicates that this is a relative file.

```
. 20:  00 00 84 11 01 54 45 53  .....TES
```

Immediately following the file type byte we have the pointer to the first block of the file. The first block is stored on track 17 ($11), sector 1 ($01). This is the same block that the TRACE FILE program gives as the first block of the four block main file.

The next bytes of interest are bytes $35 and $36.

```
. 30:  4C 45 A0 A0 A0 11 0B 14  LE......
```

The values stored here are 17 ($11) and 11 ($0B). These point to the first block in what the TRACE FILE program called the side-sector file —track 17, sector 11.

The next byte, $37, is also of interest.

```
. 30:  4C 45 A0 A0 A0 11 0B 14  LE......
```

The value stored here is 20 ($14). This is the record size we specified when we opened the relative file.

The last thing we should note is the length of the file.

. 38: 00 00 00 00 00 00 05 00 . . . .

The file is five blocks long. It seems that the length given in the directory entry is the sum of the length of the main file (four) and the length of the side-sector file (one).

Now that we know what the directory entry looks like, let's take a look at the two files themselves. We'll start with the main file. It begins on track 17, sector 1.

```
                TRACK  17     SECTOR  1

. 00:   11 0C 54 45 53 54 20 52   ..TEST.R
. 08:   45 43 4F 52 44 20 23 20   ECORD.#.
. 10:   31 20 0D 00 00 00 54 45   1.....TE
. 18:   53 54 20 52 45 43 4F 52   ST.RECOR
. 20:   44 20 23 20 32 20 0D 00   D.#.2...
. 28:   00 00 54 45 53 54 20 52   ..TEST.R
. 30:   45 43 4F 52 44 20 23 20   ECORD.#.
. 38:   33 20 0D 00 00 00 54 45   3.....TE
. 40:   53 54 20 52 45 43 4F 52   ST.RECOR
. 48:   44 20 23 20 34 20 0D 00   D.#.4...
. 50:   00 00 54 45 53 54 20 52   ..TEST.R
. 58:   45 43 4F 52 44 20 23 20   ECORD.#.
. 60:   35 20 0D 00 00 00 54 45   5.....TE
. 68:   53 54 20 52 45 43 4F 52   ST.RECOR
. 70:   44 20 23 20 36 20 0D 00   D.#.6...
. 78:   00 00 54 45 53 54 20 52   ..TEST.R
. 80:   45 43 4F 52 44 20 23 20   ECORD.#.
. 88:   37 20 0D 00 00 00 54 45   7.....TE
. 90:   53 54 20 52 45 43 4F 52   ST.RECOR
. 98:   44 20 23 20 38 20 0D 00   D.#.8...
. A0:   00 00 54 45 53 54 20 52   ..TEST.R
. A8:   45 43 4F 52 44 20 23 20   ECORD.#.
. B0:   39 20 0D 00 00 00 54 45   9.....TE
. B8:   53 54 20 52 45 43 4F 52   ST.RECOR
. C0:   44 20 23 20 31 30 20 0D   D.#.10..
. C8:   00 00 54 45 53 54 20 52   ..TEST.R
. D0:   45 43 4F 52 44 20 23 20   ECORD.#.
. D8:   31 31 20 0D 00 00 54 45   11....TE
. E0:   53 54 20 52 45 43 4F 52   ST.RECOR
. E8:   44 20 23 20 31 32 20 0D   D.#.12..
. F0:   00 00 54 45 53 54 20 52   ..TEST.R
. F8:   45 43 4F 52 44 20 23 20   ECORD.#.
```

Let's see what we've got.

. 00: 11 0C 54 45 53 54 20 52   ..TEST.R

Bytes $00 and $01 are the usual pointers to the next block in the file. In this case, track 17 ($11), sector 12 ($0C). Our first record begins at byte $02.

```
. 00:  11 0C 54 45 53 54 20 52   ..TEST.R
. 08:  45 43 4F 52 44 20 23 20   ECORD.#.
. 10:  31 20 0D 00 00 00 54 45   1.....TE
. 18:  53 54 20 52 45 43 4F 52   ST.RECOR
. 20:  44 20 23 20 32 20 0D 00   D.#.2...
```

The second record appears to start at byte $16. This means that our first record extends from byte $02 to byte $15 inclusive. A total of 20 characters. This is just what we specified as the record size when we opened the file. Note that the data we printed into the record (TEST RECORD # 1) and the carriage return character ($0D) did not completely fill the record. The data was padded with three null bytes ($00) to fill up the record.

The structure of the main file is actually quite simple. If you examine the next blocks (17,12 and 17,02) you'll find they are very similar to this one. Each contains a pointer to the next block and 254 bytes of data. The only one that is a bit different is the last block on track 17, sector 13.

```
                TRACK  17    SECTOR  13

. 00:  00 EF 53 54 20 52 45 43   ..ST.REC
. 08:  4F 52 44 20 23 20 33 39   ORD.#.39
. 10:  20 0D 00 00 54 45 53 54   ....TEST
. 18:  20 52 45 43 4F 52 44 20   .RECORD.
. 20:  23 20 34 30 20 0D 00 00   #.40....
. 28:  54 45 53 54 20 52 45 43   TEST.REC
. 30:  4F 52 44 20 23 20 34 31   ORD.#.41
. 38:  20 0D 00 00 54 45 53 54   ....TEST
. 40:  20 52 45 43 4F 52 44 20   .RECORD.
. 48:  23 20 34 32 20 0D 00 00   #.42....
. 50:  54 45 53 54 20 52 45 43   TEST.REC
. 58:  4F 52 44 20 23 20 34 33   ORD.#.43
. 60:  20 0D 00 00 54 45 53 54   ....TEST
. 68:  20 52 45 43 4F 52 44 20   .RECORD.
. 70:  23 20 34 34 20 0D 00 00   #.44....
. 78:  54 45 53 54 20 52 45 43   TEST.REC
. 80:  4F 52 44 20 23 20 34 35   ORD.#.45
. 88:  20 0D 00 00 54 45 53 54   ....TEST
. 90:  20 52 45 43 4F 52 44 20   .RECORD.
. 98:  23 20 34 36 20 0D 00 00   #.46....
. A0:  54 45 53 54 20 52 45 43   TEST.REC
```

```
. A8:  4F 52 44 20 23 20 34 37  ORD.#.47
. B0:  20 0D 00 00 54 45 53 54  ....TEST
. B8:  20 52 45 43 4F 52 44 20  .RECORD.
. C0:  23 20 34 38 20 0D 00 00  #.48....
. C8:  54 45 53 54 20 52 45 43  TEST.REC
. D0:  4F 52 44 20 23 20 34 39  ORD.#.49
. D8:  20 0D 00 00 54 45 53 54  ....TEST
. E0:  20 52 45 43 4F 52 44 20  .RECORD.
. E8:  23 20 35 30 20 0D 00 00  #.50....
. F0:  FF 00 00 00 00 00 00 00  ........
. F8:  00 00 00 00 00 00 00 00  ........
```

This time the track link is zero ($00) to indicate that this is the last block in the file.

```
. 00:  00 EF 53 54 20 52 45 43  ..ST.REC
```

Since this is the last block in the file, byte $01 is not a sector link. It is a pointer to the last byte in the sector that is part of the file.

```
. 00:  00 EF 53 54 20 52 45 43  ..ST.REC
```

In this case it has a value of 239 ($EF) which means that the 239th byte is the last byte in the file.

```
. D8:  20 0D 00 00 54 45 53 54  ....TEST
. E0:  20 52 45 43 4F 52 44 20  .RECORD.
. E8:  23 20 35 30 20 0D 00 00  #.50....
```

Note that the 239th byte is the last byte in record number 50.

The structure of the main data file part of a relative file is pretty simple. In fact, it looks just like a sequential file. The only difference is that each of the records is the same length.

Now that we have examined the main data file, let's take a look at the side-sector file. This file is only one block long and is located on track 17, sector 11. Since the side-sector file is the most complex and misunderstood part of a relative file, we'll examine it carefully.

```
         TRACK 17      SECTOR 11

. 00:  00 17 00 14 11 0B 00 00  ........
. 08:  00 00 00 00 00 00 00 00  ........
. 10:  11 01 11 0C 11 02 11 0D  ........
. 18:  00 00 00 00 00 00 00 00  ........
. 20:  00 00 00 00 00 00 00 00  ........
. 28:  00 00 00 00 00 00 00 00  ........
```

```
. 30:  00 00 00 00 00 00 00 00  ........
. 38:  00 00 00 00 00 00 00 00  ........
. 40:  00 00 00 00 00 00 00 00  ........
. 48:  00 00 00 00 00 00 00 00  ........
. 50:  00 00 00 00 00 00 00 00  ........
. 58:  00 00 00 00 00 00 00 00  ........
. 60:  00 00 00 00 00 00 00 00  ........
. 68:  00 00 00 00 00 00 00 00  ........
. 70:  00 00 00 00 00 00 00 00  ........
. 78:  00 00 00 00 00 00 00 00  ........
. 80:  00 00 00 00 00 00 00 00  ........
. 88:  00 00 00 00 00 00 00 00  ........
. 90:  00 00 00 00 00 00 00 00  ........
. 98:  00 00 00 00 00 00 00 00  ........
. A0:  00 00 00 00 00 00 00 00  ........
. A8:  00 00 00 00 00 00 00 00  ........
. B0:  00 00 00 00 00 00 00 00  ........
. B8:  00 00 00 00 00 00 00 00  ........
. C0:  00 00 00 00 00 00 00 00  ........
. C8:  00 00 00 00 00 00 00 00  ........
. D0:  00 00 00 00 00 00 00 00  ........
. D8:  00 00 00 00 00 00 00 00  ........
. E0:  00 00 00 00 00 00 00 00  ........
. E8:  00 00 00 00 00 00 00 00  ........
. F0:  00 00 00 00 00 00 00 00  ........
. F8:  00 00 00 00 00 00 00 00  ........
```

It certainly doesn't look like much.

```
. 00:  00 17 00 14 11 0B 00 00  ........  Last block, last byte pointer
```

If we can go by the usual rules, this is the last block in the file (byte $00 has a value of
zero) and only the first 23 bytes are important (byte $01 has a value of $17).

```
. 00:  00 17 00 14 11 0B 00 00  ........  Unused
```

Byte $02 is a null byte ($00). It is not used.

```
. 00:  00 17 00 14 11 0B 00 00  ........  Record size
```

Byte $03 looks somewhat familiar. It has a value of 20 ($14). It's just the record size of
our file.

```
. 00:  00 17 00 14 11 0B 00 00  ........  T & S of side sector 0
```

Bytes $04 and $05 also seem a bit familiar. They have the values 17 ($11) and 11
($0B). That's the track and sector number for this sector, the first (or zero) block in
the side-sector file. By the way, these are the bytes that the FIX BAD DIR program

checks to find side-sector files. If bytes $04 and $05 of the sector are the same as the track and sector number of the block, we have a potential side-sector file.

```
. 00:  00 17 00 14 11 0B 00 00  . . . . . . . .   Reserved for T & S numbers
                                                  of future side sectors

. 08:  00 00 00 00 00 00 00 00  . . . . . . .
```

Bytes $06 to $0F all have the value of zero ($00). They seem to be reserved for something.

```
. 10:  11 01 11 0C 11 02 11 0D  . . . . . . . .   T & S numbers of the blocks
                                                  that make up the main file
```

Bytes $10 to $17 are in use. They have the values 17 ($11), 1 ($01), 17 ($11), 12 ($0C), 17 ($11), 2 ($02), 17 ($11), and 13 ($0D). Do those numbers seem familiar? They should. They're the file chain of the main file we traced earlier.

If we expanded our relative file, the file chain stored here would be expanded. Since we need two bytes to store the track and sector numbers for each block and we have 240 bytes from byte 16 ($10) to 255 ($FF), we have space to store pointers to 240/2 = 120 blocks here.

What happens if we expand our relative file so that we need more than 120 blocks to hold the data? We'll need another block in our side-sector file to hold the rest of the file chain. When this happens, we'll notice a change in the first part of our old block. Bytes $00 and $01 will be changed to point to the new block in our side-sector file. In addition, bytes $06 and $07 will no longer be $00. They will hold the track and sector numbers of the new block in our side-sector file.

```
. 00:  00 17 00 14 11 0B tt ss  . . . . . . . .   T & S of side sector 1
```

Each block in our side-sector file really stores two file chains. Bytes $04 to $0F hold the entire file chain of the side-sector file and bytes $10 to $FF all or part of the file chain of the main data file.

```
                         ss #0 ss #1
. 00:  00 17 00 14       11 0B 00 00  . . . . . . . .

       ss #2 ss #3 ss #4 ss #5                         The entire file chain
. 08:  00 00 00 00 00 00 00 00  . . . . . . . .        of the side sector file


. 10:  11 01 11 0C 11 02 11 0D  . . . . . . . .
                                                       Part or all of the file
        :  :  :  :  :  :  :  :                         chain of the main data file
. F8:  00 00 00 00 00 00 00 00  . . . . . . . .
```

It only takes 12 bytes to hold the entire file chain of the side-sector file because it is impossible to produce a side-sector file that is more than six blocks long. Each block in the side-sector file can hold pointers to 120 blocks. With six blocks in the side-sector file we can store pointers to 6 x 120 = 720 blocks. Since a diskette only has 664 blocks free, we never need a seventh sector in the side-sector file. Note that the side sectors are numbered zero to five.

The Disk Operating System in the 1541 uses the two file chains in the side-sector file to enable it to locate any record in the file quickly and easily. It works something like this:

Problem: I have a relative file with a record size of 40. I want record number 1206. How do I locate it?

How many bytes into the file? 1206 x 40 = 48240

How many sectors into the file? 48240/254 = 189.921269 (remember each sector holds 254 data bytes). This is 234 bytes into the 190th sector.

Where is the sector pointer stored? 190/120 = 1.583333
It is the 70th pointer stored in side-sector 1.

Once the location of the pointer has been determined, it is relatively easy for the DOS to find the pointer, read in the block containing the desired record and position to the start of the record.

Now that you have a basic understanding of how relative files work, do a bit of experimenting with them yourself. Expand our test file and see what happens. As you become more familiar with relative files, you'll find them fast and easy to use. Just remember, on the 1541 drive you must *always* specify the byte parameter when you position to a record and be careful when updating records. See Section 8.6 for more details.

13.14 An Overview of the Inner Workings of the 1541

Commodore is one of the few computer manufacturers that uses intelligent disk drives. A 1541 disk drive contains some quite sophisticated electronics. It has a 6502 microprocessor, two 6522 chips to handle input/output operations, 2K of RAM memory, and a 16K Disk Operating System (DOS 2.6) contained in ROM.

The 6502 microprocessor flips back and forth between being a file manager and a floppy disk controller. In its file manager mode it:

1. Communicates with the Commodore 64 or VIC-20 computer.
2. Uses and maintains the BAM to keep track of disk storage.
3. Breaks up disk operations into simple read or write jobs.
4. Puts jobs to be done in the job queue.
5. Generates error status reports for the computer.

In its floppy disk controller mode the 6502:

1. Monitors the job queue for job requests.
2. Turns the drive motor and drive-active LED on and off.
3. Activates the stepper motor to move the read/write head.
4. Records headers and dummy data blocks to format a diskette.
5. Reads and writes encoded data.
6. Encodes and decodes data.
7. Reports the status of jobs to the file manager.

The memory map below indicates the arrangement of the disk RAM and ROM. It also highlights a few of the important areas.

```
$0000-$0011      Page 0: job queue (job & location)
$0000-$00FF              workspace for the 6502

$0100-$01B9      Page 1: 6502 stack
$01BA-$01FF              overflow buffer (encoding)

$0200-$0229      Page 2: disk command buffer
$022A-$02FF              workspace for the 6502

$0300-$03FF      Page 3: data buffer #0
                         temporary data storage

$0400-$04FF      Page 4: data buffer #1
                         temporary data storage

$0500-$05FF      Page 5: data buffer #2
                         temporary data storage

$0600-$06FF      Page 6: data buffer #3
                         temporary data storage

$0700-$07FF      Page 3: data buffer #4
                         reserved for BAM storage


$1800-$180F      6522 I/O Chip:
                 computer/disk drive communication


$1C00-$1C0F      6522 I/O Chip:
                 floppy disk controller


$C100-$F258      ROM: File manager routines

$C100-$F258      ROM: Disk controller routines
```

Some of the disk utility programs given in this book bypass the 1541's file manager and place job requests directly in the job queue. However, a discussion of this technique is beyond the scope of this book. For more details on this technique and the internal organization of the 1541 drive, see *Inside Commodore DOS*, by Richard Immers and Gerald G. Neufeld, (DATAMOST, 1984).

13.15 The Important Bugs in DOS 2.6

Several bugs have crept into DOS 2.6 and its documentation. The most important of these are listed below:

1. The byte parameter in the POSITION command is required. It is *not optional* as indicated on page 35 of the *1541 User's Manual*. It must be present or the drive will not position to the record correctly. If you leave it off, you will be positioned to the start of the record only if that record happens to span two sectors. Otherwise you will be positioned to byte 13 of the record (the DOS assumes the carriage return character at the end of the command gives the byte position). This inconsistency has generated much confusion about relative files.

2. The POSITION command can cause problems when revising records. Several articles in the popular press have indicated that there are serious problems with the POSITION command on the 2031 and 1541 Commodore disk drives. The investigations reported in Section 8.6 indicate that the problem is relatively minor and is easily fixed. Problems occur *only* when you are writing or revising records in a non-sequential manner. To fix this bug, simply issue the POSITION command twice and then create about a 0.5 second pause before using PRINT# to write data into the record. No fix is needed when reading records or writing records consecutively (as when filling a file initially). In these situations, the command appears to be completely reliable.

3. Certain record lengths of relative files are forbidden. The 1541 drive will reject any command that attempts to open a relative file with a record length of 42 (*), 58 (:) or 63 (?). The reason is that these particular lengths correspond to characters that have special meanings to the disk operating system.

4. If a replace operation aborts, the old file is lost. If a disk error occurs (including a 70, DISK FULL, error) while you are in the process of replacing a file, the old file will be lost and the new file will be incomplete. If this happens to you, turn to Section 11.8 to find out how to recover the old file.

5. The direct-access commands BLOCK-READ and BLOCK-WRITE do not work correctly. Although these commands are described in the *1541 User's Manual*, they should never be used. Use the command "U1:" to read a sector and "U2:" to write a sector instead. The correct syntax for each command is:

```
SYNTAX:
  PRINT#15,"U1:channel# drive# track# sector#"
  PRINT#15,"U2:channel# drive# track# sector#"

EXAMPLES:
  PRINT#15,"U1:0 5 18 1"      Read track 18, sector 1
```

```
PRINT#15, "U1:0 5"TR;SE
PRINT#15, "U2:0 5 18 1"      Write track 18, sector 1
PRINT#15, "U2:0 5"TR;SE
```

For practical examples of the use of "U1:" and "U2:" commands look through the listings of the disk utility programs included in this book.

6. The direct-access command BLOCK-ALLOCATE does not always work correctly. This command is used to allocate a particular sector in the BAM. If the specified sector is free, the command *will work properly*. However, if the specified sector is already allocated, an entire trackful of sectors will be allocated instead. This is why the UNSCRATCHER program reads in the BAM and checks to be sure that all the blocks are free before the blocks in the recovered file are allocated using a BLOCK-ALLOCATE command. In case you are wondering why you would ever want to allocate an already allocated sector, the reason is that this technique was used for creating random access files in the days before relative files. When you attempt to allocate an already allocated block, the drive is supposed to report the track and sector numbers of the next available block as part of the 65, NO BLOCK, error message. Not only does the drive preallocate a track full of sectors, it will even report sectors on track 18 (the reserved directory track) as the next available block.

7. The drive reset command "U" does not work. According to page 39 of the *1541 User's Manual*, you may use either PRINT#15,"U" or PRINT#15,"U;" to reset the drive to its power-on status. If you use the PRINT#15,"U" command, the drive will lock up. You will have to turn the drive OFF and ON again to recover. To reset the drive you must use the "U;", "U9", or "UI" commands.

8. The drive slow-down command "U+" does not work. According to page 39 of the *1541 User's Manual*, you can use the command PRINT#15,"U+" to set the drive's communication speed so it is compatible with the Commodore 64. If you issue this command, the drive will lock up. You will have to turn the drive OFF and ON again to recover. However, don't worry. As you have undoubtably discovered by now, your Commodore 64 and your 1541 communicate quite well without the use of this command.

Conclusion

Although the 1541 is somewhat slow and has a few flaws, it is a very sophisticated disk drive. It's low price makes it an outstanding bargain. None of the other drives in its price range provide relative file handling and make use of asynchronous I/O or read-ahead buffering. Commodore is to be congratulated for a fine product.

GLOSSARY

allocated sector—a sector (block) that is identified as being currently in use in the diskette's Block Availability Map (BAM). When a program or data file is recorded on a diskette, the status of sectors used to store the file are automatically changed from unallocated (available for use or free) to allocated (currently in use) by the 1541's Disk Operating System (DOS).

application program—a program that carries out a useful, real world task. Examples include word processors, mailing list programs, grade book programs and electronic spreadsheets.

BAM—an acronym for Block Availability Map.

binary chop—a technique for rapidly scanning a sorted list of numbers or character strings. The technique involves checking if the desired value is in the first or last half of the list. Once this is determined, the process is repeated using only the half of the list that contains the desired value. Each check splits the remaining list in half. Hence the term binary (in two) chop (to split).

block—a synonym for sector. It can store 256 characters of information.

Block Availability Map—a map which indicates which sectors (blocks) on a diskette are currently being used (in use or allocated) to store part of a program or data and which sectors are still available for use (free or unallocated). It is often referred to as the BAM. The status of each sector is represented by a single bit. If the bit corresponding to a particular sector (block) is one, the sector is unallocated. If the bit is zero, that sector has been allocated. The BAM is stored on track 18, sector 0. When a diskette is initialized, a copy of the BAM is read into the disk drive's RAM memory and resides at memory locations $0704-$078F.

buffer—an area of RAM memory inside the 1541 disk drive that is used to temporarily hold data that is being read from, or written to, a diskette. When data to be recorded on diskette is sent from the computer to the disk drive, it is stored in one of the buffers until 256 characters (bytes) of data have been received. Then all 256 bytes are encoded and recorded as the data block of one sector on the diskette. When data is to be read from diskette, the 256 bytes that make up the data block of a particular sector are read, decoded and stored in a buffer. As the data is requested by the computer, it is sent from the buffer. When all 256 bytes have been sent, another buffer full of bytes is read from the diskette. The 1541 disk drive has five buffers (#0 to #4).

close a file—when you are finished reading from or writing to a file on a diskette, the file should be closed. This breaks the communication link that was established when the file was first opened for access. It is particularly important to close a file that was opened in write mode. Unless the file is closed, the last part of the file will not be recorded onto the diskette. It will simply remain in the buffer inside the 1541. In addition, the directory entry for that file will not be completed and you will end up with an unclosed file. Unclosed files have an asterisk (*) beside their file types in a directory listing (*PRG, *SEQ or *USR).

channel number (channel#)—an integer between zero and 15. It is used in an OPEN statement to identify the type of communication link desired between the computer and the disk drive. Channel# 0 is reserved for use in loading programs. Channel# 1 is reserved for use in saving programs. Channel#'s 2 through 14 are for general use in reading or writing any type of file. Channel# 15 is the command channel and is used to send housekeeping commands to the disk drive or to read the disk drive's error status report. The channel number is also known as the secondary address.

**CHR$**—a BASIC function that allows you to convert the ASCII code for a character to the actual character itself. For example, the ASCII code for the letter A is 65. To print an A on the screen you could say either PRINT "A" or PRINT CHR$(65).

command channel—one type of communication channel that can be established between your computer and the 1541 disk drive. It is used for sending disk housekeeping commands to the disk drive and for reading the disk drive's error status. The command channel is channel# 15.

decimal notation—refers to numbers written in base 10. Numbers that we encounter in normal, everyday life are written in base 10. If you are an incurable hacker and have difficulty in expressing numbers in anything other than binary or hexadecimal notation, tune in to Sesame Street.

delimiter—a character that is used to separate the various parts (fields) of a record in a data file. For example, a delimiter might be used to separate a person's name (the name field) from his or her address (the address field). A delimiter can be any character that would never appear in either of the fields to be separated. Usually a carriage return character, CHR$(13), or a comma (,), is used as a delimiter because these characters are delimiters recognized by the INPUT statement and naturally divide the data into two fields.

device number (device#)—an integer that is used to identify a particular device. On the VIC-20 and Commodore 64, devices with numbers greater than four are assumed to be connected to computer by the serial bus. The 1541 comes from the factory as device# 8. It may be changed to device# 9, 10, 11 or 12, either temporarily or permanently.

directory—a special purpose file stored on track 18 of a diskette. It contains the diskette's Block Availability Map and a list of file entries. There is one entry for each file stored on the diskette. Each entry holds a file's name, type, size, and the track and sector numbers of the sector used to store the first block of that file. You can OPEN the directory file for read access. It is a program file and its file name is $. If you use a data channel# (2-14), you get to read the whole file. If you use channel# 0, you read the pseudo BASIC directory that is loaded by LOAD "$",8.

directory entry—refers to all the information stored in the diskette's directory about a particular file. The entry consists of the file type, the track and sector number of the first block in the file, the file name, and the length of the file (in blocks). An entry for a relative file also contains the record size, and the track and sector number of the first block in the side-sector file.

directory file—see directory.

disk—synonym for floppy diskette.

disk command—a command sent from the computer to the 1541 disk drive instructing it to carry out a specific disk operation. The 1541 commands described in detail in this book are NEW, INITIALIZE, SCRATCH, RENAME, COPY, VALIDATE and POSITION. The 1541 command set also includes "U1:" (read a sector), "U2:" (write a sector), "M-R" (memory read), "M-W" (memory write), "M-E" (memory execute), "B-A" (block allocate), "B-F" (block free), "B-E" (block execute), "U0" (reset jump vectors), "UI-" (speed up data transmission for the VIC-20), and "&" (load and execute a utility). Some of these more advanced commands are used in the disk utility programs. If you are interested in how to use these commands more effectively, see the more advanced book, *Inside Commodore DOS*, by Richard Immers and Gerald G. Neufeld, (DATAMOST, 1984).

disk error status—the 1541's Disk Operating System (DOS) monitors all disk operations. When an operation has been completed or aborted because of an error, the DOS generates a status report. The report consists of an error code number, an English language error message, and the track and sector number of where the error, if any, occurred. The status report is read using the command channel.

disk ID—a two character code used by the Disk Operating System to identify a diskette. The disk ID is specified when the diskette is formatted (newed). A diskette's ID cannot be changed unless the entire diskette is reformatted. It is good practice to have a different disk ID for every diskette you have.

disk name—an arbitrary name used to help you identify a diskette. The name is specified when the diskette is formatted. It may be changed using the MOD DISK NAME program (Appendix E).

Disk Operating System—a machine language program that directly controls the operation of the disk drive. It is often called the DOS. The 1541 uses Commodore DOS version 2.6. It is permanently stored in 16K of Read Only Memory (ROM) in the disk drive.

disk utility—a program that performs some useful task related to the preservation of the sanity of disk drive owners. Examples of disk utilities include the UNSCRATCHER, which recovers a scratched file, CHECK DISK, which checks a diskette for flaws, and CONFIRM ALL FILE, which checks to see if a diskette's BAM and directory are correct and that all files are intact.

diskette—a circular disk of thin plastic, coated on both sides with a magnetic material and encased in a protective jacket. It is used for storing computer programs or data files.

DOS—an acronym for Disk Operating System.

DOS 5.1—this is *not* a Disk Operating System. It is a short, machine language program that makes it easier to view a diskette's directory, load or save programs, send disk commands, and read the disk drive's error status. This program resides at the top of memory and does not affect the normal operation of BASIC programs in the VIC-20 or Commodore 64.

double density—describes a diskette that is designed to be used with a disk drive that uses double density recording techniques. In double density recording the data is encoded so that clock bits are not needed between data bits. The 1541 uses GCR encoding to do this. Since there are no clock bits, a double density diskette is rated at 5,876 flux changes per inch and 5,876 bits per inch along a track. Note that both single and double density diskettes can record 5,876 flux changes per inch. Since the 1541 records a maximum of 5,800 flux changes per inch, you can use either single or double density diskettes with a 1541 drive. The reason that double density diskettes are usually more expensive is that they are also designed to work with drives that write up to 80 tracks per inch. Since the 1541 only uses 40 tracks per inch, single density diskettes are adequate.

double-sided—describes a diskette that is designed to be used with a disk drive that can record on both sides of the diskette. Since the 1541 only records on one side of the diskette, you can use the less expensive, so-called single-sided diskettes.

drive-active LED—the red, Light Emitting Diode (LED) on the front of the 1541 disk drive. If this light is on, the drive is busy carrying out some disk operation. If it is flashing on and off regularly, a disk error has occurred. It is normal for the light to blink on and off occasionally as you load a long program. Normally, you should never open the drive door while the light is glowing steadily. However, if you realize you have just told the drive to NEW your only copy of a valuable diskette, quickly open the door and rescue that diskette!

end of file—when reading a file, the 1541 sends a special end-or-identify (EOI) signal to your computer along with the very last character from the file. When your computer receives this EOI signal, it sets the status variable (ST) to 64. If you check the value stored in ST after every INPUT# or GET# statement, you can tell when you read the last piece of data in your file.

file identification information—the information included in an OPEN statement that tells the disk drive the name and type of the file you want to access. For sequential, program and user files you must also specify the mode of access desired (read, write or modify). This is not necessary for relative files because these files are always opened for read/write access. However, if the OPEN statement will create a new relative file, you must specify the record length (size).

file type—identifies a file as being of a particular type. The 1541 DOS supports four different types of files: program files (PRG), sequential files (SEQ), relative files (REL), and user files (USR). An asterisk (*) in front of the file type in a directory listing identifies an unclosed file (e.g., *SEQ, *PRG, *USR). A less than sign (<) following the file type identifies a locked file (e.g., SEQ<, PRG<, REL< or USR<). A locked file cannot be scratched unless it is first unlocked.

file type byte—the single character (byte) in a file's directory entry on track 18 that identifies the type of file. Normal values are 128 ($80), a DEL file; 129 ($81), a SEQ file; 130 ($82), a PRG file; 131 ($83), a USR file; and 132 ($84), a REL file. Changing the file type byte from $8x to $Cx locks the file.

file number (file#)—an integer between one and 127 given in an OPEN statement to identify that particular file. Subsequent GET#, INPUT#, PRINT# and CLOSE statements that refer to this file must include the file#. An identifying number is needed because the VIC-20 and Commodore 64 allow the user to have up to 10 different files open simultaneously. Once a file has been closed the file# that was used to refer to that file has no further significance. The file# is also referred to as the logical file number.

flippy—a diskette that has been modified by cutting a second write protect notch in the protective jacket. This allows the second side of the diskette to be used for storing programs and data when the diskette is inserted into the drive upside down.

free sector—a sector on a diskette that is not currently being used to store part of a program or data file. It is also known as an unallocated sector. The diskette's Block Availability Map (BAM) is used to keep track of which sectors are free and which have been allocated (are in use).

format a diskette—recording a pattern of information on a new, blank diskette so that it can be used for storing programs or data. This is also known as newing a diskette. During the formatting process, an identifying header block and a dummy data block are recorded for each of the 683 sectors on the diskette. Any information previously recorded on the diskette is irretrievably lost. On the 1541 formatting a diskette takes approximately 80 seconds.

GCR—an acronym for Group Code Recording. Each 8-bit data byte is encoded into a 10-bit GCR equivalent before being recorded onto the diskette surface. The data is decoded into 8-bit form when it is read back from the diskette.

hex—short for hexadecimal notation (e.g., $0A = 10).

hexadecimal notation—refers to numbers written in base 16 rather than our more familiar base 10 (decimal) notation. A number written in hexadecimal notation is usually preceded by a dollar sign ($4F). Hexadecimal notation is used by most computer buffs because it allows all numbers between zero and 255 to be expressed as two digits ($00-$FF) and it simplifies the conversion of numbers to binary (base 2) notation. Appendix B contains a table giving all the hexadecimal numbers between $00 and $FF and their decimal equivalents.

I/O—an abbreviation for input/output.

I/O status—refers to whether an input or output operation has been completed successfully or not. In the VIC-20 and Commodore 64 the I/O status is automatically stored in the status variable, ST. If the value stored in ST is zero, the operation has been completed satisfactorily. A value of 64 after a read operation indicates that you have reached the end of the file.

index file—the file that serves as an index into another file. See indexed relative file.

indexed relative file—a way of storing and retrieving information by putting unsorted data in a large relative file and using the data in another file as an index to the relative file. The index allows the data in the relative file to be retrieved or scanned quickly in a sorted order.

initializing a diskette—reading a copy of the Block Availability Map (BAM) recorded on track 18, sector 0 of the diskette into the disk drive's RAM memory. This ensures that the disk drive recognizes the diskette properly.

link—the pointer that gives the track and sector numbers of the sector (block) on the diskette where the next part of a file is stored. For more information see Section 13.9.

LOAD—a BASIC command that reads a program that is stored on a cassette tape or diskette and stores a copy of this program in the computer's memory. The copy of the program on tape or diskette is not erased or modified in any way.

loader program—a program that is designed to load another program or other information into memory and run it. Many commercial programs use loader programs that check to make sure you have an original copy of the tape or diskette before they will load and run the main program. Usually these loader programs are written in machine code and make use of obscure programming tricks, encoding and illegal instructions to make it very difficult for someone to determine exactly what the loader does.

machine language—the native language of the 6502/6510 microprocessor in your computer and disk drive. Each line in a BASIC program must be interpreted and converted into a set of equivalent machine language instructions before the microprocessor can carry out the requested operation. Programs written in machine language run up to 1,000 times faster than an equivalent BASIC program.

machine language monitor—a program that makes it easy to examine and change the contents of various memory locations in your computer. Some machine language monitor programs include a simple assembler to make programming in machine language easier and a simple disassembler to convert machine language programs into more readable form. SUPERMON on the C-64 DISK PACK is an example of a machine language monitor.

monitor—a TV set without commercials.

opening a file—means establishing a communication link between your computer and some device so that you can output information to the device or input information from the device. A useful analogy is opening the drawer of a filing cabinet so that you can put information into it or take information out of it.

position to a record—a disk command that tells the Disk Operating System (DOS) that you want to access a particular part (record) of a relative file. You must specify the channel# you used when you opened the file and the number of the record you want. The DOS calculates where that particular record is stored on the diskette and reads it into the disk drive's RAM memory.

program—a set of instructions that tells the computer exactly how to do something (e.g., play a game). Programs can be written in the native language of the computer's microprocessor (machine language) or a language that is more understandable to humans like BASIC.

RAM—an acronym for Random Access Memory. A place where the microprocessor can store information (such as a program) and read it back later. The information is not stored permanently. When new information is stored in a particular location, any existing information stored there is lost. When the power is turned off, all the information stored in RAM memory is lost.

random access file—a data file in which any data item (record) can be read or written without having to read or write the entire file. A relative file is a random access file that has a fixed record size.

read error—occurs when the disk drive has attempted to find a particular sector on the diskette and read its data block, and found that the information recorded on diskette for this sector was incorrect in some way. An error in either the identifying header block or the data block will cause a read error.

reading a file—the disk drive plays back (reads) all or part of a group of related information (file) that has been previously recorded on a diskette.

record—the part of a file that contains all the information stored about a particular person, place or thing. In a sequential file, the length of the records usually varies according to the amount of information stored about that particular person, place or thing. In a relative file, the records are all the same length.

relative file—Commodore's name for a random access data file. All the records in a relative file must be the same length. Individual records are identified by number. When a particular record is to be accessed, the record number is specified in a POSITION command. The disk operating system accesses the appropriate sector(s) on the diskette and the record may be read or written.

replace—when an "at" sign and a colon precede the file name in a SAVE or OPEN command (e.g., SAVE "@:BIG TEST",8), the new program or data file will replace the older version stored on the diskette and use the same name. The new file is saved before the older version is replaced. If an error causes the writing of the new file to be aborted, the old file is normally lost. If the old file was normal, the old directory entry is used. If the old file was unclosed, a new directory entry is created and the old file type byte changed to $00 (scratched).

ROM—an acronym for Read Only Memory. The place where the instructions that control the basic operation of your computer or disk drive are stored. These instructions may not be changed without replacing the memory chips. This information is not erased when the power is turned off.

SAVE—a BASIC instruction that records a copy of the program currently in the computer's RAM memory onto cassette tape or diskette.

scratch a file—to delete an unwanted file from the directory of a diskette. The file itself is not erased and may be recovered if no new information has been recorded on the diskette since the file was scratched.

secondary address—a synonym for channel#.

sector—a segment of a circular ring (a track) on the surface of a diskette which contains a block of information that identifies which sector it is (the header block) and includes a block of 256 characters (bytes) of data (the data block). Sectors are identified by their track number and their sector number. The header block and a dummy data block are recorded on the diskette when a diskette is formatted.

sector number—a number which identifies a particular sector on a track. The sectors that make up a track are numbered consecutively from zero to the maximum for that track. Tracks 1 to 17 have 21 sectors (0 to 20), tracks 18 to 24 have 19 sectors (0 to 18), tracks 25 to 30 have 18 sectors (0 to 17), and tracks 31 to 35 have 17 sectors (0 to 16).

sequential file—a file of information in which the individual pieces of information (records) are packed one behind the other. The size of an individual record varies with the amount of information stored about that particular person, place or thing. To read a particular record in a sequential file you must read through all the preceding records in the file. A record cannot be modified without rewriting the entire file.

serial bus—the cable that connects the 1541 disk drive to the Commodore 64 or VIC-20 computer. Information that passes through this bundle of wires (a bus) between the two devices is transmitted one bit at a time (serially), hence the name.

side sector—one of the sectors that is used by the disk operating system of the 1541 to store the track and sector numbers of the blocks that make up a relative file. Each side sector stores the record size, the track and sector numbers of all other side sectors, and the track and sector numbers of up to 120 blocks on which the main data file is stored. Since the maximum length of any file on a 1541 formatted diskette is 664 blocks, there are a maximum of six side sectors needed to hold the pointers for a relative file.

side-sector file—a short auxiliary file set up and maintained by the disk operating system of the 1541 to keep track of the track and sector numbers of the blocks on which the main data in a relative file is stored.

single density—describes a diskette that is designed to be used with a disk drive that uses single density recording. A single density diskette is designed to record up to 5,876 flux changes per inch along a track. Since single density recording records a clock bit between each data bit, up to 2,938 data bits can be recorded per inch. The 1541 drive does not use normal single density recording. It uses GCR encoding which eliminates the need for the clock pulses. Data is recorded at 4,100 to 5,800 bits per inch. Since there is at most one flux change per bit, there are a maximum of 5,800 flux changes per inch along a track. As a result, the 1541 can use single density diskettes rated at 40 tracks per inch.

single-sided—describes a diskette that is designed to be used with a disk drive that records on only one side of the diskette (the back). Since the 1541 only records on one side of the diskette, this is the kind of diskette to purchase for your 1541.

status variable—a special variable, ST, in the VIC-20 and Commodore 64 computers that is automatically set by the computer to indicate the status of the most recent input or output operation. If ST=0, the most recent operation was completed satisfactorily. If ST=64, you have just read the last item of data in the file being read.

track—a circular ring on the surface of a diskette that is used for recording information. On a 1541 formatted diskette there are 35 concentric tracks numbered 1 to 35. Track 1 is the outermost track, closest to the outer edge of the disk. Track 35 is the innermost track, closest to the center of the disk.

track and sector link—the track and sector numbers of the sector that stores the next block of a file. The directory entry contains the link to the first sector in the file; the first two bytes stored in the first sector are the link to the second sector; the first two bytes stored in the second sector are the link to the third sector, and so on....

unallocated sector—a sector (block) that is identified as being available for use (free) in the diskette's Block Availability Map (BAM). When a program or data file is scratched, the status of sectors used to store the file is automatically changed from allocated (currently in use) to unallocated (free or available for use) by the 1541's disk operating system.

validate a diskette—creating a new copy of a diskette's Block Availability Map (BAM) by tracing through all the active files listed in the directory and marking those sectors used to store these files as allocated (currently in use). All other sectors on the diskette are marked as unallocated (free or available for use).

verify—comparing the copy of a program stored in the computer's memory with the copy stored on cassette tape or diskette. If the copies match exactly, the computer reports OK. If there is any difference between the copies, the computer reports ?VERIFY ERROR. If this happens to you after saving a program, remove the diskette, turn the drive OFF and ON, insert a different diskette and try the SAVE/ VERIFY sequence again.

wedge—a general term describing a machine language routine that modifies the part of BASIC that interprets commands so that the new routine can check for special characters or commands. Most routines of this kind are designed to add new commands to BASIC. These new commands are said to be wedged into BASIC. The DOS 5.1 routine does this.

write protect notch—the ¼ inch square notch cut out of one edge of the jacket of a floppy diskette. The presence or absence of this notch is detected by the disk drive. If the notch is present, you can record information on the diskette. If there is no notch, as on some commercially recorded diskettes, or if the notch is covered by an opaque tab, recording is disabled.

write protect tab—a small gummed tab designed to be folded over the edge of the jacket of a floppy diskette to cover the write protect notch. If the tab is in place, you cannot record any new information on the diskette.

writing a file—the procedure carried out by the disk operating system in response to OPEN, PRINT# and CLOSE commands sent by the computer, in which the DOS creates a new directory entry, records the new information on the diskette, and updates the diskette's Block Availability Map to indicate that the sectors used to store the information are now in use (allocated).

REFERENCE TABLES

Hexadecimal/Decimal Equivalents

HEX	DEC	HEX	DEC	HEX	DEC	HEX	DEC	HEX	DEC	HEX	DEC	HEX	DEC	HEX	DEC
$00	0	$20	32	$40	64	$60	96	$80	128	$A0	160	$C0	192	$E0	224
$01	1	$21	33	$41	65	$61	97	$81	129	$A1	161	$C1	193	$E1	225
$02	2	$22	34	$42	66	$62	98	$82	130	$A2	162	$C2	194	$E2	226
$03	3	$23	35	$43	67	$63	99	$83	131	$A3	163	$C3	195	$E3	227
$04	4	$24	36	$44	68	$64	100	$84	132	$A4	164	$C4	196	$E4	228
$05	5	$25	37	$45	69	$65	101	$85	133	$A5	165	$C5	197	$E5	229
$06	6	$26	38	$46	70	$66	102	$86	134	$A6	166	$C6	198	$E6	230
$07	7	$27	39	$47	71	$67	103	$87	135	$A7	167	$C7	199	$E7	231
$08	8	$28	40	$48	72	$68	104	$88	136	$A8	168	$C8	200	$E8	232
$09	9	$29	41	$49	73	$69	105	$89	137	$A9	169	$C9	201	$E9	233
$0A	10	$2A	42	$4A	74	$6A	106	$8A	138	$AA	170	$CA	202	$EA	234
$0B	11	$2B	43	$4B	75	$6B	107	$8B	139	$AB	171	$CB	203	$EB	235
$0C	12	$2C	44	$4C	76	$6C	108	$8C	140	$AC	172	$CC	204	$EC	236
$0D	13	$2D	45	$4D	77	$6D	109	$8D	141	$AD	173	$CD	205	$ED	237
$0E	14	$2E	46	$4E	78	$6E	110	$8E	142	$AE	174	$CE	206	$EE	238
$0F	15	$2F	47	$4F	79	$6F	111	$8F	143	$AF	175	$CF	207	$EF	239
$10	16	$30	48	$50	80	$70	112	$90	144	$B0	176	$D0	208	$F0	240
$11	17	$31	49	$51	81	$71	113	$91	145	$B1	177	$D1	209	$F1	241
$12	18	$32	50	$52	82	$72	114	$92	146	$B2	178	$D2	210	$F2	242
$13	19	$33	51	$53	83	$73	115	$93	147	$B3	179	$D3	211	$F3	243
$14	20	$34	52	$54	84	$74	116	$94	148	$B4	180	$D4	212	$F4	244
$15	21	$35	53	$55	85	$75	117	$95	149	$B5	181	$D5	213	$F5	245
$16	22	$36	54	$56	86	$76	118	$96	150	$B6	182	$D6	214	$F6	246
$17	23	$37	55	$57	87	$77	119	$97	151	$B7	183	$D7	215	$F7	247
$18	24	$38	56	$58	88	$78	120	$98	152	$B8	184	$D8	216	$F8	248
$19	25	$39	57	$59	89	$79	121	$99	153	$B9	185	$D9	217	$F9	249
$1A	26	$3A	58	$5A	90	$7A	122	$9A	154	$BA	186	$DA	218	$FA	250
$1B	27	$3B	59	$5B	91	$7B	123	$9B	155	$BB	187	$DB	219	$FB	251
$1C	28	$3C	60	$5C	92	$7C	124	$9C	156	$BC	188	$DC	220	$FC	252
$1D	29	$3D	61	$5D	93	$7D	125	$9D	157	$BD	189	$DD	221	$FD	253
$1E	30	$3E	62	$5E	94	$7E	126	$9E	158	$BE	191	$DE	222	$FE	254
$1F	31	$3F	63	$5F	95	$7F	127	$9F	159	$BF	192	$DF	223	$FF	255

Commodore 64/VIC-20 Internal Storage of BASIC Characters and Tokens

HEX	DEC	CHR	HEX	DEC	CHR	HEX	DEC	TOKEN	HEX	DEC	TOKEN	HEX	DEC	TOKEN
$20	32	SPC	$40	64	@	$80	128	END	$A0	160	CLOSE	$C0	192	TAN
$21	33	!	$41	65	A	$81	129	FOR	$A1	161	GET	$C1	193	ATN
$22	34	"	$42	66	B	$82	130	NEXT	$A2	162	NEW	$C2	194	PEEK
$23	35	#	$43	67	C	$83	131	DATA	$A3	163	TAB(	$C3	195	LEN
$24	36	$	$44	68	D	$84	132	INPUT#	$A4	164	TO	$C4	196	STR$
$25	37	%	$45	69	E	$85	133	INPUT	$A5	165	FN	$C5	197	VAL
$26	38	&	$46	70	F	$86	134	DIM	$A6	166	SPC(	$C6	198	ASC
$27	39	'	$47	71	G	$87	135	READ	$A7	167	THEN	$C7	199	CHR$
$28	40	(	$48	72	H	$88	136	LET	$A8	168	NOT	$C8	200	LEFT$
$29	41	)	$49	73	I	$89	137	GOTO	$A9	169	STEP	$C9	201	RIGHT$
$2A	42	*	$4A	74	J	$8A	138	RUN	$AA	170	+	$CA	202	MID$
$2B	43	+	$4B	75	K	$8B	139	IF	$AB	171	−	$CB	203	GO
$2C	44	,	$4C	76	L	$8C	140	RESTORE	$AC	172	*			
$2D	45	−	$4D	77	M	$8D	141	GOSUB	$AD	173	/	$CC	204	Values
$2E	46	.	$4E	78	N	$8E	142	RETURN	$AE	174			$CD	205	from
$2F	47	/	$4F	79	O	$8F	143	REM	$AF	175	AND	$CE	206	$CC
												$CF	207	to
$30	48	0	$50	80	P	$90	144	STOP	$B0	176	OR	$D0	208	$DA
$31	49	1	$51	81	Q	$91	145	ON	$B1	177	>	$D1	209	are
$32	50	2	$52	82	R	$92	146	WAIT	$B2	178	=	$D2	210	tokens
$33	51	3	$53	83	S	$93	147	LOAD	$B3	179	<	$D3	211	only
$34	52	4	$54	84	T	$94	148	SAVE	$B4	180	SGN	$D4	212	in
$35	53	5	$55	85	U	$95	149	VERIFY	$B5	181	INT	$D5	213	BASIC 4
$36	54	6	$56	86	V	$96	150	DEF	$B6	182	ABS	$D6	214	and are
$37	55	7	$57	87	W	$97	151	POKE	$B7	183	USR	$D7	215	unused
$38	56	8	$58	88	X	$98	152	PRINT#	$B8	184	FRE	$D8	216	on the
$39	57	9	$59	89	Y	$99	153	PRINT	$B9	185	POS	$D9	217	VIC-20
$3A	58	:	$5A	90	Z	$9A	154	CONT	$BA	186	SQR	$DA	218	& C-64
$3B	59	;	$5B	91	[	$9B	155	LIST	$BB	187	RND	$DB	219	−−−−−−
$3C	60	<	$5C	92	£	$9C	156	CLR	$BC	188	LOG			
$3D	61	=	$5D	93	]	$9D	157	CMD	$BD	189	EXP			Values from $DC
$3E	62	>	$5E	94			$9E	158	SYS	$BE	191	COS			to $FF are not
$3F	63	?	$5F	95	←	$9F	159	OPEN	$BF	192	SIN			in BASIC 2 & 4.

NOTES:

1. The hexadecimal and decimal numbers given in this table are the code numbers used internally by the Commodore 64 and VIC-20 computers to represent the character shown to the right of the pair of numbers. When you type in a program, you type characters and words such as A and PRINT. The computer's screen editor takes these characters and converts them into ASCII codes (e.g., A = 65) and BASIC tokens (e.g., PRINT = 153). It is only when you LIST a program that these internal codes are converted back to letters and words.

2. $00 (zero) is the last byte in any BASIC line.

3. If Shift-L is included in a REM statement, a LIST of the program will stop with a ?SYNTAX ERROR when this line is reached.

4. A line that contains characters other than those listed above may LIST but will halt with a ?SYNTAX ERROR during a RUN.

5. Any character may appear inside a BASIC statement provided it is preceded by a quotation mark, CHR$(34).

Number of Sectors per Track on the 1541

Zone	Tracks Numbered	Sectors Numbered	Number of Sectors
#1	1 to 17	0 to 20	21
#2	18 to 24	0 to 18	19
#3	25 to 30	0 to 17	18
#4	31 to 35	0 to 16	17

Location of Important Parts of a Directory Sector

Entry Number within a Directory Sector

	#0	#1	#2	#3	#4	#5	#6	#7
File type byte	$02	$22	$42	$62	$82	$A2	$C2	$E2
Start block (t#)	$03	$23	$43	$63	$83	$A3	$C3	$E3
Start block (s#)	$04	$24	$44	$64	$84	$A4	$C4	$E4
File name	$05-14	$25-34	$45-44	$65-74	$85-94	$A5-B4	$C5-D4	$E5-F4
Side sector (t#)	$15	$35	$55	$75	$95	$B5	$D5	$F5
Side sector (s#)	$16	$36	$56	$76	$96	$B6	$D6	$F6
Record size	$17	$37	$57	$77	$97	$B7	$D7	$F7
Length (lo byte)	$1E	$3E	$5E	$7E	$9E	$BE	$DE	$FE
Length (hi byte)	$1F	$3F	$5F	$7F	$9F	$BF	$DF	$FF

Normal Filling Sequence of the Directory Track
(8 entries/sector)

First 48 entries	18/1 → 18/4 → 18/7 → 18/10 → 18/13 → 18/16
Next 48 entries	18/2 → 18/5 → 18/8 → 18/11 → 18/14 → 18/17
Last 48 entries	18/3 → 18/6 → 18/9 → 18/12 → 18/15 → 18/18

File Type Bytes and Their Meaning

	DEL	SEQ	PRG	USR	REL
Unclosed file	$00 (0)	$01 (1)	$02 (2)	$03 (3)	$04 (4)
Normal file	$80 (128)	$81 (129)	$82 (130)	$83 (131)	$84 (132)
During replace	$A0 (160)	$A1 (161)	$A2 (162)	$A3 (163)	$A4 (164)
Locked file	$C0 (192)	$C1 (193)	$C2 (194)	$C3 (195)	$C4 (196)

DISK ERROR MESSAGES

All error messages have the following general form:

```
SYNTAX:
  error#, message,track#,sector#

EXAMPLES:
  00, OK,00,00
  21, READ ERROR,22,05
  25, WRITE ERROR,12,15
  31, SYNTAX ERROR,00,00
```

WHERE:

error#	= the error code number which indicates the exact type of error.
message	= the English language error message that indicates the general class of error.
track#	= the track number of the sector where the error, if any, occurred.
sector#	= the sector number of the sector where the error, if any, occurred.

NOTE:

Some of the errors are WRITE errors while others are READ errors.

00: OK

Disk operation completed satisfactorily.

01: FILES SCRATCHED

Informational message produced after scratching one or more files. In this case the number following the English language message is the number of files that has been scratched. Since this is not an error, the drive-active LED will not be flashing. This message may be ignored.

20: READ ERROR

When a particular sector is to be read, the disk controller creates a search image of the header block. It then attempts to find a sector header on the track that matches the image. After examining 90 headers without success, the disk controller gives up and this error is reported. This error is usually caused by switching the disk drive on or off with a diskette in it. It may also be part of a disk protection scheme.

21: READ ERROR

While searching for the desired sector header, the disk controller is unable to find a SYNC mark on the track within the allowed time. This error is usually caused by attempting to read an unformatted diskette. It may also be part of a disk protection scheme.

22: READ ERROR

The disk controller has found the desired header block. However, when attempting to read the data block, it found that the first character in the data block was not a $07 character (the data block ID character). This error is usually caused by an alignment problem or swapping diskettes between 4040 and 1541 disk drives. It may also be part of a disk protection scheme.

23: READ ERROR

The disk controller has found the desired header block and read in the data block. However, when checking the data read, the computed checksum did not match the checksum that was recorded on the diskette when the data was recorded (see Section 13.6). This error is usually caused by switching the disk drive on or off with a diskette in it. It may also be part of a disk protection scheme.

24: READ ERROR

Byte decoding error. The disk controller has read an encoded byte from diskette for which there is no hex equivalent. The 1541 drive does not check for this type of error.

25: WRITE ERROR

The disk controller found the desired header block and has written out the new data block. However, when the data block was read back from the diskette, it did not match what was just recorded. It is usually caused by a flaw on the diskette.

26: WRITE PROTECT ON

The disk controller has received a command to record some new information on the diskette. However, the write protect notch in the diskette's jacket is covered by a write protect tab. The information has *not* been written. The diskette has not been affected in any way.

27: READ ERROR

The disk controller has moved the read/write head to the desired track and read the header block of the first sector it has found to confirm that it was on the correct track (this is called a SEEK operation). The header block information has been decoded.

When the checksum of the information in the header block was calculated, it did not compute. This is usually caused by switching the disk drive on or off with a diskette in it. It is occasionally used as part of a disk protection scheme.

28: WRITE ERROR

Long data block. The disk controller found the desired header block and has written out the new data block. However, the SYNC mark at the start of the next sector's header was not detected. The 1541 drive does not check for this type of error.

29: DISK ID MISMATCH

The disk controller has moved the read/write head to the desired track and read the header block of the first sector it found to be sure that it was on the correct track (a SEEK operation in preparation for a READ). The header block information has been decoded. The header block checksum worked out properly. However, the two ID characters recorded in the header when the diskette was formatted do not match the master diskette ID stored in the disk drive's RAM memory. This is usually caused by head alignment problems or changing diskettes and failing to initialize the new diskette. It is frequently used as part of a disk protection scheme.

30: SYNTAX ERROR

General syntax error. The disk operating system cannot interpret the command sent over the command channel. This error is usually caused by using too many file names or using wild card characters improperly.

31: SYNTAX ERROR

Invalid command. The disk operating system does not recognize the command sent over the command channel. For example, the DUPLICATE command, used on the Commodore dual disk drive to make a backup copy of an entire diskette, is an invalid command on the 1541.

32: SYNTAX ERROR

Long line. The disk command sent over the command channel is more than 58 characters long.

33: SYNTAX ERROR

Invalid file name. Pattern matching is used illegally in an OPEN or SAVE command.

34: SYNTAX ERROR

Missing file name. One or more file names were omitted from a disk command that requires them. This error is usually the result of leaving a colon (:) out of a disk command.

39: FILE NOT FOUND

An unusual error. It occurs only when using the 1541 utility loader (an & disk command). The utility program named in the command was not listed in the diskette's directory.

50: RECORD NOT PRESENT

An attempt has been made to use the POSITION disk command to access a record
beyond the end of a relative file. This error may be ignored if you are writing new
records into a relative file. The only time to be concerned about this error is when you
are attempting to read a record that should exist. Note that as soon as you POSITION
to a nonexistent record, the disk operating system automatically extends the length of
the relative file to include the record requested.

51: OVERFLOW IN RECORD

You just attempted to store too much data in a relative file record using a PRINT#
statement. The first part of the data has been written into the record but the extra
characters have been deleted to protect the next record in the file.

52: FILE TOO LARGE

The record number you specified in the POSITION disk command is so large that the
file will not fit onto the diskette.

60: WRITE FILE OPEN

An attempt has been made to read a file that has not been closed properly. This error
usually occurs when you attempt to read a file that has an asterisk (*) beside its name
in the directory (e.g., *SEQ, *PRG or *USR). To read a file of this kind you must
specify the modify (M) mode in the OPEN statement.

61: FILE NOT OPEN

An attempt has been made to access a file that has not been opened. This is a very
rare message. Normally the DOS simply ignores the request.

62: FILE NOT FOUND

There is no file name in the directory that matches the one specified in the OPEN,
LOAD, COPY or RENAME command. This error does not occur if the file name as
specified in a SCRATCH command does not match any name in the directory. In this
case, the DOS simply sends the 01, FILES SCRATCHED, message indicating that
zero files have been scratched.

63: FILE EXISTS

The file name to be added to the directory as the result of an OPEN, SAVE, COPY or
RENAME command matches an existing file name in the directory.

64: FILE TYPE MISMATCH

The file type (SEQ, PRG, USR or REL) specified in a disk command does not match
the file type in the directory entry for the file named in the command.

65: NO BLOCK

This message occurs only in response to a B-A (block allocate) disk command when
the block (sector) to be allocated is already allocated in the BAM. The track and sector
numbers returned along with this error message are supposed to be those of the next

available block (sector). Unfortunately, this feature of the B-A command does not work properly on the 1541. If you get this error, VALIDATE the diskette because an entire trackful of sectors will have been allocated incorrectly in the BAM. Luckily, no sectors are freed as a result of this problem, so even if you do not notice it immediately, your files are safe. However, you will run out of storage space very rapidly.

66: ILLEGAL TRACK AND SECTOR

An attempt was made to access a block (sector) whose track or sector number was outside the allowed range. You may encounter this error (track 73, sector 1) when reading an unclosed file using modify (M) mode.

67: ILLEGAL SYSTEM T OR S

A very rare error indicating that the system has attempted to access an illegal track or sector.

70: NO CHANNEL

The requested channel is not available. A file you specified in an OPEN statement was not opened. The most common reasons for a file not being opened are an incorrectly spelled file name (in read mode), a file type mismatch, a duplicate file name (in write mode), or too many files already open. Only a few disk files can be opened simultaneously. You cannot have five sequential files opened simultaneously as specified on page 45 of the *1541 User's Manual*. The correct, maximum, allowable limits are:

Number of SEQ files	Number of REL files	Number of direct access files	TOTAL
2 SEQ	0 REL	0 or 1 D-A	2 or 3
1 SEQ	1 REL	0 or 1 D-A	2 or 3
0 SEQ	1 REL	0 to 2 D-A	1 to 3

71: DIRECTORY ERROR

A very rare error. The BAM is not internally consistent. To cure the problem re-initialize the diskette. Note that initializing the diskette will close all the data channels that are open in the disk drive. The command channel is not affected.

72: DISK FULL

Either all the storage space on the diskette has been used, or the diskette directory is full. The directory can only accomodate 144 file names. Note that the 1541 will *close the file properly* if a disk full error is encountered during a save or replace operation. However, *the file will be incomplete!* The *only* way to tell that this has happened is by reading the error status. If you look at the directory, everything will look OK. A program file will even verify as OK. *But it is not all there! Beware!* If a disk full error is encountered while writing to or appending to a file, the file will *not* be closed automatically. If you do not close it, you will have an unclosed file!

73: CBM DOS V2.6 1541

When the 1541 disk drive is first turned on, this message is generated. To see it you must check the error status as soon as you turn ON your drive.

74: DRIVE NOT READY

An unusual error that occurs mainly when using direct-access files or after doing a drive reset ("U;"). If you encounter this error while using direct-access files, change your OPEN statement to specify the buffer number explicitly. I had this problem with the MOD ENTRY program and it would not go away until I changed OPEN 2,8,5,"#" to OPEN 2,8,5,"#0"!

SUMMARY OF DISK COMMANDS

Disk commands are usually sent to the 1541 using a PRINT# statement to print the command to the command channel (previously opened as file# 15 in all our examples). However, you can also combine the PRINT# statement with the OPEN statement or use DOS 5.1 as indicated below.

```
SYNTAX:
  PRINT#15,"command"              Usual form
  OPEN 15,8,15,"command"          Combined form
  >command                        DOS 5.1 form

EXAMPLES:
  PRINT#15,"NO:TEST DISKETTE,T1"
  PRINT#15,"V"

  OPEN 15,8,15,"NO:TEST DISKETTE,T1"
  OPEN 15,8,15,"V"

  >NO:TEST DISKETTE,T1
  >V
```

NOTES:

1. Punctuation is important in these commands. Check it carefully.

2. The drive number that follows the command (e.g., N0) is always optional on the 1541 drive. It is only required when using a dual drive such as the Commodore 4040 drive.

3. Any housekeeping command may be abbreviated by using its first letter in place of the full name of the command (e.g., N=NEW).

Housekeeping Commands

1. Full NEW of a diskette.

   - Prepares a new, blank diskette for first use.
   - May be used on a previously formatted diskette to erase errors.
   - Disk error aborts command, indicates flawed diskette.
   - Recovery is possible only if command aborted, see Chapter 11.

```
SYNTAX:
  NEWO:diskname,id
```

```
EXAMPLES:
  PRINT#15,"NEWO:TEST DISKETTE,T1"
  PRINT#15,"NO:TEST DISKETTE,T1"
  OPEN 15,8,15,"N:TEST DISKETTE,T1":CLOSE15
```

2. Short NEW of a diskette.

- Prepares a previously formatted diskette for reuse.
- The diskette ID is unchanged.
- Disk error aborts command, trouble on 18/0 or 18/1.
- Recovery is possible, see Chapter 11.

```
SYNTAX:
  NEWO:diskname
```
(Note: No diskette ID specified.)

```
EXAMPLES:
  PRINT#15,"NEWO:TEST DISKETTE"
  PRINT#15,"NO:TEST DISKETTE"
  OPEN 15,8,15,"N:TEST DISKETTE":CLOSE15
```

3. VALIDATE a diskette.

- Creates a new BAM based on the files actually stored.
- Disk error aborts command, BAM is unchanged.

```
SYNTAX:
  VALIDATEO
```

```
EXAMPLES:
  PRINT#15,"VALIDATEO"
  PRINT#15,"VO"
  OPEN 15,8,15,"V":CLOSE15
```

4. SCRATCH a file.

WARNING:

Do *not* scratch an unclosed file! (*SEQ, *PRG, *USR).

- Eliminates unwanted file from the directory.
- Wild cards permitted to scratch several files.
- Disk error aborts command, BAM may be incorrect.
- Recovery is possible, see Chapter 11.

```
SYNTAX:
  SCRATCHO:filename
```

EXAMPLES:
```
PRINT#15,"SCRATCHO:OLD FILE"
PRINT#15,"SO:OLD FILE"
OPEN 15,8,15,"S:OLD FILE":CLOSE15
```

5. COPY a file.

   - Makes a second copy of a file on the same diskette.
   - No wild cards permitted.
   - Disk error aborts command, BAM may be incorrect.
   - Does not work with relative files.

   SYNTAX:
   ```
   COPYO:backupfile=O:oldfile
   ```

   EXAMPLES:
   ```
   PRINT#15,"COPYO:GAME/BU=O:GAME"
   PRINT#15,"CO:GAME/BU=O:GAME"
   OPEN 15,8,15,"C:GAME/BU=GAME":CLOSE15
   ```

6. CONCATENATE two to four files.

   - Makes new, combined file composed of contents of first file followed by contents of second, followed by contents of third...
   - No wild cards permitted.
   - Does not merge two BASIC programs.
   - Disk error aborts command, BAM may be incorrect.
   - Does not work with relative files.

   SYNTAX:
   ```
   COPYO:combofile=O:file1,O:file2,O:file3
   ```

   EXAMPLES:
   ```
   PRINT#15,"COPYO:OURS=O:YOURS,O:MINE"
   PRINT#15,"CO:OURS=O:YOURS,O:MINE"
   OPEN 15,8,15,"C:OURS=YOURS,MINE":CLOSE15
   ```

7. RENAME a file.

   - Changes the file name in the directory entry.
   - No wild cards permitted.
   - Disk error aborts command, trouble on track 18.
   - Directory may be fixed, see Chapter 11.

   SYNTAX:
   ```
   RENAMEO:newfile=oldfile
   ```

   EXAMPLES:
   ```
   PRINT#15,"RENAMEO:NEW NAME=OLD NAME"
   ```

```
PRINT#15,"RO:NEW NAME=OLD NAME"
OPEN 15,8,15:PRINT#15,"R:NEW NAME=OLD NAME"
CLOSE15
```

8. INITIALIZE a diskette.

- Read track 18, sector 0 into disk RAM ($0700-FF).
- Used to prevent 29, DISK ID MISMATCH, errors.
- Disk error aborts command, trouble on track 18, sector 0.
- Recovery is possible, see Chapter 11.

```
SYNTAX:
  INITIALIZEO

EXAMPLES:
  PRINT#15,"INITIALIZEO"
  PRINT#15,"IO"
  OPEN 15,8,15,"I":CLOSE15
```

Direct-Access Commands

These commands are used mainly by experienced programmers to create specialized
utility programs. They are not needed for normal file handling.

1. BUFFER-POINTER (B-P)

- Position to the specified byte in the data buffer to prepare to read or write data
  to the buffer.
- A direct-access channel must have been opened previously.

```
SYNTAX:
  "B-P:"channel#;byte#

EXAMPLES:
  OPEN 1,8,5,"#"
  PRINT#15,"B-P:5 O"          Position to byte zero of buffer.

  OPEN 3,8,4,"#1"
  PRINT#15,"B-P:5 25"          Position to byte 25 of data buffer #1.
```

2. BLOCK-READ (B-R)

WARNING:

The B-R command does not work properly. Use U1 below.

BLOCK-READ (U1:)

- Read specified track and sector into the 1541's RAM memory.
- A direct-access channel must have been opened previously.

SYNTAX:
```
"U1:"channel#;drive#;track#;sector#
```

EXAMPLES:
```
OPEN 1,8,5,"#"
PRINT#15,"U1:5 0 18 1"
```

Read track 18, sector 1, from drive zero into the buffer assigned to the file using data channel five.

```
OPEN 3,8,4,"#1"
TR=15:SE=10
PRINT#15,"U1:4 0"TR;SE
PRINT#15,"B-P:4 32"
GET#3,A$
```

Read track 15, sector 10 from drive zero into data buffer (one) assigned to the file using data channel four. Then position to byte 32 and read it.

3. BLOCK-WRITE (B-W)

WARNING:

This command does not work properly. Use U2 below.

BLOCK-WRITE (U2:)

- Write contents of data buffer to specified track and sector.
- A direct-access channel must have been opened previously.

SYNTAX:
```
"U2:"channel#;drive#;track#;sector#
```

EXAMPLE:
```
OPEN 1,8,5,"#"
PRINT#15,"B-P:5 0"        Position to start of buffer.
PRINT#1,M$;               Store data in buffer.
PRINT#15,"U1:5 0 18 1"
```

Record contents of the buffer assigned to the file using data channel five on drive zero, track 18, sector 1.

4. BLOCK-ALLOCATE (B-A)

Mark the specified track and sector as allocated (in use) in the diskette's BAM.

WARNING:

This command works correctly only if the designated block is free in the BAM. If the block is already allocated, an entire sector full of blocks will be allocated and the BAM will be incorrect.

```
SYNTAX:
  "B-A:"drive#;track#;sector#
```

```
EXAMPLES:
  PRINT#15,"B-A:0 17 4"          Allocate track 17, sector 4.
  TR=12:SE=5
  PRINT#15,"B-A:0"TR;SE          Allocate track 12, sector 5.
```

5. BLOCK-FREE (B-F)

Mark the specified track and sector as free (available for use) in the diskette's BAM.

```
SYNTAX:
  "B-F:"drive#;track#;sector#
```

```
EXAMPLES:
  PRINT#15,"B-F:0 17 4"          Free track 17, sector 4.
  TR=12:SE=5
  PRINT#15,"B-A:0"TR;SE          Free track 12, sector 5.
```

6. BLOCK-EXECUTE (B-E)

Read the contents of the track and sector specified into a data buffer disk RAM and then begin executing the machine language routine that begins at the start of this buffer. The 1541's microprocessor will be in file manager mode as it executes the code.

```
SYNTAX:
  "B-E:"channel#;drive#;track#;sector#
```

```
EXAMPLE:
  OPEN 1,8,5,"#1"
  PRINT#15,"B-E:5 0 24 3"
```

Read the contents of track 24, sector 3 into data buffer #1 (see OPEN) and begin executing the code that starts at memory location $0400 in RAM memory (data buffer #1 starts at $0400).

7. MEMORY-READ

- Prepares to read the contents of the 1541's RAM or ROM memory.
- Contents are actually read using GET# to read the command channel.

NOTE:

The syntax given in the *1541 User's Manual* is incorrect.

SYNTAX:
```
"M-R"CHR$(adr lo);CHR$(adr hi)
"M-R"CHR$(adr lo);CHR$(adr hi);CHR$(how many)
```

EXAMPLES:
```
PRINT#15,"M-R"CHR$(2);CHR$(7)
GET#15,A$
```

Read one byte of memory at $0702.

```
PRINT#15,"M-R"CHR$(0);CHR$(240);CHR$(32)
FOR K=0 TO 31
GET#15,MEM$(K)
NEXT
```

Read 32 bytes of memory starting at $0702.

8. MEMORY-WRITE

- Writes bytes in M$ directly into the 1541's RAM memory.
- The maximum number of bytes per "M-W" command is 32.

NOTE:

The syntax given in the *1541 User's Manual* is incorrect.

SYNTAX:
```
"M-W"CHR$(adr lo);CHR$(adr hi);CHR$(how many),M$
```

EXAMPLES:
```
PRINT#15,"M-W"CHR$(3);CHR$(0);CHR$(1);CHR$(176)
```

Stores CHR$(176) into memory at $0003.

```
FOR K=0 TO 31
READ X:C$=C$+CHR$(X)
NEXT
PRINT#15,"M-W"CHR$(0);CHR$(3);CHR$(32);M$
```

Stores 32 bytes in memory starting at $0300.

9. MEMORY-EXECUTE

Forces the 1541's microprocessor (in file manager mode) to start executing the machine language routine that begins at the location specified in the disk memory.

NOTE:

The syntax given in the *1541 User's Manual* is incorrect.

SYNTAX:
```
"M-E"CHR$(adr lo);CHR$(adr hi)
```

EXAMPLES:
```
PRINT#15,"M-E"CHR$(0);CHR$(5)
```

Execute machine language routine that begins at memory location $0500 in RAM memory.

10. RESET DRIVE ("U;", "UI", or "U9")

- Reset the 1541 drive to its power-on state.
- Note that the drive motor will *not* start up.

NOTE:

The "U" command given in the *1541 User's Manual* is incorrect.

SYNTAX:
```
"U;" or "UI" or "U9"
```

EXAMPLES:
```
PRINT#15,"U;"
PRINT#15,"UI"
PRINT#15,"U9"
```

DISK UTILITY PROGRAMS

The disk utility programs listed below are general purpose programs. More specialized utility programs are listed in the appropriate section of the book. The Table of Contents contains a complete list of the application and utility programs included herein.

WARNING

The programs listed below are very powerful disk utilities. They have been designed for ease of use and relatively foolproof operation. However, any tool may be misused. Be sure to practice using a utility on a test diskette *before* you use it with one of your important or valuable diskettes.

Summary of Programs Listed in Appendix E

Program Name	Function
FULL DIRECTORY	Expanded directory listing.
CONFIRM ALL FILE	Checks to ensure all disk files are intact.
BACKUP 1541	Backup a diskette. Does not abort on errors.
MAKE FAST COPY	BASIC program to make a working copy of the FAST COPY program from Chapter 10.
EDIT T&S	Hex or ASCII editing of any disk block.
MOD DISK NAME	Modify any diskette's name.
FIX BAD DIR	Recover files after a short NEW or if the directory has been damaged.
THE UNSCRATCHER	Recover any type of scratched files.
PRG HEX DUMP	Analysis of BASIC program showing links, etc.
PRG ANALYSIS	Detailed analysis of BASIC program file.

```
***********************
1. PROGRAM: FULL DIRECTORY
***********************
```

Produces an expanded directory listing for a diskette showing file length, file type, file name, track and sector where first block is stored, and the load address of the file. See Section 11.1 for instructions.

Compatible with C-64 or VIC-20 and 1541.

```
0 REM 1541 USER'S GUIDE   APPENDIX E
1 REM   COPYRIGHT: G. NEUFELD, 1984
2 :
3 REM   DISPLAY EXTENDED DIRECTORY
4 :
100 PRINT"{CLR}1541 FULL DIRECTORY":A$="
S"
110 DIM FX$(7),DB(1)
120 INPUT"{DOWN}OUTPUT TO SCREEN OR PRIN
TER (S/P)";A$
130 DN=3:IF A$="P" THEN DN=4
140 OPEN 3,DN
150 OPEN15,8,15,"IO"
160 OPEN 2,8,6,"#"
170 H$="0123456789ABCDEF"
180 Z$=CHR$(0)
190 FOR K=0TO5:READFX$(K):NEXT
200 DATA DEL,SEQ,PRG,REL,USR,???
210 OPEN1,8,5,"$0,P,R"
220 GET#1,A$:IFA$=""THENA$=Z$
230 DOS=ASC(A$)
240 FORK=4TO144:GET#1,A$:NEXT
250 FORK=145TO160:GET#1,A$:IFA$=""THENA$
=Z$
260 N$=N$+A$:NEXT
270 FORK=161TO162:GET#1,A$:NEXT
280 GET#1,A$:IFA$=""THENA$=Z$
290 I1=ASC(A$):I1$=A$
300 GET#1,A$:IFA$=""THENA$=Z$
310 I2=ASC(A$):I2$=A$
320 PRINT#3,"{CLR}DISK NAME: "N$
330 PRINT#3,"DOS TYPE: "DOS
340 PRINT#3,"COSMETIC DISK ID: ";
350 IF I1>31 AND I1<96 THEN PRINT#3,I1$;
:GOTO370
360 PRINT#3," ";
370 IF I2>31 AND I2<96 THEN PRINT#3,I2$;
:GOTO390
380 PRINT#3," ";
390 PRINT#3,"  ASCII ="I1;I2
400 PRINT#3,"{DOWN}BLKS   FILE NAME
 TYPE  LINK  START"
410 PRINT#3,"---- ---------------- ----
-- -- -----"
420 FOR K=165TO256:GET#1,A$:NEXT
430 GET#1,A$:IFA$=""THENA$=Z$
440 IF ST<>0 GOTO 780
450 FT=ASC(A$)
460 FT$=FX$(7ANDFT)
```

```
470 IF FT<128 THEN FT$="{RVS}"+FT$+"{ROF
F}"
480 GET#1,A$:IFA$=""THENA$=Z$
490 TR=ASC(A$)
500 TR$=RIGHT$("     "+STR$(ASC(A$)),4)
510 GET#1,A$:IFA$=""THENA$=Z$
520 SE=ASC(A$)
530 SE$=RIGHT$("    "+STR$(ASC(A$)),3)+"
":N$=""
540 IF TR=0 AND SE=0 GOTO 780
550 PRINT#15,"U1:6 0";TR;SE
560 PRINT#15,"B-P:6 2"
570 GET#2,A$:IFA$=""THENA$=Z$
580 A=ASC(A$):H=INT(A/16):L=A-16*H
590 HX$=MID$(H$,H+1,1)+MID$(H$,L+1,1)
600 GET#2,A$:IFA$=""THENA$=Z$
610 A=ASC(A$):H=INT(A/16):L=A-16*H
620 HX$="$"+MID$(H$,H+1,1)+MID$(H$,L+1,1
)+HX$
630 FOR K=1TO16:GET#1,A$:IFA$=""THEN A$=
Z$
640 N$=N$+A$:NEXT
650 N$=" "+N$+"    "
660 FORK=1TO9:GET#1,A$:NEXT
670 GET#1,A$:IFA$=""THENA$=Z$
680 BL=ASC(A$)
690 GET#1,A$:IFA$=""THENA$=Z$
700 BL=BL+256*ASC(A$)
710 IF FT<128 THEN DB(0)=DB(0)+BL
720 IF FT>127 THEN DB(1)=DB(1)+BL
730 BL$=RIGHT$("    "+STR$(BL),3)+"  "
740 PRINT#3,BL$;N$;FT$;TR$;SE$;HX$
750 ZZ=ZZ+1:IFZZ/8<>INT(ZZ/8) THEN GET#1
,A$:GET#1,A$
760 GOTO 430
770 :
780 PRINT#15,"M-R"CHR$(250)CHR$(2)CHR$(3
)
790 GET#15,A$:BF=ASC(A$+Z$)
800 GET#15,A$
810 GET#15,A$:BF=BF+256*ASC(A$+Z$)
820 PRINT"{DOWN}BLOCKS FREE PER DIRECTOR
Y ="664-DB(1)
830 PRINT"BLOCKS FREE ACCORDING TO BAM="
BF
840 PRINT"SCRATCHED BLOCKS="DB(0)
850 IF BF>(664-DB(1))THENPRINT"{DOWN}CRO
SSED FILES LIKELY"
860 IF BF<(664-DB(1))THENPRINT"{DOWN}"66
4-DB(1)-BF"NON-FILE BLOCKS ALLOCATED"
870 CLOSE1:CLOSE2:CLOSE3:CLOSE15:END
```

```
***************************
```
2. PROGRAM: CONFIRM ALL FILE
```
***************************
```

Checks all files, BAM and directory for errors. The location of any collisions between files are displayed. Output may be sent to the screen or printer. Optional display of file chains of all files and a SUPER BAM showing where all files are stored and highlighting any BAM errors. See Section 11.1 for complete instructions.

Compatible with C-64, VIC-20, 4032 and 8032 computers, 1541, 2031 and 4040 disk drives (use drive zero).

```
0 REM 1541 USER'S GUIDE   APPENDIX E
1 REM   COPYRIGHT: G. NEUFELD, 1984
2 :
3 REM   CHECK ALL FILES FOR ERRORS
4 :
100 PRINT"{CLR}CONFIRM A DISKETTE":PRINT

110 DIM M%(35,20),N$(144),S$(35),BM%(35,
20)
120 B$="":Z$=CHR$(0):SE$="ROTCES"
130 FOR K=0 TO 7:READ FT$(K):FT$(K)="...
."+FT$(K):NEXT
140 DATA DEL,SEQ,PRG,USR,REL,???,???,???

150 FOR K=0 TO 35
160 T=INT(K/10):S$(K)=CHR$(48+T)+CHR$(48
+K-10*T)
170 NEXT
180 INPUT"OUTPUT TO SCREEN OR PRINTER  S
{LEFT 3}";P$
190 DN=3:IF(ASC(P$)AND127)=80 THEN DN=4
200 OPEN 6,DN
210 PRINT:INPUT "DISPLAY FILE CHAIN (Y/N
)  Y{LEFT 3}";P$
220 FC=1:IF(ASC(P$)AND127)<>89 THEN FC=0

230 PRINT:PRINT"INSERT DISK IN DRIVE"
240 PRINT"PRESS {RVS}RETURN{ROFF} WHEN R
EADY"
250 GET A$:IF A$<>CHR$(13) GOTO 250
260 PRINT:PRINT"READING BAM (30 SECOND P
AUSE)"
270 OPEN 15,8,15,"I0"
280 GOSUB 1320
290 OPEN 1,8,4,"#"
300 GOSUB 1320
310 OPEN 2,8,5,"#"
320 GOSUB 1320
```

```
330 GOSUB 1430
340 PRINT#15,"U1:4 0 18 1"
350 DP=0:NF=0
360 :
370 REM   MAIN LOOP
380 GOSUB 500:REM TRACE NEXT ENTRY
390 IF FX=1 GOTO 380
400 :
410 CLOSE1:CLOSE2
420 INPUT#15,E,E$,T,S
430 CLOSE15
440 PRINT#6,:PRINT#6,"ALL FILES HAVE BEE
N CHECKED"
450 INPUT"{DOWN}PRINT SUPER BAM (Y/N)  Y
{LEFT 3}";X$
460 IF ASC(X$)=89 THEN GOSUB 1720
470 CLOSE6:END
480 :
490 REM: FIND NEXT FILE IN DIRECTORY
500 FD=1:SF=0:PRINT#15,"B-P:4"2+32*DP
510 GET#1,A$:FT=135ANDASC(A$+Z$)
520 IF FT>127 GOTO 540
530 SF=1
540 NF=NF+1
550 GET#1,A$:TR=ASC(A$+Z$)
560 GET#1,A$:SE=ASC(A$+Z$)
570 FOR K=1TO16
580 GET#1,A$:IF A$=B$ THEN A$=Z$
590 N$(NF)=N$(NF)+A$
600 NEXT
610 IF SF=0 GOTO 660
620 IF TR=0 AND SE=0 THEN NF=NF-1:FD=0:G
OTO900
630 PRINT:PRINT"{RVS}SCRATCHED FILE{ROFF
} ";N$(NF)
640 INPUT"TRACE IT (Y/N)  N{LEFT 3}";R$
650 IF R$<>"Y" THEN FD=0:GOTO900
660 PRINT#6,:PRINT#6,"TRACING: "N$(NF)FT
$(7ANDFT)
670 :
680 REM TRACE MAIN FILE
690 GOSUB 1090
700 IF FT<>132 GOTO 780
710 :
720 REM TRACE SIDE SECTOR FILE
730 PRINT:PRINT"SIDE SECTOR FILE: ";
740 GET#1,A$:TR=ASC(A$+Z$)
750 GET#1,A$:SE=ASC(A$+Z$)
760 GOSUB 1100
770 :
```

```
780 FD=1:PRINT#15,"B-P:4"30+32*DP
790 GET#1,A$:DB=ASC(A$+Z$)
800 GET#1,A$:DB=DB+256*ASC(A$+Z$)
810 IF FC=0 GOTO 850
820 IF DN=3 AND (ZZ/6 <> INT(ZZ/6)) THEN
 PRINT#6,
830 IF DN=4 AND (ZZ/13 <> INT(ZZ/13)) TH
EN PRINT#6,
840 IF ZZ<>DB THEN PRINT#6,"{RVS}";
850 PRINT#6,ZZ"BLOCKS FOUND,"DB"IN DIREC
TORY"
860 DP=DP+1
870 IF DP<8 GOTO 1030
880 :
890 REM: GET LINK TO NEXT DIR SECTOR
900 DP=0
910 PRINT#15,"B-P:4 0"
920 GET#1,A$:TD=ASC(A$+Z$)
930 GET#1,A$:SD=ASC(A$+Z$)
940 :
950 REM: IF NO LINK, DONE!
960 IF TD=0 THEN FX=0:RETURN
970 :
980 REM: READ NEW DIR SECTOR
990 PRINT#15,"U1:4 0"TD;SD
1000 GOSUB 1320
1010 :
1020 REM: IF NO FILE FOUND, TRY AGAIN
1030 IF FD=0 GOTO 500
1040 :
1050 FX=1:RETURN
1060 :
1070 REM: TRACE FILE BY LINKS
1080 :
1090 ZZ=0
1100 IF M%(TR,SE)<>0 THEN GOSUB 1250:RET
URN
1110 M%(TR,SE)=NF
1120 ZZ=ZZ+1:IF FC=0 GOTO 1170
1130 IF BM%(TR,SE)=1 THEN PRINT#6,"{RVS}
";
1140 PRINT#6,S$(TR)","S$(SE)"{ROFF} ";
1150 IF DN=3 AND (ZZ/6 = INT(ZZ/6)) THEN
 PRINT#6,
1160 IF DN=4 AND (ZZ/13 = INT(ZZ/13)) TH
EN PRINT#6,
1170 PRINT#15,"U1:5 0"TR;SE
1180 GOSUB 1320:IF E>19 THEN RETURN
1190 PRINT#15,"B-P:5 0"
1200 GET#2,A$:TR=ASC(A$+Z$)
```

```
1210 GET#2,A$:SE=ASC(A$+Z$)
1220 IF TR>0 AND TR<35 GOTO 1100
1230 RETURN
1240 :
1250 PRINT#6:PRINT#6,"{RVS}COLLISION WIT
H "N$(M%(TR,SE))
1260 PRINT#6,"COLLISION ON TRACK"TR"SECT
OR"SE
1270 RETURN
1280 :
1290 CLOSE1:CLOSE2:CLOSE6
1300 INPUT#15,E,E$,T,S:CLOSE15:END
1310 :
1320 INPUT#15,E,E$,T,S
1330 IF E<20 THEN RETURN
1340 PRINT:PRINT"DISK ERROR: "E;E$;T;S
1350 IF EF=1 THEN EF=0:RETURN
1360 PRINT:PRINT"PRESS C TO CONTINUE OR
Q TO QUIT"
1370 GET A$:IF A$="" GOTO 1370
1380 IF A$="C" THEN RETURN
1390 IF A$="Q" GOTO 1290
1400 GOTO 1370
1410 :
1420 REM:READ THE BAM
1430 PRINT#15,"U1:4 0 18 0"
1440 EF=1:GOSUB 1320:IF E>19 GOTO 1290
1450 PRINT#15,"B-P:4 144"
1460 FORK=1TO24:GET#1,A$:IFA$=""THEN A$=
CHR$(0)
1470 DN$=DN$+A$:NEXT
1480 PRINT#6,"{CLR}CONFIRMING {RVS} "DN$

1490 PRINT#6:PRINT#6,"CHECKING DISKETTE
BAM"
1500 PRINT#15,"B-P:4 4"
1510 FOR TR=1TO35
1520 GET#1,A$:T%=ASC(A$+Z$):B%=0
1530 NS=20+2*(TR>17)+(TR>24)+(TR>30)
1540 GET#1,A$:A=ASC(A$+Z$)
1550 FOR S=0TO7:IFAAND2^STHENBM%(TR,S)=1
:B%=B%+1
1560 NEXT S
1570 GET#1,A$:A=ASC(A$+Z$)
1580 FOR S=0TO7:IFAAND2^STHENBM%(TR,S+8)
=1:B%=B%+1
1590 NEXT S
1600 GET#1,A$:A=ASC(A$+Z$)
1610 FOR S=0TO(NS-16):IFAAND2^STHENBM%(T
R,S+16)=1:B%=B%+1
```

```
1620 NEXT S
1630 IF B%=T% GOTO 1660
1640 PRINT#6," INTERNAL {SHIFT-B}{SHIFT-
A}{SHIFT-M} ERROR, TRACK"TR:BE=1
1650 PRINT#6,"    MASTER BLOCKS FREE="T%"
ACTUAL COUNT="B%
1660 NEXT TR
1670 IF BE=0 THEN PRINT#6,"BAM IS INTERN
ALLY CONSISTENT"
1680 RETURN
1690 :
1700 REM DISPLAY SUPER BAM
1710 :
1720 IF DN=3 THEN PRINT#6,"{CLR}SUPER BA
M OF {RVS} "DN$
1730 IF DN=4 THEN PRINT#6,CHR$(19):PRINT
#6,"{CLR}SUPER BAM OF {RVS} "DN$
1740 FOR SE=20TOO STEP-1
1750 IF SE>5 THEN SX$=" ":GOTO1770
1760 SX$=MID$(SE$,SE+1,1)
1770 PRINT#6,SX$;RIGHT$(STR$(SE),2)"{COM
-Q}";
1780 FOR TR=1TO35
1790 IF SE=20 AND TR>17 THEN TR=35:GOTO
1880
1800 IF SE=19 AND TR>17 THEN TR=35:GOTO
1880
1810 IF SE=18 AND TR>24 THEN TR=35:GOTO
1880
1820 IF SE=17 AND TR>30 THEN TR=35:GOTO
1880
1830 IF TR=18 AND BM%(TR,SE)=0 THEN PRIN
T#6,"@";:GOTO1880
1840 IF M%(TR,SE)=0 AND BM%(TR,SE)=0 THE
N PRINT#6,"{RVS}{COM-+}{ROFF}";:GOTO1880

1850 IF M%(TR,SE)=0 AND BM%(TR,SE)=1 THE
N PRINT#6,"{COM-+}";:GOTO1880
1860 IF BM%(TR,SE)=1 THEN PRINT#6,"{RVS}
";
1870 PRINT#6,CHR$(64+(31ANDM%(TR,SE)))"{
ROFF}";
1880 NEXT TR:PRINT#6:NEXT SE
1890 PRINT#6,"    {COM-Z}{COM-E 35}"
1900 PRINT#6,"     12345678901234567890123
456789012345"
1910 IF DN=4 GOTO 1960
1920 PRINT#6,"    TRACK        PRESS {RVS}
RETURN{ROFF} TO END";
1930 GET A$:IF A$<>""GOTO1930
```

```
1940 GET A$:IF A$<>CHR$(13)GOTO1940
1950 RETURN
1960 PRINT#6,"                TRACK"
1970 PRINT#6:PRINT#6,"KEY TO SUPER BAM":
PRINT#6
1980 PRINT#6,"@ = DIRECTORY (TRACK 18 ON
LY)"
1990 FOR K=1 TO NF
2000 PRINT#6,CHR$(64+(31ANDK))" = ";N$(K
)
2010 NEXT
2020 RETURN
```

```
********************
```
3. PROGRAM: BACKUP 1541
```
********************
```

Makes a duplicate copy of a diskette. It takes about 25 minutes to backup a diskette. Six full tracks are read into the C-64's RAM from the master disk and then written out to the clone. A chime sounds to indicate operator attention is required. The main advantage of this backup program is that it will not abort on read or write errors. A summary of the sectors not copied is provided.

Compatible with C-64 computer and 1541 disk drive only.

```
0 REM 1541 USER'S GUIDE   APPENDIX E
1 REM   COPYRIGHT: G. NEUFELD, 1984
2 :
3 REM   BACKUP FOR THE 1541 SINGLE DISK D
RIVE
4 REM   WILL NOT ABORT ON READ OR WRITE E
RRORS
5 :
100 REM C-64/1541 BACKUP
110 PRINT"{CLR}C-64/1541 BACKUP"
120 P=PEEK(8*4096)+1:IF P>255 THEN P=0
130 POKE 8*4096,P
140 IF PEEK(8*4096)<>P THEN PRINT"NO CAR
TRIDGES ALLOWED":END
150 POKE 55,0:POKE 56,32:POKE 251,0:CLR
160 SID=54272
170 FOR K=0 TO 28:POKE SID+K,0:NEXT
180 POKE SID+24,15
190 POKE SID,34:POKE SID+1,75
200 POKE SID+5,16:POKE SID+6,249
210 DIM MT(50),MS(50),EN(50),EM$(50)
220 FOR K=0 TO 37:READ X:POKE 828+K,X:NE
XT
230 GOSUB 830
240 OPEN 15,8,15,"I0"
```

```
250 GOSUB 1010:IF ER=1 THEN STOP
260 OPEN 1,8,5,"#"
270 PRINT#15,"U1:5 0 18 0"
280 GOSUB 1010:IF ER=1 THEN STOP
290 REM DIG OUT DISK NAME
300 PRINT#15,"B-P:5 144"
310 DN$=""
320 FOR K=1 TO 16
330 GET#1,A$:IF A$="" THEN A$=CHR$(0)
340 DN$=DN$+A$
350 NEXT
360 REM DIG OUT ID
370 PRINT#15,"B-P:5 162"
380 GET#1,A$:IF A$="" THEN A$=CHR$(0)
390 ID$=A$
400 GET#1,A$:IF A$="" THEN A$=CHR$(0)
410 ID$=ID$+A$
420 CLOSE 1
430 PRINT"  DISK NAME = "DN$
440 PRINT"  DISK ID = "ID$
450 INPUT"{DOWN}CONTINUE (Y/N)  Y{LEFT 3
}";R$
460 IF R$<>"Y" THEN CLOSE 15:END
470 PRINT"{UP 3}":GOSUB 860
480 PRINT"  FORMATTING DISKETTE"
490 PRINT#15,"NO:"+DN$+","+ID$
500 GOSUB 1010:IF ER=1 THEN STOP
510 :
520 GOSUB 830:PRINT"  READING TRACKS 1-6
":T1=1:T2=6:GOSUB 1070
530 GOSUB 860:PRINT"  WRITING TRACKS 1-6
":GOSUB 1220
540 :
550 GOSUB 830:PRINT"  READING TRACKS 7-1
2":T1=7:T2=12:GOSUB 1070
560 GOSUB 860:PRINT"  WRITING TRACKS 7-1
2":GOSUB 1220
570 :
580 GOSUB 830:PRINT"  READING TRACKS 13-
18":T1=13:T2=18:GOSUB 1070
590 GOSUB 860:PRINT"  WRITING TRACKS 13-
18":GOSUB 1220
600 :
610 GOSUB 830:PRINT"  READING TRACKS 19-
24":T1=19:T2=24:GOSUB 1070
620 GOSUB 860:PRINT"  WRITING TRACKS 19-
24":GOSUB 1220
630 :
640 GOSUB 830:PRINT"  READING TRACKS 25-
30":T1=25:T2=30:GOSUB 1070
```

```
650 GOSUB 860:PRINT"  WRITING TRACKS 25-
30":GOSUB 1220
660 :
670 GOSUB 830:PRINT"  READING TRACKS 31-
35":T1=31:T2=35:GOSUB 1070
680 GOSUB 860:PRINT"  WRITING TRACKS 31-
35":GOSUB 1220
690 :
700 PRINT"{DOWN}BACKUP COMPLETE"
710 POKE SID,4:POKE SID+1,49
720 FOR L=1 TO 10
730 POKE SID+4,33:FORK=1TO10:NEXT:POKE S
ID+4,32:FORK=1TO1000:NEXT
740 NEXT
750 CLOSE 15
760 IF NE=0 THEN PRINT"{DOWN}ALL SECTORS
 COPIED":END
770 PRINT"{DOWN}THERE WERE"NE"SECTORS NO
T COPIED{DOWN}"
780 FOR K=1 TO NE
790 PRINT"T="MT(K)"S="MS(K)EN(K)EM$(K)
800 NEXT
810 END
820 :
830 PRINT"{DOWN}INSERT MASTER DISKETTE{D
OWN}"
840 POKE SID,8:POKE SID+1,98
850 GOTO 890
860 PRINT"{DOWN}INSERT DESTINATION DISKE
TTE{DOWN}"
870 POKE SID,16:POKE SID+1,195
880 GET A$:IF A$<>"" GOTO 880
890 PRINT"{UP}PRESS {RVS}RETURN{ROFF} WH
EN READY"
900 POKE SID+4,33:FORK=1TO10:NEXT:POKE S
ID+4,32
910 FOR K=1 TO 50
920 GET A$:IF A$=CHR$(13) GOTO 980
930 NEXT
940 PRINT"{UP}{RVS}PRESS {ROFF}RETURN{RV
S} WHEN READY"
950 FOR K=1 TO 50
960 GET A$:IF A$=CHR$(13) GOTO 980
970 NEXT:GOTO 890
980 PRINT"{UP}
UP}"
990 RETURN
1000 :
1010 INPUT#15,EN,EM$,ET,ES
1020 IF EN<20 THEN ER=0:RETURN
```

```
1030 PRINT"{DOWN}DISK ERROR "
1040 PRINTEN;EM$;ET;ES
1050 ER=1:RETURN
1060 :
1070 PK=32
1080 OPEN 1,8,5,"#"
1090 FOR T=T1 TO T2
1100 NS=20+2*(T>17)+(T>24)+(T>30)
1110 FOR S=0 TO NS
1120 PRINT#15,"U1:5 0"T;S
1130 GOSUB 1380
1140 PRINT#15,"B-P:5 0"
1150 POKE 252,PK:PK=PK+1
1160 SYS 828 :REM READ 256 BYTES
1170 NEXT S
1180 NEXT T
1190 CLOSE 1
1200 RETURN
1210 :
1220 PK=32
1230 OPEN 1,8,5,"#"
1240 FOR T=T1 TO T2
1250 NS=20+2*(T>17)+(T>24)+(T>30)
1260 FOR S=0 TO NS
1270 PRINT#15,"B-P:5 0"
1280 POKE 252,PK:PK=PK+1
1290 SYS 847 :REM WRITE 256 BYTES
1300 PRINT#15,"U2:5 0"T;S
1310 GOSUB 1380
1320 A=FRE(0)
1330 NEXT S
1340 NEXT T
1350 CLOSE 1
1360 RETURN
1370 :
1380 INPUT#15,EN,EM$,ET,ES
1390 IF EN<20 THEN RETURN
1400 PRINT"TRACK"ET"SECTOR"ES"NOT COPIED
"
1410 PRINT"   "EN;EM$;ET;ES
1420 NE=NE+1:IF NE>50 THEN NE=50
1430 IF NE<50 THEN MT(NE)=ET:MS(NE)=ES:E
N(NE)=EN:EM$(NE)=EM$
1440 RETURN
1450 :
1460 DATA162,  1, 32,198,255,160,  0
1470 DATA 32,207,255,145,251,200,208
1480 DATA248, 32,204,255, 96,162,  1
1490 DATA 32,201,255,160,  0,177,251
1500 DATA 32,210,255,200,208,248, 32
1510 DATA204,255, 96
```

```
**************************
```
4. PROGRAM: MAKE FAST COPY
```
**************************
```

A BASIC program that creates a working copy of the machine language FAST
COPY program given at the end of Chapter 10. To help eliminate typing errors,
the program checks each of the blocks of data before creating the disk file. The
FAST COPY program allows you to copy a file from one diskette to another
quickly and easily. Files up to about 120 blocks long may be copied. If you don't
waste time when swapping diskettes, copying takes about one second per block. It
will not copy relative files.

Compatible with C-64 computer and 1541 disk drive only.

```
0 REM 1541 USER'S GUIDE   APPENDIX E
1 REM   COPYRIGHT: G. NEUFELD, 1984
2 :
3 REM   CREATE A WORKING COPY OF THE "FAS
T COPY" PROGRAM
4 :
100 REM FAST COPY FOR THE C-64 AND 1541
110 REM MAKES PGM FILE OF FAST COPY PROG
RAM
120 DIM CK(20)
130 :
140 REM READ IN CHECKSUM VALUES
150 FOR K=1 TO 20:READ CK(K):NEXT
160 :
170 REM CHECKSUM VALUES
180 DATA 3728,4805,4391,3477,4715
190 DATA 5747,4400,4743,5805,5288
200 DATA 4852,5841,3886,3485,2016
210 DATA 2024,2350,2477,2024, 195
220 :
230 REM CHECK FOR TYPING ERRORS
240 FOR BLK=1 TO 20:SUM=0:NV=35:IF BLK=2
0 THEN NV=4
250 FOR VL=1 TO NV:READ X:SUM=SUM+X:NEXT

260 IF SUM<>CK(BLK) THEN FL=1:PRINT"ERRO
R IN BLOCK"BLK
270 NEXT
280 IF FL=1 THEN STOP
290 :
300 REM DUMP CHECKSUM VALUES
310 RESTORE:FOR K=1TO20:READ X:NEXT
320 :
330 PRINT"{DOWN}INSERT DISK FOR STORING
COPY PROGRAM"
340 INPUT"{DOWN}FILE NAME DESIRED  FAST
COPY{LEFT 11}";F$
```

```
350 PRINT"{DOWN}WORKING..... "
360 OPEN 15,8,15,"IO":GOSUB 480
370 OPEN 1,8,5,"0:"+F$+",P,W":GOSUB 480
380 :
390 REM STORE LOAD ADDRESS
400 PRINT#1,CHR$(1)CHR$(8);
410 :
420 REM STORE MAIN PROGRAM
430 FOR BLK=1 TO 20:NV=35:IF BLK=20 THEN
   NV=4
440 FOR VL=1 TO NV:READ X:PRINT#1,CHR$(X
)::NEXT VL:NEXT BLK
450 :
460 CLOSE 1:CLOSE 15:PRINT"{DOWN}ALL DON
E":END
470 :
480 INPUT#15,EN,EM$,ET,ES:IF EN<20 THEN
RETURN
490 PRINT"{DOWN}DISK ERROR":PRINT EN;EM$
;ET;ES:CLOSE 1:CLOSE 15:END
500 :
510 REM START OF BLOCK #1
520 DATA 11,  8, 10,  0,158, 50, 48
530 DATA 54, 49,  0,  0,  0, 32,204
540 DATA255, 32,231,255,160,  0,185
550 DATA215,  9, 32,210,255,200,192
560 DATA 21,208,245,160,  0, 32,207
570 REM  START OF BLOCK #2
580 DATA255,201, 13,240, 20,153, 60
590 DATA  3,200,208,243,160,  0,185
600 DATA236,  9, 32,210,255,200,192
610 DATA 21,208,245, 96,140, 52,  3
620 DATA192, 17,176,235,160,  0,185
630 REM  START OF BLOCK #3
640 DATA  1, 10, 32,210,255,200,192
650 DATA 19,208,245, 32,207,255,141
660 DATA 53,  3,201, 83,240,  4,201
670 DATA 80,208,229,172, 52,  3,169
680 DATA 44,153, 60,  3,200,173, 53
690 REM  START OF BLOCK #4
700 DATA  3,153, 60,  3,200,169, 44
710 DATA153, 60,  3,200,169, 82,153
720 DATA 60,  3,200,140, 52,  3, 32
730 DATA204,255, 32,170,  9, 32,192
740 DATA  9, 32,100,  9, 32,204,255
750 REM  START OF BLOCK #5
760 DATA165,251,240, 11,169,  1, 32
770 DATA195,255,169, 15, 32,195,255
780 DATA 96,169,  0,133,252,169, 11
790 DATA133,253,160,  0,185, 42, 10
```

```
800 DATA 32,210,255,200,192, 20,208
810 REM   START OF BLOCK #6
820 DATA245,162,  1, 32,198,255,160
830 DATA  0, 32,207,255,145,252,165
840 DATA144,208,  7,200,208,244,230
850 DATA253,208,240,132,252, 32,204
860 DATA255,169,  1, 32,195,255,169
870 REM   START OF BLOCK #7
880 DATA 15, 32,195,255,160,  0,185
890 DATA 62, 10, 32,210,255,200,192
900 DATA 49,208,245, 32,228,255,201
910 DATA 13,208,249, 32,170,  9,172
920 DATA 52,  3,169, 87,153, 59,  3
930 REM   START OF BLOCK #8
940 DATA 32,192,  9, 32,100,  9, 32
950 DATA204,255,165,251,208,142,169
960 DATA  0,133,250,169, 11,133,251
970 DATA160,  0,185,111, 10, 32,210
980 DATA255,200,192, 26,208,245,162
990 REM   START OF BLOCK #9
1000 DATA  1, 32,201,255,160,  0,177
1010 DATA250, 32,210,255,196,252,208
1020 DATA  6,165,251,197,253,240,  7
1030 DATA200,208,238,230,251,208,234
1040 DATA 32,204,255,169,  1, 32,195
1050 REM   START OF BLOCK #10
1060 DATA255,169, 15, 32,195,255,160
1070 DATA  0,185,137, 10, 32,210,255
1080 DATA200,192, 21,208,245, 32,204
1090 DATA255, 32,228,255,201, 89,240
1100 DATA  8,201, 78,208,245, 32,204
1110 REM   START OF BLOCK #11
1120 DATA255, 96, 76,215,  8, 32,204
1130 DATA255,162, 15, 32,198,255, 32
1140 DATA207,255,201, 50,144, 39,133
1150 DATA251,160,  0,185, 20, 10, 32
1160 DATA210,255,200,192, 20,208,245
1170 REM   START OF BLOCK #12
1180 DATA165,251, 32,210,255, 32,207
1190 DATA255,201, 13,240,  7, 32,210
1200 DATA255,208,244,240,242,169,  1
1210 DATA133,251, 96, 32,207,255,201
1220 DATA 13,240,  4,208,247,240,245
1230 REM   START OF BLOCK #13
1240 DATA169,  0,133,251, 96,165,  2
1250 DATA162, 40,160, 10, 32,189,255
1260 DATA169, 15,162,  8,160, 15, 32
1270 DATA186,255, 32,192,255, 96,173
1280 DATA 52,  3,162, 60,160,  3, 32
1290 REM   START OF BLOCK #14
```

```
1300 DATA189,255,169,  1,162,  8,160
1310 DATA  5, 32,186,255, 32,192,255
1320 DATA 96,142,147, 17, 70, 73, 76
1330 DATA 69, 78, 65, 77, 69, 32, 84
1340 DATA 79, 32, 67, 79, 80, 89, 63
1350 REM   START OF BLOCK #15
1360 DATA 32, 13, 13, 18, 70, 73, 76
1370 DATA 69, 78, 65, 77, 69, 32, 84
1380 DATA 79, 79, 32, 76, 79, 78, 71
1390 DATA 13, 13, 13, 70, 73, 76, 69
1400 DATA 32, 84, 89, 80, 69, 32, 40
1410 REM   START OF BLOCK #16
1420 DATA 83, 47, 80, 41, 63, 32, 13
1430 DATA 13, 18, 70, 65, 84, 65, 76
1440 DATA 32, 68, 73, 83, 75, 32, 69
1450 DATA 82, 82, 79, 82, 13, 73, 48
1460 DATA 13, 13, 82, 69, 65, 68, 73
1470 REM   START OF BLOCK #17
1480 DATA 78, 71, 32, 68, 73, 83, 75
1490 DATA 32, 70, 73, 76, 69, 13, 13
1500 DATA 73, 78, 83, 69, 82, 84, 32
1510 DATA 79, 84, 72, 69, 82, 32, 68
1520 DATA 73, 83, 75, 69, 84, 84, 69
1530 REM   START OF BLOCK #18
1540 DATA 13, 13, 80, 82, 69, 83, 83
1550 DATA 32, 18, 82, 69, 84, 85, 82
1560 DATA 78,146, 32, 87, 72, 69, 78
1570 DATA 32, 82, 69, 65, 68, 89, 13
1580 DATA145, 87, 82, 73, 84, 73, 78
1590 REM   START OF BLOCK #19
1600 DATA 71, 32, 68, 73, 83, 75, 32
1610 DATA 70, 73, 76, 69, 32, 32, 32
1620 DATA 32, 32, 32, 13, 13, 65, 78
1630 DATA 79, 84, 72, 69, 82, 32, 67
1640 DATA 79, 80, 89, 32, 40, 89, 47
1650 REM   START OF BLOCK #20
1660 DATA 78, 41, 63, 13
```

****
5. PROGRAM: EDIT T&S/C-64
****

Allows you to read or edit any block on a diskette. The display shows half a sector
at a time. You may toggle back and forth between the two halves. The left side of
the screen shows a hex dump of the sector. The right side shows the corresponding
ASCII characters. You may edit either the hex or the ASCII side. This is particularly useful when editing the diskette name or file names in the directory.
Since the sectors are read and written by bypassing the 1541's file management
routines, you may write out an edited block onto any position on any diskette.
NOTE: The disk ID's do not have to match.

Compatible with C-64 computer and 1541 disk drive only.

```
0 REM 1541 USERS' GUIDE   APPENDIX E
1 REM  COPYRIGHT: G. NEUFELD, 1984
2 :
3 REM EDIT ANY BLOCK ON A DISKETTE
4 :
100 REM EDIT T&S C-64
110 POKE 53280,11:POKE 53281,11:POKE650,
255
120 PRINTCHR$(14)CHR$(144)"{CLR}{SHIFT-E
}DIT {SHIFT-T}RACK & {SHIFT-S}ECTOR (C)
{SHIFT-G}. {SHIFT-N}EUFELD,1984"
130 TR=18:SE=0:SX=16:FH=240:FL=15:CO=48:
C9=57:N2=2:N7=7:SS=1024:SC=55296:NC=40
140 D$="{HOME}{DOWN 18}"
150 B$="":ZC$=CHR$(0):CR$=CHR$(13):TB=29

160 CI$=CHR$(148)+CHR$(34)+CHR$(20)
170 CD$=CHR$(34)+CHR$(20):QT$=CHR$(34)
180 DIM HX(255),HX$(255)
190 DIM HT$(32),CH$(255)
200 GOSUB 3280:REM ZERO SID CHIP
210 FOR K=0 TO 63:CH$(K)=CHR$(K+A1):CH$(
K+A2)=RV$+CH$(K)+RO$:NEXT
220 FOR K=64 TO 95:CH$(K)=CHR$(K+A2):CH$
(K+A2)=RV$+CH$(K)+RO$:NEXT
230 FOR K=96 TO 127:CH$(K)=CHR$(K+A1):CH
$(K+A2)=RV$+CH$(K)+RO$:NEXT
240 FOR K=0 TO 31 :Z=K*8:GOSUB2440:HT$(K
)="$"+Z$+": ":NEXT
250 B$=" ":NT=TR:GOTO 270
260 PRINT"{CLR}{SHIFT-E}DIT {SHIFT-T}RAC
K & {SHIFT-S}ECTOR (C) {SHIFT-G}. {SHIFT
-N}EUFELD,1984"
270 PRINT"{DOWN} {SHIFT-W}HICH TRACK "NT

280 PRINT"{UP}"TAB(12);:INPUT NT
290 IF NT<1 OR NT>35 THENPRINT"{UP}"TAB(
20)"{SHIFT-B}AD TRACK":GOSUB3540
300 IF NT<1 OR NT>35 THEN GOSUB2860:NT=T
R:GOTO 260
310 MS=20+2*(NT>17)+(NT>24)+(NT>30)
320 PRINT"{DOWN} {SHIFT-W}HICH SECTOR "S
E
330 PRINT"{UP}"TAB(13);:INPUT NS
340 IF NS<0 OR NS>MS THENPRINT"{UP}"TAB(
20)"{SHIFT-B}AD SECTOR":GOSUB3540
350 IF NS<0 OR NS>MS THEN GOSUB2860:GOTO
 260
```

```
360 OPEN 15,8,15,"IO"
370 GOSUB 2500
380 OPEN 1,8,5,"#0"
390 GOSUB 2500
400 JOB=128:GOSUB 2930:REM SAME AS: PRIN
T#15,"U1:5 0"TR;SE
410 IF GF=1 THEN CLOSE1:NT=TR:NS=SE:GOTO
 260
420 PRINT"{DOWN} {SHIFT-O}NE MOMENT PLEA
SE...":TR=NT:SE=NS
430 FOR K=0 TO 255:GET#1,A$:Z=ASC(A$+ZC$
):GOSUB 2440:HX(K)=Z:HX$(K)=Z$:NEXT
440 CLOSE 1
450 HF=0:GOSUB 2570
460 GOSUB 2700
470 GET A$:IF A$<>""GOTO470
480 GET A$:IF A$="" GOTO 480
490 A=ASC(A$)-132
500 IF A<1 OR A>8 THEN GOSUB3540:GOTO 47
0
510 GOSUB 3440
520 ON A GOTO 570,1450,1730,2070,1040,15
10,1820,2210
530 :
540 REM EDIT (HEX)
550 GOSUB3540:GOTO 570:REM ERROR
560 GOSUB 3350
570 CC=PEEK(SS+N2+NC*ER+3*EC+EH)
580 POKE(SS+N2+NC*ER+3*EC+EH),CCOR128
590 FOR K=1 TO 30
600 GET A$:IF A$<>"" GOTO 670
610 NEXT
620 POKE(SS+N2+NC*ER+3*EC+EH),CCAND127
630 FOR K=1 TO 30
640 GET A$:IF A$<>"" GOTO 670
650 NEXT
660 GOTO 570
670 A=ASC(A$)
680 POKE(SS+N2+NC*ER+3*EC+EH),CC
690 IF A<133 OR A>140 GOTO 730
700 A=A-132:GOSUB 3440
710 ON A GOTO 570,1450,1730,2070,1040,15
10,1820,2210
720 :
730 IF A=19 THEN EC=1:EH=0:ER=2:GOTO560
740 IF A=29 AND EH=0 THEN EH=1:GOTO 560
750 IF A=29 AND EH=1 AND EC<8 THEN EH=0:
EC=EC+1:GOTO 560
760 IF A=29 AND EH=1 AND EC=8 AND ER>=17
 GOTO 550
```

```
770 IF A=29 AND EH=1 AND EC=8 THEN EH=0:
EC=1:ER=ER+1:GOTO560
780 IF A=157 AND EH=1 THEN EH=0:GOTO560
790 IF A=157 AND EH=0 AND EC>1 THEN EH=1
:EC=EC-1:GOTO 560
800 IF A=157 AND EH=0 AND EC=1 AND ER<=2
 GOTO 550
810 IF A=157 AND EH=0 AND EC=1 THEN EH=1
:EC=8:ER=ER-1:GOTO 560
820 IF A=17 AND ER<17 THEN ER=ER+1:GOTO
560
830 IF A=145 AND ER>2 THEN ER=ER-1:GOTO
560
840 IF A=13 THEN EC=1:EH=0:IF ER<17 THEN
 ER=ER+1:GOTO 560
850 IF(A<48)OR(A>57ANDA<65)OR(A>70) GOTO
 550
860 POKE(SS+N2+NC*ER+3*EC+EH),AAND63
870 N=A-C0:IF A>C9 THEN N=N-N7
880 P=(ER-2)*8+EC-1:GOSUB 3350
890 C=HX(P+HF*128)
900 IF EH=0 THEN C=(C AND 15)+16*N
910 IF EH=1 THEN C=(C AND 240)+N
920 POKE(SS+TB+NC*ER+EC),C
930 HX(P+HF*128)=C
940 Z=C:GOSUB 2440:HX$(P+HF*128)=Z$
950 IF EH=0 THEN EH=1:GOTO 990
960 IF EH=1 AND EC<8 THEN EH=0:EC=EC+1:G
OTO 990
970 IF ER>=17 GOTO 990
980 EC=1:EH=0:ER=ER+1
990 GOTO 570
1000 :
1010 REM EDIT (ASCII)
1020 GOSUB3540:GOTO1040:REM ERROR
1030 GOSUB 3350:REM KEY CLICK
1040 CC=PEEK(SS+29+NC*ER+EC)
1050 POKE(SS+29+NC*ER+EC),CCOR128
1060 FOR K=1 TO 30
1070 GET A$:IF A$<>"" GOTO 1140
1080 NEXT
1090 POKE(SS+29+NC*ER+EC),CCAND127
1100 FOR K=1 TO 30
1110 GET A$:IF A$<>"" GOTO 1140
1120 NEXT
1130 GOTO 1050
1140 A=ASC(A$)
1150 POKE(SS+29+NC*ER+EC),CC
1160 IF A<133 OR A>140 GOTO 1200
1170 A=A-132:GOSUB 3440
```

```
1180 ON A GOTO 570,1450,1730,2070,1040,1
510,1820,2210
1190 :
1200 IF A=19 THEN EC=1:EH=0:ER=2:GOTO 10
30
1210 IF A=29 AND EC<8 THEN EC=EC+1:GOTO
1030
1220 IF A=29 AND EC=8 AND ER=17 GOTO 102
0
1230 IF A=29 AND EC=8 THEN EC=1:IFER<17T
HEN ER=ER+1:GOTO1030
1240 IF A=157 AND EC>1 THEN EC=EC-1:GOTO
 1030
1250 IF A=157 AND EC=1 AND ER=2 GOTO 102
0
1260 IF A=157 AND EC=1 THEN EC=8:IFER>2T
HEN ER=ER-1:GOTO 1030
1270 IF A=17 AND ER<17 THEN ER=ER+1:GOTO
 1030
1280 IF A=145 AND ER>2 THEN ER=ER-1:GOTO
 1030
1290 IF A=13 THEN EC=1:IF ER<17 THEN ER=
ER+1:GOTO 1030
1300 IF(A<32)OR(A>95ANDA<160)OR(A>223) G
OTO 1020
1310 POKE(SS+TB+NC*ER+EC),A
1320 GOSUB 3350
1330 CL=(A AND 15)+48:IF CL>C9 THEN CL=C
L+N7
1340 CH=(A AND 240)/SX+C0:IF CH>C9 THEN
CH=CH+N7
1350 PRINTLEFT$(D$,ER+1)TAB(3*EC+2)CHR$(
CH)CHR$(CL)
1360 P=(ER-2)*8+EC-1
1370 HX(P+HF*128)=A
1380 Z=A:GOSUB 2440:HX$(P+HF*128)=Z$
1390 IF EC<8 THEN EC=EC+1:GOTO 1420
1400 IF EC=8 AND ER=17 GOTO 1040
1410 EC=1:IF ER<17 THEN ER=ER+1
1420 GOTO 1040
1430 :
1440 REM DISPLAY OTHER HALF
1450 IF HF=0 THEN HF=1:GOTO 1470
1460 HF=0
1470 GOSUB 2570
1480 GOTO 460
1490 :
1500 REM PRINT SECTOR
1510 GOSUB 2780
1520 OPEN 3,4
```

```
1530 PRINT#3:IF ST=0 GOTO 1590
1540 GOSUB3540
1550 PRINT" {SHIFT-D}EVICE #4 NOT PRESEN
T":CLOSE3
1560 INPUT" {DOWN}{SHIFT-C}ONTINUE (Y/N)
  N{LEFT 3}";A$
1570 IF A$<>"Y" THEN GOSUB 2780:GOSUB 27
00:GOTO470
1580 GOTO 1510
1590 GOSUB 2780
1600 INPUT" {SHIFT-I}S THE PAPER ADJUSTE
D (Y/N)   Y{LEFT 3}";A$
1610 IF A$<>"Y" THEN GOSUB 2780:GOSUB 27
00:GOTO470
1620 PRINT#3,"    {SHIFT-T}RACK"MID$(STR$
(TR),2)",  {SHIFT-S}ECTOR"SE"{SHIFT-T}RAC
K ID="QT$ID$QT$
1630 PRINT#3
1640 FOR K=0 TO 248 STEP 8
1650 PRINT#3,"{DOWN}"HT$(K/8)HX$(K)HX$(K
+1)HX$(K+2)HX$(K+3);
1660 PRINT#3,HX$(K+4)HX$(K+5)HX$(K+6)HX$
(K+7);" ";
1670 FOR C=0 TO 7:PRINT#3,CH$(HX(K+C));:
NEXT:PRINT#3
1680 NEXT:PRINT#3
1690 CLOSE 3:GOSUB 2780:GOSUB 2700
1700 GOTO 470
1710 :
1720 REM EXIT PROGRAM
1730 GOSUB 2780
1740 INPUT" {SHIFT-E}XIT PROGRAM NOW (Y/
N)   N{LEFT 3}";A$
1750 IF A$<>"Y" GOTO460
1760 PRINT#15,"U;"
1770 CLOSE 1
1780 CLOSE 15
1790 GOSUB 2780:GOSUB 3280:END
1800 :
1810 REM WRITE SECTOR
1820 GOSUB 2780:NT=TR
1830 INPUT" {SHIFT-W}RITE SECTOR TO DISK
 (Y/N)   N{LEFT 3}";A$
1840 IF A$<>"Y" GOTO460
1850 GOSUB 2780:NS=SE:PRINT" {SHIFT-W}RI
TE TO TRACK "NT
1860 PRINT"{UP}"TAB(15);:INPUT NT
1870 IF NT<1 OR NT>35 THENPRINT"{UP}"TAB
(20)"{SHIFT-B}AD TRACK"
```

```
1880 IF NT<1 OR NT>35 THENGOSUB3540:GOSU
B 2860:NT=TR:GOTO1830
1890 MS=20+2*(NT>17)+(NT>24)+(NT>30)
1900 PRINT"          SECTOR "NS
1910 PRINT"{UP}"TAB(16);:INPUT NS
1920 IF NS<0 OR NS>MS THENPRINT"{UP}"TAB
(20)"{SHIFT-B}AD SECTOR":GOSUB3540
1930 IF NS<0 OR NS>MS THEN NS=SE:GOSUB28
60:GOTO1830
1940 PRINT"{DOWN} {SHIFT-O}NE MOMENT PLE
ASE..."
1950 OPEN 1,8,5,"#0"
1960 PRINT#15,"B-P:5 0"
1970 FOR K=0 TO 255:PRINT#1,CHR$(HX(K));
:NEXT
1980 JOB=144:GOSUB 2930:REM SAME AS: PRI
NT#15,"U2:5 0"TR;SE
1990 CLOSE1:IF GF=1 GOTO460
2000 TR=NT:SE=NS
2010 PRINT"{HOME} {RVS}{SHIFT-T}RACK"TR"
{LEFT}, {SHIFT-S}ECTOR"SE"{LEFT}";
2020 IF HF=0 THEN PRINT" (FIRST HALF) ID
="CD$ID$
2030 IF HF=1 THEN PRINT" (LAST HALF) ID=
"CD$ID$
2040 GOTO 460
2050 :
2060 REM READ NEXT SECTOR
2070 GOSUB 2780
2080 IF HX(0)=0 THEN PRINT" {SHIFT-T}HIS
 SECTOR WAS THE LAST":GOSUB3540
2090 IFHX(0)=0 THEN GOSUB2860:GOTO460
2100 PRINT" {SHIFT-N}EXT TRACK = "HX(0)
2110 IF HX(0)<1 OR HX(0)>35 THEN PRINT"{
UP}"TAB(20)"{SHIFT-B}AD TRACK":GOSUB3540

2120 IF HX(0)<1 OR HX(0)>35 THEN GOSUB28
60:GOTO460
2130 PRINT" {SHIFT-N}EXT SECTOR ="HX(1)
2140 MS=20+2*(HX(0)>17)+(HX(0)>24)+(HX(0
)>30)
2150 IF HX(1)<0 OR HX(1)>MS THEN PRINT"{
UP}"TAB(20)"{SHIFT-B}AD SECTOR":GOSUB354
0
2160 IF HX(1)<0 OR HX(1)>MS THEN GOSUB28
60:GOTO460
2170 NT=HX(0)
2180 NS=HX(1)
2190 GOTO 2320
2200 :
2210 REM READ NEW SECTOR
```

```
2220 NT=TR
2230 GOSUB 2780:NS=SE:PRINT" {SHIFT-W}HI
CH TRACK "NT
2240 PRINT"{UP}"TAB(12);:INPUT NT
2250 IF NT<1 OR NT>35 THEN PRINT"{UP}"TA
B(20)"{SHIFT-B}AD TRACK":GOSUB3540
2260 IF NT<1 OR NT>35 THEN GOSUB2860:GOT
O2220
2270 PRINT" {SHIFT-W}HICH SECTOR "NS
2280 MS=20+2*(NT>17)+(NT>24)+(NT>30)
2290 PRINT"{UP}"TAB(13);:INPUT NS
2300 IF NS<0 OR NS>MS THEN PRINT"{UP}"TA
B(20)"{SHIFT-B}AD SECTOR":GOSUB3540
2310 IF NS<0 OR NS>MS THEN GOSUB2860:GOT
O2230
2320 OPEN 1,8,5,"#0"
2330 JOB=128:GOSUB 2930:REM SAME AS: PRI
NT#15,"U1:5 0"TR;SE
2340 IF GF=1 THEN CLOSE1:GOTO460
2350 TR=NT:SE=NS
2360 PRINT"{DOWN} {SHIFT-O}NE MOMENT PLE
ASE..."
2370 PRINT#15,"B-P:5 0"
2380 FOR K=0 TO 255:GET#1,A$:Z=ASC(A$+ZC
$):GOSUB 2440:HX(K)=Z:HX$(K)=Z$:NEXT
2390 CLOSE 1
2400 HF=0:GOSUB 2570
2410 GOTO 460
2420 :
2430 REM CONVERT TO HEX
2440 ZH=(FHANDZ)/SX+CO:IF ZH>C9 THEN ZH=
ZH+N7
2450 ZL=(FLANDZ)+CO:IF ZL>C9 THEN ZL=ZL+
N7
2460 Z$=CHR$(ZH)+CHR$(ZL)+B$
2470 RETURN
2480 :
2490 REM READ DISK ERROR CHANNEL
2500 INPUT#15,EN,EM$,ET,ES
2510 IF EN<19 THEN RETURN
2520 PRINT"{DOWN}{SHIFT-D}ISK ERROR:":GO
SUB3540
2530 PRINTEN;EM$;ET;ES
2540 CLOSE 1:CLOSE 15:END
2550 :
2560 REM DISPLAY SECTOR
2570 PRINT"{CLR} {RVS}{SHIFT-T}RACK"TR"{
LEFT}. {SHIFT-S}ECTOR"SE"{LEFT}";
2580 IF HF=0 THEN PRINT" (FIRST HALF) ID
="CD$ID$
```

```
2590 IF HF=1 THEN PRINT" (LAST HALF) ID=
"CD$ID$
2600 PRINT
2610 FOR K=HF*128 TO HF*128+120 STEP 8
2620 PRINTHT$(K/8)HX$(K)HX$(K+1)HX$(K+2)
HX$(K+3);
2630 PRINT HX$(K+4)HX$(K+5)HX$(K+6)HX$(K
+7)
2640 L=KAND127:PS=SS+110+5*L:PC=SC+110+5
*L
2650 FOR C=0 TO 7:POKE PC+C,0:POKE PS+C,
HX(K+C):NEXT
2660 NEXT
2670 RETURN
2680 :
2690 REM DISPLAY COMMANDS
2700 PRINTD$"{DOWN} F1 = {SHIFT-E}DIT (H
EX)    F2 = {SHIFT-E}DIT ({SHIFT-A}{SHIF
T-S}{SHIFT-C}{SHIFT-I 2})
2710 PRINT" F3 = {SHIFT-O}THER HALF     F
4 = {SHIFT-P}RINT SECTOR
2720 PRINT" F5 = {SHIFT-E}XIT PROGRAM   F
6 = {SHIFT-W}RITE SECTOR
2730 PRINT" F7 = {SHIFT-N}EXT SECTOR    F
8 = {SHIFT-N}EW SECTOR
2740 EC=1:EH=0:ER=2
2750 RETURN
2760 :
2770 REM CLEAR LOWER SCREEN
2780 PRINT D$
2790 FOR K=1TO4
2800 PRINT"
                "
2810 NEXT
2820 PRINT D$
2830 RETURN
2840 :
2850 REM WAIT FOR RETURN
2860 PRINT"{DOWN}  {SHIFT-P}RESS {RVS}{S
HIFT-R}{SHIFT-E}{SHIFT-T}{SHIFT-U}{SHIFT
-R}{SHIFT-N}{ROFF} TO CONTINUE"
2870 GET A$:IF A$<>"" GOTO 2870
2880 GET A$:IF A$<>CR$ GOTO 2880
2890 PRINT"{UP}
  "
2900 RETURN
2910 :
2920 REM READ/WRITE SECTOR USING JOB QUE
UE
2930 TY=0
```

```
2940 PRINT#15,"M-W"CHR$(6)CHR$(0)CHR$(2)
CHR$(NT)CHR$(NS)
2950 PRINT#15,"M-W"CHR$(0)CHR$(0)CHR$(1)
CHR$(176):REM SEEK TRACK
2960 PRINT#15,"M-R"CHR$(0)CHR$(0):REM WA
IT TILL JOB COMPLETE
2970 GET#15,A$:A=ASC(A$+ZC$)
2980 IF A>127 GOTO 2960
2990 IF A=1 GOTO 3060
3000 TY=TY+1:IF TY<5 GOTO 2940
3010 GOSUB 2780:IF JOB=128 THEN PRINT"{S
HIFT-R}EAD JOB ABORTED"
3020 IF JOB=144 THEN PRINT"{SHIFT-W}RITE
 JOB ABORTED"
3030 PRINT"{DOWN} {SHIFT-T}ROUBLE ON THI
S TRACK"
3040 GOSUB3540:GOSUB 2860
3050 GF=1:RETURN
3060 PRINT#15,"M-R"CHR$(18)CHR$(0)CHR$(2
)
3070 GET#15,A$:IF A$="" THEN A$=ZC$
3080 ID$=A$
3090 GET#15,A$:IF A$="" THEN A$=ZC$
3100 ID$=ID$+A$
3110 TY=0
3120 PRINT#15,"M-W"CHR$(6)CHR$(0)CHR$(2)
CHR$(NT)CHR$(NS)
3130 PRINT#15,"M-W"CHR$(0)CHR$(0)CHR$(1)
CHR$(JOB):REM READ/WRITE SECTOR
3140 PRINT#15,"M-R"CHR$(0)CHR$(0):REM WA
IT TILL JOB COMPLETE
3150 GET#15,A$:A=ASC(A$+ZC$)
3160 IF A>127 GOTO 3140
3170 IF A=1 GOTO 3240
3180 TY=TY+1:IF TY<5 GOTO 3120
3190 GOSUB 2780:IF JOB=128 THEN PRINT"{S
HIFT-R}EAD JOB ABORTED"
3200 IF JOB=144 THEN PRINT"{SHIFT-W}RITE
 JOB ABORTED"
3210 PRINT"{DOWN} {SHIFT-T}ROUBLE WITH T
HIS SECTOR"
3220 GOSUB3540:GOSUB 2860
3230 GF=1:RETURN
3240 PRINT#15,"B-P:5 0"
3250 GF=0:RETURN
3260 :
3270 REM SET-UP SID CHIP
3280 SID = 54272
3290 FOR K=SID TO SID+24
3300 POKE K,0
```

```
3310 NEXT
3320 RETURN
3330 :
3340 REM DO KEY CLICK
3350 POKE SID+13,240
3360 POKE SID+24,15
3370 POKE SID+8,40
3380 POKE SID+11,17
3390 FOR K=1 TO 30:NEXT
3400 POKE SID+11,0
3410 RETURN
3420 :
3430 REM DO COMMAND TONE
3440 POKE SID+1,20
3450 POKE SID+5,11
3460 POKE SID+6,10
3470 POKE SID+24,15
3480 POKE SID+4,21
3490 FOR K=1 TO 600:NEXT
3500 POKE SID+4,0
3510 RETURN
3520 :
3530 REM DO ERROR TONE
3540 POKE SID+1,60
3550 POKE SID+5,11
3560 POKE SID+6,10
3570 POKE SID+24,15
3580 POKE SID+4,21
3590 FOR K=1 TO 750:NEXT
3600 POKE SID+4,0
3610 RETURN
```

```
***********************
```
6. PROGRAM: MOD DISK NAME
```
***********************
```

Allows you to modify the diskette name of any diskette. To use run program, insert diskette and edit.

Compatible with C-64, VIC-20, 4032 and 8032 computers, 1541, 2031 and 4040 disk drives.

```
0 REM  1541 USER'S GUIDE  APPENDIX E
1 REM   COPYRIGHT: G. NEUFELD, 1984
3 REM   MODIFY A DISKETTE'S NAME
4 :
100 REM MOD DISK NAME
110 PRINT"{CLR}{DOWN} MODIFY DISKETTE NA
ME"
120 PRINT"{DOWN} INSERT DISKETTE TO BE M
ODIFIED"
```

```
130 PRINT"{DOWN} PRESS RETURN WHEN READY
"
140 GET A$:IF A$<>CHR$(13) GOTO 140
150 PRINT"{UP} WORKING......
"
160 OPEN 15,8,15,"IO"
170 GOSUB 470
180 OPEN 1,8,5,"#"
190 PRINT#15,"U1:5 0 18 0"
200 PRINT#15,"B-P:5 144"
210 DN$=""
220 FOR K=1 TO 16
230 GET#1,A$:IF A$="" THEN A$=CHR$(0)
240 DN$=DN$+A$
250 NEXT
260 PRINT"{CLR}{DOWN} EDIT DISK NAME"
270 PRINT"{DOWN 2}     "DN$
280 PRINT"     ----------------"
290 PRINT"{UP 2} ";:INPUT NN$
300 IF LEN(NN$)<17 GOTO 360
310 IF RIGHT$(NN$,1)=CHR$(160) THEN NN$=
LEFT$(NN$,LEN(NN$)-1):GOTO 300
320 PRINT"{DOWN} ** NAME TOO LONG **"
330 PRINT"{DOWN} PRESS RETURN TO GO ON"
340 GET A$:IF A$<>CHR$(13) GOTO 340
350 GOTO 260
360 INPUT"{DOWN 2} CHANGE ON DISKETTE (Y
/N)   N{LEFT 3}";X$
370 IF ASC(X$)<>89 THEN CLOSE 1:CLOSE 15
:END
380 IF LEN(NN$)<16 THEN NN$=NN$+CHR$(160
):GOTO 380
390 PRINT#15,"B-P:5 144"
400 PRINT#1,NN$;
410 PRINT#15,"U2:5 0 18 0"
420 GOSUB 470
430 PRINT#15,"IO"
440 CLOSE 1:CLOSE 15
450 PRINT"{DOWN}DONE":END
460 :
470 INPUT#15,EN,EM$,ET,ES
480 IF EN<20 THEN RETURN
490 PRINT"{DOWN} DISK ERROR"
500 PRINTEN;EM$;ET;ES
510 CLOSE 1:CLOSE 15:END


***********************
7. PROGRAM: FIX DIRECTORY
***********************
```

Provides automated recovery of files lost due to a damaged directory sector or inadvertent issuance of a "short NEW" command.

To recover files after a "short NEW" command specify "1", the sector to be recovered.

To recover files lost because of a read error on track 18, you must know which sector is causing the problem. Use this short program to scan track 18 for this.

```
100 REM FIND ERRORS ON TRACK 18
110 PRINT"{CLR}FIND ERRORS IN THE DIRECT
ORY"
120 PRINT"{DOWN}INSERT DISKETTE"
130 PRINT"{DOWN}PRESS {RVS}RETURN{ROFF}
TO CONTINUE"
140 GET A$:IF A$<>CHR$(13) GOTO 140
150 PRINT"{CLR}ERROR ANALYSIS OF TRACK 1
8{DOWN}"
160 OPEN 15,8,15,"IO"
170 OPEN 1,8,5,"#"
180 DIM SE(20)
190 SE(1)=0:KT=1:NE=0
200 FOR K=2 TO 19
210 SE(K)=KT
220 KT=KT+3:IF KT>18 THEN KT=KT-17
230 NEXT
240 FOR K=1 TO 19
250 PRINT#15,"U1:5 0 18"SE(K)
260 INPUT#15,EN,EM$,ET,ES$
270 IF EN<20 GOTO 300
280 NE=NE+1
290 PRINT"SECTOR #"SE(K)"ERROR #"EN" - "
EM$
300 NEXT
310 CLOSE 1:CLOSE 15
320 IF NE=0 THEN PRINT"{DOWN}NO ERRORS F
OUND ON TRACK 18"
```

Once you have found the problem sector, write down the sector number. Load and run the FIX BAD DIR program and specify this sector as the one to be recovered.

Compatible with C-64 and VIC-20 computers and the 1541 disk drive.

```
100 REM DIR-FIX FOR 1541 AND C-64/VIC-20

110 PRINT"{CLR}   {RVS}    RECOVER DIRECT
ORY SECTOR    "
120 PRINT"{DOWN}THIS UTILITY WILL RECOVE
R A SECTOR"
```

```
130 PRINT"OF THE DIRECTORY. TO RECOVER A
FTER A"
140 PRINT"SHORT NEW ENTER '1' AS THE SEC
TOR TO"
150 PRINT"BE RECOVERED. NOTE THAT YOU CA
NNOT"
160 PRINT"RECOVER ANY FILES AFTER A FULL
 NEW."
170 PRINT"{DOWN}INSERT DISKETTE WITH BAD
 DIRECTORY"
180 PRINT"{DOWN}PRESS {RVS}RETURN{ROFF}
TO CONTINUE"
190 GET A$:IF A$<>"" GOTO 190
200 GET A$:IF A$<>CHR$(13) GOTO 200
210 INPUT"{UP}WHICH SECTOR TO RECOVER  1
{LEFT 3}";A$
220 DX=INT(VAL(A$))
230 IF DX>0 AND DX<19 GOTO 270
240 PRINT"{DOWN}I DON'T DO SECTOR #"DX
250 GOTO 210
260 :
270 Z$=CHR$(0)
280 DIM TL(200),SL(200),BM(35,24),B%(35,
2),BF(35)
290 B0=1:B1=2:B2=4:B3=8:B4=16:B5=32:B6=6
4:B7=128
300 OPEN 15,8,15,"IO"
310 GOSUB 3190:IF FZ=1 THEN STOP
320 OPEN 1,8,5,"#"
330 GOSUB 3190:IF FZ=1 THEN STOP
340 :
350 IF DX=1 GOTO 870
360 :
370 REM NOT SECTOR 18/1, SO CORRECT ANY
BAD LINKS
380 REM AND UNSCRATCH ANY SCRATCHED FILE
S IN THE
390 REM PRECEEDING DIRECTORY BLOCKS
400 PRINT"{DOWN}CHECKING FOR CORRECT LIN
KS AND"
410 PRINT"SCRATCHED FILES IN PREVIOUS BL
OCKS"
420 ZD=1
430 PRINT#15,"U1:5 0 18"ZD
440 PRINT"CHECKING SECTOR 18,"ZD
450 GOSUB 3190:IF FZ=1 THEN STOP
460 :
470 REM CHECK LINK TO NEXT SECTOR
480 PRINT#15,"B-P:5 0"
490 GET#1,A$:TL=ASC(A$+Z$)
```

```
500 GET#1,A$:SL=ASC(A$+Z$)
510 IF TL=18 AND SL>1 AND SL<19 GOTO 630

520 :
530 REM CORRECT BAD LINK
540 SL=ZD+3:TL=18
550 IF SL>18 THEN SL=SL-17
560 PRINT#15,"B-P:5 0"
570 PRINT#1,CHR$(TL)CHR$(SL);
580 PRINT#15,"U2:5 0 18"ZD
590 PRINT"FIXING LINK ON 18/"ZD
600 GOSUB 3190:IF FZ=1 THEN STOP
610 :
620 REM SCAN FOR SCRATCHED FILES
630 WF=0:FOR K=0 TO 7
640 PRINT#15,"B-P:5"2+K*32
650 GET#1,A$:FT=ASC(A$+Z$)
660 IF FT>128 GOTO 770
670 :
680 REM UNSCRATCH FILE ENTRY AND CREATE
690 REM DUMMY ENTRY IF NECESSARY
700 GET#1,A$:ZT=ASC(A$+Z$)
710 GET#1,A$:ZS=ASC(A$+Z$)
720 WF=1:NT=FT OR 128
730 PRINT#15,"B-P:5"2+K*32
740 PRINT#1,CHR$(NT);
750 IF ZT=0 OR ZT>35 THEN PRINT#1,CHR$(1
7)CHR$(0)"- DUMMY ENTRY - ";
760 IF FT>0 THEN PRINT#1,CHR$(17)CHR$(0)
"- DUMMY ENTRY - ";
770 NEXT K
780 :
790 REM REWRITE SECTOR IF ANY CHANGES
800 IF WF=1 THEN PRINT#15,"U2:5 0 18"ZD
810 GOSUB 3190:IF FZ=1 THEN STOP
820 :
830 ZD=SL
840 IF ZD<>DX GOTO 430
850 :
860 REM COMPUTE FILE NUMBERS FOR NEW FIL
ES
870 NF=0
880 IF (DX-2)/3=INT((DX-2)/3) THEN NF=48

890 IF DX/3=INT(DX/3) THEN NF=96
900 NF=NF+8*INT((DX-1)/3)
910 DY=DX+3:IF DY>18 THEN DY=DY-17:REM D
Y=NEXT DIR SECTOR
920 PRINT"{DOWN}STARTING WORK ON TRACK 1
8, SECTOR"DX
```

```
930 :
940 REM CHECK FOR READ ERROR ON SECTOR
950 PRINT#15,"U1:5 0 18"DX
960 INPUT#15,EN,EM$,ET,ES
970 IF EN<19 GOTO 1650
980 PRINT"{DOWN}DISK ERROR WHEN READING
SECTOR"
990 PRINT" "EN;EM$;ET;ES
1000 :
1010 IF EN<22 OR EN>24 GOTO 1080
1020 :
1030 PRINT"{DOWN}NOTE: MOST 22, 23, AND
24 READ ERRORS"
1040 PRINT"          CAN BE CORRECTED BY NUL
LING OUT"
1050 PRINT"          THE SECTOR AND THEN REC
OVERING."
1060 GOTO 1130
1070 :
1080 PRINT"{DOWN}NOTE: 20, 21, AND 27 RE
AD ERRORS ARE"
1090 PRINT"          DUE TO ERRORS IN THE HE
ADER AND"
1100 PRINT"          SO ARE NOT USUALLY CURE
D IF YOU"
1110 PRINT"          NULL OUT THE SECTOR."
1120 :
1130 PRINT"{DOWN}YOUR OPTIONS ARE:"
1140 PRINT"{DOWN}1. NULL OUT THIS SECTOR
"
1150 PRINT"2. BRIDGE OVER THIS SECTOR"
1160 PRINT"3. TERMINATE THE PROGRAM"
1170 INPUT"{DOWN}YOUR CHOICE IS (1-3)   1
{LEFT 3}";A$
1180 A=ASC(A$)-48
1190 IF A<1 OR A>3 THEN PRINT"ENTER ONLY
 1, 2, OR 3":GOTO 1170
1200 :
1210 IF A=3 THEN CLOSE1:CLOSE15:END
1220 IF A=1 GOTO 1570
1230 :
1240 REM BRIDGE OVER TROUBLED SECTOR
1250 IF DX=1 THEN PRINT"{DOWN}YOU CAN'T
BRIDGE OVER 18/1":GOTO 1140
1260 DW=DX-3:IF DW<1 THEN DW=DW+18:REM P
REVIOUS SECTOR
1270 PRINT#15,"U1:5 0 18"DW
1280 GOSUB 3190:IF FZ=1 THEN STOP
1290 PRINT#15,"B-P:5 0"
1300 PRINT#1,CHR$(18)CHR$(DY);
```

```
1310 PRINT#15,"U2:5 0 18"DW
1320 GOSUB 3190:IF FZ=1 THEN STOP
1330 :
1340 PRINT"{DOWN}SECTOR 18,"DX"NO LONGER
 IN DIRECTORY"
1350 PRINT"{DOWN}VALIDATING DISKETTE TO
CORRECT BAM"
1360 PRINT#15,"V0"
1370 GOSUB 3190:IF FZ=1 THEN STOP
1380 CLOSE 1:OPEN 1,8,5,"#"
1390 GOSUB 3190:IF FZ=1 THEN STOP
1400 GOSUB 4490
1410 :
1420 REM FIND LAST BLOCK IN DIRECTORY FI
LE
1430 ZD=1
1440 PRINT#15,"U1:5 0 18"ZD
1450 GOSUB 3190:IF FZ=1 THEN STOP
1460 PRINT#15,"B-P:5 0"
1470 GET#1,A$:ZT=ASC(A$+Z$)
1480 GET#1,A$:ZS=ASC(A$+Z$)
1490 IF ZT=18 AND ZS<19 AND ZS>0 THEN ZD
=ZS:GOTO 1440
1500 IF ZT<>0 OR ZS<>255 THEN PRINT"{DOW
N}BAD DIR LINK ON SECTOR"ZD:GOTO 1540
1510 ZD=ZD+3:IF ZD>19 THEN ZD=ZD-18
1520 PRINT"{DOWN}TO RECOVER LOST FILES R
UN PROGRAM AGAIN"
1530 PRINT"AND SPECIFY RECOVERY OF SECTO
R #"ZD
1540 CLOSE1:CLOSE15:END
1550 :
1560 REM NULL OUT THE SECTOR AND TRY AGA
IN
1570 PRINT#15,"B-P:5 0"
1580 PRINT#1,Z$;CHR$(255);
1590 FOR K=2 TO 255:PRINT#1,Z$;:NEXT
1600 PRINT#15,"U2:5 0 18"DX
1610 GOSUB 3190:IF FZ=1 THEN STOP
1620 GOTO 950
1630 :
1640 REM CHECK IF SECTOR IS ALL NULLS
1650 PRINT#15,"B-P:5 2"
1660 M$="DIRECTORY SECTOR NOT BLANK"
1670 FOR K=2 TO 255
1680 GET#1,A$:IF A$<>"" THEN K=255:NEXT:
PRINT"{DOWN}"M$:GOTO 1130
1690 NEXT
1700 :
1710 REM CHECK IF FOLLOWING SECTOR HAS E
NTRIES
```

```
1720 PRINT#15,"U1:5 0 18"DY
1730 GOSUB 3190:IF FZ=1 THEN STOP
1740 PRINT#15,"B-P:5 0"
1750 GET#1,A$:A=ASC(A$+Z$)
1760 GET#1,A$:B=ASC(A$+Z$)
1770 DF=0
1780 IF A=0 AND B=0 GOTO 1910:REM VIRGIN
  SECTOR
1790 IF A=75 AND B=1 GOTO 1910:REM VIRGI
N SECTOR
1800 :
1810 REM RELINK DIRECTORY TO NEXT SECTOR

1820 PRINT#15,"U1:5 0 18"DX
1830 GOSUB 3190:IF FZ=1 THEN STOP
1840 PRINT#15,"B-P:5 0"
1850 PRINT#1,CHR$(18)CHR$(DY);
1860 PRINT#15,"U2:5 0 18"DX
1870 GOSUB 3190:IF FZ=1 THEN STOP
1880 PRINT"{DOWN}VALIDATING DISKETTE TO
RECOVER ALL"
1890 PRINT"FILES EXCEPT THE 8 DAMAGED EN
TRIES."
1900 GOTO 1920
1910 PRINT"{DOWN}VALIDATING BAM FOR STAR
T OF DIRECTORY"
1920 CLOSE1
1930 PRINT#15,"V0":REM ALLOCATE RECOVERE
D FILES
1940 GOSUB 3190:IF FZ=1 THEN STOP
1950 GOSUB 4490
1960 OPEN 1,8,5,"#"
1970 :
1980 REM READ IN THE BAM
1990 PRINT"{DOWN}READING IN BAM. 15 SECO
ND PAUSE..."
2000 GOSUB 3600
2010 :
2020 REM RE-CREATE FIRST EIGHT ENTRIES
2030 MN=17:MX=19
2040 FOR F=0 TO 7:Z1=0
2050 PRINT#15,"U;":REM RESET 1541 DRIVE
2060 CLOSE 1:REM CLOSE FILE IN COMPUTER
2070 PRINT#15,"I0"
2080 PRINT"{DOWN}WORKING ON FILE ENTRY #
"NF+F+1
2090 REM OPEN NEW FILE TO FOR NEW ENTRY
2100 OPEN 2,8,4,"FILE #"+STR$(NF+F+1)+",
P,W"
2110 INPUT#15,E,E$:IF E<20 GOTO 2170
```

```
2120 Z1=Z1+1:IF Z1<5 THEN CLOSE 2:GOTO 2
050
2130 PRINT"{DOWN}JOB ABORTED":PRINTE;E$:
CLOSE2:CLOSE 15:STOP
2140 :
2150 REM NOTE: BAM IS NOW OVER ALLOCATED

2160 REM FORCE NEW ENTRY TO BE UNCLOSED
FILE
2170 PRINT#15,"M-W"CHR$(43+4)CHR$(2)CHR$
(1)CHR$(255)
2180 CLOSE 2:CLOSE 15:REM IN COMPUTER ON
LY
2190 :
2200 REM REOPEN FILES AND GRAB NEW ENTRY

2210 OPEN 15,8,15,"IO"
2220 OPEN 1,8,5,"#"
2230 PRINT#15,"U1:5 0 18"DX
2240 GOSUB 3190:IF FZ=1 THEN STOP
2250 PRINT#15,"B-P:5"3+32*F
2260 GET#1,A$:TL=ASC(A$+Z$)
2270 IF TL<MN THEN MN=TL
2280 IF TL>MX THEN MX=TL
2290 GET#1,A$:SL=ASC(A$+Z$)
2300 GOSUB 3320:REM TRACE NEW ENTRY FILE
 CHAIN
2310 REM SET UP LENGTH OF NEW ENTRY
2320 BH=INT(NB/256):BL=NB-256*BH
2330 PRINT#15,"U1:5 0 18"DX
2340 GOSUB 3190:IF FZ=1 THEN STOP
2350 PRINT#15,"B-P:5"30+32*F
2360 PRINT#1,CHR$(BL)CHR$(BH);
2370 PRINT#15,"U2:5 0 18"DX
2380 GOSUB 3190:IF FZ=1 THEN STOP
2390 IF FL=1 GOTO 2050:REM BAD FILE
2400 IF NB>6 GOTO 2430:REM CAN'T BE A SI
DE SECTOR FILE
2410 GOSUB 3940:REM CHECK IF THIS IS A S
IDE SECTOR FILE
2420 IF RF=1 THEN F=F-1:RF=0:GOTO 2770
2430 GOSUB 3810:REM ALLOCATE NEW FILE IN
 BAM
2440 REM GET LOAD ADDRESS OF THE NEW FIL
E
2450 PRINT#15,"U1:5 0"TL(1)SL(1)
2460 GOSUB 3190:IF FZ=1 THEN STOP
2470 PRINT#15,"B-P:5 2"
2480 GET#1,A$:A=ASC(A$+Z$)
2490 GET#1,A$:B=ASC(A$+Z$)
2500 LA=256*B+A
```

```
2510 LA$="("+MID$(STR$(256*B+A),2)+")"
2520 H=(240ANDB)/16+48:IF H>57 THEN H=H+
7
2530 REM CONVERT LOAD ADDRESS TO HEX NOT
ATION
2540 LH$="$"+CHR$(H)
2550 H=(15ANDB)+48:IF H>57 THEN H=H+7
2560 LH$=LH$+CHR$(H)
2570 H=(240ANDA)/16+48:IF H>57 THEN H=H+
7
2580 LH$=LH$+CHR$(H)
2590 H=(15ANDA)+48:IF H>57 THEN H=H+7
2600 LH$=LH$+CHR$(H)
2610 PRINT" LOAD ADDRESS OF FILE = "LH$"
 "LA$
2620 FT=1:FT(F)=1
2630 :
2640 IF LA=1025 OR LA=2049 OR LA=4097 TH
EN FT=2:FT(F)=2
2650 IF LA=4097 OR LA=4609 OR LA=16270 T
HEN FT=2:FT(F)=2
2660 IF LA=32768 OR LA=36864 OR LA=40960
 THEN FT=2:FT(F)=2
2670 IF FT=1 THEN PRINT" ASSUMED TO BE A
 SEQUENTIAL FILE"
2680 IF FT=2 THEN PRINT" ASSUMED TO BE A
 PROGRAM FILE"
2690 REM PUT FILE TYPE IN DIRECTORY ENTR
Y
2700 PRINT#15,"U1:5 0 18"DX
2710 GOSUB 3190:IF FZ=1 THEN STOP
2720 PRINT#15,"B-P:5"2+32*F
2730 PRINT#1,CHR$(128+FT);
2740 PRINT#15,"U2:5 0 18"DX
2750 GOSUB 3190:IF FZ=1 THEN STOP
2760 :
2770 NEXT F
2780 :
2790 REM SEE IF WE HAVE ANY SEQ FILES AN
D NEED
2800 REM TO CHECK FOR POSSIBLE SIDE SECT
OR FILES
2810 FOR K=0 TO 7:IF FT(K)=1 THEN K=7:NE
XT:GOTO 2860
2820 NEXT
2830 GOTO 3040: REM DON'T BOTHER CHECKIN
G
2840 :
2850 REM CHECK FOR SIDE SECTOR FILES
2860 PRINT"{DOWN}CHECKING FOR ANY SIDE S
ECTOR FILES"
```

```
2870 FOR TX=17 TO MN STEP-1
2880 FOR SX=0 TO 20
2890 IF BM(TX,SX)=0 GOTO 2940
2900 TL(1)=TX
2910 SL(1)=SX
2920 NB=1
2930 GOSUB 3940
2940 NEXT SX:NEXT TX
2950 FOR TX=19 TO MX
2960 FOR SX=0 TO 20
2970 IF BM(TX,SX)=0 GOTO 3020
2980 TL(1)=TX
2990 SL(1)=SX
3000 NB=1
3010 GOSUB 3940
3020 NEXT SX:NEXT TX
3030 :
3040 CLOSE 1
3050 PRINT"{DOWN}SCRATCHING ANY DUMMY EN
TRIES CREATED"
3060 PRINT#15,"SO:- DUMMY ENTRY -*"
3070 PRINT"{DOWN}DOING FINAL VALIDATION
TO UPDATE BAM"
3080 PRINT#15,"V0"
3090 INPUT#15,EN,EM$,ET,ES
3100 IF EN<20 THEN PRINT"{DOWN}JOB COMPL
ETED":CLOSE 15:END
3110 PRINT"FINAL VALIDATION ABORTED, BAM
 INCORRECT"
3120 PRINT"{DOWN}"EN;EM$;ET;ES
3130 PRINT"COPY ALL FILES TO ANOTHER DIS
KETTE.":END
3140 :
3150 REM ------------------------
3160 REM          SUBROUTINES
3170 REM ------------------------
3180 REM CHECK DISK STATUS
3190 INPUT#15,EN,EM$,ET,ES
3200 IF EN<20 THEN FZ=0:RETURN
3210 PRINT"{DOWN}JOB ABORTED"
3220 PRINT"  "EN;EM$;ET;ES
3230 CLOSE 1:CLOSE 15
3240 FZ=1:RETURN
3250 :
3260 REM FOLLOW FILE, STORE LINKS, & CHE
CK BAM
3270 REM ON ENTRY: TL = TRACK LINK; SL =
 SECTOR LINK
3280 REM ON EXIT: NB = NUMBER OF BLOCKS
3290 REM             TL() & SL() = LIST OF
T & S LINKS
```

```
3300 REM           FL = 0 IF ALL BLOCKS F
REE
3310 REM           FL = 1 IF NOT ALL BLOC
KS FREE
3320 NB=1
3330 IF BM(TL,SL)=0 THEN M$="FIRST BLOCK
 IN USE":GOTO 3510
3340 TL(NB)=TL:SL(NB)=SL
3350 PRINT#15,"U1:5 0"TL;SL
3360 GOSUB 3190:IF FZ=1 THEN STOP
3370 PRINT#15,"B-P:5 0"
3380 GET#1,A$:TL=ASC(A$+Z$)
3390 GET#1,A$:SL=ASC(A$+Z$)
3400 IF TL=0 AND SL>0 GOTO 3480:REM LAST
 BLOCK
3410 IF TL=0 AND SL=0 THEN M$="VIRGIN SE
CTOR":GOTO 3510
3420 IF TL=75 AND SL=1 THEN M$="VIRGIN S
ECTOR":GOTO 3510
3430 IF TL>35 THEN M$="BAD LINK":GOTO 35
10
3440 IF BM(TL,SL)=0 THEN M$="IN USE":GOT
0 3510
3450 NB=NB+1
3460 TL(NB)=TL:SL(NB)=SL
3470 GOTO 3350
3480 PRINT" FILE WITH"NB"BLOCKS TRACED O
K"
3490 FL=0
3500 RETURN
3510 PRINT" TROUBLE: "M$
3520 PRINT" AT TRACK"TL(NB)", SECTOR"SL(
NB)
3530 ZZ=ZZ+1:IF ZZ>5 THEN CLOSE 15:PRINT
"JOB ABORTED!"
3540 PRINT"{DOWN}VALIDATING AGAIN"
3550 PRINT#15,"V0":CLOSE 1:OPEN 1,8,5,"#
"
3560 FL=1
3570 RETURN
3580 :
3590 REM READ IN & STORE THE BAM
3600 PRINT#15,"U1:5 0 18 0"
3610 GOSUB 3190:IF FZ=1 THEN STOP
3620 PRINT#15,"B-P:5"4
3630 FOR TR=1 TO 35
3640 GET#1,A$:BF(TR)=ASC(A$+Z$)
3650 FOR K=0 TO 2
3660 GET#1,A$:A=ASC(A$+Z$):K8=8*K
3670 B%(TR,K)=A
3680 IF A AND B0 THEN BM(TR,K8)=1
```

```
3690 IF A AND B1 THEN BM(TR,1+K8)=1
3700 IF A AND B2 THEN BM(TR,2+K8)=1
3710 IF A AND B3 THEN BM(TR,3+K8)=1
3720 IF A AND B4 THEN BM(TR,4+K8)=1
3730 IF A AND B5 THEN BM(TR,5+K8)=1
3740 IF A AND B6 THEN BM(TR,6+K8)=1
3750 IF A AND B7 THEN BM(TR,7+K8)=1
3760 NEXT K
3770 NEXT TR
3780 RETURN
3790 :
3800 REM ALLOCATE FILE IN BAM
3810 FOR K=1 TO NB
3820 BM(TL(K),SL(K))=0
3830 BY=INT(SL(K)/8)
3840 BI=SL(K)-8*BY
3850 B%(TL(K),BY)=B%(TL(K),BY) AND (255-
2^BI)
3860 BF(TL(K))=BF(TL(K))-1
3870 IF TL(K)<MN THEN MN=TL(K)
3880 IF TL(K)>MX THEN MX=TL(K)
3890 NEXT
3900 GOSUB 4610:REM PUT GOOD BAM TO DISK
ETTE
3910 RETURN
3920 :
3930 REM CHECK IF REL FILE
3940 RF=1
3950 PRINT#15,"U1:5 0"TL(1)SL(1)
3960 GOSUB 3190:IF FZ=1 THEN STOP
3970 PRINT#15,"B-P:5 4"
3980 GET#1,A$:TL=ASC(A$+Z$)
3990 IF TL<>TL(1) THEN RF=0:RETURN
4000 GET#1,A$:SL=ASC(A$+Z$)
4010 IF SL<>SL(1) THEN RF=0:RETURN
4020 PRINT"{DOWN} FOUND WHAT MAY BE PART
 OF A REL FILE"
4030 INPUT" IS THIS POSSIBLE (Y/N)  N{LE
FT 3}";A$
4040 IF (ASC(A$)AND127)<>89 THEN RF=0:RE
TURN
4050 PRINT#15,"B-P:5 3"
4060 GET#1,A$:RS=ASC(A$+Z$)
4070 PRINT#15,"B-P:5 16"
4080 GET#1,A$:FT=ASC(A$+Z$)
4090 GET#1,A$:FS=ASC(A$+Z$)
4100 PRINT#15,"U1:5 0 18"DX
4110 GOSUB 3190:IF FZ=1 THEN STOP
4120 FOR KX=0 TO F-1
4130 PRINT#15,"B-P:5"3+32*KX
4140 GET#1,A$:A=ASC(A$+Z$)
```

```
4150 IF A<>FT GOTO 4440
4160 GET#1,A$:B=ASC(A$+Z$)
4170 IF B<>FS GOTO 4440
4180 PRINT"{DOWN} SIDE SECTOR FILE FOR F
ILE #"KX+1
4190 PRINT" FILE #"KX+1"CONVERTED TO REL
 FILE"
4200 PRINT" RECORD SIZE IS"RS"CHARACTERS
"
4210 FT(KX)=4
4220 PRINT#15,"B-P:5"2+32*KX
4230 PRINT#1,CHR$(128+4);:REM REL FILE T
YPE
4240 PRINT#15,"B-P:5"21+32*KX
4250 PRINT#1,CHR$(TL)CHR$(SL)CHR$(SS);:R
EM SIDE SECTOR LINK
4260 PRINT#15,"B-P:5"30+32*KX
4270 GET#1,A$:BL=ASC(A$+Z$)
4280 GET#1,A$:BH=ASC(A$+Z$)
4290 PRINT#15,"U2:5 0 18"DX
4300 GOSUB 3190:IF FZ=1 THEN STOP
4310 GOSUB 3320:REM TRACE SIDE SECTOR CH
AIN
4320 IF FL=0 THEN GOSUB 3810:REM ALLOCAT
E IT
4330 PRINT#15,"U1:5 0 18"DX
4340 BL=BL+NB
4350 IF BL>255 THEN BL=BL-256:BH=BH+1
4360 PRINT#15,"B-P:5"30+32*KX
4370 PRINT#1,CHR$(BL)CHR$(BH);
4380 KX=F-1:NEXT:IF F>7 GOTO 4410
4390 PRINT#15,"B-P:5"2+32*F
4400 PRINT#1,CHR$(0)CHR$(0)CHR$(0);
4410 PRINT#15,"U2:5 0 18"DX
4420 GOSUB 3190:IF FZ=1 THEN STOP
4430 RETURN
4440 NEXT KX
4450 PRINT" DOESN'T FIT WITH ANY OTHER F
ILE"
4460 RF=0:RETURN
4470 :
4480 REM FORCE WRITE OF BAM TO DISKETTE
4490 TZ=0
4500 PRINT#15,"M-W"CHR$(14)CHR$(0)CHR$(2
)CHR$(18)CHR$(0)
4510 PRINT#15,"M-W"CHR$(4)CHR$(0)CHR$(1)
CHR$(144)
4520 PRINT#15,"M-R"CHR$(4)CHR$(0)
4530 GET#15,A$:A=ASC(A$+CHR$(0))
4540 IF A>127 GOTO 4520
4550 IF A=1 THEN RETURN
```

```
4560 TZ=TZ+1:IF TZ<10 GOTO 4500
4570 PRINT"JOB ABORTED, PROBLEMS WITH 18
/0"
4580 CLOSE 1:CLOSE 15:STOP
4590 :
4600 REM STORE CORRECT BAM IN DRIVE RAM
4610 FOR ZT=1 TO 35
4620 M$=CHR$(BF(ZT))+CHR$(B%(ZT,0))+CHR$
(B%(ZT,1))+CHR$(B%(ZT,2))
4630 PRINT#15,"M-W"CHR$(4*ZT)CHR$(7)CHR$
(4)M$
4640 NEXT
4650 GOSUB 4490
4660 RETURN
```

```
**************************
```
8. PROGRAM: THE UNSCRATCHER
```
**************************
```

This program recovers any scratched file. It displays a list of all scratched files on the diskette and you may choose which one to unscratch. The file is traced to ensure that it does not contain any read errors and that it has not been overwritten. The program works with any type of file, including relative files.

Compatible with C-64, VIC-20, 4032 and 8032 computers, and 1541, 2031 and 4040 disk drives (use drive zero).

```
0 REM  1541 USER'S GUIDE   APPENDIX E
1 REM   COPYRIGHT: G. NEUFELD, 1984
3 REM   UNSCRATCH ANY TYPE OF SCRATCHED F
ILE
4 :
100 DIM BM%(35,2),TL(50),SL(50),F$(50)
110 DIM SD(50),DE(50)
120 Z$=CHR$(0)
130 OPEN 15,8,15
140 PRINT"{CLR} 1541 FILE UNSCRATCHER"
150 PRINT"{DOWN}INSERT DISKETTE WITH SCR
ATCHED FILE"
160 PRINT"{DOWN}PRESS {RVS}C{ROFF} TO CO
NTINUE"
170 PRINT"        {RVS}Q{ROFF} TO QUIT"
180 GET A$:IF A$<>"" GOTO 180
190 GET A$:IF A$="" GOTO 190
200 IF A$="C" GOTO 230
210 IF A$="Q" THEN PRINT"{CLR}":CLOSE15:
END
220 GOTO 190
230 PRINT"{DOWN}OK. READING DIRECTORY...
"
```

```
240 PRINT#15,"IO"
250 GOSUB 1290:IF FL=1 GOTO 140
260 REM READ THE DIRECTORY
270 SE=1:NE=0
280 OPEN1,8,4,"#"
290 PRINT#15,"U1:4 0 18"SE
300 GOSUB 1290:IF FL=1 THEN CLOSE 1:GOTO
 140
310 FOR K=0 TO 7
320 PRINT#15,"B-P:4"2+K*32
330 GET#1,A$:FT=ASC(A$+Z$)
340 GET#1,A$:TL=ASC(A$+Z$)
350 GET#1,A$:SL=ASC(A$+Z$)
360 IF (SL=0 AND TL=0) OR FT<>0 GOTO 470

370 NE=NE+1
380 TL(NE)=TL
390 SL(NE)=SL
400 SD(NE)=SE
410 DE(NE)=K
420 F$(NE)=""
430 FOR L=1TO15
440 GET#1,A$:IFA$=""THENA$=Z$
450 F$(NE)=F$(NE)+A$
460 NEXT L
470 NEXT K
480 PRINT#15,"B-P:4"0
490 GET#1,A$:TL=ASC(A$+Z$)
500 GET#1,A$:SE=ASC(A$+Z$)
510 IF TL=18 GOTO 290
520 :
530 PRINT"{CLR} 1541 FILE UNSCRATCHER"
540 IF NE<>0 GOTO 600
550 PRINT"{DOWN}NO SCRATCHED FILES FOUND
"
560 PRINT"{DOWN}PRESS {RVS}RETURN{ROFF}
TO CONTINUE"
570 GET A$:IF A$<>"" GOTO 570
580 GET A$:IF A$<>CHR$(13) GOTO 580
590 CLOSE 1:GOTO 140
600 PRINT"{DOWN}"NE"SCRATCHED FILES FOUN
D{DOWN}"
610 FOR K=1 TO NE
620 PRINTK"{LEFT}. "F$(K)
630 NEXT
640 PRINT"{DOWN}WHICH FILE TO UNSCRATCH
(1"NE*-1"{LEFT})";
650 INPUT X$:X=INT(VAL(X$))
660 IF X<1 OR X>NE THEN CLOSE 1:GOTO 140

670 PRINT"{DOWN}READING THE BAM PRIOR TO
 CHECK...."
```

```
680 PRINT#15,"U1:4 0 18 0"
690 PRINT#15,"B-P:4 4"
700 FOR T=1 TO 35
710 GET#1,A$:REM DUMP BLK COUNT
720 GET#1,A$:BM%(T,0)=ASC(A$+Z$):REM SEC
T 0-7
730 GET#1,A$:BM%(T,1)=ASC(A$+Z$):REM SEC
T 8-15
740 GET#1,A$:BM%(T,2)=ASC(A$+Z$):REM SEC
T 16-23
750 NEXT T
760 PRINT"CHECKING IF ALL BLOCKS ARE FRE
E..."
770 TL=TL(X):SL=SL(X):NB=0
780 SN=2+(SL<8)+(SL<16)
790 NB=NB+1
800 SP=SL-8*SN
810 IF (2^SP AND BM%(TL,SN))=0 GOTO 1200

820 PRINT#15,"U1:4 0"TL;SL
830 GOSUB 1290
840 PRINT#15,"B-P:4 0"
850 GET#1,A$:TL=ASC(A$+Z$)
860 GET#1,A$:SL=ASC(A$+Z$)
870 IF TL<>0 GOTO 780
880 PRINT"{DOWN}FILE IS"NB"BLOCKS LONG A
ND"
890 PRINT"CAN BE UNSCRATCHED"
900 INPUT"{DOWN}SHALL I UNSCRATCH IT (Y/
N)";A$
910 IF (ASC(A$)AND127)<>89 THEN CLOSE 1:
GOTO 140
920 PRINT#15,"U1:4 0 18"SD(X)
930 GOSUB 1290
940 PRINT#15,"B-P:4"23+32*DE(X)
950 GET#1,A$:A=ASC(A$+Z$)
955 PRINT#15,"B-P:4"2+32*DE(X)
960 IF A=0 GOTO 990
970 PRINT"{DOWN}THIS IS A RELATIVE FILE"

971 PRINT"  RECORD SIZE="A:FT=132:GOTO10
70
990 T$="P":INPUT"{DOWN}FILE TYPE (P/S/U)
";T$
1000 T$=LEFT$(T$,1)
1010 IF T$="P" THEN FT=130:GOTO 1070
1020 IF T$="S" THEN FT=129:GOTO 1070
1030 IF T$="U" THEN FT=131:GOTO 1070
1040 PRINT"{DOWN}ENTER ONLY P, S, OR U"
1050 PRINT"P=PRG  S=SEQ  U=USR"
1060 GOTO 990
```

```
1070 PRINT#1,CHR$(FT);
1080 PRINT#15,"B-P:4"31+32*DE(X)
1090 BH=INT(NB/256)
1100 BL=NB-256*BH
1110 PRINT#1,CHR$(BH);
1120 PRINT#1,CHR$(BL);
1130 PRINT#15,"U2:4 0 18"SD(X)
1140 PRINT"{DOWN}NOW VALIDATING DISKETTE
.....
1150 PRINT#15,"VO"
1160 GOSUB 1290:IF FL=1 THEN CLOSE1:GOTO
140
1170 CLOSE1
1180 PRINT"{DOWN}ALL DONE!"
1190 GOTO 1220
1200 PRINT"{DOWN}CAN NOT UN-SCRATCH THIS
 FILE"
1210 PRINT"{DOWN}FOUND ALLOCATED BLOCK I
N BAM."
1220 PRINT"{DOWN}PRESS {RVS}RETURN{ROFF}
 TO CONTINUE"
1230 GET A$:IF A$<>"" GOTO 1230
1240 GET A$:IF A$<>CHR$(13) GOTO 1240
1250 CLOSE 1:GOTO 140
1260 :
1270 REM READ DISK STATUS
1280 :
1290 INPUT#15,EN,E$,ET,ES
1300 IF EN<20 THEN FL=0:RETURN
1310 PRINT"{DOWN}{RVS}DISK ERROR{ROFF}"
1320 PRINTEN;E$;ET;ES
1330 PRINT"{DOWN}PRESS {RVS}RETURN{ROFF}
 TO CONTINUE"
1340 GET A$:IF A$<>"" GOTO 1340
1350 GET A$:IF A$<>CHR$(13) GOTO 1350
1360 FL=1:RETURN
```

```
**********************
9. PROGRAM: PRG HEX DUMP
**********************
```

This program produces a hex dump to the screen of any program file on disk. The important features of the inner structure of BASIC (line link bytes, line numbers, and null bytes marking the end-of-line) are highlighted in color. The decimal equivalents of the line numbers are shown on the right of the display. Illegal bytes are highlighted in blue. Because of the color highlights this program is most effective when used with the Commodore 64.

Compatible with C-64, VIC-20, 4032 and 8032 computers, and 1541, 2031 and 4040 disk drives (use drive zero).

```
0 REM 1541 USER'S GUIDE   APPENDIX E
1 REM   COPYRIGHT: G. NEUFELD, 1984
2 :
3 REM   HEX DUMP OF PROGRAM FILE WITH LIN
E LINKS, LINE
4 REM   NUMBERS, ILLEGAL BYTES, AND LINE
ENDS HIGHLIGHTED
5 :
100 REM HEX ANAL
110 DIM C(255)
120 C1=30:C2=158:C3=152:C4=144:BC=11
130 POKE53280,BC:POKE53281,BC
140 N$=CHR$(0):BL$=CHR$(154):OL=-1
150 PRINTCHR$(C3)"{CLR}{DOWN}    HEX DUMP
 OF PROGRAM FILE"
160 INPUT"{DOWN}    PGM FILE NAME";F$
170 OPEN15,8,15,"IO"
180 GOSUB650:IFF=1THENSTOP
190 OPEN1,8,5,"0:"+F$+",P,R"
200 GOSUB650:IFF=1THENSTOP
210 PRINTCHR$(C3)"{CLR}{DOWN}    HEX DUMP
 OF "F$"{DOWN}"
220 GET#1,C$:L=ASC(C$+N$)
230 GET#1,C$:H=ASC(C$+N$)
240 HA=L+256*H-1:N=0
250 GOSUB 570:Z=0:PRINT"{RVS}"CHR$(C4);:
GOSUB700:PRINT"{ROFF} ";
260 GET#1,C$:PL=ASC(C$+N$):REM POINTER
270 GET#1,C$:PH=ASC(C$+N$):REM POINTER H
I
280 QA=256*PH+PL-2:IFQA=-2 THEN C1=154
290 IFQA<>-2AND(QA<HAOR(QA-HA)>256)THENM
$="{LEFT}BAD LINK":C1=154
300 Z=PL:PRINT"{RVS}"CHR$(C1);:GOSUB700
310 IF N<>0 THEN PRINT"{RVS} {ROFF}";
320 Z=PH:PRINT"{RVS}"CHR$(C1);:GOSUB700:
IFN<>OTHENPRINT"{ROFF} ";
330 IF QA=-2 THENPRINT:PRINTTAB(8)"{DOWN
}{RVS} END OF PROGRAM ":CLOSE1:CLOSE15:E
ND
340 GET#1,C$:LL=ASC(C$+N$):REM LINE# LO
350 GET#1,C$:LH=ASC(C$+N$):REM LINE# HI
360 Z=LL:PRINT"{RVS}"CHR$(C2);:GOSUB700
370 IFM$=""THENM$="#"+MID$(STR$(256*LH+L
L),2)
380 IF OL>(256*LH+LL)THENM$=BL$+"{<--}"+
MID$(STR$(256*LH+LL),2)
390 OL=(256*LH+LL)
400 IF N<>0 THEN PRINT"{RVS} {ROFF}";
410 Z=LH:PRINT"{RVS}"CHR$(C2);:GOSUB700:
IFN<>OTHENPRINT"{ROFF} ";
```

```
420 Q=0:FORK=HATOQA
430 GET#1,C$:Z=ASC(C$+N$):REM CHARACTER
440 IF Z=0 GOTO 500
450 IF Q=0 AND (Z<31 OR Z>219) GOTO 500
460 IF Q=0 AND (Z>95 AND Z<128) GOTO 500

470 IF Z=34 THEN Q=2+NOTQ
480 PRINTCHR$(C3);:GOSUB700:IFN<>OTHEN P
RINT" ";
490 GOTO 510
500 PRINT"{RVS}"BL$;:M$=BL$+"ERROR":GOSU
B700:IFN<>OTHENPRINT"{ROFF} ";
510 NEXT
520 GET#1,C$:LL=ASC(C$+N$):REM LINE END
530 IFLL=OTHENZ=LL:PRINT"{RVS}"CHR$(C4);
:GOSUB700:IFN<>OTHENPRINT"{ROFF} ";
540 IFLL=OGOTO560
550 Z=LL:PRINT"{RVS}"BL$;:M$=BL$+"ERROR"
:GOSUB700:IFN<>OTHENPRINT"{ROFF} ";
560 GOTO 260
570 XL=XL+1:IF XL=20THENGOSUB750
580 ZH=INT(HA/256):ZL=HA-256*ZH
590 Z1=(ZHAND240)/16+48:IFZ1>57THENZ1=Z1
+7
600 Z2=(ZHAND15)+48:IFZ2>57THENZ2=Z2+7
610 Z3=(ZLAND240)/16+48:IFZ3>57THENZ3=Z3
+7
620 Z4=(ZLAND15)+48:IFZ4>57THENZ4=Z4+7
630 PRINTCHR$(C3)":  $"CHR$(Z1)CHR$(Z2)CH
R$(Z3)CHR$(Z4)" ";
640 RETURN
650 INPUT#15,E,E$,T,S
660 IF E<20 THEN F=0:RETURN
670 PRINT"{DOWN}DISK ERROR"
680 PRINT"  "E;E$;T;S:CLOSE1:CLOSE15
690 F=1:RETURN
700 ZH=(ZAND240)/16+48:IFZH>57THENZH=ZH+
7
710 ZL=(ZAND15)+48:IFZL>57THENZL=ZL+7
720 PRINTCHR$(ZH);CHR$(ZL);
730 HA=HA+1:N=N+1:IFN>7THENN=O:PRINTCHR$
(C2)"{ROFF} "M$:M$="":GOSUB570
740 RETURN
750 PRINTCHR$(C3)"{RVS} PRESS G TO GO ON
 OR Q TO QUIT {ROFF}"
760 GET A$:IFA$=""GOTO760
770 IF A$="Q"THENCLOSE1:CLOSE15:END
780 IF A$<>"G"GOTO760
790 PRINT"{UP}
          "
800 PRINT"{UP}";:XL=0:RETURN
```

```
***************************
```
10. PROGRAM: PROGRAM ANALYZER
```
***************************
```

This program produces a detailed line by line analysis of any program file on disk.
Each byte of the program is analyzed. All the line links, line numbers, BASIC
tokens, ASCII characters, and null bytes marking the end-of-line are displayed
and interpreted. A useful program for studying the inner structure of any BASIC
program. Assumes at least a 40 column display.

Compatible with C-64, VIC-20, 4032 and 8032 computers, and 1541, 2031 and 4040
disk drives (use drive zero).

```
0 REM 1541 USER'S GUIDE   APPENDIX E
1 REM   COPYRIGHT: G. NEUFELD, 1984
2 :
3 REM   BYTE BY BYTE ANALYSIS OF BASIC PR
OGRAM FILE
4 :
100 DIM A$(2,255)
110 PRINT"{CLR}{DOWN}"TAB(10)"PROGRAM FI
LE SCAN"
120 PRINT"{DOWN}EXCUSE ME WHILE I SET UP
 SOME TABLES"
130 REM SET UP ASCII TABLE (WITHIN QUOTE
S)
140 RESTORE
150 N$=CHR$(0):D$="{HOME}{DOWN 23}"
160 FORK=0TO4:A$(1,K)=CHR$(K):NEXT
170 FORK=5TO31:READA$(1,K):NEXT
180 FORK=32TO132:A$(1,K)=CHR$(K):NEXT:A$
(1,129)="ORANGE"
190 FORK=133TO160:READA$(1,K):NEXT
200 FORK=161TO255:A$(1,K)=CHR$(K):NEXT
210 :
220 REM SET UP BASIC BYTES & KEYWORDS TA
BLE
230 FORK=1TO33:A$(0,K)="?SYNTAX ERROR":N
EXT:A$(0,32)="  "
240 FORK=34TO95:A$(0,K)=CHR$(K):NEXT
250 FORK=96TO127:A$(0,K)="?SYNTAX ERROR"
:NEXT
260 FOR K=128TO218:READA$(0,K):NEXT
270 FORK=219TO255:A$(0,K)="?SYNTAX ERROR
":NEXT
280 :
290 REM TABLE OF SPECIAL ASCII CHARACTER
S
300 DATA WHITE,,,DISABLE,ENABLE,,,,RETUR
N,LOWER CASE,,
310 DATA DOWN,RVS ON,HOME,DEL,,,,,,,,,RED
,RIGHT,GREEN,BLUE
```

```
320 DATA FUNC#1,FUNC#3,FUNC#5,FUNC#7,FUN
C#2,FUNC#4,FUNC#6,FUNC#8
330 DATA SHIFTED RETURN,UPPER CASE,,BLAC
K,UP,RVS OFF,CLR SCREEN,INSERT
340 DATA BROWN,LT RED,GREY1,GREY2,LT GRE
EN,LT BLUE,GREY3
350 DATA PURPLE,LEFT,YELLOW,CYAN,SHIFT S
PC
360 :
370 REM TABLE OF BASIC KEYWORDS
380 DATA END,FOR,NEXT,DATA,INPUT#,INPUT,
DIM,READ,LET,GOTO,RUN,IF,RESTORE
390 DATA GOSUB,RETURN,REM,STOP,ON,WAIT,L
OAD,SAVE,VERIFY,DEF,POKE,PRINT#
400 DATA PRINT,CONT,LIST,CLR,CMD,SYS,OPE
N,CLOSE,GET,NEW,TAB(,TO,FN,SPC(
410 DATA THEN,NOT,STEP,+,-,*,/,^,AND,OR,
>,=,<,SGN,INT,ABS,USR,FRE,POS
420 DATA SQR,RND,LOG,EXP,COS,SIN,TAN,ATN
,PEEK,LEN,STR$,VAL,ASC,CHR$,LEFT$
430 DATA RIGHT$,MID$,GO,CONCAT,DOPEN,DCL
OSE,RECORD,HEADER,COLLECT,BACKUP
440 DATA COPY,APPEND,DSAVE,DLOAD,CATALOG
,RENAME,SCRATCH,DIRECTORY
450 :
460 PRINT"{CLR}{DOWN}"TAB(10)"PROGRAM FI
LE SCAN"
470 INPUT"{DOWN}PGM FILE NAME";F$
480 OPEN 15,8,15
490 GOSUB 1190:IF DF=1 THEN STOP:REM DIS
K ERROR STATUS
500 OPEN 1,8,5,"0:"+F$+",P,R"
510 GOSUB 1190:IF DF=1 THEN STOP:REM DIS
K ERROR STATUS
520 GET#1,P$:LL=ASC(P$+N$)
530 GET#1,P$:LH=ASC(P$+N$)
540 PRINT"{DOWN}THE FIRST TWO BYTES IN T
HE FILE ARE:"
550 Z=LL:GOSUB1240:PRINTTAB(8)"{DOWN}$"Z
$;
560 Z=LH:GOSUB1240:PRINT" AND $"Z$
570 LD=LL+256*LH
580 PRINT"{DOWN}THE LOAD ADDRESS IS:"LD"
($";
590 Z=LH:GOSUB1240:PRINTZ$;:Z=LL:GOSUB12
40:PRINTZ$")"
600 IFLD=1025THEN PRINT"{DOWN}PROGRAM WR
ITTEN ON A PET":GOTO650
610 IFLD=2049THENPRINT"{DOWN}PROGRAM WRI
TTEN ON A 64":GOTO650
```

```
620 IFLD=2049THENPRINT"{DOWN}PROGRAM WRI
TTEN ON A VIC-20":GOTO650
630 IFLD=4609THENPRINT"{DOWN}PROGRAM WRI
TTEN ON AN EXPANDED VIC-20":GOTO650
640 PRINT"{DOWN}THIS IS NOT A BASIC PROG
RAM":CLOSE1:CLOSE15:END
650 M$="FIRST LINE":GOSUB1270
660 SA=LD+4:AD=LD
670 L=0:GET#1,P$:PL=ASC(P$+N$)
680 GET#1,P$:PH=ASC(P$+N$)
690 QA=PH*256+PL-1
700 PRINT"{CLR} PREAMBLE TO NEXT LINE"
710 PRINT" {COM-U 22}"
720 PRINT"{DOWN}NEXT LINE POINTER BYTES:
"
730 PRINT"{DOWN}{RVS}     ADDRESS          V
ALUE "
740 Z=AD:GOSUB1320:PRINTAD;Z$;:AD=AD+1
750 Z=PL:GOSUB1240:PRINTRIGHT$("        "+S
TR$(PL),5)" ($"Z$")"
760 Z=AD:GOSUB1320:PRINTAD;Z$;:AD=AD+1
770 Z=PH:GOSUB1240:PRINTRIGHT$("        "+S
TR$(PH),5)" ($"Z$")"
780 PRINT"{DOWN}NEXT LINE STARTS AT:"
790 PRINT"{DOWN}  256 *"PH"+"PL"="256*PH
+PL" ($";
800 Z=PH:GOSUB1240:PRINTZ$;:Z=PL:GOSUB12
40:PRINTZ$")"
810 IF PH<>0 OR PL<>0 GOTO 860
820 PRINT"{DOWN}END OF BASIC PROGRAM"
830 IFST=64THENPRINT"{DOWN}ALSO END OF P
ROGRAM FILE":GOTO850
840 PRINT"{DOWN}BUT, NOT THE END OF THE
PGM FILE."
850 CLOSE1:CLOSE15:END
860 GET#1,P$:LL=ASC(P$+N$)
870 GET#1,P$:LH=ASC(P$+N$)
880 PRINT"{DOWN}LINE NUMBER BYTES:"
890 PRINT"{DOWN}{RVS}     ADDRESS          V
ALUE "
900 Z=AD:GOSUB1320:PRINTAD;Z$;:AD=AD+1
910 Z=LL:GOSUB1240:PRINTRIGHT$("        "+S
TR$(LL),5)" ($"Z$")"
920 Z=AD:GOSUB1320:PRINTAD;Z$;:AD=AD+1
930 Z=LH:GOSUB1240:PRINTRIGHT$("        "+S
TR$(LH),5)" ($"Z$")"
940 PRINT"{DOWN}LINE NUMBER IS: "
950 PRINT"{DOWN}  256 *"LH"+"LL"="256*LH
+LL" ($";
960 Z=LH:GOSUB1240:PRINTZ$;:Z=LL:GOSUB12
40:PRINTZ$")"
```

```
970 M$="LINE ANALYSIS":GOSUB1270
980 PRINT"{CLR}ANALYSIS OF LINE #"256*LH
+LL
990 PRINT"{DOWN}{RVS}    ADDRESS       VAL
UE    MEANING   {DOWN}"
1000 L=0:Q=0
1010 FOR MA=SATOQA
1020 Z=AD:GOSUB1320:PRINTAD;Z$;:AD=AD+1
1030 GET#1,P$:P=ASC(P$+N$)
1040 Z=P:GOSUB1240:PRINTRIGHT$("       "+ST
R$(P),4)" ($"Z$")";
1050 IF P=0 THEN PRINT" {RVS}LINE END":G
OTO1100
1060 IF Q=1 THEN PRINT" ASC- "A$(1,P)
1070 IF Q=0 AND P>127 THEN PRINT" TOK- "
A$(0,P)
1080 IF Q=0 AND P<128 THEN PRINT" CHR- "
A$(0,P)
1090 IF P=34 THEN Q=2+NOTQ
1100 L=L+1:IF L/18<>INT(L/18)ORMA=QA GOT
O1150
1110 M$="MORE ANALYSIS":GOSUB1270
1120 PRINT"{CLR}ANALYSIS OF LINE #"256*L
H+LL
1130 PRINT"{DOWN}{RVS}    ADDRESS       VA
LUE    MEANING   {DOWN}"
1140 L=0
1150 NEXT
1160 SA=AD+4:M$="NEXT LINE":GOSUB1270
1170 GOTO670
1180 NEXT:STOP
1190 INPUT#15,E,E$,T,S
1200 IF E<20 THEN DF=0:RETURN
1210 PRINT"{DOWN}DISK ERROR"
1220 PRINT"  "E;E$;T;S
1230 DF=1:RETURN
1240 ZH=48+(ZAND240)/16:IFZH>57THENZH=ZH
+7
1250 ZL=48+(ZAND15):IFZL>57THENZL=ZL+7
1260 Z$=CHR$(ZH)+CHR$(ZL):RETURN
1270 PRINTD$;"PRESS C FOR "M$;" OR Q TO
QUIT"
1280 GETX$:IFX$<>""GOTO1280
1290 GETX$:IFX$="Q"THENCLOSE1:CLOSE15:EN
D
1300 IFX$<>"C"GOTO1290
1310 RETURN
1320 ZH=INT(Z/256):Z1=48+(ZHAND240)/16:I
FZ1>57THENZ1=Z1+7
1330 Z2=48+(ZHAND15):IFZ2>57THENZ2=Z2+7
```

```
1340 ZL=Z-256*ZH:Z3=48+(ZLAND240)/16:IFZ
3>57THENZ3=Z3+7
1350 Z4=48+(ZLAND15):IFZ4>57THENZ4=Z4+7
1360 Z$="($"+CHR$(Z1)+CHR$(Z2)+CHR$(Z3)+
CHR$(Z4)+")"
1370 RETURN
```

INDEX

1541 User's Guide

All the programs listed in *1541 User's Guide* on one diskette! Save yourself hours of typing and debugging.

Only $24.95 with this coupon!

Available only to readers of this book. Send $24.95 plus $2.00 shipping and handling (California residents add 6½% sales tax) to:

19821 Nordhoff Street, Northridge, CA 91324
(818) 709-1202

Please RUSH me *1541 User's Guide* diskette. I have enclosed my check or money order for $24.95 plus $2.00 shipping and handling (California residents add $1.62 for sales tax).

Name ____

Address ____

City _______________________ State _________ Zip _________

Phone (____)____________________________________

MORE GREAT BOOKS FROM DATAMOST

Inside Commodore DOS — Now you can get the inside story on the 1541 disk operating system. This valuable tool for the intermediate and advanced programmer includes complete information on correcting errors and omissions in Commodore's *1541 User's Manual*, diskette formatting, file storage, reading and writing data in non-standard ways, backing up protected disks, recovering damaged data, and more. Includes an analysis of 1541's ROM, completely disassembled and annotated. *$19.95*

The Elementary Commodore

Explains the Commodore 64 in simple, everyday language. How to hook it up, use the keyboard, and program in BASIC. Teaches about word processing, utilities and peripherals. *$14.95*

Games Commodores Play

A collection of classic computer games that teaches BASIC using a games and graphics approach. Simply type them in and make your own modifications. *$14.95*

Intermediate Commodore

Takes you from being a fledging programmer and teaches important principles so you can handle more complicated problems. Helps you take that step from elementary BASIC programming to machine language programming. *$14.95*

C-64 Game Construction Kit

Shows you how to write your own BASIC games! This unique book gives examples of different games and teaches fundemental lessons of quality game programming. *$14.95*

Computers & Writing

An innovative approach to teaching children to write using the computer. Topics discussed include computers in the classroom, adapting traditional teaching methods to include computers, setting up a creative environment at home and more. For both parents and teachers. *$9.95*

A Shortcut Through Adventureland, Volume I

Contains answers to 14 of the most popular hi-res puzzle solving adventures including *Wizard and the Princess, Cranston Manor, The Dark Crystal, Escape from Rungistan, Time Zone* and more. *$9.95*

The C-64 Home Companion

This is the book that should have come with your Commodore 64. Straight answers to home computing questions, dozens of software reviews, BASIC and more! *$19.95*

The Musical Commodore

Introduces you to music theory and computing at the same time. For beginners as well as pros, this book helps you turn your C-64 into a musical instrument. *$14.95*

Super Computer Snooper (C-64)

Learn how the computer "thinks." Investigate memory, screens, programs and variables, keyboards, printers, and expansion boards. *$14.95*

Programming for Profit

Aimed at the programmer who wants to get his or her software published. This is a unique guidebook through the maze of traditions, rules and standards in the software industry. Contains hints and tricks of the trade and much more! *$14.95*

C-64 Logo Workbook

Teaches children in grades 2-6 how the Logo language can be used for problem solving. Learn about the "turtle," variables, geometry and recursion. *$12.95*

Kids to Kids on the C-64

Written *by* kids *for* kids, explains BASIC programming in simple, straight-forward language. Two chapters are devoted to sound and graphics, and another shows how to write an original game. *$9.95*

A Shortcut Through Adventureland, Volume II

The cheater's guide to all of Infocom's text adventures to date: The *Zork* Trilogy, *Infidel, The Witness, Deadline* and *Enchanter* to name a few. *$9.95*

Available at better book and computer stores, or contact

DATAMOST®

19821 Nordhoff Street, Northridge, CA 91324
(818) 709-1202